TM

BESTSELLING BOOK SERIES

References for the Rest of Us! ®

Are you intimidated and confused by computers? Do you find that traditional manuals are overloaded with technical details you'll never use? Do your friends and family always call you to fix simple problems on their PCs? Then the *...For Dummies*® computer book series from IDG Books Worldwide is for you.

...For Dummies books are written for those frustrated computer users who know they aren't really dumb but find that PC hardware, software, and indeed the unique vocabulary of computing make them feel helpless. *...For Dummies* books use a lighthearted approach, a down-to-earth style, and even cartoons and humorous icons to dispel computer novices' fears and build their confidence. Lighthearted but not lightweight, these books are a perfect survival guide for anyone forced to use a computer.

> *"I like my copy so much I told friends; now they bought copies."*
>
> — Irene C., Orwell, Ohio

> *"Quick, concise, nontechnical, and humorous."*
>
> — Jay A., Elburn, Illinois

> *"Thanks, I needed this book. Now I can sleep at night."*
>
> — Robin F., British Columbia, Canada

Already, millions of satisfied readers agree. They have made *...For Dummies* books the #1 introductory level computer book series and have written asking for more. So, if you're looking for the most fun and easy way to learn about computers, look to *...For Dummies* books to give you a helping hand.

DYNAMIC
HTML
FOR
DUMMIES®
2ND EDITION

DYNAMIC HTML FOR DUMMIES®
2ND EDITION

by Michael I. Hyman

IDG BOOKS WORLDWIDE

IDG Books Worldwide, Inc.
An International Data Group Company

Foster City, CA ◆ Chicago, IL ◆ Indianapolis, IN ◆ New York, NY

Dynamic HTML For Dummies® 2nd Edition
Published by
IDG Books Worldwide, Inc.
An International Data Group Company
919 E. Hillsdale Blvd.
Suite 400
Foster City, CA 94404
www.idgbooks.com (IDG Books Worldwide Web site)
www.dummies.com (Dummies Press Web site)

Library of Congress Catalog Card No.: 99-60731

ISBN: 0-7645-0467-3

Printed in the United States of America

10 9 8 7 6 5 4 3 2 1

1O/QY/QU/ZZ/IN

Distributed in the United States by IDG Books Worldwide, Inc.

Distributed by CDG Books Canada Inc. for Canada; by Transworld Publishers Limited in the United Kingdom; by IDG Norge Books for Norway; by IDG Sweden Books for Sweden; by Woodslane Pty. Ltd. for Australia; by Woodslane (NZ) Ltd. for New Zealand; by TransQuest Publishers Pte Ltd. for Singapore, Malaysia, Thailand, Indonesia, and Hong Kong; by ICG Muse, Inc. for Japan; by Norma Comunicaciones S.A. for Colombia; by Intersoft for South Africa; by Le Monde en Tique for France; by International Thomson Publishing for Germany, Austria and Switzerland; by Distribuidora Cuspide for Argentina; by Livraria Cultura for Brazil; by Ediciones ZETA S.C.R. Ltda. for Peru; by WS Computer Publishing Corporation, Inc., for the Philippines; by Contemporanea de Ediciones for Venezuela; by Express Computer Distributors for the Caribbean and West Indies; by Micronesia Media Distributor, Inc. for Micronesia; by Grupo Editorial Norma S.A. for Guatemala; by Chips Computadoras S.A. de C.V. for Mexico; by Editorial Norma de Panama S.A. for Panama; by American Bookshops for Finland. Authorized Sales Agent: Anthony Rudkin Associates for the Middle East and North Africa.

For general information on IDG Books Worldwide's books in the U.S., please call our Consumer Customer Service department at 800-762-2974. For reseller information, including discounts and premium sales, please call our Reseller Customer Service department at 800-434-3422.

For information on where to purchase IDG Books Worldwide's books outside the U.S., please contact our International Sales department at 317-596-5530 or fax 317-596-5692.

For consumer information on foreign language translations, please contact our Customer Service department at 1-800-434-3422, fax 317-596-5692, or e-mail rights@idgbooks.com.

For information on licensing foreign or domestic rights, please phone +1-650-655-3109.

For sales inquiries and special prices for bulk quantities, please contact our Sales department at 650-655-3200 or write to the address above.

For information on using IDG Books Worldwide's books in the classroom or for ordering examination copies, please contact our Educational Sales department at 800-434-2086 or fax 317-596-5499.

For press review copies, author interviews, or other publicity information, please contact our Public Relations department at 650-655-3000 or fax 650-655-3299.

For authorization to photocopy items for corporate, personal, or educational use, please contact Copyright Clearance Center, 222 Rosewood Drive, Danvers, MA 01923, or fax 978-750-4470.

About the Author

Michael Hyman is the author of numerous computer books, including *Borland C++ For Dummies, Visual C++ For Dummies,* and *Visual J++ For Dummies,* all published by IDG Books Worldwide, Inc. He is an award-winning industry columnist and works on Internet technology at a large software company. In his spare time, Michael hangs out with his family, watches the waves, and dreams of being an over-idolized rock and roll star.

ABOUT IDG BOOKS WORLDWIDE

Welcome to the world of IDG Books Worldwide.

IDG Books Worldwide, Inc., is a subsidiary of International Data Group, the world's largest publisher of computer-related information and the leading global provider of information services on information technology. IDG was founded more than 30 years ago by Patrick J. McGovern and now employs more than 9,000 people worldwide. IDG publishes more than 290 computer publications in over 75 countries. More than 90 million people read one or more IDG publications each month.

Launched in 1990, IDG Books Worldwide is today the #1 publisher of best-selling computer books in the United States. We are proud to have received eight awards from the Computer Press Association in recognition of editorial excellence and three from Computer Currents' First Annual Readers' Choice Awards. Our best-selling ...For Dummies® series has more than 50 million copies in print with translations in 31 languages. IDG Books Worldwide, through a joint venture with IDG's Hi-Tech Beijing, became the first U.S. publisher to publish a computer book in the People's Republic of China. In record time, IDG Books Worldwide has become the first choice for millions of readers around the world who want to learn how to better manage their businesses.

Our mission is simple: Every one of our books is designed to bring extra value and skill-building instructions to the reader. Our books are written by experts who understand and care about our readers. The knowledge base of our editorial staff comes from years of experience in publishing, education, and journalism — experience we use to produce books to carry us into the new millennium. In short, we care about books, so we attract the best people. We devote special attention to details such as audience, interior design, use of icons, and illustrations. And because we use an efficient process of authoring, editing, and desktop publishing our books electronically, we can spend more time ensuring superior content and less time on the technicalities of making books.

You can count on our commitment to deliver high-quality books at competitive prices on topics you want to read about. At IDG Books Worldwide, we continue in the IDG tradition of delivering quality for more than 30 years. You'll find no better book on a subject than one from IDG Books Worldwide.

John Kilcullen
Chairman and CEO
IDG Books Worldwide, Inc.

Steven Berkowitz
President and Publisher
IDG Books Worldwide, Inc.

Eighth Annual Computer Press Awards ≥1992

Ninth Annual Computer Press Awards ≥1993

Tenth Annual Computer Press Awards ≥1994

Eleventh Annual Computer Press Awards ≥1995

Dedication

To Miriam Beth.

Author's Acknowledgments

Writing a book is, in many ways, like running a marathon. It takes endurance, lots of carbs, and a cheering crowd. I am especially grateful to my wife, who put up with my disappearing late into the night to work on this book. My daughter Miriam was not only a constant source of inspiration and amusement but helped out when I wasn't looking and aklj;skfkj. A special thanks to my parents, for much needed babysitting, meals, and everything else. Thanks to my sister, Betsy, and fellow nerd b-i-l Jerry. And of course, thanks to all the fine folks at IDG Books, including Nate Holdread and Sherri Morningstar, who picked this project up midway. Finally, I am especially grateful to D. Wayne Ruehling for his hard work, excellent comments, and samples when reviewing this book.

Publisher's Acknowledgements

We're proud of this book; please register your comments throught our IDG books Worldwide Online Registration Form located at http://my2cents.dummies.com.

Some of the people who helped bring this book to marke include the following:

Acquisitions, Editorial, and Media Development

Project Editor: Nate Holdread
(*Previous Edition: Kelly Oliver*)

Acquisitions Editors: Sherri Morningstar, Jill Pisoni

Senior Copy Editor: Christine Meloy Beck

Technical Editor: D. Wayne Ruehling

Media Development Editor: Joell Smith

Associate Permissions Editor: Carmen Krikorian

Media Development Coordinator: Megan Roney

Editorial Manager: Mary C. Corder

Media Development Manager: Heather Heath Dismore

Editorial Assistant: Alison Walthall

Production

Project Coordinator: Regina Snyder

Layout and Graphics: Linda Boyer, Lisa Harrington, Angela F. Hunckler, Ted Perada, Brent Savage, Kathie Schutte, Janet Seib, Mark Shirar, Kate Snell, Michael Sullivan, Brian Torwelle

Proofreaders: Kelli Botta, Melissa D. Buddendeck, Nancy Price, Rebecca Senninger, Ethel M. Winslow

Indexer: Ty Koontz

Special Help
Publication Services

General and Administrative

IDG Books Worldwide, Inc: John Kilcullen, CEO; Steven Berkowitz, President and Publisher

IDG Books Technology Publishing: Brenda McLaughlin, Senior Vice President and Group Pubisher

Dummies Technology Press and Dummies Editorial: Diane Graves Steele, Vice President and Associate Publisher, Mary Bednarek, Director of Acquisitions and Product Development; Kristin A. Cocks, Editorial Director

Dummies Trade Press: Kathleen A. Welton, Vice President and Publisher; Kevin Thornton, Acquisitions Manager

IDG Books Production for Dummies Press: Michael R. Britton, Vice President of Production and Creative Services; Cindy L. Phipps, Manager of Project Coordination, Production Proofreading, and Indexing, Kathie S. Schutte, Supervisor of Page Layout; Shelley Lea, Supervisor of Graphics and Design; Debbie J. Gates, Production Systems Specialist; Robert Springer, Supervisor of Proofreading, Debbie Stailey, Special Projects Coordinator; Tony Augsburger, Supervisor of Reprints and Bluelines

Dummies Packaging and Book Design: Patty Page, Manager, Promotions Marketing

◆

The publisher would like to give special thanks to Patrick J. McGovern,
without whom this book would not have been possible

◆

Contents at a Glance

Cartoons at a Glance

By Rich Tennant

The 5th Wave — By Rich Tennant

"Hello, smart-home maintenance? Can you send someone out? Our den is acting really stupid."

page 5

The 5th Wave — By Rich Tennant

AND TO COMPLETE THE MULTIMEDIA EXPERIENCE, WE WANT TO SHIP EACH WORKSTATION WITH THIS SCRATCH 'N SNIFF MOUSE PAD AND A SCENT-RESIDENT RAM CARD

page 323

The 5th Wave — By Rich Tennant

"HONEY! OUR WEB BROWSER GOT OUT LAST NIGHT AND DUMPED THE TRASH ALL OVER MR. BELCHER'S HOME PAGE!"

page 153

The 5th Wave — By Rich Tennant

"We're researching molecular/digital technology that moves massive amounts of information across binary pathways that interact with free agent programs capable of making decisions and performing logical tasks. We see applications in really high-end doorbells."

page 263

The 5th Wave — By Rich Tennant

"Can someone please tell me how long 'Larry's Lunch Truck' has had his own page on the intranet?"

page 339

Fax: 978-546-7747 • E-mail: the5wave@tiac.net

Table of Contents

Introduction

A long, long time ago, there was a world without the Internet. People hung around at corner soda stores wondering what their neighbors were up to. Now, they hang around at corner Internet bars and can check out their neighbor's Web cam. (I don't mean one of *those* Web cams. What were you thinking?) Anyway, just as the world has changed with the evolution of the Internet, so has the Web with the evolution of browsers. Web pages aren't only places to put lists of your favorite books or pictures of your salt and pepper shaker collection. You can create amazingly interactive pages, pages that look like magazine layouts, and even full-fledged business applications, all using Web technology. At least, you can do so if you understand Dynamic HTML. That's where this book comes in. Understanding Dynamic HTML is not like knowing HTML. You need to know far more than a set of tags for organizing a page. Rather, you need to understand many new techniques for creating pages, and must know how to control your Web browser's object model through scripts. In short, you need to understand enough to make your head spin. It's no wonder that the technical documentation for browsers takes hours to download and that good Web consultants drive fancy cars.

This book walks you through everything that you need to know to create hot Microsoft Internet Explorer 5.0 and Netscape Navigator 4.5 pages. You find out how to use the Dynamic HTML Object Model, how to lay out pages, and how to process events. You modify pages on the fly, incorporate cool multimedia, connect to databases, and more — without too much pain and with tons of sample pages that you can cut and paste to create your own sites.

Now, at this point you may be saying, "Wait a minute. I thought Internet Explorer 5.0 and Navigator 4.5 were as similar as cherry ice cream and corn chowder." Well, you may be correct. Both provide something called Dynamic HTML, and both are about the same when it comes to plain old HTML support — at least for supporting early HTML features. Both let you create HTML pages and use a cool feature called *Cascading Style Sheets* (CSS) to move elements across the page in two dimensions. Both let you set font styles and other text aspects with CSS. But as soon as you try to make a page dynamic, the two are completely different.

Internet Explorer 5.0 lets you change just about anything on a page in reaction to just about anything you can imagine. You can change font sizes and colors, you can change the text on the page, and you can even create new tags and behaviors. You can make Web pages that are as sophisticated as any Windows program or game you may have encountered. Navigator 4.5 is more restrictive, primarily letting you change the 2-D position of specific elements.

Regardless, this book shows how to create pages in both environments. Sometimes one page works in both places. Sometimes I show how to apply the same techniques in each environment. And sometimes I show capabilities that only work with Internet Explorer 5.0.

Who This Book Is For

This book is for anyone who wants to create rich pages that feature Dynamic HTML, especially if you want a book that provides tons of sample pages to give you a starting point for your own work. It assumes that you are familiar with HTML and are also familiar with the fundamentals of JavaScript — or at least that you have some elementary knowledge of programming. Now, if you are used to books such as *Beer For Dummies,* you may say, "Yeah, right. It's a *...For Dummies* book. What's this programming goo?" Well, be forewarned. To make Dynamic HTML Web pages rock, you need to put on your pocket protector, take out your slide rule, and write some small programs. Of course, I help you the whole way, so it shouldn't be too painful and you probably won't end up with high-waters and Band-Aids on your glasses. (Unless, like me, you already have them.)

So, if you've never turned on a computer before, you may want to start with a different book, such as *HTML For Dummies,* 3rd Edition, by Ed Tittel and Stephen N. James (IDG Books Worldwide, Inc.). But if you've created a few (or many) Web pages and now want to find out what Dynamic HTML and interactive Web pages are all about, this is the book for you.

This book not only goes over all the key techniques, but it provides numerous sample pages as well. You can thus easily apply what you've read.

How This Book Is Organized

This book is broken into four parts. Part I covers the fundamentals of Dynamic HTML. You find out what an object model is and read about the key objects that let you control the browser. You pick up layout techniques that can help you improve your Web site's organization. You read all about events and how you can use them to modify a page based on a user's actions. In Part I, you also discover 2-D layout. You gather input from users and read about a variety of Dynamic HTML tricks.

In Part II, you find out how to add multimedia to your pages. You change how text looks through visual filters and transitioning elements in and out. You also read about sound, synchronization, and vector graphics.

In Part III, you delve into data-focused techniques, including persisting information and using data binding. You also learn how to create and use behaviors.

Finally, in Part IV, you get the top ten lists of a variety of key HTML features, including the top ten objects, top ten style attributes, and top ten HTML tags.

Appendix A provides a quick overview of HTML, Appendix B shows you a quick overview of JavaScript, and Appendix C outlines what's on the CD-ROM that accompanies this book.

About the CD

The CD-ROM that accompanies this book contains all the samples from the text, ready for you to cut and paste to use in your own projects. The CD also contains some extra samples, great shareware to help you create your pages, and of course, Internet Explorer 5.0 itself.

Icons Used in This Book

The following icons are used in this book.

The Tip icon means that I'm about to tell you one of those tidbits I learned the hard way. Some tips show you shortcuts and better approaches to solving certain problems. Others help you work around bugs (not that they really exist). And of course, there is the ultimate tip: plastics.

Be careful when you see this icon. It warns you of things you shouldn't do or dangerous things you should watch out for.

The Technical Stuff icon warns you that the next set of text is for hard-core nerds. When you see it, throw up your hands, yell "Danger! Danger, Will Robinson!" and then dig in to some advanced details.

The Netscape Version icon indicates that the text discusses the differences between Internet Explorer 5.0 and Netscape Navigator 4.5. You see these icons throughout the book to point out why a particular page won't work with Navigator 4.5.

Part I

Everything You Wanted to Know about Dynamic HTML

The 5th Wave   By Rich Tennant

"Hello, smart-home maintenance? Can you send someone out? Our den is acting really stupid."

In this part . . .

You need to know many things to create great Web pages: the basic techniques, the important tags, scripting techniques, and the number of a great pizza joint for late-night authoring sessions.

This part discusses the first three of these fundamental needs. You find out what an object model is and the key objects that let you control how a Web page acts. From there, you discover a variety of layout techniques that you can use to organize your pages.

You also read about events, which let you react to users as they cruise through a page. Then, you find out all about 2-D layout. You see how to get input from the user by using forms, and you discover tricks, such as adding search engines to your page.

Finally, you discover how to use Dynamic HTML to make all types of modifications to your page, such as changing fonts and colors on the fly and even typing directly into an HTML page.

Chapter 1

Introducing . . . Dynamic HTML!

In This Chapter

▶ What is Dynamic HTML?

▶ Using an object model in Dynamic HTML

▶ Using a script

▶ Discovering the key Dynamic HTML objects

▶ Creating a simple Dynamic HTML Web page

*B*ack in the dark ages — that is, last year, last month, or maybe even a couple of minutes ago — the World Wide Web was static. The only things that were truly animated about surfing the Internet were watching the modem lines blink and cursing all the busy signals. And even with the introduction of Java applets, the information on the page is basically constant. To see something different, you click a link, and the browser downloads another page.

Dynamic HTML changes that. The page is no longer static. Practically everything on the page can change at runtime. What exactly does this mean? Think about it this way. You're sitting at the keyboard of a computer that's powerful enough to do your taxes, keep track of your business, and run Doom. Then you surf to the Internet, and what does your machine do? It just sits there, waiting for bits to come across the modem, and then displays them on the screen. It may as well be one of those green terminals in the movies that goes click-click-click each time the letters appear on the screen. Meanwhile, all the processing power of the computer is going to waste. It's like hiring Einstein to copy all the names from the Los Angeles phone book. He could do it, but it may not be the best use of his time.

Dynamic HTML shifts more activity to the client computer. Instead of having the computer simply wait for new data to come down the modem, Dynamic HTML pages contain information that tells the page how to interact with the user. For example, suppose you want the color of a word to change when you move the mouse over it. (Why would you want to change the color? To draw

---

What is HTML?

HTML stands for Hypertext Markup Language. It's a set of commands that get mixed in with text to describe how a Web page should appear. When you look at a Web page, you don't see the HTML tags — instead, Microsoft Internet Explorer reads the tags and uses them to decide how the text should appear. HTML tags are all enclosed within angle brackets. For example, the bold command looks like this: <B>. So if you see a sentence such as "I am **happy**" on a Web page, the underlying HTML would be I am <B>happy</B>. If you're new to HTML, you may want to glance through Appendix A, which provides a quick overview of the key HTML features and concepts.

---

attention to the word, thereby waking up the reader and making the page feel more like a cool CD-ROM.) You couldn't do this in the dark ages. At best, you could click on a link to download a different page with different highlighting. Of course, by the time the download finished, you had probably long since moved the mouse or surfed to a different page.

Or maybe you want to sort data in a table, rearrange a chart, or have animated bears run across the page. Again, in the dark ages, all these activities would require asking the server for a new page. This constant querying of the server, even for mundane tasks, not only results in slower Web pages but also slows down the whole Internet.

With Dynamic HTML, everything on the page can change at any time. For example, you can change the color or size of the text. You can hide and show regions. You can add or delete text based on user interactions. You can move items across the page over time. You can sort data. You can have animated lights illuminate text. All these effects are accomplished by using Dynamic HTML and scripting, without the need to fetch a new page from the server every time you want to make a slight change.

The Knights Who Say OM

Unlike regular HTML (okay, what is officially called HTML 3.2), Dynamic HTML lets you add functions to a Web page program that can change all aspects of the page. That's why it's called *Dynamic HTML* — anything about the HTML document can change dynamically, which means that instead of having to download new information every time something on the page changes, the change can be done by the HTML document. As a result, pages are richer and more interactive, respond faster, and don't need to consume as much bandwidth.

The fundamental concept behind Dynamic HTML is that it includes an *object model* that describes the page. The object model exposes all the features of the page to script so that you can dynamically change the page by simply writing scripts.

"Groovy," you say. "It has an object model. I always wanted one of those. Does it come with mud flaps?"

Even though the term *object model* sounds as if it were invented by the bearded UNIX guru who hangs out with Dilbert, it really describes a simple concept that provides a way for you to change anything you want on a Web page. Before jumping into the specifics, let me describe an analogy. Suppose you're typing a letter using your favorite word processor. Your letter has an address and three paragraphs. If you want, you can change the margin for the entire document. Or you can select just the first paragraph and change the style and size of the font. That first paragraph is also composed of a set of sentences. You can just go in and delete one of those sentences. Or better yet, you can select the third word in the second sentence and make it boldface.

In short, your letter has a natural hierarchy. First, you have the document itself. Changing its properties, such as the margin, affects the entire document. The document contains an address and a set of paragraphs. The paragraphs contain sentences. The sentences contain words. Finally, the words contain letters. Sometimes you want to make changes that affect the entire document. Other times, you want to change a whole paragraph. And sometimes, you just want to modify a single word or character.

Now, when you change the document in your word processor, you don't explicitly think about the hierarchy. You just click on the word or select the paragraph that you want to change. But suppose you want to change the document *programmatically*. That is, you want to create a program that does the work for you. In this case, you need a way to describe the document as something that a program can understand. In short, you need to create a set of hierarchical objects that a program can talk to. Each object needs to represent part of the document. You can break the document into the hierarchy shown in Figure 1-1.

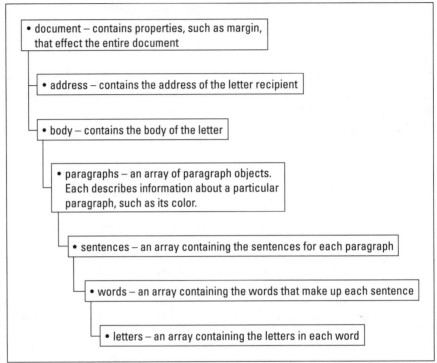

Figure 1-1:
Hierarchical
objects for
your
document.

If you want to change the margin for the document, you can write this line into the code for the program:

```
document.margin = 3
```

This line sets the margin property of the document to 3.

To make the third paragraph blue, you can use this code:

```
document.body.paragraphs(3).color = blue
```

This line changes the color property of the third paragraph in the body of the document.

Having a set of commands you can execute to control a document, as in the previous snippets, is what an object model is. It's a way to break up a complex thing (such as a Web page) into a set of components. Each component has a set of properties (color, margin, and so on) and can contain additional components (such as sentences inside a paragraph).

Are you sure this object model stuff is new?

If you wrote scripts for Netscape Navigator 3.0 or Internet Explorer 3.0, you may say to yourself, "Ho hum, I've seen this object model stuff before. What's the big deal?" Internet Explorer 3.0 and Navigator 3.0 both provide an object model. In fact, the two browsers provide the same object model. Not only that, but the object model from the 3.0 browsers is the starting point for the Dynamic HTML object model.

But there is one big difference. With the 3.0-level browsers, you can find out some aspects about the Web page, and you can change some aspects of the page, such as the background color. But outside of that, you can change very little. With Dynamic HTML, you can change pretty much anything on a Web page, which makes browsers that support Dynamic HTML very exciting to write Web pages for.

And just in case that explanation sounds straightforward, let me confuse you by telling you that there are actually three object models. Navigator 4.5 has one object model, and Internet Explorer 5.0 has another one. They are kind of like distant cousins. And then there is a third object model, which was developed by the W3C, a committee that creates standards for use on the Web. Internet Explorer 5.0 implements the W3C-approved object model in addition to the one that is similar to the Internet Explorer 4.0 object model. At some point, maybe Navigator will implement the W3C object model as well, and you'll be able to share code across browsers. But until that time, the two browsers remain incompatible.

Dynamic HTML provides an object model that describes the Web page. By doing so, it enables you to programmatically change just about anything that is on a Web page. Thus, the page is dynamic — anything can change at any time. This capability is extremely powerful because it lets you, as a Web author, have the page react to user activity without having to download a new page. It also lets you do cool things, such as make animated text or add sound effects.

Script Writing? Sure, See My Agent

By itself, an object model is boring. True, you could share object model facts with others at parties in hopes of getting a date, but realistically, you probably wouldn't have much luck. Instead, the way to make an object model interesting is to manipulate it with scripts. That way, you can use it to make a Web page come alive. If you want to have some text fly across the page or you want to import data from a database and create a chart from it, you need to write scripts. Internet Explorer 5.0 provides two built-in scripting languages: VBScript and JScript. As you may guess, VBScript is based on VisualBasic, and JScript is based on Java. Navigator 4.5 provides JavaScript.

In case you're wondering whether there's a difference between JScript and JavaScript, the answer is yes and no. JScript comes from Microsoft, and JavaScript comes from Netscape. Their lawyers probably didn't want them calling the language the same thing — at least, that's usually what happens when you put a bunch of lawyers together in a sandbox. Regardless, JScript and JavaScript are technically just about the same thing, and all the samples in this book are written in JScript/JavaScript.

If you haven't written much script, don't panic. I step through the early samples so that you can get the hang of what is going on. You can also check out Appendix B, which provides a quick JScript/JavaScript tutorial, or read *JavaScript For Dummies,* 2nd Edition, by Emily A. VanderVeer (IDG Books Worldwide, Inc.).

The unbearable lightness of scripting

Scripts and scripting languages are so named because they are designed to enhance the capabilities of an application — such as Microsoft Word or Internet Explorer — without requiring the services of a hard-core, expensive programmer. The idea is that, if a language is called a *scripting language* rather than a *programming language,* it must somehow seem easier. It's like saying that Greenland must be warm and sunny because it's called Greenland.

Actually, writing scripts is much like writing programs. There are fewer commands, and you don't have as many low-level details to worry about, but the fundamental concepts are the same.

You find one big difference, though, between writing a full-fledged program and writing a script to manipulate a Web page. With full-fledged programs, everything — and I mean *everything* — that happens is because of your code. If you want the word *Hello* to appear on the screen, you write code to do so. If you want a menu to appear or a beep to sound when the user clicks, you write code.

By contrast, when you write a script for a Web page, the script just enhances the Web page. In other words, a scripted Web page consists of a lot of HTML — for example, for the title, the layout, the text, the images, and so on — and some scripts that define how the page responds to user input. Thus, the majority of the work is done by the application — the browser — and not by the scripts that you need to write. What takes a few lines of script may take hundreds or thousands of lines of C++ or Java. That's because the script simply controls how Internet Explorer 5.0 and Navigator 4.5 behave. The browsers themselves are extremely powerful; therefore, you can do many things with very little scripting.

So what exactly is a script? A *script* is a small program that's designed to manipulate a Web page. Now, this manipulation doesn't just happen out of the blue. You don't bring up a Web page and have a script spring into action whenever it feels like it. Rather, scripts are triggered in response to some action. For example, you could write a script that runs when the user moves the mouse over an image on the page. Or you could write a script that runs when the user clicks on a button or selects an option from a drop-down list. The thing that triggers the script is called an *event*. (Programmers also call events *messages*.) Many different events can occur when the user interacts with a Web page; these events are covered in detail in Chapter 3.

When the event occurs, the script that's designed to process the event runs. The script itself is called an *event handler* because it's designed to handle (that is, respond to) any actions that need to happen when the event occurs.

The script can do any number of things:

- ✔ Read or write properties from the Dynamic HTML object model
- ✔ Call (or invoke) Dynamic HTML methods
- ✔ Perform calculations

Think of *properties* as adjectives that describe part of the Web page. (If you are familiar with object-oriented programming, properties are simply *data members*.) For example, properties include the width and height of HTML elements, the URL of the document that's being displayed, and the number of frames that are on the page.

Scripts can read and write properties. (Often these actions are called *getting* and *setting* properties rather than *reading* and *writing* properties, but the terms mean the same thing.) For example, you could write a script that changes the color of some text. Or you could write a script that moves a button across the screen by changing its position properties.

Scripts can also *call* Dynamic HTML methods. *Calling* a method (or script) is also called *invoking* or *executing*. *Methods* are like verbs — they cause some action to occur. (If you have done object-oriented programming, you may have heard methods referred to as *member functions*.) For example, the object model contains an object called the `window` object. Among other things, it contains a method called `setTimeout`, which tells the browser to call some script after a specific delay.

And finally, scripts can call other scripts, an action known as *calling a function*. In short, it's usually easier to tackle programming challenges by breaking a problem into smaller pieces. That's how things operate in the real world. When you cook dinner, you break the task into specific tasks. Pick the beans. Wash the tofu. Chop the onions. Wave a newspaper at the smoke detector until it stops beeping. Essentially, a function is a script that accomplishes a specific task. Scripts call functions to do various specific tasks, and when all those tasks are completed, the larger job is finished, and you have dinner.

To write Dynamic HTML pages, you create scripts that manipulate the Dynamic HTML object model.

A quick example

The following is a quick look at a Dynamic HTML page to see what these object-model-manipulating scripts really look like. Start your browser and, using the CD-ROM at the back of this book, load the simple.html file from the ch01 folder.

If you're using Navigator, load simple_nn.html instead of simple.html.

This page looks boring. You simply see some text on the screen, as shown in Figure 1-2. Now click on the page. Suddenly, some of the text moves. In fact, each time you click on the page, the words *Hello World Wide Web!* move down and to the right. Figure 1-3 shows what the page looks like after clicking several times.

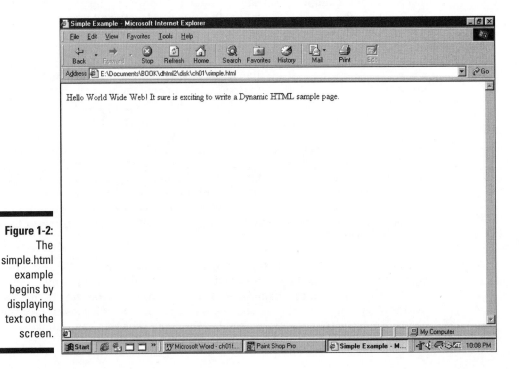

Figure 1-2:
The simple.html example begins by displaying text on the screen.

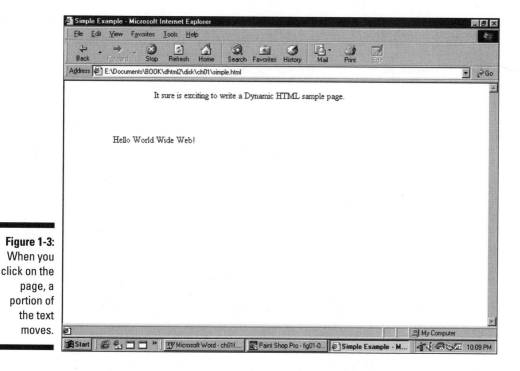

Figure 1-3:
When you
click on the
page, a
portion of
the text
moves.

In the rest of this section, I describe how this page works.

Take a look at the HTML file. You can examine the file in one of two ways. From Internet Explorer, choose View⇨Source to display the HTML file using Notepad. From Navigator, choose View⇨Page Source to display the source using the Netscape source browser. For another approach, load the HTML file the into an HTML editor, such as Microsoft Visual InterDev or Allaire HomeSite. For example, if you have installed HomeSite from the *Dynamic HTML For Dummies,* 2nd Edition, CD, follow these steps:

1. **Start HomeSite.**

2. **Use the drive selector drop-down box to select the CD-ROM drive.**

3. **Use the directory tree to switch to the samples\ch01 folder.**

4. **Double-click on the simple.html file in the file list.**

   The simple.html file opens in the HomeSite editor.

The HTML that you see is shown in Listing 1-1.

Listing 1-1	The simple.html File

```
<HTML>
<HEAD>
<TITLE>Simple Example</TITLE>
<SCRIPT>
function moveText() {
 myText.style.posLeft += 10;
 myText.style.posTop += 10;
}
</SCRIPT>
</HEAD>
<BODY onclick="moveText()">
<SPAN id=myText style="position:relative" >Hello World Wide Web!</SPAN> It sure is
             exciting to write a Dynamic HTML sample page.
</BODY>
</HTML>
```

What is going on here? The page starts with the usual <HTML> tag, and then a <TITLE> tag appears inside the <HEAD> tags. Nothing interesting so far, but note the <SCRIPT> tag — that's where the interesting stuff happens. Skip the <SCRIPT> tag for a moment so that you have a chance to examine the rest of the page. After the script comes the body. You can immediately see something special — the <BODY> tag contains the following code:

```
onclick="moveText()"
```

When the user clicks on an element on the Web page, the onclick event occurs. This line in the <BODY> tag tells the browser to call the script function moveText whenever the onclick event happens for the <BODY>. In other words, whenever a viewer clicks somewhere inside the page, the function moveText is called. That's how you get the text to move when the viewer clicks inside the page.

Note that with the Navigator version, you process events in a slightly different fashion, as you can see in the setup function. Instead of indicating the event to handle on the object, you do so with script:

```
function setup() {
   document.onclick = moveText;
}
```

This approach actually works with Internet Explorer as well. Sometimes I use it for the examples in this book to create versions of pages that work in both browsers. But most of the time, I show the simplest approaches for both browsers.

If this explanation seems a little nerdy to you, that's okay. As you progress through the book, creating event handlers is going to become second nature. On the other hand, if you're wondering what the heck an ⟨HTML⟩ tag is, you may want to brush up on HTML before continuing.

Next, you see a ⟨SPAN⟩ tag. This tag groups a set of HTML commands and gives them a name. In this case, you can see that the words *Hello World Wide Web!* are contained between the ⟨SPAN⟩ and the ⟨/SPAN⟩ tags. The ⟨SPAN⟩ tag has an id parameter that gives a name to the span (I use the generic name *span* for the ⟨SPAN⟩ tag) so that it can easily be modified from a script. Note the following example:

```
<SPAN id=myText style="position:relative" >
```

In this case, the span's name is myText. Its name is used shortly when I go back to examine the script.

You can also see that the ⟨SPAN⟩ tag has a style parameter. This very powerful parameter was introduced with Internet Explorer 4.0 and Navigator 4.0. The style parameter lets you control many aspects of how an item is displayed, including its position, color, and size. I discuss using the style parameter in more detail in Chapters 2 and 4. Here, it indicates that the position of the span can change and that its coordinate system is relative to the body of the page.

After the ⟨/SPAN⟩ tag, you find more plain text and then the closing tags for the page.

In short, the page is composed of some scripts and a body with some text in it. The body contains a named span and reacts to mouse clicks.

Next, I review the scripts themselves. A moment ago, you saw that the function moveText gets called when the body is clicked on. The function moveText is created with JavaScript. (Or JScript. Take your pick on what to call this scripting language. I don't care.) If you look inside the ⟨SCRIPT⟩ tags, you can see moveText, as follows:

```
function moveText() {
  myText.style.posLeft += 10;
  myText.style.posTop += 10;
}
```

When a user clicks on the body, this function is called, meaning that the lines within it are executed. In this case, the lines manipulate the style properties for myText, which is the name of the span. Thus, when the mouse is clicked, moveText manipulates some of the myText properties. In particular, it adds 10 to the posLeft and posTop properties of the style.

Pretty complex, huh? Let me give you more detail. An object named `myText` is on the page; this object represents a span. Objects can have styles. So `myText.style` indicates the style object that helps describe `myText`. It's just like asking for the formatting information for a paragraph. The style object itself contains many properties and some objects. The property `posLeft` indicates the position of the left corner of the object. Similarly, `posTop` indicates the position of the top of the object. By adding 10 to `posLeft`, you move the left corner of the object 10 units to the right. By adding 10 to `posTop`, you move the top corner of the object 10 units down. Thus, every time the user clicks on the page, the span moves right and down.

The Navigator code for moving the object looks slightly different. Here's the `moveText` function:

```
function moveText() {
   document.myText.left += 10;
   document.myText.top += 10;
}
```

The code does the same thing as the Internet Explorer version, only instead of manipulating `myText.style.posLeft`, you manipulate `document.myText.left`.

Guess what? You've now manipulated the Dynamic HTML object model!

When you look at scripts that control Dynamic HTML, you see many periods throughout. For example, the `moveText` function manipulates `myText.style.posLeft`. The period is a way of separating objects. It means "Look for the object (or property) to the right of the period within the object to the left of the period." So `myText.style` indicates the style object that is part of `myText`. And `style.posLeft` indicates the `posLeft` property of the `style` object. Thus, `myText.style.posLeft` denotes the `posLeft` property of the `style` object of the `myText` span.

Note that the period doesn't let you arbitrarily combine together objects that have no relationship. It lets you navigate through a hierarchy of objects. The `style` object is part of the `myText` object. It didn't just show up arbitrarily. Likewise, `posLeft` is part of `style`.

Note that JavaScript is *case-sensitive,* which means that when you type in one of the programs in this book, you need to make sure that you don't change the capitalization of any of the commands. For example, Dynamic HTML has a command called `window.setInterval`. You need to type it in with the same case shown here. `Window.SetInterval` doesn't work because too many letters are capitalized. Note, however, that VBScript is not case-sensitive. With VBScript programs you can use whatever mix of capital and lowercase letters you want.

Unidentified Flying Objects

In the preceding section, you got a taste of what creating a Dynamic HTML page is all about. In this section, I discuss more about some of the key objects that make up the Dynamic HTML object model. I start with the window object — the top-level object for the whole browser. Then I examine the most important of the other objects. Throughout the book, you find out more about the various objects that you can use to control a Web page. Figure 1-4 shows the full Dynamic HTML object hierarchy.

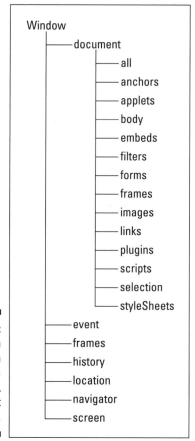

Figure 1-4:
The main objects in the Dynamic HTML object model.

Window
— document
———— all
———— anchors
———— applets
———— body
———— embeds
———— filters
———— forms
———— frames
———— images
———— links
———— plugins
———— scripts
———— selection
———— styleSheets
— event
— frames
— history
— location
— navigator
— screen

Remember that the object model is simply a set of objects that describes the browser and what is displayed on a page. Nothing is magical here. The various objects provide a way to organize and access the information that is necessary to have complete control over a Web page.

Window on the world

The window is the top-level object in the object model. It contains objects that provide complete information about the browser, including objects that indicate what page is being examined (location), the size of the computer display (screen), the page content (document), and information about frames (frames), if there are any. You can also use the window object to change the property of the status bar (which is along the bottom of the browser) or to perform simple timing.

Location, screen, document, and frames are all full-fledged objects, so I examine them later. Of the various properties and methods on the window object, four are particularly useful: status, setTimeout, setInterval, and clearInterval.

status

The status property lets you set the text that is displayed in the status line — the bar along the bottom of the browser where various messages appear. The browser uses this area to update you on its progress in finding a particular URL. You can use it to display messages as well.

To display a message in the status bar, just set the status property. For example, to display the message *Hi Mom,* you could use the following line of script:

```
window.status = "Hi Mom";
```

setTimeout

The setTimeout method calls a function after a specified amount of time has elapsed. The format is as follows:

```
window.setTimeout("function name", milliseconds)
```

For example, suppose you want to change the color of certain text in five seconds. You could write the following code:

```
window.setTimeout("changeColor()", 5000);
```

This code calls the changeColor function after 5,000 milliseconds (5 seconds) have elapsed.

You may have noticed that setTimeout is a method, although status is a property. Thus, you set (or get) the value of the status property, and you call the setTimeout method. You may wonder, why treat status as a property rather than have a getStatus and setStatus method? Values that are both read and written are usually treated as properties — that makes one less thing for you to remember.

setInterval and clearInterval

The `setInterval` and `clearInterval` methods are similar to `setTimeout`, except that they repeatedly call a function. The `setInterval` method starts the process. You specify what to call and the delay between invocations. That function is then called indefinitely. The `setInterval` method returns a number that identifies that particular `setInterval` call. If you want to stop a particular `setInterval`, call `clearInterval`, passing in the number returned from the `setInterval`.

For example, the following code calls a function named `updateClock` every 3.5 seconds:

```
myInterval = window.setInterval("updateClock()", 3500);
```

To stop the repeated calling of `updateClock`, you can write the following code:

```
window.clearInterval(myInterval);
```

A simple, out-of-the-way clock

You can use the timing methods I describe in the preceding section to create a simple timer. This timer updates the status bar by showing how many seconds you've looked at the particular page, as shown in Figure 1-5.

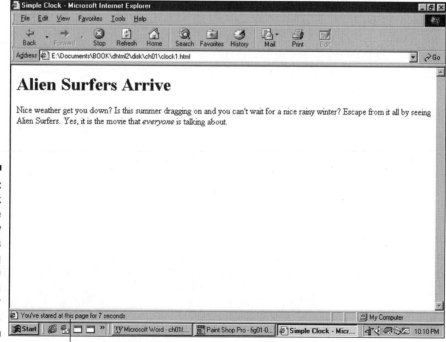

Figure 1-5:
The clock page regularly updates how long you've looked at a particular Web page.

The timer updates the status bar.

If you look at the <BODY> tag, you can see that two functions are called based on body events. In particular, the function startClock is called when the page finishes loading (that's when the onload event fires), and the endClock function is called when the page goes away — whether from shutting down the browser, requesting a page refresh, or going to another page. The following is the HTML code that establishes this behavior:

```
<BODY onload="startClock()" onunload="endClock()">
```

The function startClock uses setInterval to update the clock every second with the following line of script:

```
myTick = window.setInterval("updateClock()", 1000);
```

As you can see, this line simply calls another function, updateClock, every second. The function updateClock, in turn, updates a counter and displays the counter value in the status line, as follows:

```
cntTime++;
window.status = "You've stared at this page for " + cntTime + " seconds";
```

You can see the complete code in Listing 1-2. To load the page, load the clock1.html file from the ch01 folder on the enclosed CD-ROM.

Listing 1-2   The clock1.html Page

```
<HTML>
<HEAD>
<TITLE>Simple Clock</TITLE>
<SCRIPT>
var myTick;
var cntTime = 0;
function startClock() {
 myTick = window.setInterval("updateClock()", 1000);
}
function updateClock() {
 cntTime++;
window.status = "You've stared at this page for " + cntTime + " seconds";
}
function endClock() {
 window.clearInterval(myTick);
}
</SCRIPT>
</HEAD>
<BODY onload="startClock()" onunload="endClock()">
<H1>Alien Surfers Arrive</H1>
Nice weather get you down? Is this summer dragging on and you can't wait for a nice
          rainy winter? Escape from it all by seeing Alien Surfers. Yes, it is
          the movie that <I>everyone</I> is talking about.
</BODY>
</HTML>
```

Whoa! What's going on here?

If you're not used to JavaScript programs, the code in Listing 1-2 may look scary. The best way to approach it is to walk through it a section at a time. The program starts with the `<SCRIPT>` tag.

This tag tells the browser that all the lines up to the `</SCRIPT>` tag are a program. The program begins by defining some variables named `myTick` and `cntTime`:

```
var myTick;
var cntTime = 0;
```

Variables let you store information. For example, the variable named `cntTime` stores how many seconds have elapsed. You can name variables pretty much anything you want.

Notice that both lines end with a semicolon, which is the JavaScript way of indicating that a line has ended. The semicolons aren't really necessary (the script still works if you leave them out), but it's stylistically better to put them in.

The next set of lines start with `function`:

```
function startClock() {
  myTick = window.setInterval
    ("updateClock()", 1000);
}
```

Surprisingly enough, when a section of script starts with the word `function`, it means that the next few lines define a function — a named

group of lines that can be called from another script. The word `function` is followed by the name of the function. In this case, the function is called `startClock`. How do you know which lines are part of the function? They are all enclosed within curly braces (the { and the }).

You can see that the function `startClock` sets the value of the variable `myTick` to the value returned by calling the `setInterval` method. In other words, when `startClock` is called, it calls the `setInterval` method on the `window` object. `setInterval` returns a value — and that value, in turn, is stored in the variable named `myTick` so that it can be used later.

The script continues by defining a few more functions.

Later in the HTML, in the `<BODY>` tag, the scripts are hooked up to events:

```
<BODY onload="startClock()"
    onunload="endClock()">
```

This line says that when the `onload` event occurs for the page, call the script named `startClock`. When the `onunload` event occurs, call the script named `endClock`.

Be sure to check out Appendix B, which provides a quick overview of JavaScript.

Location, location, location

The `location` object shows you information about the URL for the page that's being viewed. The `location` object is available from the `window`, `document`, and `frames` objects.

The `location` object contains several key properties. Of these, `href` returns the full URL for the document that's being viewed. The others contain part of the URL, such as the filename or the protocol.

The following are the key properties of the location object:

  ✔ `hostname`. The name of the server that the Web page being viewed is located on. For example, if the document viewed is `www.nwlink.com/~tigger/index.html`, the `hostname` is `www.nwlink.com`.

  ✔ `href`. The full URL of the document being displayed. For example, if the document viewed is `www.nwlink.com/~tigger/index.html`, the `href` is `http://www.nwlink.com/~tigger`.

  ✔ `pathname`. The path and filename for the object. For example, if the document viewed is `www.nwlink.com/~tigger/index.html`, the `pathname` is `~tigger/index.html`.

  ✔ `protocol`. The protocol used for accessing the document. Typically, the protocol is `http:` or `file:`. For example, if the document viewed is `http://www.nwlink.com/~tigger/index.html`, the `protocol` is `http:`.

  ✔ `hash`. The fragment associated with queries, or anchor name(s) within a specific document. For example `http://www.nwlink.com/~tigger/index.html#Page3` (would refer to a named anchor Page3, within the document referred to in the URL).

By changing the `href` (or any of the other location properties), you change what page is viewed in the browser. Changing the `href` through script lets you write code that makes the browser jump to various pages. If you have a page with several frames on it, you can also set the `href` property on a particular frame to display a different page within that frame.

For an example of using the `location` object, check out the location.html file in the ch01 folder. It starts by displaying the values of the `protocol`, `host`, `path`, and `href` properties, as shown in Figure 1-6. Clicking on the page changes the `href`, thereby forcing a jump to a different page. You force a jump with the following line:

```
window.location.href = "ch1mars.jpg";
```

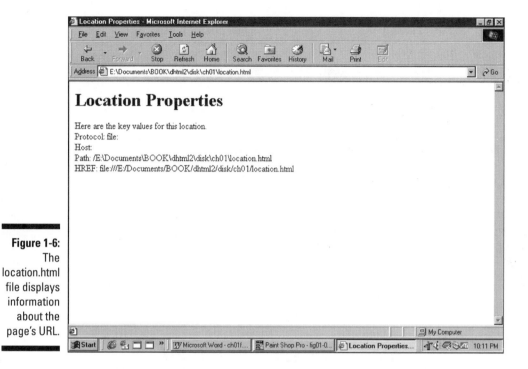

Figure 1-6:
The
location.html
file displays
information
about the
page's URL.

This line changes the href to ch1mars.jpg. As a result, when the viewer clicks on the page, the browser jumps to display the JPEG file. You could also have the browser jump to an HTML file, such as alien.html or to a Web site such as www.microsoft.com.

You can see the complete code in Listing 1-3.

If you run the location.html page locally (that is, off the CD-ROM or your hard drive), you note that the host property is blank because your page isn't being read from a Web host. If, on the other hand, you upload the page to your Web site and then check it out, the host is filled in.

If you're running Navigator, load location_nn.html instead. Internet Explorer lets you insert new HTML into the middle of an HTML page whenever you like, using a function called innerHTML. (See Chapter 6 for more information.) Navigator lets you write into sections only during page load, using the function document.writeln, as you can see in location_nn.html.

Listing 1-3	The location.html File

```
<HTML>
<HEAD>
<TITLE>Location Properties</TITLE>
<SCRIPT>
function changeURL() {
  window.location.href = "ch1mars.jpg";
}
function showLocation() {
  var theLoc;
  theLoc = "Protocol: " + window.location.protocol + "<BR>";
  theLoc += "Host: " + window.location.host + "<BR>";
  theLoc += "Path: " + window.location.pathname + "<BR>";
  theLoc += "HREF: " + window.location.href + "<BR>";
  myText.innerHTML = theLoc;
}
</SCRIPT>
</HEAD>
<BODY onclick="changeURL()" onload="showLocation()">
<H1>Location Properties</H1>
Here are the key values for this location.<BR>
<SPAN id=myText></SPAN>
</BODY>
</HTML>
```

I screen, you screen, we all screen for ice screen

Use the `screen` object to determine the size of the computer display. The key properties are `height` and `width`, which return the height and width of the computer display, in pixels. You can use this to aid in changing the size and layout of your Web page to adjust for the user's screen resolution.

Back to our documentary

By itself, the `document` object isn't too interesting. It is, however, the jumping-off point for finding most of the worker objects that relate to a page. In particular, the `document` object contains the following key objects; you find out about most of these in more detail in later chapters:

- ✔ `all`. Gives you access to all the items within the page. You use this object in Chapter 3 to read radio buttons and in Chapter 6 to create a Web-based form letter.

- ✔ `anchors`. Gives you access to all the named anchor tags in the document.

- ✔ `body`. Contains information regarding the text that's displayed on the page and the size of the browser window.

- ✔ forms. Gives you access to all the forms in the document. You use this object in Chapter 5 to read and set the values of checkboxes and to edit fields on a Web page.

- ✔ images. Gives you access to all the images that are displayed in the document.

- ✔ frames. Gives you access to all the frames on the page. This object is frequently used to change what documents are displayed in a particular frame. You use this object in Chapter 3 to create a page that displays restaurant menus.

- ✔ layers. Gives you access to all the <LAYER>, <SPAN>, and <DIV> tags on a page.

- ✔ links. Gives you access to all the anchor tags in the documents that are used to link to other files or Web pages.

- ✔ styleSheets. Gives you access to all the styleSheets on the page. You use this object in Chapter 6 to change the font that's used for items of a particular style.

Navigator does not provide the all or styleSheets collections or the body object. Internet Explorer does not provide the layers collection. (In case you are wondering what the heck a collection is, read on.)

Help me understand that code!

The showLocation function provides the heart of the page: It checks the various location properties and then displays them. The showLocation function starts by creating a variable to store the location information:

```
var theLoc;
```

Next, it reads the various location properties, which all return text values. The script adds the value to the name of the property and then adds an HTML line break to the end of the string.

For example, the following line creates a new string formed by the word "Protocol: ", followed by the value of the protocol property, followed by a <BR> tag:

```
theLoc = "Protocol: " +
    window.location.protocol +
    "<BR>";
```

The next three lines add more information to this string. Finally, the resulting string is displayed in the Web page, using a very cool Dynamic HTML method called innerHTML. The innerHTML method inserts new HTML into part of a Web page. In this case, I set the HTML that is displayed inside the span named myText:

```
myText.innerHTML = theLoc;
```

You can read more about the innerHTML method in Chapter 6.

Collections

In addition to modifying objects by name, you can enumerate all the items in a particular collection. For example, most of the objects on the document object (especially those ending in *s,* such as forms and frames) are *collection objects.* A collection object contains an array that refers to all the items of a particular type.

For example, suppose that you have two images on your page. In that case, `document.images` is a two-element array. `document.images[0]` refers to the first image in the document, and `document.images[1]` refers to the second image in the document. You use collections to modify a group of elements all at once or when elements aren't named. By using collections rather than individually named elements, you can write scripts that work regardless of the number of elements that are on the page. For example, in Chapter 5, you create a page that reads which radio button is set, regardless of how many radio buttons are on the page.

Collections provide a very powerful way to group items on a page. You can give the same name to multiple elements and then get a collection for all the elements of that name. For example, if you want to manipulate four different objects at the same time, you could give them the same name, get the collection of those objects, and programmatically enumerate through them. You see this technique used in Chapter 6.

The following is a quick example of using collections; you can find collections.html in the ch01 folder on the enclosed CD-ROM. This page contains a set of images. When you click on the button on the page, the script displays the names of each image on the page — regardless of how many images are on the page. Looking at the code in Listing 1-4, you can see that the function `showNames` uses the images collection to display the names of all the images in the document. It doesn't need to refer to the images by name. Furthermore, the same function works regardless of the number of images.

Listing 1-4	The collections.html File

```
<HTML>
<!--From Dynamic HTML for Dummies by Michael I. Hyman-->
<HEAD>
<TITLE>Collection Demo</TITLE>
<SCRIPT>
function showNames() {
   for (i = 0; i < document.images.length; i++)
      alert(document.images[i].src)
}
</SCRIPT>

</HEAD>
<BODY>
```

```
<H1>Demonstrates Using Collections</H1>
When you click on the button below, all of the image source names will be
            displayed.<FORM>
<input type=button value="Show names" onclick="showNames()">
</FORM>
<IMG src="../media/img1.jpg">
<IMG src="../media/img2.jpg">
<IMG src="../media/img3.jpg">
</BODY>
</HTML>
```

Chapter 2

The Best Laid-Out Pages
of Mice and Men

· ·

· ·

*N*ewspapers are not Web pages. When you read a newspaper, the layout is exactly predetermined. If you fold the paper because you're sitting on a crowded subway, the paper doesn't recognize that change. None of the words move across the page to allow you to read the article with a much narrower column (unless, of course, you've had a little too much pancake syrup and the sugar buzz is making you see things).

By contrast, Web pages *reflow* automatically — the browser can move text around on the page to fit the size of the browser window. If you aren't sure what this explanation means, browse to one of your favorite pages. Maximize the browser window so that it takes up the whole screen, and look at where the text and images end up. Now shrink the browser so that it takes up only half the screen. The text and images show up in a different configuration. In particular, text doesn't get cut from the sides of the page the way it does when you fold a newspaper. The text flows as if it had always been designed for a smaller space.

Browsers are able to reflow the text in HTML pages because of the HTML tags that tell the browser how the page should appear. For example, the `<BR>` tag indicates that there should be a break between two lines. The `<H1>` tag indicates that the text down to the corresponding `</H1>` is a level-1 heading and thus should be displayed using the heading 1 style. The `<TABLE>` tag indicates that a multirow, multicolumn table is about to begin. You control how a page looks through your use of the various HTML tags.

As an HTML author, you add tags to your page to control how it appears. These tags not only help organize your page, but they indicate how it reflows depending on the size of the browser window. Because this book assumes that you already have created some HTML pages and is not about HTML basics, I'm not going to explain what the various tags are (although you can find a quick guide in Appendix A). Instead, I go through some common layout needs and show you how to achieve them by using various HTML approaches and tricks. Then I cover using Cascading Style Sheets (CSS) to provide more control over how a page appears. By the end of this chapter, you're going to know much more about how to make a page look the way you want it to.

Heading to the Beach

Books and articles usually have a natural hierarchical organization. Take this book . . . please. (Okay, perhaps you should *buy* it.) This book has a title, which is clearly visible across the yellow front cover. It has five parts, and each part is further broken down into chapters or appendixes. Finally, each chapter has sections, and some sections even have further subsections within them.

Correspondingly, HTML pages can have titles (which appear in the title bar of the browser) and heading levels. Each heading level is displayed using a different style. For example, heading level 1 (`<H1>`) is the topmost heading. Therefore, it is displayed using a large font. Heading level 2 (`<H2>`) uses a smaller font, and so on. Because HTML takes care of the formatting for you, creating pages for content that naturally falls into heading groups is easy.

To display content that is broken into headings and subheadings, simply use the standard HTML heading tags. Spruce things up by changing font and background colors, and use some centered text or numbered lists where needed. You can get some reasonably cool-looking pages created very quickly. Which brings up Mike's Web Authoring Rule No. 1:

Rule No. 1: Avoid temptation.

Sound deep? I hope so. After all, why have a rule that doesn't sound ominous and important? It's the only way to have disciples flock to you and shower you with money. Another way of stating Rule No. 1 is "Sometimes simple solutions are the best solutions." If you don't need text swirling around, fancy 3-D animations, or blinking buttons to get your point across, don't use them. After all, they just take time and money to create and, when overused, can detract from the content.

As an example of a page that uses a simple layout, take a look at the simpleflow.html page in the ch02 folder on the enclosed CD-ROM. This page describes a bed-and-breakfast hotel (see Figure 2-1). You don't need fancy graphics or glitz. Instead, the key thing is to convey information about the hotel. The page has an <H1> and two <H2> tags in it. It uses a centered image at the top as a visual draw, and it uses an unnumbered list to display information. The only fancy thing about the page is that the background is black and the text is white, which makes the page and its graphic stand out more. You can find the full source code for the page in Listing 2-1.

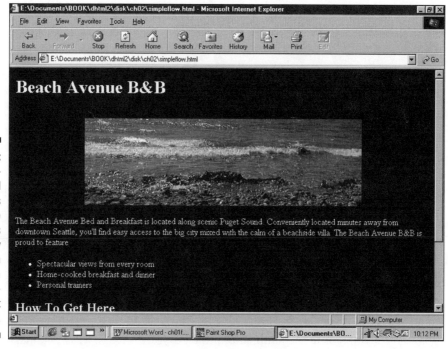

Figure 2-1:
The simple-flow.html file uses very simple HTML tags to display information about a bed-and-breakfast hotel.

Listing 2-1	The simpleflow.html Source Code

```
<HTML>
<!--Chapter 2 -- Simple flow-->
<BODY BGCOLOR=black TEXT=white>
<H1>Beach Avenue B&B</H1>
<BR>
<CENTER><img src="SURF.JPG"></CENTER>
<BR>
The Beach Avenue Bed and Breakfast is located along scenic Puget Sound. Conveniently
           located minutes away from downtown Seattle, you'll find easy access to
           the big city mixed with the calm of a beachside villa. The Beach
           Avenue B&B is proud to feature
<UL>
<LI>Spectacular views from every room
<LI>Home-cooked breakfast and dinner
<LI>Personal trainers
</UL>
<H2>How To Get Here</H2>
Finding the Beach Avenue B&B is easy. From I5 heading North, take the 12th Street
           exit. Turn right on C Street. After two stop lights, take a left on
           Jupiter Drive. Drive along the coast for a mile until you see our
           sign.
<H2>Room Rates</H2>
Our standard rates start at $250/night. Group discounts are available. Reservations
           are required during the summer months.
</BODY>
</HTML>
```

Using headings to break up a page works well for many home pages and other relatively small pages. This layout style has a number of advantages:

- ✔ The page is simple and easy to read.
- ✔ The page is easy to write.
- ✔ The information reflows nicely as the page size changes.

Two limitations exist with the simpleflow.html page, though. If the browser window is small, the graphic consumes too much space. And more importantly, this layout technique doesn't hold up well if the page needs to convey significantly more information. You see how to account for these needs in "Curses, Framed Again," later in this chapter.

Size Me Up, Size Me Down

If you look at the simpleflow.html file, you notice that, as you make the browser window smaller, the image of the water consumes more space. It's not that the picture is growing; its size stays constant regardless of the screen size. So if you have shrunk the browser window, what used to be a nice image to draw a user into the page becomes the only thing that's visible. In short, it's no longer an effective graphic.

You can get around this limitation by adding sizing information. By default, images appear using their natural size — that is, a 100-x-200-pixel image is drawn as a 100-x-200-pixel image. You can override this default by giving an explicit width and height. The browser then scales the image to the size that you specify.

Use the style parameter to specify the width and height of an element. This parameter is part of what is called *Cascading Style Sheets* (CSS). CSS is a rich specification that lets you provide broad visual control over HTML elements, including their location, size, color, background images, and much more. You discover many of the CSS capabilities throughout this book.

First, however, I describe how to use CSS to specify a width and height. You simply add the following to an element that you want to size:

```
style="width: desiredwidth; height: desiredheight"
```

For example, suppose that you want the surf.jpg image to be 20 pixels wide and 40 pixels high. You could use the following HTML code:

```
<img src="SURF.JPG" style="width:20; height:40">
```

You can specify size using the following measurements:

Value	Meaning
px	Pixels
in	Inches
cm	Centimeters
em	Em dashes (a typographic measurement representing the width of the letter *m*)
%	Percentage of the window size

If you specify width and height, the image is sized to match what you specify. If, on the other hand, you only specify one parameter, the other parameter is adjusted to preserve the *aspect ratio*. In other words, if you change the height of the image, the width changes proportionately. For example, suppose that you have an image that is 20 pixels wide and 10 pixels high. If you specify the height to be 20 and don't give a value for the width, the width is scaled to be 40. Why? The height is now twice as large, so the width is also twice its original size. As a result, the proportions of the image remain intact.

To check out sizing in action, look at the sizing.html file in the ch02 folder (see Listing 2-2). This page takes an image and displays it in a variety of different sizes. For the most part, it sets only the width and lets the browser adjust the height accordingly. In one case, it sets the width and the height. As you can see from browsing the page or from Figure 2-2, the images change size according to the values that are passed in the style parameters.

Netscape Navigator lets you use CSS information for `<DIV>`, `<SPAN>`, and `<LAYER>` tags, but not for images. You can set an image's width and height to a pixel or percentage value by using the `WIDTH=` and `HEIGHT=` notation, as shown in sizing_nn.html.

Listing 2-2   The sizing.html Source Code

```
<HTML>
<BODY BGCOLOR=black TEXT=white>
Default: <img src="SURF.JPG"><BR>
50 pixels: <img src="SURF.JPG" style="width:50"><BR>
1 inch: <img src="SURF.JPG" style="width:1in"><BR>
4 cm: <img src="SURF.JPG" style="width:4cm"><BR>
5 em: <img src="SURF.JPG" style="width:5em"><BR>
10%: <img src="SURF.JPG" style="width:10%"><BR>
50 x 50 pixels: <img src="SURF.JPG" style="width:50; height:50"><BR>
</BODY>
</HTML>
```

Figure 2-2:
The sizing.html file resizes a single image in a variety of ways.

You can use this technique to improve the simpleflow.html page. First, specify the image size as a percentage of the page size. As a result, whenever the page size changes, the image shrinks or grows accordingly. That way, you can make sure that it doesn't consume too much of the screen.

Making this change is easy. You simply change the following line of HTML code:

```
<img src="SURF.JPG">
```

After revision, the code is as follows:

```
<img src="SURF.JPG" style="height:25%">
```

Now, regardless of the size of the page, the image height is always 25 percent of the screen height. You can see this adjustment in Figure 2-3, which shows how the page looks for three different sizes of the browser. To check out the page, load the simpleflow2.html file from the ch02 folder.

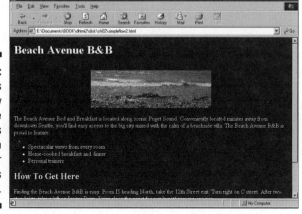

Figure 2-3: The figures show how the image changes size when the browser changes size.

Stupid Table Tricks

To display information in rows and columns, use the `<TABLE>` tag. For example, suppose that you want to show the measurement units that you can use for CSS. You could create a two-column table, with one column indicating the abbreviation and the other the meaning, as shown in Listing 2-3. The browser automatically scales the column width and the row height based on the content. Figure 2-4 shows the resulting table.

Figure 2-4:
CSS units
displayed in
a table.

CSS measurement units	
	pixels
px	pixels
in	inches
em	em's
cm	centimeters
%	percentage of window size

Listing 2-3   **The table.html Source Code**

```
<HTML>
<HEAD>
     <TITLE>Simple Table Example</TITLE>
</HEAD>
<BODY>
<TABLE BORDER=1>
     <CAPTION>CSS measurement units</CAPTION>
<TR>
     <TD> </TD>
     <TD>pixels </TD>
</TR>
<TR>
     <TD>px</TD>
     <TD>pixels</TD>
</TR>
<TR>
     <TD>in</TD>
     <TD>inches</TD>
</TR>
<TR>
     <TD>em</TD>
     <TD>em's</TD>
</TR>
<TR>
     <TD>cm</TD>
     <TD>centimeters</TD>
</TR>
<TR>
     <TD>%</TD>
     <TD>percentage of window size</TD>
</TR>
</TABLE>
</BODY>
</HTML>
```

Tables are also very useful for layout. In particular, you can use them to create multicolumn displays. For example, suppose that you want to show a set of images and have text that describes those images. One approach would be to have the images, a line break, and then the text. Unfortunately, this approach uses a great deal of vertical space, and sometimes it becomes hard to determine whether the text is associated with the image that is above or below it. With tables, you can have the text appear in a column to the side of an image. For example, check out Figure 2-5. You see a set of images in one column and text describing each image in another.

The table's border is set to 0 so that the page appears more like annotations to an illustration rather than a standard table. To see the page, load table2.html from the ch02 directory. You can find the source code in Listing 2-4.

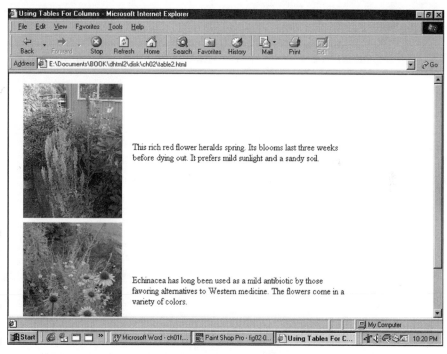

Figure 2-5:
A table is used to make the text appear in columns.

Table manners

Tables are a powerful but underutilized aspect of HTML. You use three key table tags — <TABLE>, <TR>, <TD> — and of course the corresponding </TABLE>, </TR>, and </TD>. <TABLE> starts the table. You don't specify how many rows and columns that it has. Instead, you use <TR> to start each new row. (Guess what? TR stands for Table Row.) Then you use <TD> to create each cell that you want in that row. (And what does TD stand for? Ta da, of course. It's an abbreviation for Table Data.) You can have as many cells as you want within a row, and you don't need to have the same number of cells in every row in the table.

Many properties are available to manipulate the table appearance. You can set the background color, justification for cells (not why you need them but whether the contents are left-justified, centered, or right-justified), and whether lines are drawn between rows and columns to demarcate cells.

Listing 2-4	The table2.html Source Code

```
<HTML>
<HEAD>
      <TITLE>Using Tables For Columns</TITLE>
</HEAD>
<BODY>
<TABLE WIDTH="80%" BORDER=0>
<TR>
     <TD ALIGN="CENTER" WIDTH=35% ><img src="img2.jpg" ></TD>
     <TD>This rich red flower heralds spring. Its blooms last three weeks before
           dying out. It prefers mild sunlight and a sandy soil.
     </TD>
</TR>
<TR>
     <TD ALIGN="CENTER" ><img src="img3.jpg" ></TD>
     <TD>Echinacea has long been used as a mild antibiotic by those favoring alter-
           natives to Western medicine. The flowers come in a variety of colors.
     </TD>
</TR>
</TABLE>
</BODY>
</HTML>
```

Variation No. 1: Sizing the image

As a variation to the columnar layout, you may want to change the size of the image that's displayed in one column to fill the vertical space that is consumed by the text in the column describing the image. Making the image the same height as the text provides a much denser use of screen real estate. To do so, simply set the image height to 100%.

"Wait a minute," you may say. "Doesn't setting the image size to 100% fill the whole screen?" Not necessarily. When you specify image sizes in percents, the measurement is always with respect to the containing element. If the element is inside a table, the percent size is with respect to the size of the table cell. So specifying a 100% height means setting the image to the height of the table cell. The tallest item in the row determines the height of the table cell. In this case, the row contains only two columns, so the height of the text in the second column determines the height of the cell.

Likewise, if you use percent measurements for an element that is inside a span, the measurements are with respect to the size of the span.

To check out an example of this technique, load table3.html from the ch02 folder. The images size to match the height of each row, as shown in Figure 2-6.

To achieve this effect, the image has its height specified as 100%, as you can see in the following line:

```
<img src="img3.jpg" style="height:100%">
```

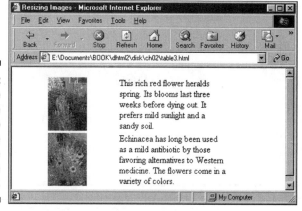

Figure 2-6:
This page resizes the images to match the height of the text in the row.

Navigator doesn't let you use CSS with images.

Variation No. 2: Central columns

You can easily use the table trick to provide central columns. For example, you may want to have images in a column with descriptive text to the left and the right. To do so, simply create three columns, as shown in Figure 2-7. This page is very similar to table3.html, except that it now uses three columns. The image is displayed in the central column, with descriptive text to the left and right. You can examine the page by loading table4.html from the ch02 folder.

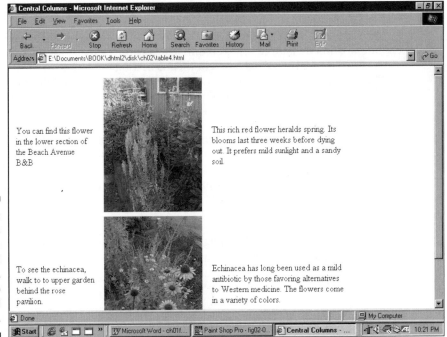

Figure 2-7:
The images
now are in a
central
column,
with text to
the left and
the right.

Variation No. 3: Alignment

Tables let you control the vertical and horizontal alignment. By default, table elements are left-justified and vertically centered. You can change this by setting the ALIGN and VALIGN parameters for the <TD> tag, as indicated in Tables 2-1 and 2-2.

Table 2-1	ALIGN Options
Option	*Result*
CENTER	Centers the cell contents horizontally
LEFT	Left-justifies the cell contents
RIGHT	Right-justifies the cell contents

Table 2-2	VALIGN Options
Option	*Result*
TOP	Starts the cell contents at the top of the cell
CENTER	Centers the cell contents vertically
BOTTOM	Aligns the cell contents to the bottom of the cell

You can get nice visual effects by altering alignment. For example, look at Figure 2-8. Here the text is right-justified so that it abuts the image. The exact word breaks are set by using <BR> tags. Check out the page by loading table5.html from the ch02 folder or by examining Listing 2-5.

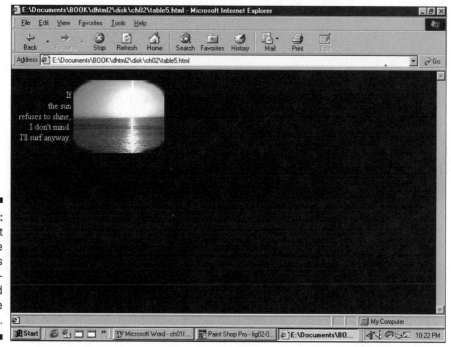

Figure 2-8: The text from the poem is right-justified against the image.

Listing 2-5	The table5.html Source Code

```
<HTML>
<BODY BGCOLOR=black TEXT=white>
<TABLE BORDER=0>
<TR ><TD ALIGN="RIGHT">If<BR>the sun<BR>refuses to shine,<BR>
I don't mind.<BR>I'll surf anyway.</TD>
<TD><IMG SRC="sun.jpg"></TD>
</TR>
</TABLE>
</BODY>
</HTML>
```

Curses, Framed Again

Web pages have an innate tendency to grow. You start off with a list of your favorite restaurants, and before you know it, you've added your favorite movies and songs. And then images of all your favorite T-shirts. And then pictures of your pet cow on your cross-country tour following the Grateful Dead. What began as a simple list has turned into a big mess. This brings up Mike's Web Authoring Rule No. 2:

Rule No. 2: Good things come in small packages.

Note the following three reasons for avoiding long Web pages:

✔ **They are hard to read.**

Or rather, it's easy to lose context when scrolling down through large amounts of text. Users can get more information if they need to look at only one screen at a time.

✔ **They take a while to download.**

A long download time is okay if the user is going to read the whole page, from top to bottom, and at a slower rate than the download rate. But if the user wants to skip ahead and the page hasn't finished loading, he or she gets frustrated.

✔ **They make it hard to find information.**

Except in a few cases, such as alphabetical reference material, users end up reading far more than they need to find specific information. Long Web pages are like a book without a table of contents: good for fiction, bad for facts.

If you need to display more than a few screens of information on a single page, try one of the following techniques:

✔ **Get rid of information that you don't need.**

   For example, use small images rather than full-page pictures.

✔ **Add links. Provide short descriptions with links to more information.**

   Essentially, construct a table of contents that is similar to what you would find in a magazine. Move the majority of the material into separate pages. The user gets a live overview but needs to return to the table of contents page each time she wants to jump to a different section.

✔ **Use frames.**

   Frames let you add a small table of contents area that is present regardless of what page is being viewed.

Combining the last two techniques works well. You can see this approach on many Web sites.

Frames let you break the Web page into several distinct areas, each of which can display its own URL. For example, you can have a table of contents list in a small area to the left of the page and the linked-to material occupying the main portion of the page. By using frames, users always have a sense of the content that's available. Each content page can be authored separately and isn't large. Therefore, a reader wanting information on cuttlefish doesn't need to download information on albacore, Atlantic Ocean currents, or anything else that may come before cuttlefish for a particular site.

Breaking up is easy to do

To use frames, you first create the main page. It contains the frame definitions that describe how many frames are on the page and how they are positioned. But the main page doesn't contain any text to display on the screen. Instead, each frame refers to a URL that it can display. That's where the content comes from. Essentially, you get several Web pages all wrapped up in one.

Setting up frames is similar to setting up a table. You need to tell the browser what the frames are and how they are configured, which you do by using two HTML tags: <FRAMESET> and <FRAME>. <FRAMESET> establishes a row or a column of frames. <FRAME> provides specifics for the frames that are within a <FRAMESET>. For example, the following creates a page with two frames in it:

```
<HTML>
<FRAMESET COLS="100%" ROWS="20%,*" >
<FRAME SRC="surf5indx.html">
    <FRAME SRC="who.html">
</FRAMESET>
</HTML>
```

This page is broken into two rows. The first uses 20 percent of the screen and is filled by surf5indx.html. The second uses the rest of the screen and is filled by who.html. (The asterisk {*} means *Use all the remaining space, please.*)

If, instead, you want the page to be broken into two columns, you can do the following:

```
<HTML>
<FRAMESET COLS="40%, *" ROWS="100%" >
<FRAME SRC="surf5indx.html">
    <FRAME SRC="who.html">
</FRAMESET>
</HTML>
```

Now the page is broken into two columns. The first, filled by surf5indx.html, uses 40 percent of the screen. The rest is filled by who.html.

You can also create a grid. For example, the following breaks the page into four frames:

```
<HTML>
<FRAMESET COLS="40%, *" ROWS="20%,*" >
<FRAME SRC="surf5indx.html">
    <FRAME SRC="who.html">
    <FRAME SRC="what.html">
    <FRAME SRC="where.html">
</FRAMESET>
</HTML>
```

The surfindx.html file appears in the upper left; it consumes 40 percent of the width and 20 percent of the height. The who.html file appears in the upper right, what.html appears in the lower left, and where.html shows up in the lower right.

Each frameset can be separated into further framesets. For example, the following HTML code creates a page with three frames in it:

```
<HTML>
<FRAMESET COLS="100%" ROWS="20%,*" >
    <FRAME SRC="surf5title.html" >
    <FRAMESET COLS="15%,*" >
<FRAME SRC="surf5indx.html">
        <FRAME SRC="who.html">
    </FRAMESET>
</FRAMESET>
</HTML>
```

The first frame stretches across the entire width of the page. The second and third split the bottom part of the page. You use this configuration in the surf5.html example later in this chapter.

Of course, you don't have to stop there. You can put framesets within framesets within framesets. In fact, if you nest enough frames, you can even create fractal frame patterns. That is surely going to impress your friends, although the Web page will be unusual, if not unusable.

For example, the following breaks the page into four frames and then breaks the upper-left frame into four more frames:

```
<HTML>
<FRAMESET COLS="40%,*" ROWS="40%,*">
<FRAMESET COLS="40%,*" ROWS="40%,*" >
<FRAME SRC="who.html">
    <FRAME SRC="who.html">
        <FRAME SRC="who.html">
    <FRAME SRC="who.html">
</FRAMESET>
    <FRAME SRC="who.html">
    <FRAME SRC="who.html">
    <FRAME SRC="who.html">
</FRAMESET>
</HTML>
```

"No way," you say? You can see what the result looks like in Figure 2-9. Or you can load the file framemania.html from the ch02 folder.

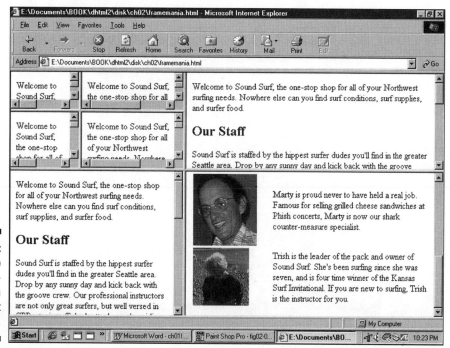

Figure 2-9:
This Web page contains seven different frames.

Who framed Web Page Rabbit?

You can use frames to help organize a page. The surf5.html page contains information about a mythical surfing store. To check it out, load the surf5.html page from the ch02 folder (see Figure 2-10). At first glance, it looks like any other Web page. But note that if you click on one of the links on the left, it updates what is displayed on the area in the right. That's because the page is composed of three frames. The title is one frame, the index (the set of links on the left) is another, and the main body of the page is a third. Each is a view of a different URL. By breaking the page up in this fashion, each topic can live on a page by itself. The user can find out information about one topic — for example, bleach — without having to download information on all the topics.

If you choose View⇨Source, you see the frame definitions rather than the HTML code that you see displayed on the screen (see Listing 2-6). Note that FRAMEBORDER and FRAMESPACING are set to 0, and BORDER is set to NO. These settings prevent lines from appearing between the various frames, making the page seem as if it is one continuous page rather than three separate frames. Also note that the title frame has scrollbars turned off by setting SCROLLING="No" NORESIZE, and the margins are set to 0.

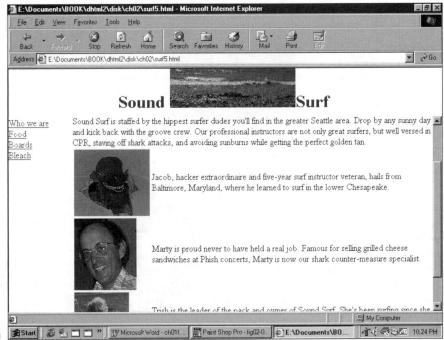

Figure 2-10:
The surf5.html page uses three frames: one for the title, one for the index, and one for the main body.

Listing 2-6	The surf5.html Source Code

```
<HTML>
<FRAMESET COLS="100%" ROWS="20%,*" FRAMEBORDER=0 FRAMESPACING=0 BORDER=NO>
    <FRAME NAME="frTitle" SRC="surf5title.html"        SCROLLING="NO" NORESIZE MARGIN-
            HEIGHT=0 MARGINWIDTH=0>
<FRAMESET COLS="15%,*" FRAMEBORDER=0 FRAMESPACING=0 BORDER=NO>
<FRAME NAME="frIndex" SRC="surf5indx.html" SCROLLING="AUTO" MARGINHEIGHT=0 MARGIN-
            WIDTH=0>
    <FRAME NAME="frBody" SRC="who.html" SCROLLING="AUTO" MARGINHEIGHT=0 MARGIN-
            WIDTH=0>
    </FRAMESET>
</FRAMESET>
</HTML>
```

To see the HTML code for a frame, right-click on the frame and choose View Source from the shortcut menu.

Normally, when you click on a link, the URL that you jump to appears on the same page as the link. When you create a page using frames, you override this behavior. That way, clicking on a link in one frame can update what is displayed in another frame. To do so, you use the `<BASE TARGET>` tag to determine in what frame the new URLs should be displayed. You can see an example in the surf5indx.html file, as shown in Listing 2-7. In this case, the `BASE TARGET` is set to `"frBody"`. Looking at surf5.html (refer to Listing 2-6), you can see that `frBody` is the name of the lower-right frame on the page.

Listing 2-7	The surf5indx.html Source Code

```
<HTML>
<BODY>
<BASE TARGET="frBody">
<A HREF="who.html">Who we are</A><BR>
<A HREF="food.html">Food</A><BR>
<A HREF="board.html">Boards</A><BR>
<A HREF="bleach.html">Bleach</A><BR>
</BODY>
</HTML>
```

When you specify frames, you must not do so within a `<BODY>` tag. If you put the frame definitions within a body, nothing shows up. This rule is different from Microsoft Internet Explorer 3.0, where you can put frames within a body.

Fine-Tuning Font Size

Earlier in this chapter, I tell you about a few major layout techniques. I tell you how to create different styles of pages by using headings, tables, and frames. Next, I show you some layout techniques that can help fine-tune a page's appearance. In particular, I describe how to use CSS to take control of your fonts.

I show you how to use CSS to set the width and height of images in "Size Me Up, Size Me Down." You can also use CSS to establish complete control over how text appears. In fact, you can control more than 50 different display properties with CSS.

The most important properties for controlling text are shown in Table 2-3.

Table 2-3	The Key CSS Font Properties	
Property	*Meaning*	*Sample*
font-family	Specifies the name of the font to use, such as Arial or Times. You can specify as many fonts as you like — the system uses the first one it can match. That way, if the desired font isn't available on a user's machine, a suitable alternate can be used. You can also specify one of the following generic family names: serif, sans-serif, cursive, fantasy, or monospace. Separate the names with a comma. If the font name has a space in it, contain the whole name within single quotation marks.	style = "font-family:arial, sans-serif"
font-style	Determines whether a font is italicized. Valid values are *italic* and *normal.* The default is normal. You can always use the <I> tag instead of this value.	style="font-style:italic"
font-size	Specifies the size of the font. You can set the size in inches (in), centimeters (cm), pixels (px), or points (pt) or use any of the following: xx-large, x-large, large, medium, small, x-small, xx-small. Check out fonts.html in the ch02 folder for a sample of using different font sizes (see Listing 2-8). As you can see from Figure 2-11, CSS provides great control over font size.	style="font-size:25pt"
color	Specifies the color of the font. It can be one of the color constants, such as red and green, or a hex color value, such as #FF00FF.	style= "color:yellow"
font-weight	Specifies whether a font is bold. Possible values are *normal* or *bold.* You can always use the <B> tag instead of this value.	style="font-weight:bold"

Property	*Meaning*	*Sample*
letter-spacing	Specifies the amount of spacing between letters. Typically specified in em's (the width of the letter *m*), but can also be specified in any of the other measurement units. The default is *normal*. Load fontspacing.html from the ch02 folder or check out Listing 2-9 for a sample that alters letter spacing. You can see the result in Figure 2-12.	style="letter-spacing:.5em"

Navigator does not support `letter-spacing`; thus, fontspacing.html doesn't work on Navigator.

If you don't know for certain that the requested font is on all users' machines, specify a generic font as the last font in the list. The browser can always find one of them. For example, suppose that you want to use Arial. Arial is a sans-serif font (meaning that it doesn't have any squiggles and twists at the edges of letters). Instead of asking only for Arial, you could ask for Arial and sans-serif. That way, if Arial isn't found, you still get a sans-serif font.

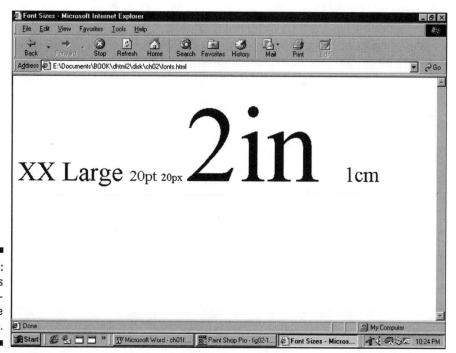

Figure 2-11: CSS allows great control over the size of fonts.

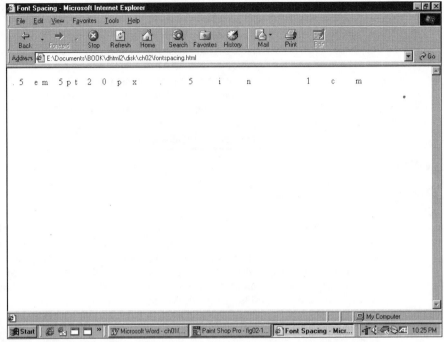

Figure 2-12:
CSS lets you
control the
spacing
between
letters.

You set the font style the same way that you set the width and height of an element: Just include the style parameter inside the element tag. For example, the following uses a 20-point font for all the text inside the span:

```
<SPAN style="font-size:20pt">The text here will use a 20pt font</SPAN>
```

When you set font size with Navigator, be sure to include units, such as *pt* or *px*.

Listing 2-8 **The fonts.html Source Code**

```
<HTML>
<HEAD>
<TITLE>Font Sizes</TITLE>
<BODY>
<SPAN style="font-size:xx-large">XX Large </SPAN>
<SPAN style="font-size:20pt">20pt </SPAN>
<SPAN style="font-size:20px">20px </SPAN>
<SPAN style="font-size:2in">2in </SPAN>
<SPAN style="font-size:1cm">1cm </SPAN>
</BODY>
</HTML>
```

Listing 2-9	The fontspacing.html Source Code

```
<HTML>
<HEAD>
<TITLE>Font Spacing</TITLE>
<BODY>
<SPAN style="letter-spacing:.5em">.5 em </SPAN>
<SPAN style="letter-spacing:5pt">5pt </SPAN>
<SPAN style="letter-spacing:20px">20px </SPAN>
<SPAN style="letter-spacing:.5in">.5in </SPAN>
<SPAN style="letter-spacing:1cm">1cm </SPAN>
</BODY>
</HTML>
```

Combining things

The samples that I have shown you so far just set a single font parameter. In fact, you can set as many parameters as you like at one time. For example, to use a 2-inch italic Arial font, you can use the following HTML code:

```
<SPAN style="font-size:2in; font-family:arial, sans-serif; font-style: italic">Hi!</SPAN>
```

As you can see, you simply combine as many characteristics as you want, separated by semicolons.

Using style sheets

You can control the style of individual page elements by adding the style parameter to those elements. You've added the style parameter to elements in fonts.html and fontspacing.html. Doing so works great when you want to control specific elements in the page. On the other hand, you often want to create a style that applies to an entire page. For example, you may want all your level-1 headings to use a 30-point green font. Or you may want the normal text on the page to be an italicized Arial font. To do so, you create a style sheet. The style sheet contains a collection of style parameters that associates with a particular HTML tag. Most typically, you set the style for headings and paragraph text.

Although you can set up a style sheet in several different ways, the easiest way is to do something called *creating an inline style sheet*. In this case, you include a <STYLE> tag in the document head. Inside the style section, you list the various tags that you want to define a style for. You then include style definitions, using the same format as you would for setting individual elements. For example, the following defines the appearance for H1 text.

```
<STYLE TYPE="text/css">
    H1 { font-size: 100pt; font-family: Arial;font-weight: bold; font-style:
            italic }
</STYLE>
```

To define the default font — that is, the font that's used when no tag is given — use a period (.) as the tag. Every style inherits from this default font, so if you set it to blue, every font on the page is blue. (Well, that's not quite true. A different style could change the color. The color of an individual element can also be set to any color. But all elements whose style doesn't override the color and whose color is not set via HTML tags or style values will be blue.)

Creating style sheets makes it easy to set the style for a whole set of elements at one time. And, as you find in Chapter 6, you can also change style sheets dynamically to do things such as reduce font size when the window is small.

Figure 2-13 shows a page that uses style sheets to define several styles. Here I set the default text to be blue. I changed the spacing for paragraph text and made it italicized and yellow. Finally, I made the headings nice and large and requested special fonts. Just check out the code in Listing 2-10 or load styles from the ch02 folder.

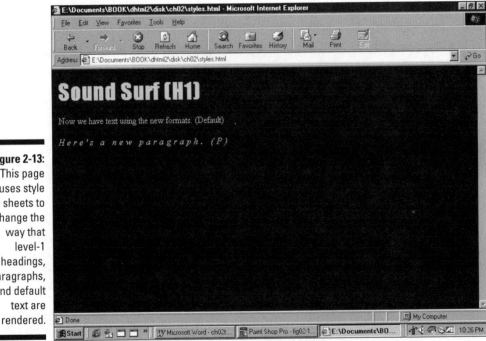

Figure 2-13:
This page uses style sheets to change the way that level-1 headings, paragraphs, and default text are rendered.

Listing 2-10	The styles.html Source Code

```
<HTML>
<BODY BGCOLOR=black TEXT=white>
<STYLE TYPE="text/css">
H1 { font-size: 30pt; font-family: impact, sans-serif}
    P { font-style: italic; letter-spacing: .3em; color: yellow }
    . { color: aqua }
</STYLE>
<H1>Sound Surf (H1)</H1>
Now we have text using the new formats. (Default)
<P>Here's a new paragraph. (P)
</BODY>
</HTML>
```

Creating new styles

In addition to changing how existing styles appear, you can use style sheets to create new styles. For example, you may want three different types of level-1 headings. Or perhaps you want a few different types of built-in formats to use for paragraphs.

To do so, you can create substyles. Simply follow the style name with a period and then a name for the substyle. For example, to create a new type of paragraph that is always italicized, you can do the following:

```
<STYLE TYPE="text/css">
P.1 { font-style: italic }
</STYLE>
```

Substyles always inherit from the parent style. So in this case, the new type of paragraph looks just like a normal paragraph, only it is italicized. You can create as many substyles as you want. For example, the following example creates a new type of paragraph style and several level-1 heading styles:

```
<STYLE TYPE="text/css">
H1 { font-family: impact, sans-serif}
    H1.big { font-size: 30pt}
    H1.realbig {font-size: 40 pt}
    P.1 { font-style: italic; letter-spacing: .3em; color: yellow }
</STYLE>
```

To use the new styles, you specify the class parameter within the element tag. For example, the following uses the large H1 style:

```
<H1 class=big>Whoa!</H1>
```

To see custom styles in action, check out styles2.html in the ch02 folder. (You can see the HTML in Listing 2-11.) As you can see in Figure 2-14, the file displays text using three different heading styles and two paragraph styles. Using custom styles is a technique that you can easily use to enhance the appearance of your pages. By centralizing style information into a style sheet, you can change a font or size in one location and have the change ripple throughout the page.

Listing 2-11	The styles2.html Source Code

```
<HTML>
<BODY BGCOLOR=black TEXT=white>
<STYLE TYPE="text/css">
     H1 { font-family: impact, sans-serif}
     H1.big { font-size: 30pt}
     H1.realbig {font-size: 40 pt}
     P.1 { font-style: italic; letter-spacing: .3em; color: yellow }
</STYLE>
<H1 class=big>Sound Surf (big H1)</H1>
<P>Here's a new paragraph.</P> <P class=1>And here's a special paragraph.</P>
<H1 class=realbig>A really big H1</H1>
<H1>A normal H1</H1>
</BODY>
</HTML>
```

This page doesn't work with Navigator.

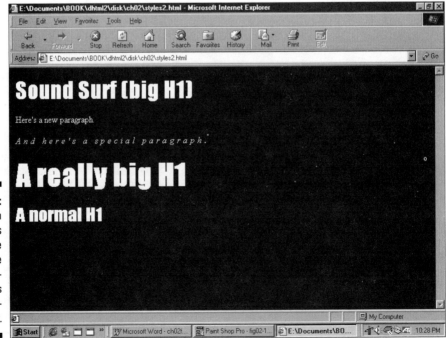

Figure 2-14:
Custom
styles
change the
appearance
of the level-
1 headings
and para-
graph text.

Changing styles programmatically

Just for fun, the chapter ends on an advanced note. So far, I've shown you how to manipulate styles through HTML tags. You can also manipulate styles through script by accessing the Dynamic HTML object model. Check out jump.html in the ch02 folder (see Listing 2-12). This page programmatically changes the font size for a series of words. To do so, it uses the setInterval method repeatedly to call a function:

```
setInterval("jump()", 500);
```

The function loops through all the anchors in the page. In this case, I created anchor tags for a number of words on the page so that I can access them programmatically, but because I haven't added an HREF parameter, clicking on the words doesn't cause a jump to a link.

The function jump begins by finding out how many anchors are on the page:

```
var cntA = document.anchors.length;
```

It then loops through each of these anchors and changes the font size. It does so by accessing the style.fontSize property. This is the object model way of doing the same thing that style="font-size: x" does through HTML code. The following is the script:

```
document.anchors(i).style.fontSize=10*(1 + (i + cnt) % cntA);
```

As you may guess, document.anchors(0) lets you access the first anchor on the page. Likewise, document.anchors(1) lets you access the second anchor on the page. Thus, the loop goes through every anchor on the page. For each anchor encountered, the font size changes. The program loops through font sizes, essentially causing the size of the text to ripple. Be sure to run the program to watch the text in animated action.

Navigator doesn't let you dynamically change font size, so this page doesn't work with Navigator. In Chapter 6, I show you a Netscape trick to get the same effect.

Listing 2-12	The jump.html Source Code

```
<HTML>
<HEAD>
    <TITLE>Animated text</TITLE>
<SCRIPT>
var cnt = 0;
function init() {
    setInterval("jump()", 500);
}
function jump() {
    var cntA = document.anchors.length;
    for (i = 0; i < cntA; i++)
document.anchors(i).style.fontSize=10*(1 + (i + cnt) % cntA);
    cnt = (++cnt % (2*cntA));
}
</SCRIPT>
</HEAD>
<BODY onload="init()">
<A id=a1>What </A><A id=a2>is </A><A id=a3>going </A><A id=a4>on </A><A
            id=a5>here?</A>
</BODY>
</HTML>
```

Chapter 3

A Surprising Turn of Events

*B*y themselves, Web pages are passive. They don't suddenly jump up, grab a piece of cheesecake off a table, or run into a corner screaming. In fact, the only screaming that occurs is when you're halfway through downloading a really large file (such as Microsoft Internet Explorer 5.0 or Quake) and someone else in the house picks up the phone.

On the other hand, users — that is, people who are browsing Web pages — are active. Half of the users are jittery from drinking too many caffeine-laden beverages or sitting in rush-hour traffic all day. The other half have just finished a 48-hour network Doom marathon session, and they expect Web pages to provide the same adrenaline rush.

So what happens when the jittery Web surfer meets the passive Web page? About the same thing that happens if you jump at a brick wall. The wall moves a tiny bit. At least, physics professors tell you that it does. But you move a bunch more as you bounce off it. In short, if the page isn't interesting, the user heads somewhere else.

Now, I don't mean that the only pages that people visit are the ones with flashing lights and naked bodies. I mean that people spend time at pages where they get a positive experience: quick answers to questions, interesting or challenging information without painful navigation, an entertaining experience, and the illusion of control.

These ideas bring us to Mike's Web Authoring Rule No. 3, which I have handily swiped from some long-dead rock star:

Rule No. 3: Feedback is everything.

Now, that rule doesn't mean that every time the user clicks on a link or moves the mouse, you should fire rockets toward the edge of the screen or explode the status bar. It does mean, however, that small reactions to user actions can make a big difference. For example, you can highlight links as the user moves over them. This reaction provides the extra information that the user has moved on a link and reminds him that your page is interesting. If your site relates to the entertainment industry, you may want even more interaction, showing the user that the related product is bound to be hip because the Web site is hip.

Dynamic HTML lets you react to user actions. When the user does something — such as move a mouse, click on a mouse button, or press a key — that action sends an *event* — a notification that something has happened. (Okay, so the mouse itself doesn't send the event. What happens is the user moves the mouse. The computer hardware detects this movement and tells Windows that the mouse has moved. Windows sends an event to the browser notifying it that the mouse has moved. The browser decides whether it wants to do something special with the event, and if not, passes the event on to the page. As a result, any script on the page can detect that the mouse has moved. Whew.) You can write a script that jumps into action when that event has fired. For example, you can write a script that starts a timer when the page is loaded or that changes the cursor when the user moves it over a particular area of the screen.

You can process many different events. The most important of these are mouse events, keyboard events, and page-related events. You find out about all these events in this chapter.

All Is Quiet Except for the Mouse

Mouse events are probably the most important events to process. After all, the mouse is the primary Web-navigation tool for most users. Users click on links to jump to new pages and click on images to find hot spots, and users are generally used to clicking on icons and toolbars from Windows and Macintosh applications.

You can use several key mouse events:

- onmouseover
- onmouseout
- onclick
- onmousemove

The first two mouse events, onmouseover and onmouseout, occur when you move the mouse pointer across elements on the page. As soon as you move the pointer over an element, the onmouseover message fires. The onmouseout fires when you move away from the element. As you may guess, onclick fires when you click on the mouse button, and onmousemove fires each time you move the mouse.

Mouse events are always relative to a particular object. For example, suppose that you have a button on the page and a piece of text. Whenever the mouse moves, onmousemove messages are sent to the body. Why? Because the body fills the browser window (or frame). So no matter where you move across a Web page, you are always in the body. Whenever the mouse moves over the button, the button gets onmousemove events — the body does as well. Likewise, if you move the mouse pointer over the text, the body and the text get onmousemove messages. (Of course, the object must be visible to get the events. So if you have a button that is completely covered by an image, you won't be able to click on the button.)

At first glance, you may think that onmouseover and onmousemove are the same event. Nope. Suppose that you move the mouse across a button. The onmousemove event fires the whole time that you are moving the mouse. The onmouseover event, on the other hand, fires only once — when you first move over the button. After you move away from the button, onmouseout fires.

Unfortunately, Netscape Navigator handles events in a very different fashion than Internet Explorer. Thus, most pages that handle events either need to be written separately for each browser or incorporate special code so as to work with both. In general, Navigator is far more restrictive as to what elements can process events.

Table 3-1 shows how the different events are handled with each browser.

Table 3-1	Event Processing with Internet Explorer and Navigator	
Event	**Internet Explorer**	**Navigator**
onclick	You can process for any element	You can process for document, anchors, and most <INPUT> types.
onmousemove	You can process for any element	You must capture mouse movement before you can track mouse movement. To see an example, check out surfcond_nn.html in Chapter 6.
onmouseover	You can process for any element	You can process for <AREA>, <LAYER>, and links. To see an example, check out food3_nn.html in this chapter.
onmouseout	You can process for any element	You can process for <AREA>, <LAYER>, and links.

Get right on it

In order for your Web page to react to events, you need to write script that watches for a particular event. You can do so in three ways. For HTML elements (except <OBJECT>, <APPLET>, and <EMBED>), you can list the events and the scripts to call within the tag itself. For example, suppose that you want to call the clickMe function when the user clicks on a button. (In other words, the function named clickMe does something interesting. You want to run that set of interesting stuff whenever the user clicks on a button.) You could use the following HTML code:

```
<INPUT type=BUTTON onclick="clickMe()">
```

Likewise, if you want to call the function named moveMe when the user moves the mouse pointer over the page, you could use the following code:

```
<BODY onmousemove="moveMe()">
```

When you use this technique to associate functions with events, you can easily see what events are processed for any of the elements on the page. Thus, it is easy to read the HTML and see what is going to happen. Most of the sample programs in this book will hook up events directly on the element.

The second approach is to use script to set up your event handlers. For example, if you want to process clicks on the window, you could use script such as the following:

```
document.onclick = clickMe;
```

This script indicates that when a click occurs on the document, the `clickMe` function is called. You can see an example of using this technique in the "City clickers" section.

Remember to examine Table 3.1 to see which events you can process with Navigator. It doesn't provide event handling on as many objects as does Internet Explorer.

When you set up an event handler using script, be sure that you don't put parentheses after the function name. That is, do:

```
document.onclick = clickMe;
```

Not:

```
document.onclick = clickMe();
```

If you put the parentheses after the name, the function is called immediately, not when the event occurs.

The third approach is to use the `FOR EVENT` syntax with the `<SCRIPT>` tag. This approach is the only way to associate functions with events that relate to ActiveX controls and Java applets. In other words, to process an event that is associated with an `<OBJECT>`, `<EMBED>`, or `<APPLET>` tag, you need to use the following syntax:

```
<SCRIPT FOR="object name" EVENT="event name" >
    JScript code goes here
</SCRIPT>
```

For example, suppose you want to process the `onmousemove` event for a button named Mo. You could write the following code:

```
<SCRIPT FOR="Mo" EVENT="onmousemove" >
    alert("You clicked on Mo");
</SCRIPT>
```

Internet Explorer lets you set up event handlers with the `FOR EVENT` syntax. Navigator doesn't support that syntax and immediately executes any script inside a `FOR EVENT` handler. With Navigator, you must set up the event processing on the element itself or through script.

Over and out, good buddy

The `onmouseover` and `onmouseout` events let you easily highlight regions of the screen. For example, you may want to change the color of a link or some text when the user moves the mouse pointer over it.

You can see an example of doing just that by loading food.html from the ch03 folder on the enclosed CD-ROM (see Listing 3-1). When you move the mouse over certain words in the file, the words change color. In this case, one set of words turns blue and the other turns green. When you move away from the words, they return to their original color (see Figure 3-1).

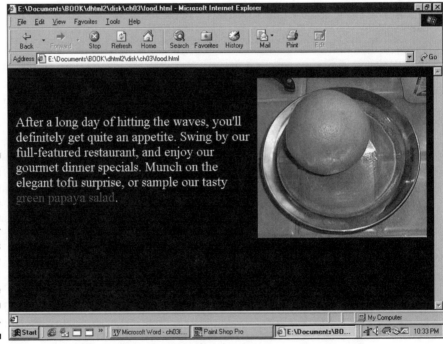

Figure 3-1: When you move the mouse pointer over the words *green papaya salad,* the words turn green.

Listing 3-1	The food.html Source Code

```
<HTML>
<HEAD>
<SCRIPT>
function tofuHigh() {
    tofu.style.color = "blue";
}
function tofuBack() {
    tofu.style.color = "white";
}
function papHigh() {
    papaya.style.color = "green";
}
function papBack() {
    papaya.style.color = "white";
}
</SCRIPT>
</HEAD>
<BODY BGCOLOR=black TEXT=white>
<TABLE>
<TR>
<TD><FONT SIZE=5>After a long day of hitting the waves, you'll definitely get quite
            an appetite. Swing by our full-featured restaurant, and enjoy our
            gourmet dinner specials. Munch on the elegant <A name=tofu
            onmouseover="tofuHigh()" onmouseout="tofuBack()">tofu surprise</A>, or
            sample our tasty <A name=papaya onmouseover="papHigh()"
            onmouseout="papBack()">green papaya salad</A>.
</TD>
<TD><img src="plate.jpg">
</TD>
</TR>
</TABLE>
</BODY>
</HTML>
```

Now that you've experimented with using the page, let's see how the page works. First, use the following HTML code to set up the event processing for the text *green papaya salad:*

```
<A name=papaya onmouseover="papHigh()" onmouseout="papBack()">green papaya salad</A>
```

You can see that two things are happening. First, you gave a name — papaya — to the text that's between the anchor tags. The name makes it easy to change the text color later. Second, you specified that the function papHigh should be called when the mouse pointer is moved over the text that's inside the anchor and that the function papBack should be called when the mouse pointer is moved away from the text that's inside the anchor.

That's all you need to do to set up event processing. Now, you need script to process the events. For the onmouseover event, you turn the color of the text green. Because you gave the text a name, you simply need to change the text's color; you can do so with the following script:

```
function papHigh() {
    papaya.style.color = "green";
}
```

For the `onmouseout` event, just change the color back to white, as follows:

```
function papBack() {
    papaya.style.color = "white";
}
```

You can create a similar page for Navigator, but with a few differences. First, in order to process the `onmouseover` and `onmouseout` events on the anchor, you need to specify an `HREF`. Because clicking on the anchor jumps to the `HREF`, you can just specify the anchor itself as the `HREF`, as follows:

```
<A onmouseover="papHigh()" onmouseout="papBack()" href="#papaya">green papaya salad</A>
```

Because this link is now active, it shows up with the ALINK color, so set the ALINK color to white so that the text doesn't stand out too much from the rest of the page.

Navigator also doesn't let you change the color of text dynamically, although it does let you control the background color of positioned elements (`<P>`, `<DIV>`, `<SPAN>`, and `<LAYER>` elements in particular). But you can't trap the `onmouseover` event for these tags. So I put a `<SPAN>` tag inside the `<A>` tag. That way, I trap the `onmouseover` event on the `<A>` tag and then change the color of a `<SPAN>` located inside it. Admittedly, this workaround is a bit kludgy. You can find the Navigator equivalent by loading food_nn.html from the ch03 folder (Listing 3-2).

Listing 3-2   **The food_nn.html Source Code**

```
<HTML>
<HEAD>
<SCRIPT>
function tofuHigh() {
   document.tofu.bgColor = "blue";
}

function tofuBack() {
   document.tofu.bgColor = "black";
}

function papHigh() {
   document.papaya.bgColor = "green";
}

function papBack() {
   document.papaya.bgColor = "black";
```

```
}
</SCRIPT>
</HEAD>
<BODY BGCOLOR=black TEXT=white ALINK=white VLINK=white LINK=yellow>
<TABLE>
<TR>
<TD><FONT SIZE=5>After a long day of hitting the waves, you'll definitely get quite
            an appetite. Swing by our full-featured restaurant, and enjoy our
            gourmet dinner specials. Munch on the elegant <A name="tofu"
            onmouseover="tofuHigh()" onmouseout="tofuBack()" href="#tofu"
            style="position:relative">tofu surprise</A>, or
sample our tasty <A name="papaya" onmouseover="papHigh()" onmouseout="papBack()"
            href="#papaya" style="position:relative">green papaya salad</A>.
</TD>
<TD><img src="../media/plate.jpg">
</TD>
</TR>
</TABLE>
</BODY>
</HTML>
```

With some versions of Navigator, changing the background color of a span will cause bizarre side effects. In particular, other words on or near the line may disappear when the background color changes. You can get around this by ensuring that the lines that will be highlighted are separated out from the other text on the page. You can see an example of this in the foodwa_nn.html file on the CD-ROM. foodwa_nn.html puts the items that get highlighted inside of an unnumbered list. Each item in the unnumbered list stands by itself.

You may decide that you want to make a version of the page that works with both browsers. To do so, you first need to write a script that detects which brower is running. I talk about this kind of script in more detail in Chapter 15. In the interim, the following line of code will do:

```
ieLoc = window.navigator.userAgent.indexOf("MSIE");
```

The variable ieLoc is less than 0 if the user is viewing your page with Navigator and greater than 0 if the user is viewing your page with Internet Explorer.

Detect which browser is being used. Then write code that decides whether to change the page using the Navigator commands or the Internet Explorer commands. For example, the following function highlights the word *tofu* in Internet Explorer or changes the word's background color in Navigator:

```
function tofuHigh() {
   if (ieLoc > 0)
      tofu.style.color = "blue"
   else
      document.tofu.bgColor = "blue"
}
```

Check out the food_both.hmtl page in the ch03 folder to see a complete version of the food page that works in both Internet Explorer and Navigator.

City clickers

Processing mouse clicks is just as easy as processing the onmouseover and onmouseout events. Mouse clicks typically mean "jump" or "act." For example, users expect that clicking on a button invokes some action and that clicking on an image somehow changes the image. Processing clicks is also a great way to create interactive presentations. For example, the Microsoft Internet Software Development Kit uses mouse clicks to expand the table of contents that is displayed on the left side of the page. Many presentation packages use mouse clicks to display important points.

As with the other events, Internet Explorer lets you process click events on any element, whereas Navigator is more restrictive. (Refer to Table 3-1.)

To process clicks with Navigator, use the script method for capturing events. The following simple program, shown in Listing 3-3, works with both Navigator and Internet Explorer. When you click on the page, it pops up an alert. (You can load the program by opening events.html from the ch03 folder.)

Listing 3-3   The events.html Source Code

```
<html>
<title>Captures events through script</title>
<script>
function clickMe() {
   alert("clicked");
}

function init() {
   document.onclick = clickMe;
}
</script>
<body onload="init()">
Click on me.
</body>
</html>
```

As you can see, the program is simple. It sets up the click handler in the init function. Whenever you click, the clickMe function is called.

Of course, pages are more interesting if you do something a little fancier when the user clicks with the mouse. The following example shows you how to make a page in which clicking on the mouse advances you through bullet points. Such a page can be adopted for a corporate presentation. Load the page food2.html in the ch03 folder, or look at Listing 3-4.

Navigator doesn't let you change the visibility of anchors, but it does let you change the visibility of `<DIV>` and `<SPAN>` tags, as long as they have their style set to absolute or relative positioning. You can check out a Navigator version of this file by loading food2_nn.html. It uses spans for the bullet points and the `layers` collection instead of the `anchors` collection to access the bullet points. Navigator doesn't provide a style object, and you can't change many object properties. You make an object invisible or visible by changing the object's `visibility` property to `"hide"` or `"show"`.

Listing 3-4	The food2.html Source Code

```
<HTML>
<HEAD>
<SCRIPT>
var curBullet = 0;
function nextBullet() {
     //Make the next bullet visible
document.anchors(curBullet).style.visibility = "visible";
     //Increment the counter
     if (curBullet < document.anchors.length-1)
curBullet += 1;
}
function init() {
     //Hide all bullets
     for (i = 0; i < document.anchors.length; i++)
document.anchors(i).style.visibility = "hidden";
}
</SCRIPT>
</HEAD>
<BODY BGCOLOR=black TEXT=white onclick="nextBullet()" onload="init()">
<TABLE>
<TR>
<TD><FONT SIZE=5><A id=b1>Elegant meals</A><BR><A id=b2>Fast service</A><BR>
<A id=b3>Good vibes</A>
</TD>
<TD><img src="plate.jpg">
</TD>
</TR>
</TABLE>
</BODY>
</HTML>
```

First, you need to put the various bullet points on the screen. Because you want to selectively show and hide the points, you give each one an `id`. Using `id`s lets you address the points programmatically:

```
<A id=b1>Elegant meals</A><BR><A id=b2>Fast service</A><BR>
<A id=b3>Good vibes</A>
```

Next, you set up the event processing. You need to process two events: `onload` and `onclick`. The `onload` event fires when the page is finished loading. Processing the event enables you to initialize elements; you find out more about processing events later in this chapter. You process `onclick` to show bullet points each time that the user clicks on the page. The following HTML code sets up the event handling:

```
<BODY BGCOLOR=black TEXT=white onclick="nextBullet()" onload="init()">
```

When the page first loads, all the elements are visible, but that's not what you want. You want to start with none of the bullets visible and then make one visible each time that the user clicks.

You can go about setting up this result in several ways. One way is to set the visibility property for each object. For example, the following HTML code makes the first bullet initially invisible:

```
<A id=b1 style="visibility:hidden">Elegant meals</A>
```

The downside of this approach is that you need to type the same style setting repeatedly, regardless of how many bullets you have. For a small set of bullets, it's not a big deal. But if you have 10 or 20, repeatedly typing `style="visibility:hidden"` gets tedious. You may even forget what you're doing and start typing **all work and no play makes Jack a dull boy.** Before you know it, you're running down hotel hallways swinging an ax. That would be bad.

Remember, however, that Dynamic HTML lets you access each of the elements programmatically. As I explain in Chapter 1, the document object has the following objects within it:

- ✔ all
- ✔ anchors
- ✔ applets
- ✔ embeds
- ✔ filters
- ✔ forms
- ✔ frames
- ✔ images
- ✔ links
- ✔ plugins
- ✔ scripts
- ✔ styleSheets

Each of these items is a *collection object*. In other words, each one is like an array through which you can access all the anchors, all the applets, all the links, and so on in a document.

I'd like to make a comment, please

You notice that the script in Listing 3-4 contains lines that start with //. These two slashes mean that the words that follow on the line are a *comment*. Comments are a way for you to indicate what is going on in a particular section of code. JScript ignores all the text in the comments, so you can write them in normal people language rather than in computer language.

Navigator doesn't support all, filters, scripts, or styleSheets. It provides layers to access <DIV>, <SPAN>, and <LAYER> tags.

Remember that JavaScript is case-sensitive. So if you want to access the anchors collection, you examine document.anchors, not document.Anchors, document.ANchOrs, or any other variations. Likewise, if you want to access the style sheet collection, you access document.styleSheets. Usually, if Dynamic HTML has a two-word property, such as for style sheets or font weight, the two words are combined together, and the first word is lowercase and the second starts with an uppercase letter. (The official technical term for this style of capitalization is *camel capping*, because the words kind of look like they have camel humps in them. Aren't you glad I told you that?)

In this example, you have a set of anchors. (Why? Because when you use the anchor tag and specify a name or id for the anchor tag, it shows up in the anchors collection.) Thus, anchors(0) refers to the first anchor on the page, and anchors(1) refers to the second element on the page. You can use the anchors object to make all the elements invisible by using the following lines, which are found in the init function:

```
for (i = 0; i < document.anchors.length; i++)
    document.anchors(i).style.visibility = "hidden";
```

You can find out how many elements are in a collection by looking at its length property. You find the number of anchors on the page by using document.anchors.length.

You then loop through the array, setting the visibility parameter on each one to "hidden".

Now you only need to show a new bullet point each time the user clicks, which is easy. You create a counter that indicates which bullet to show next. The counter begins with value 0. Each time the user clicks, you find the element to show by using the collection, which is indexed by the counter. That is, the first time through, you get element 0 from the collection. Then you increment the counter. The next time through, you get element 1 from the collection.

After you have the element, make it visible by changing its visibility property, as shown in the following script:

```
document.anchors(curBullet).style.visibility = "visible";
```

This script is kind of long. It means: Find the collection of anchors, which is part of the document object. Look for the `curBullet` anchor from this collection. Find its style object. Change the visibility to visible. Whew!

After you show the bullet, you increment the counter so that the next click reveals the next bullet.

To review what happens, when the page loads, the `init` function is called. The `init` function contains script that makes all the bullets invisible. When the user clicks on the page, the `nextBullet` function is called. This function contains script that makes a bullet visible. Thus, clicking on the page shows bullets one at a time, much as you would see from a presentation done with an application such as Microsoft PowerPoint.

In Figure 3-2, you can see what the page looks like when it loads. In Figure 3-3, you can see how, three mouse clicks later, three bullet points have appeared on the screen.

Figure 3-2:
The screen initially shows a picture but no bullet points.

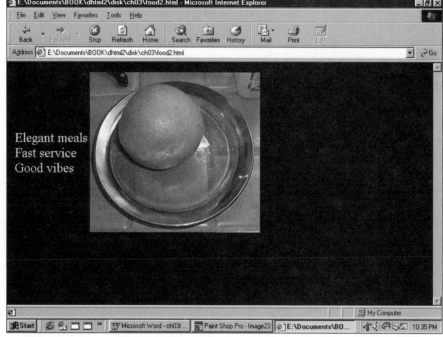

Figure 3-3:
Each time
the user
clicks,
another
bullet point
appears.
Here, the
user has
clicked
three times.

When you access elements by using the `collections` objects, remember that the first element in the collection is item 0. The second element is item 1. And if there are *n* elements in the collection, the last is item *n*–1. If you are a C++ or Java programmer, you're saying, "Duh. All arrays are 0 subscripted." If you're kind of new to this JScript thing, though, you may think that computer people are wacky. After all, why call the first thing 0?

Although you may be right about computer people, there's a good reason why the first element in a collection is item 0. It relates to how arrays are stored in memory. It's a little complex to get into here, but if you read the section on pointers in my book *Visual C++ 6 For Dummies* (IDG Books Worldwide, Inc.), you then know more than you ever wanted to about why arrays start with 0.

Client-side image maps

Another great use of processing mouse events is for creating *client-side image maps*. Image maps create hot spots for parts of an image. For example, you can have an image that's a picture of a shopping mall. Clicking on the shoe store jumps you to a shoe store site. Clicking on a movie theater takes you to a page that lists current movies.

Doing it with style

The style property is one of the most important properties of HTML elements. You can use it to control almost all aspects of an element's appearance. Chapter 2 covers many of the font properties that you can set with the style parameter. The following are some other key properties that you can set using the style object:

Property	Meaning
posLeft	Position of the left side of the element. The units of measurement are the same as those used when the element was initially positioned. For example, if the element were positioned with `style="left:2in"`, it returns 2.
posTop	Position of the top side of the element.
posWidth	Width of the element.
posHeight	Height of the element.
pixelLeft	Similar to posLeft, only the measurement is always in pixels. For example, if the element were positioned with `style="left:2in"`, the value returned by pixelLeft would be equal to the number of pixels that corresponds to 2 inches.
pixelTop	Same as posTop, but in pixels.
pixelWidth	Same as posWidth, but in pixels.
pixelHeight	Same as posHeight, but in pixels.
color	Color of the text.
background-color	Background color of the element.
visibility	Whether the element is visible. Using "visible" means that it is displayed, and using "hidden" means that it is not visible.

The style object is not supported by Navigator. Instead, the object itself has certain properties that can be manipulated. Note that these properties are available on objects that are positioned (with `style="position: relative"` or `style="position: absolute"`). That restricts these properties to `<P>`, `<SPAN>`, `<DIV>`, `<A>`, `<LAYER>` and a few other tags:

Property	Meaning
left	Position of the left side of the element.
top	Position of the top side of the element.
clip.width	Visible width of the element.
clip.height	Visible height of the element.
bgColor	Sets the background color.
visibility	Whether the element is visible. Using "show" means that it is displayed, and using "hide" means that it is not visible.

You can easily set up jumps such as these by using an image map. Typically, an image map associates a URL with clicking on regions of the image. But by processing the mouse events themselves, you can do fancier things. For example, you can call functions on mouse movement as well as click events.

Check out food3.html from the ch03 folder or look at Listing 3-5. Here you find a client-side image map. But instead of associating an HREF with the map areas, functions are called for the onmouseover, onmouseout, and onclick events, as you can see in the following HTML code:

```
<AREA SHAPE="CIRCLE" COORDS="126,101, 76,24" onclick="orangeClick()"
            onmouseover="orangeOver()" onmouseout="orangeOut()">
```

With Navigator, you can only process events on <AREA> tags if you set an HREF for the <AREA> tag. The name of the HREF is displayed when you mouse over the area. Although you can change the status line from a mouseover handler, you don't see the results on the screen. You can see an example client-side image map with Navigator in food3_nn.html.

Listing 3-5	The food3.html Source Code

```
<HTML>
<HEAD>
<SCRIPT>
function orangeClick() {
     alert("ta da!");
}
function orangeOver() {
     window.status = "Entering Orange County";
}
function orangeOut() {
     window.status = "Leaving Orange County";
}
</SCRIPT>
</HEAD>
<BODY BGCOLOR=black TEXT=white>
<MAP NAME="map1">
<AREA SHAPE="CIRCLE" COORDS="126,101, 76,24" onclick="orangeClick()"
            onmouseover="orangeOver()" onmouseout="orangeOut()">
</map>
<img src="plate.jpg" USEMAP="#map1" ISMAP BORDER=0>
</BODY>
</HTML>
```

When the mouse pointer moves over the circle (which happens to corre-spond to the orange in the image), the status bar is updated. Likewise, a different message appears when the user moves away from the orange. Clicking on the orange brings up an alert.

Where am I? How did I get here?

Whenever an event fires, a special object that is part of the window object, called *event,* gets filled in. You can query the event object to find out more information about the event. In particular, event provides the following properties:

Event	Meaning
altKey	Whether Alt is pressed.
ctrlKey	Whether Ctrl is pressed.
shiftKey	Whether Shift is pressed.
keyCode	UNICODE value for key pressed.
srcElement	The element that is the source for the event. For example, if you click on a button, the source element is the object that refers to that button. You can access srcElement as if it were the object itself. For example, you can make the element blue by using window.srcElement.style.color = "blue".
type	The type of the event. This is the same thing as the event name, without the on. For example, if you clicked on an object, type would be "click".
offsetX	The x coordinate where the mouse was clicked, with respect to the upper-left corner of the element. For example, if you click on the upper-left corner of an image, the x coordinate is 0.
offsetY	The same as offsetX but provides the y coordinate.
screenX	The x coordinate where the mouse was clicked on, with respect to the entire screen. The upper-left corner of the monitor is 0,0. This value, therefore, changes depending on the click and the position of the browser.
screenY	The same as screenX but provides the y coordinate.
clientX	The x coordinate of the mouse with respect to the left of the page.
clientY	The same as clientX but provides the y coordinate.

Navigator provides a completely different set of properties for the event object, including layerX, layerY, pageX, pageY, target, which, type, and modifiers. Unfortunately, Navigator does not indicate the element that triggered the event, making it harder to use a single event processor for multiple elements.

You may remember the scene in the movie *Blade Runner* in which Harrison Ford finds photographs left in the apartment where the replicants were living. He puts them in a computer device and tells it to zoom in repeatedly until he is able to identify an unknown mark. You can do something similar by processing mouse events. Of course, unlike Ford's device, you don't give the commands vocally. And worse, you don't get to meet Daryl Hannah.

What are image maps?

Image maps provide a cool way to create hot spots on a graphic. You create an image map with the <MAP> tag and describe the hot spots with the <AREA> tag. You can use three basic image map shapes: circle, rectangle, and polygon. You set the shape to use with the SHAPE parameter and then set the coordinates that describe the shape with the COORDS parameter. For circles and rectangles, you set COORDS to left, top, width, and height. For polygons, you input the *x,y* coordinates of the endpoints of the polygon.

For example, the following code creates two hot spots. The first is a circle with a left corner at 126,101; a width of 76; and a height of 24. The second is a polygon formed by connecting the points at (10,10), (20,10), (30,40), and (10,10).

```
<AREA SHAPE="CIRCLE"
    COORDS="126,101, 76,24">
<AREA SHAPE="POLYGON"
    COORDS="10,10, 20,10,
    30,40, 10,10">
```

The easiest way to create image maps is with a tool such as SoftQuad MetalWorks or FractalDesign Painter 5.0.

To make the Web page zoom in on photos, first check where the mouse was clicked on. Move that location to the center of the screen and then change the width and height of the image. Check out food4.html in the ch03 folder, or look at Listing 3-6.

This sample doesn't work in Navigator.

Listing 3-6	The food4.html Source Code

```
<HTML>
<HEAD>
<SCRIPT>
function doClick() {
    //Zoom in or out
    if (window.event.shiftKey) {
        imgPlate.style.pixelWidth -= 40;
        imgPlate.style.pixelHeight -= 40;
    }
    else {
        imgPlate.style.pixelWidth += 40;
        imgPlate.style.pixelHeight += 40;
    }
    //Move the point clicked to the window center
    imgPlate.style.pixelLeft = document.body.offsetWidth/2 - window.event.offsetX;
    imgPlate.style.pixelTop = document.body.offsetHeight/2 - window.event.offsetY;
}
function init() {
    //center it
    imgPlate.style.pixelLeft = document.body.offsetWidth/2 - imgPlate.style.pixelWidth/2;
    imgPlate.style.pixelTop = document.body.offsetHeight/2 - imgPlate.style.pixelHeight/2;
}
```

(continued)

Listing 3-6 (continued)

```
</SCRIPT>
</HEAD>
<BODY BGCOLOR=black TEXT=white onload="init()">
<img src="plate.jpg" id="imgPlate" onmousedown="doClick()"
         style="position:absolute;width:200;height:200">
</CENTER>
</BODY>
</HTML>
```

The most interesting code is inside the `doClick` function. It starts by checking to see whether the Shift key is pressed. If so, the image width and height are made 40 pixels smaller. Otherwise, the image width and height are increased. In short, clicking on the image zooms in. Shift-clicking zooms out.

Next, the position on which the user clicks is moved to the center of the screen. That's done by calculating the center of the screen — found by (`document.body.offsetWidth/2, document.body.offsetHeight/2`) — and moving the point that is clicked on to that location.

When the page loads, the image is centered (see Figure 3-4). Try clicking on the image several times to zoom in (see Figure 3-5), and then Shift-click several times to shrink it (see Figure 3-6).

Figure 3-4:
The image
starts out
being
centered.

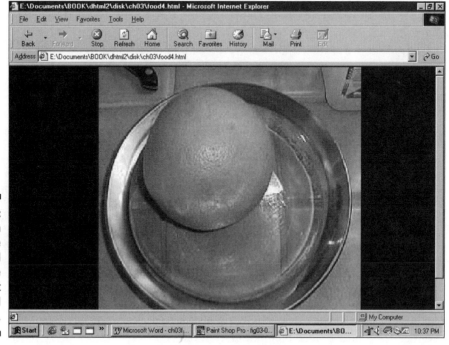

Figure 3-5:
Clicking on the image zooms and centers the point that was clicked on.

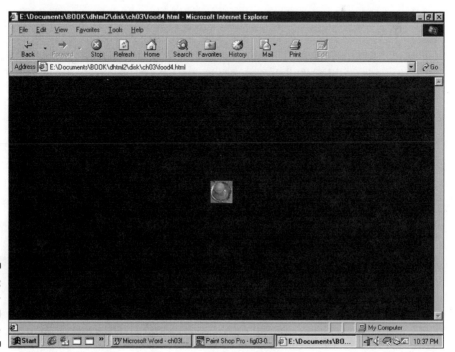

Figure 3-6:
Shift-clicking zooms out.

Note that `document.body.offsetWidth` returns the width of the page, and `document.body.offsetHeight` returns the height of the page. These properties are also available on any page element. For example, if `foo` is a button, `foo.offsetWidth` returns the width of the button.

Menu highlighting

You can use mouse event processing, along with a table trick, to create a pretty cool HTML toolbar. You can display a set of options in a row across the top of the screen. Moving the mouse pointer over these items highlights them. Clicking on them brings up a different URL into an `<IFRAME>` that's inside the page. The result is a menu system that gives direct feedback as the user moves the mouse pointer over the various potential jumps.

You need to use a table with centered elements to make the text menu items appear across the top of the screen. Because you use a table, the elements always space nicely, regardless of the window size.

`<IFRAME>` is an Internet Explorer-only extension. You can get similar functionality with the Navigator-only `<LAYER>` tag.

Be sure to load menu.html from the ch03 folder to see this page in action. It's a nice effect that you can use in your pages.

Figure 3-7 shows what the page looks like when the user has moved the mouse pointer over one of the menu items.

You should note several things in menu.html. First, instead of breaking the page into several frames, you need to use an `<IFRAME>`. (See the accompanying sidebar, "An IFRAME for an IFRAME," for the details about the `<IFRAME>` tag.)

To have links show up inside the `IFRAME`, use the `<BASE TARGET>` tag, as follows:

```
<BASE TARGET = menuFrame>
```

An IFRAME for an IFRAME

The `<IFRAME>` tag creates a new frame on a page. Unlike a frame created with the `<FRAME>` tag, an `<IFRAME>` can occur anywhere within a page. In fact, you can position it or have it flow just like any other HTML element. But, like a frame, it shows the contents of a particular URL.

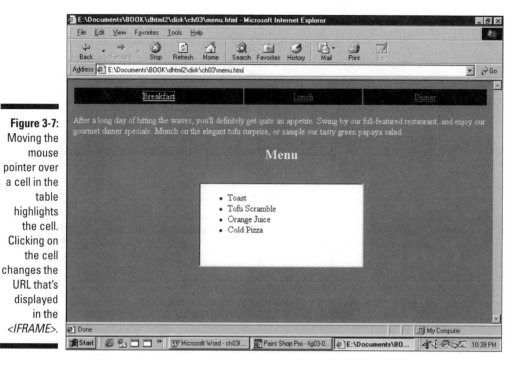

Figure 3-7:
Moving the
mouse
pointer over
a cell in the
table
highlights
the cell.
Clicking on
the cell
changes the
URL that's
displayed
in the
<IFRAME>.

Here, I gave it the name of the <IFRAME>. Any links then display the URL inside the <IFRAME>.

Next, set up event handlers for the elements in the table, as shown in the following HTML code:

```
<TABLE onMouseOver="mHigh()" onMouseOut="mBack()" BGCOLOR=black BORDERCOLOR=gray
        FRAME=VSIDES CELLPADDING=5 CELLSPACING = 0 style="width:100%">
```

These handlers change the color of the elements that are being moved over, as you can see in the following code:

```
function mHigh() {
    event.srcElement.style.color = "white";
}
function mBack() {
    event.srcElement.style.color = "gray";
}
```

Note the use of srcElement. By checking the value of srcElement, you can use the same event handler for many different elements. That's because event.srcElement returns the element to which the event applied.

So what exactly happens? The page displays a bunch of links in a table. Because they're in a table, they space nicely. Because they're links, clicking on them automatically brings a new URL into the <IFRAME>. (Of course, you can also use a span instead of a link and call some script instead of changing the URL that's displayed in the <IFRAME>.) The interesting part is that moving the mouse pointer over the cells in the tables highlights the table element. The result looks more like a CD-ROM than a typical Web page.

If you're feeling adventurous, try changing the background color of the text as well as the text itself. Also, replace the text with a series of images, thereby making a toolbar similar to the one that's at the top of Internet Explorer 4.0. See Listing 3-7.

Listing 3-7	The menu.html Source Code

```
<HTML>
<HEAD>
<BASE TARGET = menuFrame>
<SCRIPT>
function mHigh() {
     event.srcElement.style.color = "white";
}
function mBack() {
     event.srcElement.style.color = "gray";
}
</SCRIPT>
</HEAD>
<BODY ALINK=gray LINK=gray VLINK=gray BGCOLOR=gray>
<TABLE onMouseOver="mHigh()" onMouseOut="mBack()" BGCOLOR=black BORDERCOLOR=gray
            FRAME=VSIDES CELLPADDING=5 CELLSPACING = 0 style="width:100%">
<FONT COLOR=white>
<TR>
<TD ALIGN=CENTER><A HREF="choice1.html">Breakfast</A></TD>
<TD ALIGN=CENTER><A HREF="choice2.html">Lunch</A></TD>
<TD ALIGN=CENTER><A HREF="choice3.html">Dinner</A></TD>
</TR>
</TABLE>
<BR>
<FONT COLOR=yellow>
After a long day of hitting the waves, you'll definitely get quite an appetite. Swing
            by our full-featured restaurant, and enjoy our gourmet dinner spe-
            cials. Munch on the elegant tofu surprise, or sample our tasty green
            papaya salad.
<BR>
</CENTER>
<H2>Menu</H2>
<BR>
<IFRAME name=menuFrame>
</IFRAME>
</BODY>
</HTML>
```

<IFRAME>s are funny critters. To use <BASE TARGET> or otherwise specify that a URL should appear inside an <IFRAME>, you must set the name property for the <IFRAME>. But you can't access any of the <IFRAME>'s properties via this name. Instead, to change the <IFRAME>'s properties, such as its size or location, you must set an id property. You can then access the properties via the id. Note that the name and the id cannot be the same. For example, you can do the following:

```
<IFRAME name=menuFrame id=ifMenuFrame>
</IFRAME>
```

Now you can cause links to jump to the <IFRAME> with the following statement:

```
<BASE TARGET = menuFrame>
```

And you can change its visibility with this statement:

```
ifMenuFrame.style.visibility = "hidden";
```

Unfortunately, the menu example doesn't work with Navigator as is. But you can easily make a version that does work in Navigator by using a few tricks. Instead of using an <IFRAME>, use a Netscape-only tag called <LAYER>. A <LAYER>, like an <IFRAME>, lets you display HTML from an external source right in the middle of your page:

```
<LAYER name=menuFrame>
</LAYER>
```

You can then set the source for this layer whenever the user clicks on the menu item:

```
document.menuFrame.src = obj;
```

Also, as you did with food_nn.html, you can surround the menu text with an anchor tag so that you can process the onmouseover, onmouseout, and onclick events. Put a span inside the anchor tag so that you can change its background color as the user moves over it.

To examine the Netscape version of the program, load menu_nn.html from the ch03 folder, or check out Listing 3-8. Also, take a look at menu_nn2.html in the ch03 folder for a variation of this program that is closer in look and feel to the Internet Explorer counterpart.

Listing 3-8	The menu_nn.html page

```
<HTML>
<HEAD>
<SCRIPT>
function mHigh(obj) {
  obj.bgColor = "white";
}

function mBack(obj) {
  obj.bgColor = "black";
}

function mClick(obj) {
  document.menuFrame.src = obj;
}

</SCRIPT>
</HEAD>
<BODY ALINK=gray LINK=gray VLINK=gray BGCOLOR=gray>
<TABLE BGCOLOR=black BORDERCOLOR=gray FRAME=VSIDES CELLPADDING=5 CELLSPACING = 0
        style="width:100%">
<FONT COLOR=white>
<TR>
<TD ALIGN=CENTER><A id=choice1 style="position:relative"
        onclick="mClick('choice1.html')" onmouseover="mHigh(choice1)" onmouse-
        out="mBack(choice1)" HREF="#choice1">Breakfast</A></TD>
<TD ALIGN=CENTER><A id=choice2 style="position:relative"
        onclick="mClick('choice2.html')" onmouseover="mHigh(choice2)" onmouse-
        out="mBack(choice2)" HREF="#choice2">Lunch</A></TD>
<TD ALIGN=CENTER><A id=choice3 style="position:relative"
        onclick="mClick('choice3.html')" onmouseover="mHigh(choice3)" onmouse-
        out="mBack(choice3)" HREF="#choice3">Dinner</A></TD></TR>
</TABLE>
<BR>
<FONT COLOR=yellow>
After a long day of hitting the waves, you'll definitely get quite an appetite. Swing
        by our full-featured restaurant, and enjoy our gourmet dinner spe-
        cials. Munch on the elegant tofu surprise, or sample our tasty green
        papaya salad.
<BR>
<CENTER>
<H2>Menu</H2>
<BR>
<LAYER name=menuFrame>
</LAYER>
</BODY>
```

</HTML>I'll Try Not to Sing Out of Key

Just as you can process mouse events, you can also process keyboard events. Processing keyboard events lets you check out what keys the user has pressed. You can use this technique to jump to elements in a list, provide keyboard equivalents for mouse events, or process the keystrokes for navigation or for creating games such as Tetris.

Keyboard messages are onkeypress, onkeyup, and onkeydown. The onkeypress message fires when the users click on one of the character keys, such as a letter, number, or punctuation mark. The onkeyup and onkeydown messages fire when any key is pressed, including Shift, Ctrl, and Alt.

To determine what character a key is, you need to examine the keyCode. For English language systems, the keyCode is the same as the ASCII value of the character, as shown in Table 3-2.

Table 3-2		keyCode **Values for English Key Sets**			
keyCode	*Character*	keyCode	*Character*	keyCode	*Character*
32	(space)	33	!	34	"
35	#	36	$	37	%
38	&	39	'	40	(
41	)	42	*	43	+
44	,	45	-	46	.
47	/	48	0	49	1
50	2	51	3	52	4
53	5	54	6	55	7
56	8	57	9	58	:
59	;	60	<	61	=
62	>	63	?	64	@
65	A	66	B	67	C
68	D	69	E	70	F
71	G	72	H	73	I
74	J	75	K	76	L
77	M	78	N	79	O
80	P	81	Q	82	R
83	S	84	T	85	U
86	V	87	W	88	X
89	Y	90	Z	91	[

(continued)

Table 3-2 *(continued)*

keyCode	*Character*	keyCode	*Character*	keyCode	*Character*
92	\	93	]	94	^
95	_	96	'	97	a
98	b	99	c	100	d
101	e	102	f	103	g
104	h	105	i	106	j
107	k	108	l	109	m
110	n	111	o	112	p
113	q	114	r	115	s
116	t	117	*	118	v
119	w	120	x	121	y
122	z	123	{	124		
125	}	126	~		

You can use the `String.fromCharCode` method to convert the `keyCode` value to an ASCII. For example, look at keys.html in the ch03 folder (or see Listing 3-9). This source code brings up a letter where the addressee is blank. As you type on the keyboard, the key that you press appears in the middle of the letter.

Listing 3-9   **The keys.html Source Code**

```
<HTML>
<HEAD>
<TITLE>Typing Sample</TITLE>
<SCRIPT>
function typeMe() {
   nameField.innerText = nameField.innerText +
             String.fromCharCode(window.event.keyCode)
}
</SCRIPT>  </HEAD>
<BODY onkeypress="typeMe()">
Dear <A id=nameField></A>,<BR>
Thank you for your interest in the smash hit <B>Surf Aliens</B>. We are sure you
             would like to know more about the sequel, <B>Surf Aliens Return, And
             Boy Are They Bummin' This Time</B>.
<BR>
Sincerely,<BR><BR>
The Producer
</BODY>
</HTML>
```

The event processing is set up with the following HTML code:

```
<BODY onkeypress="typeMe()">
```

The `typeMe` function converts the `keyCode` to an ASCII value and then adds it to the end of the text inside a named area, as follows:

```
nameField.innerText = nameField.innerText +
            String.fromCharCode(window.event.keyCode)
```

You find out more about `innerText` in Chapter 6.

Can you do this same thing in Navigator? Of course. Do you need to write different code? Yup. Navigator also lets you capture keyboard events. But instead of adding the event to the `<BODY>` tag or to some other element on the page, you must set up an event handler by using script:

```
window.captureEvents(Event.KEYPRESS)
window.onkeypress = typeMe;
```

The handler — in this case, `typeMe` — is passed a parameter that contains information about the event that happened. For key press events, the `which` property of the argument contains the keycode. As with the Internet Explorer version, you convert the keycode using the `String.fromCharCode` function:

```
str += String.fromCharCode(evt.which);
```

Navigator doesn't provide the `innerText` function that you use in the Internet Explorer version. Instead, you need to put a `<LAYER>` on the page and write into the layer using script. Because you don't have a way to find out what is currently in the layer, create a string to store all the keys that the user presses. Each time the user presses a key, add the character to the end of the string. Then you can blast that string into the layer, as you can see in Listing 3-10. To load this program, open keys_nn.html from the ch03 folder.

Listing 3-10	The keys_nn.html program

```
<HTML>
<HEAD>
<TITLE>Typing Sample</TITLE>
<SCRIPT>
var str = "";

function typeMe(evt) {
   str += String.fromCharCode(evt.which);
   document.nameField.document.open()
   document.nameField.document.writeln(str)
   document.nameField.document.close()


}

function init() {
```

(continued)

Listing 3-10 *(continued)*

```
    window.captureEvents(Event.KEYPRESS)
    window.onkeypress = typeMe;
}
</SCRIPT>
</HEAD>

<BODY onload="init()">
Dear <LAYER id=nameField style="position:relative"></LAYER><BR>
Thank you for your interest in the smash hit <B>Surf Aliens</B>. We are sure you
            would like to know more about the sequel, <B>Surf Aliens Return, And
            Boy Are They Bummin' This Time</B>.
<BR>
Sincerely,<BR><BR>
The Producer
</BODY>
</HTML>
```

Page Events

Three events relate to page loading. You already used one of these: `onload`.
The `onload` event fires when the page is finished loading. By processing it, you
can initialize elements on the screen. When it fires, you know that all the elements on the page have loaded and you can therefore access them via script.

The `onunload` event fires when the document is unloaded. Unloading occurs
when the browser is shut down, the user refreshes the page, or the user goes
to a different page. Process the event to perform cleanup code.

The `onreadystatechange` event (not to be confused with `onreadysetgo`)
fires twice when a page loads. It first fires when enough of the page has
loaded that you can begin to scroll through the page. You can see the effect
of this event with large pages: At first, you can't do anything with the document. Then you can begin to scroll through the page and click on links, even
though not everything has loaded. The event fires again when the page is
fully loaded.

`onreadystatechange` is not available in Navigator.

Typically, you process the `onload` and `onunload` events for the body or the
window, but you can also process them for individual elements on the page.

You can process the `onload` and `onunload` messages for the page via the
body, as shown in the following HTML code:

```
<BODY onload="init()" onunload="cleanUp()">
```

The events, however, are really happening in the window. So to handle the
events by using the `FOR`, `EVENT` syntax instead, you need to do the following:

```
<SCRIPT FOR="window" EVENT="unload" >
</SCRIPT
```

Chapter 4

Cosi Fan 2-D

. . . .

In This Chapter

▶ Setting the *x* and *y* position for elements

▶ Creating overlapping elements

▶ Finding out how containment affects coordinates

▶ Discovering relative and absolute positioning

▶ Setting the *z*-index for elements

▶ Animating objects

. . . .

Close your eyes for a moment and imagine a world in which nothing is still. You go to take a glass from a shelf, but the shelf moves, and your hand waves in the empty air. You sit down, but the chair is a few inches from where you expected it, so you end up on the ground. Have you just entered a Picasso painting? Did you breathe too deeply at the last rock concert you went to? Perhaps. Or you may just be using the Web.

Until the version 4.0 browsers, the Web was a one-dimensional medium. That doesn't mean that it always used to be concerned with one thing and that now its mind is out of the gutter. Instead, it means that there was no way to specify the exact location of an object. Everything was always relative to the item that came before it. So you couldn't exactly position text next to an image. You couldn't guarantee that an image would appear in a particular location. And you certainly couldn't have overlapping images and text.

The version 4.0 and beyond browsers change that through the use of Cascading Style Sheet (CSS) positioning. You get a taste of using CSS in Chapter 2: The style object lets you specify the exact position of an element as well as the width and height of that element. The change is dramatic. You can animate objects by moving them across the screen. You can put text on top of images, thereby calling out key points and increasing screen density. You can create pages that duplicate any layout, just as if you were using a desktop publishing package. In short, you can create far richer pages than ever before.

In this chapter, you find out how to position objects on a page by using CSS. You also discover a couple of tricks of the trade that you can use throughout your own pages.

Why Bother?

You may say to yourself, "What's the big deal? My page looks fine as it is." But two-dimensional (2-D) layout opens a whole world of possibilities for Web design. You're soon hooked!

For an example of the types of things that you can do, check out alien2.html in the ch04 folder on the enclosed CD-ROM. As you can see in Figure 4-1, it's a slick layout. You can achieve a similar look with earlier browsers by creating a bunch of bitmaps and playing a lot of table tricks. But this page uses only two bitmaps and was easy to create.

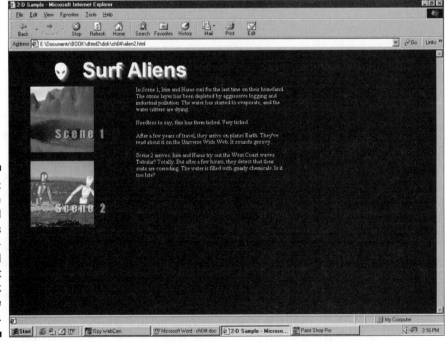

Figure 4-1:
The alien2.html page uses 2-D positioning and filters to get a great look for very little bandwidth.

My position is...

Micrsoft Internet Explorer lets you attach a position to any element. Netscape Navigator is more restrictive, but still allows a broad set of tags to be positioned. Here is a list:

`<A>`	`<OL >`
`<ADDRESS >`	`<PLAINTEXT >`
`<BIG >`	`<PRE >`
`<CAPTION >`	`<S >`
`<CITE >`	`<SAMP >`
`<CODE>`	`<SMALL >`
`<DIR >`	`<SPAN >`
`<DIV >`	`<STRIKE >`
`<EM >`	`<STRONG >`
`<H1 >`	`<SUB >`
`<H2 >`	`<SUP >`
`<I >`	`<TABLE>`

Warning: Tables don't work well when positioned. You are better off putting them inside of a positioned element.

`<LAYER >`	`<TT >`
`<ILAYER >`	`<U >`
`<KBD >`	`<UL >`
`<MENU >`	`<VAR >`

Navigator doesn't support the WebDings font, letter spacing, or filters. Navigator doesn't let you supply positioning to any page element. In particular, `<IMG>` tags must be positioned within other tags, such as a `<P>` or a `<DIV>`. For a version of this page that runs on both Navigator and Internet Explorer, load alien2_both.html. For a list of tags that you can position using Navigator, see the sidebar, "My position is..."

In Figure 4-1, the alien landscape and the ocean scene are JPEG files. They are positioned to specific 2-D locations on the screen. The words *Scene 1* and *Scene 2* are plain text, positioned on top of the bitmaps. These words have an alpha filter applied to them, so the image behind bleeds through slightly, giving a much smoother look. The words also have a drop shadow applied to them, giving a letterbox feel. You can see this shadow if you look closely at the bottom-right portion of the letters. You find out about applying filters such as the alpha and drop shadow in Chapter 7.

The column that describes the movie is positioned so that it's to the right of the images by a specified amount. And the title bar (across the top) is also positioned in 2-D so that the left edge is centered over the images. A shadow filter gives it the green glow. Believe it or not, the alien head is not a bitmap. It's a character from the WebDings font.

As you can see, 2-D positioning gives you superb control over a page's layout.

2-D or Not 2-D, That Is the Question

Giving an element a 2-D position is easy. You simply specify the position of the upper-left corner by setting the left and top values for the style property. For example, the following HTML code makes an image appear 50 pixels over and 60 pixels down from the upper-left corner of the page:

```
<IMG src="scene1.jpg" style="position:absolute; left:50; top:60">
```

You can use any measurement units when specifying a position. For example, to make a button appear 2 inches from the left of the page and 20 percent down, use the following HTML code:

```
<INPUT type=BUTTON style="position:absolute; left:2in; top:20%">
```

You can also specify the width and height. For example, the following code makes an image appear 50 pixels over and 60 pixels down from the upper-left corner of the page; the image is 10 centimeters wide and 10 centimeters high:

```
<IMG src="scene1.jpg" style="position:absolute; left:50; top:60; width:10cm; height:10cm">
```

You can specify values for the style property in any order. However, you must always give the name of the parameter, followed by a colon, followed by the value, followed by a semicolon.

Navigator lets you apply positions only to <P>, <DIV>, <SPAN>, and the Navigator-only <LAYER> tags. To give a position to a different type of an element, place the element inside a <DIV> and position the <DIV>. (Of course, you can also put the element inside a <P>, <SPAN>, or <LAYER>.)

For example, to position an image, you may use HTML such as the following:

```
<DIV style="position:absolute; left:50; top:60"><IMG src="scene1.jpg"></DIV>
```

You can easily put one object on top of another. Just set the coordinates for the second object so that it overlaps the first.

For example, check out rainbow.html from the ch04 folder (shown in Listing 4-1). Many different text elements are displayed on top of each other, giving a rainbow effect (see Figure 4-2). You can create this illusion by placing one group of text elements on top of the other by using 2-D positioning. Note that each copy of *Rainbow Page* is placed 5 pixels down and to the right of the previous copy. Also note that the style property is used to change the color for each set of text elements.

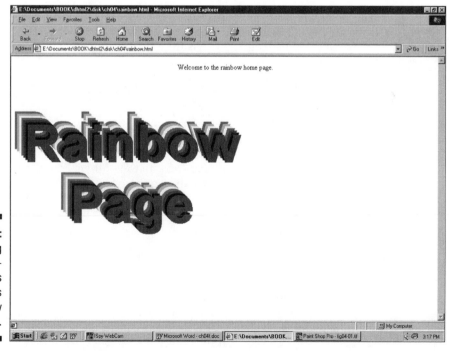

Figure 4-2: Overlapping text of various colors creates this rainbow pattern.

Listing 4-1	The rainbow.html Source Code

```
<HTML>
<BODY>
<STYLE TYPE="text/css">
</STYLE>
<CENTER>
<DIV style="position:absolute; left:0; top:100; color:red">
<P>Rainbow<BR>Page</DIV>
<DIV style="position:absolute; left:5; top:105; color:orange">
<P>Rainbow<BR>Page</DIV>
<DIV style="position:absolute; left:10; top:110; color:yellow">
<P>Rainbow<BR>Page</DIV>
<DIV style="position:absolute; left:15; top:115; color:green">
<P>Rainbow<BR>Page</DIV>
<DIV style="position:absolute; left:20; top:120; color:blue">
<P>Rainbow<BR>Page</DIV>
<DIV style="position:absolute; left:25; top:125; color: fuchsia">
<P>Rainbow<BR>Page</DIV>
<DIV style="position:absolute; left:30; top:130; color:purple">
<P>Rainbow<BR>Page</DIV>
<FONT COLOR = black>
Welcome to the rainbow home page.
</BODY>
</HTML>
```

You can create a column of text by specifying the width of a div or a span. For example, the following code creates a column of text that starts 2 inches from the left of the screen and 20 pixels from the top and consumes 30 percent of the width of the screen:

```
<SPAN style="position:absolute; left:2in; top:20; width:30%">
This text will now appear in a column.
</SPAN>
```

Try using 2-D positioning with a simplified version of the alien2.html page. You can see what this page looks like in Figure 4-3. First, you position two images on the page and then place text on top of them. You then set up a column to the right. As you can see from the HTML code in Listing 4-2 (or from loading alien3.html from the ch04 folder), all the positioning is achieved by specifying the left and top positions of the objects. For example, the following code places the first image:

```
<IMG src="scene1.jpg" style="position:absolute; left:50; top:80">
```

Remember that in Navigator you can't set the position of an image. Instead, put the image inside a positioned `<LAYER>`, `<P>`, `<DIV>`, or `<SPAN>`. Load alien3_nn.html for a version that works in Navigator.

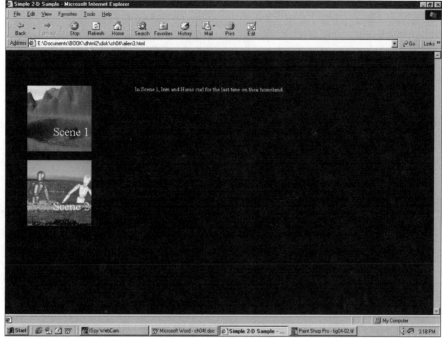

Figure 4-3:
In this example, 2-D positioning causes the text to overlap the images and creates a column of text to the right of the images.

Listing 4-2   **The alien3.html Source Code**

```
<HTML>
<HEAD>
<TITLE>Simple 2-D Sample</TITLE>
</HEAD>
<BODY BGCOLOR=black text=white>
<IMG src="scene1.jpg" style="position:absolute; left:50; top:80">
<IMG src="scene2.jpg" style="position:absolute; left:50; top:250">
<SPAN style="position:absolute; left:110; top:170; font-size:20pt">Scene 1</SPAN>
<SPAN style="position:absolute; left:110; top:340; font-size:20pt">Scene 2</SPAN>
<SPAN style="position:absolute; width:35%; top:80; left:300; font-size:10pt">
In Scene 1, Irim and Haras curl for the last time on their homeland.
</SPAN>
</BODY>
</HTML>
```

Position the text that appears on top of the image with the following HTML code:

```
<SPAN style="position:absolute; left:110; top:170; font-size:20pt">Scene 1</SPAN>
```

What are divs and spans?

Divs (created with the <DIV> tag) and *spans* (created with the <SPAN> tag) let you break your page into regions. All the elements within a div or a span take on the values specified by the div or span's style values. For example, if you set the font to be Impact, then the default font for any elements in the div or span is Impact.

Likewise, the coordinate system of any elements within a div or span is with respect to the div or span. For example, suppose you position a div so that its left side is 2 inches from the left side of the page. If you position an element within the div to a left position of 0, it appears 0 pixels away from the left side of the div — and, therefore, 2 inches away from the left side of the page. If you move a div or span, all the elements within it move as well. Thus, divs and spans help you organize groups of related elements.

The image is 150 pixels high and 150 pixels wide. (How do I know? I created it. If I hadn't created it, I could look at the size with an image editor such as Paint Shop Pro.) The image appears from (50,80) to (200,230). Thus, the text, which starts at (110,170), is obviously on top of the image.

The text column is created by placing a span and setting its width, which you do with the following HTML code:

```
<SPAN style="position:absolute; width:35%; top:80; left:300; font-size:10pt">
In Scene 1, Irim and Haras curl for the last time on their homeland.
</SPAN>
```

As you can see, by adding a few extra parameters to HTML elements, you get an incredible amount of control over how a page looks.

My position on the issue is . . .

To check where an object is on the screen, examine its position properties. For example, the following code finds the *x* and *y* position of an item named *foo*, in pixels:

```
foo_x = foo.currentStyle.pixelLeft;
foo_y = foo.currentStyle.pixelTop;
```

You can use a variation of this code to modify an object's location. For example, the following shifts an object 5 pixels to the left:

```
foo.style.pixelLeft -= 5;
```

Internet Explorer 5.0 provides two different objects for setting and retrieving style. The first is the `style` object. You can always use it to set the position of an element. But if you want to find where an element is located, you're better off checking `currentStyle`. You may wonder what the heck the difference is. Well, the `style` object returns the position only if you have set the position with a CSS style directly on the HTML element (or through script). If the position of the element was set by a global style sheet, `style` returns 0. Thus, you may see an element clearly positioned on the page but not be able to find out where it is located. `currentStyle` tells you where it is located regardless of whether the position was set from an inline or global style sheet. So why even have `style`? It's the only way you could get and set position in Internet Explorer 4.0, so it still lives on from those days.

Now, to make things a little more confusing, `currentStyle` doesn't always return the position either. If you look at the position.html sample in the ch04 folder, you see that `currentStyle.left` returns `auto` for the image that is contained within a positioned element. By contrast, `offsetLeft` returns the offset of the image from the container. You can also use `offsetTop`, `offsetWidth`, and `offsetHeight` to retrieve the top, and height of an object, even if it wasn't positioned with CSS.

In Navigator, check the `left` and `top` properties on the object — for example, `myObj.left`. Note that you can only check the position of an object that is positioned with a CSS style. For example, if you try to check the position of an `<IMG>` within a positioned `<DIV>`, you get a script error. You can check the position of the `<DIV>`, though.

You can see an example of checking position with Internet Explorer and Navigator by looking at the position.html file in the ch04 folder.

Containment vessels

You can use the `<TD>`, `<DIV>`, and `<SPAN>` tags to create HTML regions that can contain other tags. In alien3.html, I used a span to create a column. That column contained HTML text. It could just as easily have contained images and other HTML tags as well. When you create a table cell, span, or div, any 2-D positions that are established on elements within it are relative to the cell, span, or div. In other words, suppose that you place a span at (80,300). Within that span, you put an image at (20,10). This image is positioned relative to the location of the span. Therefore, it shows up at (100,310) with respect to the page. Why? The span started at (80,300). The image starts at (20,10) with respect to that. Adding the coordinates, you get (100,310).

To see containment in action, check out container.html in the ch04 folder (see Listing 4-3). In this example, you can see three spans. The first — which is set up with a red background — contains another span. The span inside it is placed at (20,20) and contains the text *Inside container.*

Look at Figure 4-4. The text *Inside container* and *Outside container* are both placed at the same position. However, only the text inside the container is with respect to a span, whereas *Outside container* is placed with respect to the page. Notice also that the text shows up inside the span with the red background. That's because it is placed 20 units to the right and 20 units down from the span that it's contained in. By contrast, the span with the text *Outside container* is not inside another span. It's just part of the page itself. It, too, is placed at (20,20), but it is positioned relative to the page. Thus, it appears outside of the span with the red background.

Listing 4-3　　　　　**The container.html Source Code**

```
<HTML>
<HEAD>
      <TITLE>Containment</TITLE>
</HEAD>
<BODY>
<SPAN style="position:absolute; left:50; top:50; height: 200; width: 200; background-
            color:red">Container
<SPAN style="position:absolute; left:20; top:20">Inside container</SPAN></SPAN>
<SPAN style="position:absolute; left:20; top:20">Outside container</SPAN>
</BODY>
</HTML>
```

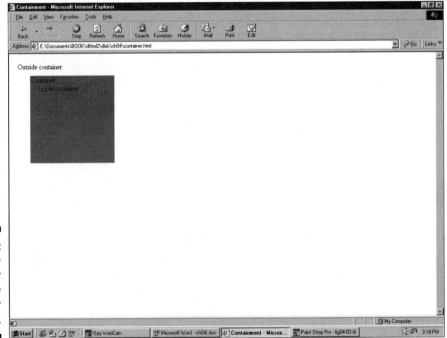

Figure 4-4:
The *Inside container* and *Outside container* example.

Relatively speaking

You can position objects either relatively or absolutely. In this book, I have used absolute positioning. *Absolute positioning* means that the coordinates are placed with respect to the container. An element that is part of a span is positioned with respect to the upper-left corner of the span. An element that is not contained in a cell, div, or a span is positioned with respect to the upper-left corner of the page.

To specify absolute positioning, use the following HTML code:

```
<SPAN style="position:absolute">
```

With *relative positioning,* the coordinates are placed with respect to the previous HTML element that wasn't positioned absolutely. When you don't supply absolute position information, the HTML code determines the position of objects automatically by reflowing the text and images to fit the size of the page. When you specify relative positioning, the browser places the object as if no positioning information is provided — in other words, as if it were just part of the normal flow of HTML elements. Then the browser offsets the position by the specified amount.

Why is relative positioning useful? Suppose that you have a group of text and images. They are part of a column, so you want the browser to flow them to fit the size of the page. Therefore, you don't specify any 2-D positioning information. Now you want some text to appear on top of the image, but you don't know exactly where the image is on the page. Using relative positioning, you can make the text appear on top of the image by specifying a negative left and top value — thereby moving the text up and to the left from where it normally would appear.

To specify relative positioning, use the following HTML code:

```
<SPAN style="position:relative">
```

For an example of relative and absolute positioning, look at relabs.html in the ch04 folder (see Listing 4-4). This page starts with some simple HTML text: *Hello. And welcome to the absolute and relative sample page.* Some new text, *Absolutely correct,* is then placed at (10,10) using absolute positioning. As a result, the new text appears 10 pixels over and 10 pixels down from the upper-left corner of the page. In fact, it overlaps the other text on the page. Another span places the words *Relatively reasonable* at (10,10) using relative positioning. *Relatively reasonable* shows up 10 pixels to the right and down from the end of the last element that didn't have absolute positioning. In this case, that makes *Relatively reasonable* show up 10 pixels down and to the right of the word *page,* as you can see in Figure 4-5.

Figure 4-5:
The absolutely positioned text appears relative to the page. The relatively positioned text shows up relative to the normal HTML flow.

What happens if you have two relatively positioned elements? The second element is positioned relatively to the position of the first, but as if the first wasn't offset by any left or top value. In other words, if the first element is relatively positioned with `left` set to 10, the second element is positioned with respect to the first, but as if `left` were set to 0. Sound confusing? It is. But there's no way around it.

Listing 4-4   **The relabs.html Source Code**

```
<HTML>
<HEAD>
    <TITLE>Absolute and Relative</TITLE>
</HEAD>
<BODY>
Hello. And welcome to the absolute and relative sample page.
<SPAN style="position:absolute; left:10; top:10">Absolutely correct</SPAN>
<SPAN style="position:relative; left:10; top:10">Relatively reasonable</SPAN>
</BODY>
</HTML>
```

Zzzzz . . . wake up!

When you use 2-D positioning, some elements can appear on top of others.
For example, the following HTML code, taken from the alien3.html page,
places text on top of an image:

```
<IMG src="scene1.jpg" style="position:absolute; left:50; top:80">
<SPAN style="position:absolute; left:110; top:170; font-size:20pt">Scene 1</SPAN>
```

The text appears on top of the image because the text occurs later in the
HTML page. If, instead, you had the following code, the image would appear
on top of the text:

```
<SPAN style="position:absolute; left:110; top:170; font-size:20pt">Scene 1</SPAN>
<IMG src="scene1.jpg" style="position:absolute; left:50; top:80">
```

In other words, as elements are read, new elements appear on top of previous
elements (only if the elements overlap, of course). In a way, the Web page is
constructed similarly to early animated cartoons. With cartoons, each character is drawn on a separate piece of film, called a *cel*. The cels are then
stacked on top of each other. The cels on the top of the stack can obscure
images from the cels toward the bottom of the stack. A Web page is quite similar. Each element essentially creates a new cel — and the cel is placed at the
top of the stack. This top-to-bottom ordering is called *z-ordering*. That's
because, in 3-D coordinate systems, *x* is the horizontal coordinate, *y* is vertical coordinate, and *z* represents the depth coordinate.

You can specify that certain elements should be on top of others. To do so,
you set a z-index. By default, elements appear at z-index 0. Elements with
a higher z-index appear on top of elements with a lower z-index. For example, you may have the following HTML code:

```
<SPAN style="position:absolute; left:110; top:170; font-size:20pt">Scene 1</SPAN>
<IMG src="scene1.jpg" style="position:absolute; left:50; top:80">
```

In this case, the image appears on top of the text. But, if you set the z-index
for the text, you can make the text appear on top of the image, even though it
occurs earlier in the HTML code:

```
<SPAN style="position:absolute; left:110; top:170; font-size:20pt; z-index:1">Scene
          1</SPAN>
<IMG src="scene1.jpg" style="position:absolute; left:50; top:80">
```

Within any given z-index, a *z-order* exists. For example, you have seen that
when you place two elements in a row, the last one that's created appears on
top of the other. The order in which elements appear in a document establishes a *z*-order for elements at z-index 0. Likewise, suppose that you
created several elements and gave them a z-index of 1. The most recently
added elements would be higher in the *z*-order. For example, the following
code has four elements. Two are at z-index 0, and two are at z-index 1.

```
<SPAN id=sp1 style="position:absolute; left:110; top:170; font-size:20pt; z-index:
        1">Scene 1</SPAN>
<IMG id=img1 src="scene1.jpg" style="position:absolute; left:50; top:80; z-index: 1">
<SPAN id=sp2 style="position:absolute; left:190; top:170; font-size:20pt">Scene
        2</SPAN>
<IMG id=img2 src="scene2.jpg" style="position:absolute; left:130; top:80">
```

The span sp1 and the image img1 appear on top of the other two elements.
That's because the other elements are at the default z-index of 0, whereas
sp1 and img1 are at z-index 1. Image img1 appears on top of span sp1
because img1 appears later in the HTML code than sp1 does. Likewise, img2
appears on top of sp2 because img2 appears later in the code than sp2.

The z-index values can be positive or negative. Negative values place
objects behind the default z-index of 0. In other words, if you have some
text on the page with no z-index set and you add an element with a negative, that added element appears behind the text. Using a negative z-index is
a nice way to create background elements that appear behind the main text
on the page.

As an example, check out zindex.html from the ch04 folder (see Listing 4-5).
You see some text describing the pretext of the *Surf Aliens* movie. The text
appears on top of a background that consists of the words *Scene 1* and an
image, as shown in Figure 4-6. By setting the z-index to –1, the page has a
much richer look than it otherwise would. The density of the page is also
increased. In short, the page looks much more like an excerpt from a magazine than a standard Web page.

Navigator doesn't support negative values for z-index. Also note that you
can only set the z-index on a <DIV>, <SPAN>, or <LAYER>. You can see a
Netscape version of zindex.html by loading zindex_nn.html.

Listing 4-5	The zindex.html Source Code

```
<HTML>
<HEAD>
    <TITLE>Z-Index Sample</TITLE>
</HEAD>
<BODY bgcolor=black text=cyan>
<SPAN style="width:45%">
Haras and Irim valiantly tried to save their home planet. Alas, it was beyond repair.
            That's why they decided to escape to other worlds to continue their
            endless summer of surfing.<BR><BR>
Meanwhile, planet Earth itself was undergoing drastic changes. As the temperature
            warmed, coastal cities experienced colder winters and hotter summers.
</SPAN>
<SPAN style="position:absolute; top: 10; left: 150; font-family: impact; font-size:
            30pt; color: gray; z-index: -1">Scene 1<IMG src="scene1.jpg"></SPAN>
</SPAN>
</BODY>
</HTML>
```

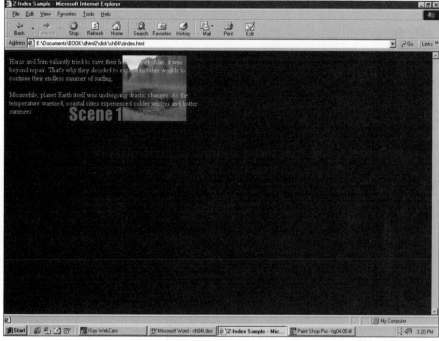

Figure 4-6:
By setting
the *z-*
index, the
image and
the words
Scene 1
appear
behind the
explanatory
text.

Animating an Object

Not only does 2-D positioning allow you to create richer-looking pages, but it
lets you animate pages by enabling you to change the 2-D location of any element over time. You simply change the object's position from script.

You see animation happen in the food4.html file that I discuss in Chapter 3.
There, every time that the mouse clicked, an image's size and position
changed. You can also animate text to create slides. In Chapter 3, you create
a slide presentation by showing text when the user clicks. Another approach
is to have the text slide in. Of course, you can get fancier. You can move text
or images across the page to grab a user's attention. Moving an animated GIF
file lets you create cartoon-style animations.

Take a look at alien4.html in the ch04 folder (see Listing 4-6). The text elements *Scene 1* and *Scene 2* slide across the page when the page loads. To do
so, the page uses the `setInterval` method repeatedly to call a function
called `moveText`. The `setInterval` method moves the two spans with the
following code:

```
sc1.style.pixelLeft -= 10;
sc2.style.pixelLeft -= 10;
```

Load alien4_nn.html for a Navigator version of this page.

The `setInterval` method also increments a counter and shuts down the loop after 20 iterations, as follows:

```
cnt++;
if (20 == cnt)
    window.clearInterval(intNum);
```

Look at Figure 4-7, and you can see the text moving across the page.

Figure 4-7:
The two text
spans slide
across the
page when
the page
first
appears.

Listing 4-6	The alien4.html Source Code

```
<HTML>
<HEAD>
<TITLE>Simple 2-D Sample</TITLE>
<SCRIPT>
var cnt = 0;
var intNum;
function init() {
    intNum = window.setInterval("moveText()", 100);
}
function moveText() {
    sc1.style.pixelLeft -= 10;
    sc2.style.pixelLeft -= 10;
    cnt++;
    if (20 == cnt)
        window.clearInterval(intNum);
}
</SCRIPT>
</HEAD>
<BODY BGCOLOR=black text=white onload="init()">
<IMG src="scene1.jpg" style="position:absolute; left:50; top:80">
<IMG src="scene2.jpg" style="position:absolute; left:50; top:250">
<SPAN id=sc1 style="position:absolute; left:310; top:170; font-size:20pt">Scene 1</SPAN>
<SPAN id=sc2 style="position:absolute; left:310; top:340; font-size:20pt">Scene 2</SPAN>
<SPAN style="position:absolute; width:35%; top:80; left:300; font-size:10pt">
In Scene 1, Irim and Haras curl for the last time on their homeland.
</SPAN>
</BODY>
</HTML>
```

Chapter 5

Input Your Right Foot In

*W*eb pages entertain. Web pages provide information. And Web pages gather data. After all, that's how sites get your name and address so that if you buy something from the site, such as a book, they can send it to you. Or, just as likely, so that they can pester you with junk mail.

HTML code provides a set of elements that you can use to gather input from the user. These elements include checkboxes, radio buttons, text entry fields, and pushbuttons. In this chapter, you find out how to use these input elements to enhance your pages.

Red Alert

Before you find out how to get input from the user, you need to know how to display information back to the user. There are many ways to do so. For example, in Chapter 6 you find out how to write text directly into the page. But right now, I'm going to tell you about the easiest technique of all: showing alerts. *Alerts,* also known as *message boxes,* are dialog boxes that appear on the screen with some text and an OK button. They pop up on top of everything else and stay there until the user clicks on the OK button. Using alerts is a great way to get the attention of the user or to provide some important information. You see alerts used throughout this chapter.

Creating an alert is easy. You call the alert command and pass in the text that you want to display. For example, the following line of script displays an alert with the text *Hello Mom*:

```
alert("Hello Mom");
```

Forms, Forms, Everywhere Forms

There are two main ways to get user input. Chapter 3 discusses how to get user input by processing mouse events and keystrokes. You can certainly process these events to gather input, but there is a much easier way. HTML provides a variety of elements that are already designed for getting input: the form elements.

There are six key form elements:

- ✔ button. This element is a pushbutton that processes an onclick event when the user clicks on it.
- ✔ checkbox. Use a checkbox to let a user choose whether a value is true or false.
- ✔ password. This element is a text entry field that displays asterisks instead of the actual characters that the user types. This form element is usually used for entering passwords.
- ✔ radio. Use the radio button element to allow the user to select a single item from a series of choices.
- ✔ reset. This element is a pushbutton that, when clicked on, automatically resets all elements on the form to their initial values.
- ✔ text. Use a text entry field to provide a place for the user to enter text.

All these elements are created using the <INPUT> tag, as follows:

```
<INPUT type=type of button value=text for element>
```

In addition, for text and password fields, you can specify the maximum number of characters that can be typed with maxLength, and you can define the number of characters that are displayed at once with size.

You can set a radio button or checkbox initially by adding checked=true to the <INPUT> tag. For example, the following code makes the checkbox initially checked:

```
<INPUT type="CHECKBOX" checked=true>
```

Checkboxes and radio buttons don't display text in them. Text and password elements can display initial text, but they don't have labels. Thus, you need to add text to the page to indicate which elements do what. Do so simply by adding HTML code. In other words, if you want *Name:* to appear before a text entry field, use the following HTML code:

```
Name: <INPUT type="text">
```

If you want a picture to appear before a radio button, use the following HTML code:

```
<IMG src="jelly.jpg"><INPUT type="radio" name="grp1">
```

Thus, if you know how to design a page, you don't need to learn anything special to design a page with input elements.

Microsoft Internet Explorer lets you use the form elements anywhere on a page. With Netscape Navigator, you need to put them inside <FORM> and </FORM> tags. If you're designing a page for both browsers, keep this difference in mind.

Input family values

After you add input elements to a page, you surely want to find their values. After all, getting the values lets you process the data that the user has entered. You need to make sure that you have given a `name` or `id` to the elements that you want to query.

For text and password fields, the entered data is in the `value` field. For checkboxes and radio buttons, the `checked` property is true if the elements are selected and false if they are not.

To look at a sample, open query.html in the ch05 folder on the enclosed CD-ROM (see Listing 5-1). This file creates a form with a text field, a password field, a checkbox, and a button. When the user clicks on the button, the values of the input elements are displayed in a message box (see Figure 5-1).

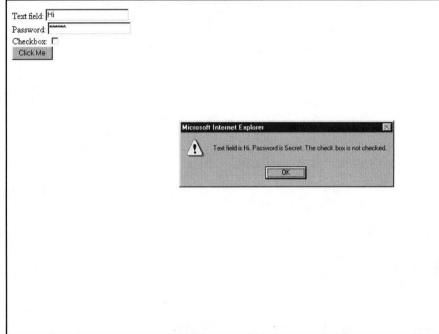

Figure 5-1:
When the
user clicks
on the
button, the
page dis-
plays the
values of
the other
input
elements.

Listing 5-1　　　　　　The query.html Source Code

```
<HTML>
<HEAD>
<TITLE>Element values</TITLE>
<SCRIPT>
function showValues() {
    var answer;
    answer = "Text field is " + document.form1.txt1.value
    + ". ";
    answer += "Password is " + document.form1.pass1.value
    + ". ";
    answer += "The check box is ";
    if (!document.form1.chk1.checked)
        answer += "not ";
    answer += "checked.";
    alert(answer);
}
</SCRIPT>
</HEAD>
<BODY>
<FORM name="form1">
Text field: <INPUT name=txt1 type="TEXT" value="Hi"><BR>
Password: <INPUT name=pass1 type="PASSWORD"
value="Secret"><BR>
Checkbox: <INPUT name=chk1 type="CHECKBOX"><BR>
```

```
<INPUT type="BUTTON" value="Click Me"
onclick="showValues()">
</FORM>
</BODY>
</HTML>
```

Here's how the code works. When the user clicks on the button, the function showValues is called. This function examines the values of the other <INPUT> elements. The following code checks the value of the text field:

```
answer = "Text field is " + document.form1.txt1.value + ".";
```

As you can see, document.form1.txt1.value returns the text that is inside the text field. This value is added to the string named answer.

The value of the checkbox is read with the following code:

```
if (!document.form1.chk1.checked)
    answer += "not ";
```

After all the values are checked, answer is displayed with an alert.

Why don't any radio buttons appear in the sample? They are handled a bit differently, and I cover them shortly.

If you place input elements inside a form, give the form a name to make accessing the input elements easier. For example, suppose you have a form named form1 and a text field named street. You can find values of elements in the form with the following line of script:

```
txtStreet = document.form1.street.value;
```

Without a name, you would need to use script such as the following:

```
txtStreet = document.forms(0).street.value;
```

Note that you must set a *name* for the form, not an id.

Internet Explorer lets you assign a name and/or id to an <INPUT> element. Navigator only lets you assign a name.

Setting the values

Setting the values of input fields is as easy as querying them. Instead of getting the values, simply set them. For example, take a look at form.html in the ch05 folder (see Listing 5-2). This page has a number of input fields inside a form. Clicking on the Prefill button sets several of these fields, as you can see in Figure 5-2.

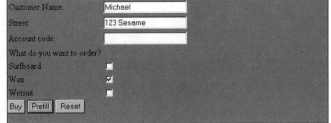

Figure 5-2:
Clicking on
the Prefill
button fills
in several
input values
on the form.

Listing 5-2   The form.html Source Code

```
<HTML>
<HEAD>
<TITLE>Form Example</TITLE>
<SCRIPT>
function doBuy() {
   alert("Thanks for the order, " + document.order.CustName.value);
}

function doPrefill() {
   document.order.CustName.value = "Michael";
   document.order.Street.value = "123 Sesame";
   document.order.Wax.checked = true;
}
</SCRIPT>
</HEAD>

<BODY>
<FORM name=order>
<TABLE style="background-color:gray;width:70%" cellspacing=0 border=0>
<TR>
   <TD WIDTH="25%">Customer Name: </TD>
   <TD WIDTH="75%"><INPUT TYPE="TEXT" NAME="CustName" VALUE="" MAXLENGTH=20></TD>
</TR>
<TR>
   <TD>Street:</TD>
   <TD><INPUT TYPE="TEXT" NAME="Street" VALUE="" MAXLENGTH=20></TD>
</TR>
<TR>
   <TD>Account code:</TD>
   <TD><INPUT TYPE="PASSWORD" NAME="Password" VALUE="" MAXLENGTH=8></TD>
</TR>
<TR>
   <TD COLSPAN=2>What do you want to order?</TD>
</TR>
<TR>
   <TD>Surfboard</TD>
   <TD><INPUT TYPE="CHECKBOX" NAME="Board" ></TD>
</TR>
<TR>
   <TD>Wax</TD>
```

```
    <TD><INPUT TYPE="CHECKBOX" NAME="Wax" ></TD>
</TR>
<TR>
  <TD>Wetsuit</TD>
  <TD><INPUT TYPE="CHECKBOX" NAME="Wetsuit"  ></TD>
</TR>
<TR><TD COLSPAN=2><INPUT TYPE="BUTTON" VALUE="Buy" onclick="doBuy()">
<INPUT TYPE="BUTTON" VALUE="Prefill" onclick="doPrefill()">
<INPUT TYPE="RESET" VALUE="Reset"><BR> 
</TD></TR>
</TABLE>
</FORM>
</BODY>
</HTML>
```

The page is simple. When the user clicks on the Prefill button, the doPrefill function springs into action. The function fills in text values with the following lines:

```
document.order.CustName.value = "Michael";
document.order.Street.value = "123 Sesame";
```

The doPrefill function also automatically checks the Wax checkbox with the following line:

```
document.order.Wax.checked = true;
```

The page also has a reset button. Clicking on it automatically clears all the values on the form. Be sure to try it out!

To restrict the width of a form or to set its background color, put the form inside a div. Set the background color and position for the div using the style parameter.

Note: An easy way to get all the input elements in a form to line up is to put them inside a table. Use one column for the field labels and another column for the input values.

Video killed the radio star

Radio buttons behave a little differently than the other input elements. Radio buttons are always used in groups, and only one radio button in a group can be set. (After all, these buttons are used for choosing mutually exclusive options.) For example, you can use radio buttons to select whether you want an item shipped normally or by an overnight service.

When you use radio buttons, use the same name for all the radio buttons that you want to be together. Use a different value for each button. For example, the following HTML code, taken from the radio.html page in the ch05 folder, sets up two groups of radio buttons (see Figure 5-3). One contains a list of lunch specials, and the other displays a list of drinks. I show the source code for the entire radio.html file later in this chapter.

Figure 5-3:
This page
contains
two groups
of radio
buttons.

Please select your lunch:
- ⊙ Chicken Delight
- ○ Tofu Supreme
- ○ Random Roadkill

Please select your drink:
- ○ Tequila Sunrise
- ⊙ Lemon Twister
- ○ Caffo Pop

[Click Me]

NETSCAPE VERSION

Navigator doesn't let you create a collection of similarly named objects. As a result, you need to a look at all elements within a form, see whether the name is the name of the radio button group, and see whether the element is checked. You can see how to do this in radio_nn.html.

```
<FORM name="form1">
<EM>Please select your lunch:</EM><BR>
<INPUT type="RADIO" name="grp1" value="Chicken Delight"
checked=true> Chicken Delight<BR>
<INPUT type="RADIO" name="grp1" value="Tofu Supreme"> Tofu
Supreme<BR>
<INPUT type="RADIO" name="grp1" value="Random Roadkill">
Random Roadkill<BR>
<EM>Please select your drink:</EM><BR>
<INPUT type="RADIO" name="grp2" value="1"> Tequila
Sunrise<BR>
<INPUT type="RADIO" name="grp2" value="2" checked=true>
Lemon Twister<BR>
<INPUT type="RADIO" name="grp2" value="3"> Caffo Pop<BR>
<INPUT type="BUTTON" value="Click Me"
onclick="showValues()">
</FORM>
```

Notice that each group shares the same name, but the various radio buttons within that group each have different values. Only one radio button in a group can be on at once.

TIP

It is good practice to set `checked=true` for one of the radio buttons in a group.

Although setting up radio buttons is easy, finding out which was checked is more difficult. There are two basic approaches. First, you can give an `id` to each radio button. The `id` should be set to a name that's different than the group name. For example, you could use the following HTML code:

```
<INPUT id="drink1" type="RADIO" name="grp2" value="1">
Tequila Sunrise<BR>
<INPUT id="drink2" type="RADIO" name="grp2" value="2"
checked=true> Lemon Twister<BR>
```

You can then see whether a particular radio button is checked by using the following script:

```
if (document.form1.drink1.checked)
    alert("It's drink one");
```

A second, more general approach to finding out which radio button was checked is to create a collection for all the radio buttons in a particular group. This uses a fancy feature of Dynamic HTML that I discuss further in Chapters 6 and 13. In short, you can get a collection of all the elements on a page with a particular name with the following script:

```
radioSet = document.all.item(groupName);
```

This script essentially says "Look at all the elements in the page and grab for me those with a particular name." In this case, groupName is set to a value such as grp1.

This is a trick that you can exploit in many ways. To access a group of elements programmatically, you can give them the same name, get a collection of elements with that name as shown here, and then loop through the collection to access the group. But remember that this trick only works with Internet Explorer.

After you have this collection, you can go through it one element at a time to find out which item was checked. Then you can return the value for the checked item. You can use the following code:

```
function getClicked(groupName) {
    var radioSet;
    radioSet = document.all.item(groupName);
    for (i = 0; i < radioSet.length; i++)
        if (radioSet(i).checked)
            return radioSet(i).value;
}
```

"Whoa," you say. "You're making my head hurt!" Well, radio buttons are tricky. Allow me to walk you through this code one more time. It begins by creating a collection for all the elements on the page that have a particular name. For example, if groupName is grp1, the code returns all the elements on the page named grp1. In the sample page radio.html, all the radio buttons in the first group are named grp1. As a result, the collection contains all the radio buttons in the first group.

Next, the loop goes through every item in the collection. How does it do this? The loop variable i goes from 0 to 1 less than the length of the collection. Thus, radioSet(i) starts with the first element in the collection (item 0) and continues to the last (item length–1). If the particular radio button is checked, the function returns the value that is associated with that radio button.

You can see this code in action by looking at radio.html in the ch05 folder (see Listing 5-3). It has two groups of radio buttons and a button. When the button is clicked on, a script like the following checks each group of radio buttons to see which is pressed.

```
answer = "Your meal is " + getClicked("grp1") + ". ";
answer += "Your drink is " + getClicked("grp2") + ".";
```

Listing 5-3   The radio.html Source Code

```
<HTML>
<HEAD>
<TITLE>Element values</TITLE>
<SCRIPT>
function getClicked(groupName) {
    var radioSet;
    radioSet = document.all.item(groupName);
    for (i = 0; i < radioSet.length; i++)
        if (radioSet(i).checked)
            return radioSet(i).value;
}
function showValues() {
    var answer;
    answer = "Your meal is " + getClicked("grp1") + ". ";
    answer += "Your drink is " + getClicked("grp2") + ".";
    alert(answer);
}
</SCRIPT>
</HEAD>
<BODY>
<FORM name="form1">
<EM>Please select your lunch:</EM><BR>
<INPUT type="RADIO" name="grp1" value="Chicken Delight"
checked=true> Chicken Delight<BR>
<INPUT type="RADIO" name="grp1" value="Tofu Supreme"> Tofu
Supreme<BR>
<INPUT type="RADIO" name="grp1" value="Random Roadkill">
Random Roadkill<BR>
<EM>Please select your drink:</EM><BR>
<INPUT type="RADIO" name="grp2" value="1"> Tequila
Sunrise<BR>
<INPUT type="RADIO" name="grp2" value="2" checked=true>
Lemon Twister<BR>
<INPUT type="RADIO" name="grp2" value="3"> Caffo Pop<BR>
<INPUT type="BUTTON" value="Click Me"
onclick="showValues()">
</FORM>
</BODY>
</HTML>
```

You are allowed to think that this code is awfully twisted and complex. But that's okay. You can just cut and paste the getClicked code and use it whenever you need to check which radio button in a group was checked.

When you use radio buttons with submit forms, the submit form automatically sends the name of the radio button group followed by the value of the radio button that was selected.

To find the radio button that is set with Navigator, you must cycle through all the elements on the form looking for a checked element that has the same name as the group you're trying to examine. You can see such a page by looking at radio_nn.html in the ch05 folder. Or check out the following code. Be sure to compare it to the equivalent Internet Explorer code in Listing 5-3:

```
function getClicked(groupName) {
    for (i = 0; i < document.form1.elements.length; i++)
        if ((document.form1.elements[i].checked) && (document.form1.elements[i].name ==
            groupName))
            return document.form1.elements[i].value;
    return 0;
}
```

Another way to find the value of a radio button is to put an event handler on each radio button. When the radio button is clicked, set a global variable indicating which one was clicked, as shown in the code that follows:

```
<SCRIPT>
var Rb1Grp = null;
</SCRIPT>
<FORM NAME=Aform>
<INPUT TYPE=Radio value="One" onClick="javascript:Rb1Grp=this.value" Name=Rb1Grp>
<INPUT TYPE=Radio value="Two" onClick="javascript:Rb1Grp=this.value" Name=Rb1Grp >
</FORM>
```

The Select Few

Selection fields are another useful input element. They let you display a drop-down list of choices. Like radio buttons, only one item from a select group can be chosen at any time. But unlike radio buttons, selections don't use much screen real estate. Instead, the list of choices shows up only when you click on the drop-down button. Selection fields are particularly useful when you have a large variety of choices. Figure 5-4 shows what a selection list looks like.

Figure 5-4:
Selections
display a set
of choices
in a drop-
down list.

Start a selection list with the `<SELECT>` tag. Then add the `<OPTION>` tags for each item in the drop-down list. The `<OPTION>` tag contains a value to return when the drop-down list is queried. Follow it by the text that you want to have displayed in the drop-down list. For example, the following code creates a drop-down list with a set of lunch options:

```
<SELECT NAME=selectList>
<OPTION VALUE=1 SELECTED>Tofu Supreme
<OPTION VALUE=2>Chicken Delight
<OPTION VALUE=3>Random Roadkill
</SELECT>
```

Note that the text that follows the `<OPTION>` tag is treated as plain text. Any HTML tags that you include, such as `<B>` or `<FONT>`, are ignored.

Add `SELECTED` to the `<OPTION>` tag for the item that you want to have selected by default.

To find the value of the item that is selected, just query the `value` property for the selection list. This query returns the value for the `<OPTION>` that is selected.

To see selection lists in action, check out Listing 5-4. This page contains a selection list that contains a set of lunch choices and a button. Clicking on the button displays the value of the selected item. Note that in this case, I set the value to be a number, but it could just as easily have been the name of the item ordered.

You must use code such as the following to find the value of a select box with Navigator:

```
document.form1.selectList.options[document.form1.selectList.selectedIndex].value
```

With Internet Explorer, you can use the following shortcut instead:

```
document.form1.selectList.value
```

Listing 5-4	**The select.html Source Code**

```
<HTML>
<HEAD>
<TITLE>Select Sample</TITLE>
<SCRIPT>
function showValues() {
     var answer;
   answer = "The selected item is " +
             document.form1.selectList.options[document.form1.selectList.selectedIn
             dex].value + ". ";      selectList.value + ". ";
     alert(answer);
}
</SCRIPT>
</HEAD>
<BODY>
<FORM name="form1">
Please choose your lunch:
<SELECT NAME=selectList>
<OPTION VALUE=1 SELECTED>Tofu Supreme
<OPTION VALUE=2>Chicken Delight
<OPTION VALUE=3>Random Roadkill
</SELECT>
<BR>
<INPUT type="BUTTON" value="Click Me" onclick=
"showValues()">
</FORM>
</BODY>
</HTML>
```

Justice Is Served

Originally, forms were created so that you could easily send data to servers. The server would then process the data and return new information for the page. This is how search engines such as Yahoo! and AltaVista work. You place data in a form, the data is sent to a server, and then the server processes the information and returns the answer. How does the server figure out what to send back? Only Dilbert's mom really understands that stuff.

Even if you aren't Dilbert's mom, you can take advantage of the way that servers process forms by using the snarf trick. Essentially, you find a page that has an interesting query in it, and then you choose View⇨Source from Internet Explorer 5.0 or View⇨Page Source from Navigator. You see the source code for the Web page. You can then read the HTML code to see what data needs to be filled out for the query. Next, you add the appropriate form elements to your page.

To add a form query to your page, add a submit button or an image button. Both of these are special buttons that, when pressed, gather the data from the form elements and send it to the server as a query. A submit button looks like any other pushbutton. With an image button, you specify the image to show, so a graphic appears for the button rather than a normal gray pushbutton.

Some queries also have many parameters that need to be passed; these parameters are often too complex or ugly to bother users with. For these parameters, you use hidden input fields. A *hidden input field* is just like a text field, but it's invisible. Usually, the values for the hidden fields are set statically, but you can also set them using code just as you would for any other text field.

Finally, you need to enter some extra values in the `<FORM>` tag. In particular, you need to set the `ACTION` parameter to indicate what the query is supposed to do and the `METHOD` parameter to indicate the type of the query. Rather than scratch your head for a few years, just look inside the snarfed HTML code for an existing query to see what these values should be.

Take the following steps:

1. **Find a page with the query that you want to incorporate into your page.**

2. **View the source code.**

3. **Look for the `<FORM>` tag to see the `ACTION` and `METHOD` values.**

4. **Look for `<INPUT>` elements to see the names and types of data to include.**

5. **Snarf it.**

For example, suppose that you want to create a query that links to the Yahoo! search engine. Maybe you have a page that's devoted to the movie *Surf Aliens*. You may want users to click on a button and instantly get a Yahoo! search for any other sites that are devoted to *Surf Aliens*. This search would be much easier than maintaining all the links yourself. Or you may want to add a search for people who share your name, your birthday, or anything else that strikes your fancy.

You add this each capability by first looking at the source code for the `www.yahoo.com` home page. Among many tags, you find the following code:

```
<form action="http://search.yahoo.com/bin/search">
<input size=30 name=p> <input type=submit value=Search>
```

This code tells you all you need to know to hook up a Yahoo! search. You need a text input called `p` that contains the text to search for and a form tag with the action that's shown in the HTML code.

Because that was so simple, look at AltaVista, too. The following is the relevant HTML code from that site:

```
<FORM method=GET action="/cgi-bin/query"><INPUT TYPE=hidden
NAME=pg VALUE=q>
<B>Search <SELECT NAME=what><OPTION VALUE=web SELECTED>the
Web<OPTION VALUE=news >Usenet</SELECT>
<B> in </B><SELECT NAME=kl>
<OPTION VALUE=XX SELECTED>any language
<OPTION VALUE=zh >Chinese
<OPTION VALUE=cz >Czech
<OPTION VALUE=da >Danish
<OPTION VALUE=nl >Dutch
<OPTION VALUE=en >English
<OPTION VALUE=et >Estonian
<OPTION VALUE=fi >Finnish
<OPTION VALUE=fr >French
<OPTION VALUE=de >German
<OPTION VALUE=el >Greek
<OPTION VALUE=he >Hebrew
<OPTION VALUE=hu >Hungarian
<OPTION VALUE=is >Icelandic
<OPTION VALUE=it >Italian
<OPTION VALUE=ja >Japanese
<OPTION VALUE=ko >Korean
<OPTION VALUE=lv >Latvian
<OPTION VALUE=lt >Lithuanian
<OPTION VALUE=no >Norwegian
<OPTION VALUE=pl >Polish
<OPTION VALUE=pt >Portuguese
<OPTION VALUE=ro >Romanian
<OPTION VALUE=ru >Russian
<OPTION VALUE=es >Spanish
<OPTION VALUE=sv >Swedish
</SELECT> and Display <SELECT NAME=fmt><OPTION VALUE="."
SELECTED>in Standard Form<OPTION VALUE=c >in Compact
Form<OPTION VALUE=d >in Detailed Form</SELECT></B><BR>
<INPUT NAME=q size=55 maxlength=800 VALUE="">
<INPUT TYPE=submit VALUE="Submit">
</FORM>
```

From this code, you find out that, for an AltaVista query, you need to fill in fields named pg, what, kl, fmt, and q. You don't need to use the drop-down lists like AltaVista does. Instead, you can use hidden fields to fill in the language and format fields with the values that you want.

Note that the action for the AltaVista page is action="/cgi-bin query", which means, "Run the program named query in the cgi-bin directory." Now, that doesn't mean the cgi-bin directory where your page is but rather the one at the AltaVista site. So to use the AltaVista query, you need to enter the full URL for the file to run — that is,
http://altavista.digital.com/cgi-bin/query.

Next, create a page that uses the Yahoo! and AltaVista searches. (You can load it by looking at search.html in the ch05 folder or by checking out Figure 5-5. Also, refer to Listing 5-5.) In particular, the page searches for other pages that refer to a particular name. I'm going to use mine; of course, you should change this to your own name.

This page finds other Web sites for people with my name.

Search Yahoo for my name. [Search]

Search AltaVista for anything.   Search for: Michael Hyman   [AltaVista search]

Listing 5-5   **The search.html Source Code**

```
<HTML>
<HEAD>
<TITLE>Demos Submit Forms</TITLE>
</HEAD>
<BODY>
This page finds other Web sites for people with my name.
<form action="http://search.yahoo.com/bin/search">
Search Yahoo for my name.
<input type="hidden" value="Michael Hyman" name=p>
<input type="submit" value=Search>
</FORM>
<FORM method=GET action="http://altavista.digital.com/
cgi-bin/query">
Search AltaVista for anything.
<INPUT TYPE="hidden" NAME=pg VALUE=q>
<INPUT type="hidden" NAME=what VALUE=web>
<INPUT type="hidden" NAME=kl VALUE=XX>
<INPUT type="hidden" NAME=fmt VALUE=".">
Search for: <INPUT NAME=q VALUE="Michael Hyman">
<INPUT TYPE="submit" VALUE="AltaVista search">
</FORM>
</BODY>
</HTML>
```

The page has one form for the Yahoo! query and another for the AltaVista query. For the Yahoo! query, you must force it to search for pages with a particular name. To do so, you prefill all the values using HIDDEN elements rather than TEXT elements. The following is the HTML code:

```
<form action="http://search.yahoo.com/bin/search">
Search Yahoo for my name.
<input type="hidden" value="Michael Hyman" name=p>
<input type="submit" value=Search>
</FORM>
```

For the AltaVista query, you fill in most of the query values with HIDDEN elements, but you let the user change the text that he searches for. In this case, I prefill the search text to look for *Michael Hyman.* The following is the HTML code for the AltaVista query:

```
<FORM method=GET action="http://altavista.digital.com/
cgi-bin/query">
Search AltaVista for anything.
<INPUT TYPE="hidden" NAME=pg VALUE=q>
<INPUT type="hidden" NAME=what VALUE=web>
<INPUT type="hidden" NAME=k1 VALUE=XX>
<INPUT type="hidden" NAME=fmt VALUE=".">
Search for: <INPUT NAME=q VALUE="Michael Hyman">
<INPUT TYPE="submit" VALUE="AltaVista search">
</FORM>
```

With a little hunting through Web pages, you can add all types of interesting searches to your page, such as links to phone directories, maps, and much more.

Chapter 6

Textual Healing

. . . .

In This Chapter

▶ Dynamically changing text color, size, and style

▶ Dynamically showing and hiding areas

▶ Automatically adjusting font size when a page resizes

▶ Changing HTML code on the fly

▶ Typing directly into an HTML page

. . . .

*W*hen it comes to Web pages, life is a stream of text. And in the old days, you often got caught up the stream without a paddle. What you had was what you got. And you liked it. Yeah. But with Dynamic HTML, you can change any aspect of the Web page at any time. You can dynamically adjust the appearance of the page as well as its content in response to user actions. For example, you can highlight text as the user moves over it. You can change the data in a table on the fly, perhaps sorting it in different ways. You can expand areas of the page to provide more detail. Or you can move and hide areas for a multimedia presentation.

In this chapter, you discover all types of tricks and techniques for manipulating Web pages.

In the Zone

To manipulate a page, you must first set up areas that you can access from scripts. I show this procedure several times in the earlier chapters of this book: Elements are given names and are then manipulated by scripts.

For manipulating blocks of text (or really, any block of HTML code), set up a named span, div, or anchor. Then change its properties by using a script.

Use a <DIV> or a <SPAN> tag to set the position or size of the area. To allow the area to flow normally, you can use a <SPAN>, <DIV>, or <A> tag. If you want a click on an area to cause a jump to a link, use an <A> tag.

Naming a span, div, or anchor is easy. Just add an id parameter, as you would for any other element on the page. For example, the following excerpt from surfcond.html (located in the ch06 folder on the enclosed CD-ROM) sets up a named anchor for the sentence starting with *Temperatures*:

```
Today's surf conditions are superb. There is a light southwesterly breeze. <A
        id=myText onclick="highlight()">Temperatures are expected to reach the
        low 80s, and the water is a mild 72 degrees.</A> Wave height is three
        feet in the outer swell.
```

Note that Microsoft Internet Explorer lets you dynamically control the appearance of just about every element on the page. Netscape Navigator is more restrictive. Although you can position <DIV>, <SPAN>, and <P> tags, you can't do much with them except change their background color. You can, however, dynamically rewrite the contents of a <LAYER> tag. So some of the samples in this chapter use the <LAYER> tag in Navigator. Of course, the <LAYER> tag doesn't do anything in Internet Explorer. Sometimes getting Web pages to work on both browsers seems harder than going on a long car trip with a hungry 2-year-old.

Changing color

After you have named a text area, you can manipulate it in many ways. An easy way to draw attention to text is to change its color or the background color. You can see this technique in action by loading surfcond.html from the ch06 folder (see Listing 6-1). This page manipulates the text in two ways. If you click on the sentence describing the temperature of the air and the water, its background changes to yellow, simulating the effect of a highlighting marker. As you move the mouse pointer around the screen, the color of the text itself changes (see Figure 6-1). The red value changes with the x position of the mouse pointer, and the blue value varies with the y position of the mouse pointer. Figure 6-1 shows how the page looks with the text highlighted and the mouse pointer toward the upper-right corner of the page.

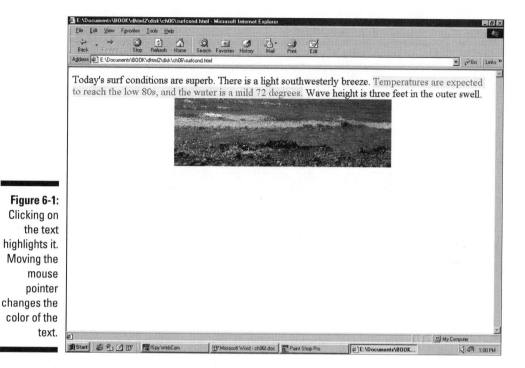

Figure 6-1:
Clicking on
the text
highlights it.
Moving the
mouse
pointer
changes the
color of the
text.

Listing 6-1	**The surfcond.html Source Code**

```
<HTML>
<HEAD>
<SCRIPT>
//Convert a decimal number to a two digit hex string
function toHex(n) {
    var tempVal;
    tempVal = n.toString(16);
    if (tempVal.length < 2)
        tempVal = "0" + tempVal;
    return tempVal;

}
function changeText() {
    //Calculate R and B values based on mouse position
    r = Math.round(event.x * 255 / document.body.offsetWidth);
    b = Math.round(event.y * 255 / document.body.offsetHeight);
    myText.style.color = toHex(r) + "00" + toHex(b);
}
function highlight() {
    myText.style.backgroundColor = "yellow";
}
</SCRIPT>
</HEAD>
```

(continued)

Listing 6-1 *(continued)*

```
<BODY onmousemove="changeText()">
<FONT SIZE=5>
Today's surf conditions are superb. There is a light southwesterly breeze. <A
          id=myText onclick="highlight()">Temperatures are expected to reach the
          low 80s, and the water is a mild 72 degrees.</A> Wave height is three
          feet in the outer swell.
<CENTER><IMG src=surf.jpg></CENTER>
</BODY>
</HTML>
```

The tricky part about this page is calculating the color values based on the mouse pointer position. Therefore, you start with the easy stuff: highlighting. First, set up a script to call when the user clicks on the text area. You process the `onclick` event for the text area as follows:

```
<A id=myText onclick="highlight()">
```

The `highlight` function changes the background color for the area as follows:

```
myText.style.backgroundColor = "yellow";
```

That's all. Not bad, huh?

Figuring out how to script style properties is easy. If the property doesn't have a dash in it, its name is unchanged. For example, to set the color in a tag, use this code:

```
<A id=myText style="color:red">
```

And in script, use the following code:

```
myText.style.color = "red";
```

If the property has a dash in it, remove the dash and capitalize the first letter after the dash. For example, to set the background color in a tag, use this code:

```
<A id=myText style="background-color:red">
```

And in script, use the following code:

```
myText.style.backgroundColor = "red";
```

To change the color of the text, the page simply changes the color property for the anchor, as follows:

```
myText.style.color = toHex(r) + "00" + toHex(b);
```

Pass the value, please

You may have noticed that the function has the letter *n* between the (and the). This isn't a funny reference to the game Hexen. Rather, the *n* is an *argument*. An argument is a value that gets *passed* to a function by the script that calls the function. Within the function, the argument takes on the value that is passed in. In other words, the argument provides a way for the script calling the function to provide information that the function may need. The argument is just like any other variable that you use inside the function.

For a real-world example, suppose you are keeping track of which baseball player is at bat. I could call you up and say, "Edgar is at bat." You would then write that down in your book. A few minutes later I may call you and say, "Ken is at bat." You would dutifully write that down. The name of the player is a value that I pass to you.

Because `toHex` has an argument, when you call `toHex`, you pass it a value. For example, you may call `toHex(3)`. That passes the value 3 to the function `toHex`, thereby setting the value of the variable n to 3. Arguments are very useful because they let you use a function over and over again to modify different values. For example, `toHex(3)` returns the hex value of 3 and `toHex(44354)` returns the hex value of 44354. You don't have to write a special function just for converting 3 to hex and just for converting 44354 to hex.

Of course, Navigator does things differently. Although you can set positions and CSS attributes with the style attribute on an element, you can't do the same programmatically. Depending upon the type of element, you may or may not be able to change all the attributes. In general, if the element has been positioned, you can change the position by setting the left and top properties of the element. You can change the background color of certain elements by setting the bgColor property. You can't change the color of text dynamically, although I describe a trick that lets you get the same effect shortly.

The interesting part is calculating the color based on the mouse position. To make this calculation, the script processes the onmousemove event for the entire page. That way, the color varies as the mouse pointer moves over the page. (If you had processed the onmousemove event for the text area itself, the color would change only when the mouse pointer moved over the text area. That wouldn't be as interesting.)

When the mouse pointer moves, a script calculates a red and blue value to correspond to the mouse pointer position. Red, green, and blue values can range from 0 to 255. The code takes the current *x* position, multiplies it by 255, and divides by the width of the page to calculate the red value. As a result, when the mouse is at the left of the page, the red value is 0. When the mouse is at the far right, the value is 255. (Why? The *x* position for the far right is the same as the width of the page. So the current position divided by the width is thus 1. One times 255 is 255.) Use a similar calculation to find a blue value, based on the *y* position of the mouse pointer and the height of the page. The code is as follows:

```
r = Math.round(event.x * 255 / document.body.offsetWidth);
b = Math.round(event.y * 255 / document.body.offsetHeight);
```

After the red and blue values are calculated, they need to be converted to a hex color. That's because HTML code expects style colors to be set using hex notation. (For more information on HTML color values, check out the sidebar "Color my HTML world.") The function `toHex` takes the color value and converts it to a two-character hex string. The string must have two characters in it, because the color value needs to have six characters in it: rrggbb. Thus, a pure red would be FF0000. If you didn't convert to a two-character string and you had a red of FF and a green and blue of 0, you would get FF00. (Here, the green and blue are represented by single zeros.) That is not the same as FF0000. In fact, it *is* the same as 00FF00, or pure green. By having two characters for each hex string, you always get the right number.

You need to play a bunch of tricks to get close to equivalent functionality in Navigator. Navigator doesn't let you change the color of text dynamically. To get around this limitation, you can create a layer and rewrite the text inside the layer. The first time through, the layer contains the normal text. Each time the mouse moves, you rewrite the text into the layer, adding a `<FONT>` tag to set the color:

```
function changeText(e) {
    //Calculate R and B values based on mouse position
    r = Math.round(e.pageX * 255 / window.screen.width);
    b = Math.round(e.pageY * 255 / window.screen.height);
    //Dynamically write in the new text.
    writeIt("<FONT COLOR=" + toHex(r) + "00" + toHex(b) + ">" + theText);
}
```

Note also that Navigator doesn't tell you the actual size of the document. Instead, you have to change the color calculation to base itself on the size of the screen, as I do in the preceding example.

Unfortunately, layers don't smoothly flow in the text the way spans do. Text that follows a layer flows as if the layer wasn't there, so you get overlapping text. To get around this problem, I add some `<BR>`s to move text after the layer. The look is similar to but not quite as nice as the Internet Explorer page:

```
<FONT SIZE=5>Today's surf conditions are superb. There is a light southwesterly breeze.
<BR>
<LAYER id=myText></LAYER>
<!--manually break the text-->
<BR><BR>Wave height is three feet in the outer swell.
```

In an earlier example, you see how to use an anchor tag to wrap a span so as to trap mouse clicks on the span. You can use this trick to highlight text after it is clicked on. When I first used this trick, I established an onclick handler for the anchor. That doesn't work when you dynamically insert text into a layer. Instead, you need to set the href to call a JavaScript function:

```
<A href='javascript:highlight()'>
```

You can see the Navigator version by loading surfcond_nn.html or by looking at Listing 6-2.

Listing 6-2   The surfcond_nn.html Source Code

```
<HTML>
<HEAD>
<SCRIPT>
//Note: need to set the font size manually
var theText = "<FONT SIZE=5><A href='javascript:highlight()'>Temperatures are
               expected to reach the low 80s, and the water is a mild 72
               degrees.</A>";

//Convert a decimal number to a two digit hex string
function toHex(n) {
  var tempVal;

  tempVal = n.toString(16);
  if (tempVal.length < 2)
     tempVal = "0" + tempVal;
  return tempVal;

}

function changeText(e) {
  //Calculate R and B values based on mouse position
  r = Math.round(e.pageX * 255 / window.screen.width);
  b = Math.round(e.pageY * 255 / window.screen.height);
  //Dynamically write in the new text.
  writeIt("<FONT COLOR=" + toHex(r) + "00" + toHex(b) + ">" + theText);
}

function writeIt(t) {
  document.myText.document.open();
  document.myText.document.write(t);
  document.myText.document.close();
}

function highlight() {
  document.myText.bgColor = "yellow";
}

function init() {
  writeIt(theText);
  document.onmousemove = changeText;
  document.captureEvents(Event.MOUSEMOVE);
}
```

(continued)

Listing 6-2 *(continued)*

```
</SCRIPT>
</HEAD>
<BODY onload="init()">
<FONT SIZE=5>Today's surf conditions are superb. There is a light southwesterly
              breeze.
<BR>
<LAYER id=myText></LAYER>
<!--manually break the text-->
<BR><BR>Wave height is three feet in the outer swell.
<P>
<CENTER><IMG src=../media/surf.jpg></CENTER>
</BODY>
</HTML>
```

Changing font characteristics

Another way to draw attention to text is to change its size. Changing the text size is just as easy as changing the color. To set a font size, use HTML code such as the following:

```
<A id=myTxt style="font-size:20pt">
```

Therefore, to change the font size programmatically, use the following script:

```
myTxt.style.fontSize = "20pt";
```

Color my HTML world

You can represent colors in HTML code in two ways. The first is through the color constants, such as red, green, cyan, and yellow. The other way is by setting an RGB (red, green, blue) value. An RGB value is a hexadecimal value in the form of #RRGGBB. Here, RR represents the red value, GG is the green value, and BB is the blue value. Each value can range from 00, meaning no color, to FF, meaning as much color as possible.

The following are some examples of hexadecimal values:

#000000 is black.

#FF0000 is bright red, because it has a full amount of red and no other colors.

#008000 is a medium-intensity green.

#FFFFFF is bright white — it combines full strength red, green, and blue.

#202020 is a dark gray.

#800080 is a medium purple.

To see this technique in action, check out surfcond2.html in the ch06 folder (see Listing 6-3). In this case, the text size is calculated based on the *x* position of the mouse pointer, using the same technique that surfcond.html shows for calculating the red value of the color. However, instead of changing a color value, the font size is changed, as shown in the following script:

```
myText.style.fontSize = txtSize;
```

As you move the mouse pointer, the font size for the text area changes. Toward the left of the screen, the font is very small. Toward the right, the font becomes quite large, as you can see in Figure 6-2.

You can't dynamically change font properties with Navigator, so to create an equivalent effect, you need to use the layer-writing technique I use in surf-cond_nn.html. You can find the Navigator equivalent by loading surfcond2_nn.html. The key line from this file is:

```
writeIt("<SPAN style='font-size:" + txtSize + "px'>" + theText + "</SPAN>");
```

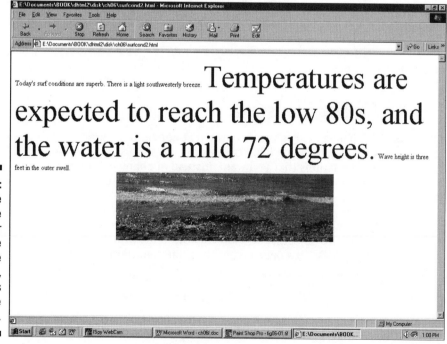

Figure 6-2: Moving the mouse pointer changes the size of the text. Here, the font has become very large.

This line dynamically writes text into the layer, wrapping it in a `<SPAN>` tag. The span includes the style information for changing the font size.

When using font size with Navigator, be sure to specify the units of measurement. Internet Explorer defaults to pixels, but Navigator ignores the size if no units are specified.

Listing 6-3	The surfcond2.html Source Code

```
<HTML>
<HEAD>
<SCRIPT>
function changeText() {
    //Calculate size based on mouse position
    txtSize = event.x * 100 / document.body.offsetWidth;
    myText.style.fontSize = txtSize;
}
</SCRIPT>
</HEAD>
<BODY onmousemove="changeText()">
Today's surf conditions are superb. There is a light southwesterly breeze. <A
            id=myText style="font-size:12">Temperatures are expected to reach the
            low 80s, and the water is a mild 72 degrees.</A> Wave height is three
            feet in the outer swell.
<CENTER><IMG src=surf.jpg></CENTER>
</BODY>
</HTML>
```

Changing style

To change many aspects of the text appearance at one time, consider using style sheets instead. In other words, create a style sheet with the different text variations that you want. Instead of changing individual style properties in response to an event, change the style class that's used for the text. (Chapter 2 covers the style sheet with the `class` parameter on a tag.)

To change the style sheet programmatically, you change the `className` property of the object. Take a look at surfcond3.html in the ch06 folder (see Listing 6-4). This page defines two different paragraph styles:

```
P.1 {font-size:20; font-family:times; font-weight:bold}
P.2 {font-size:40; font-family:arial; letter-spacing:.3em}
```

The following HTML code makes the page initially use paragraph style 1 for the text:

```
<P id=myText CLASS=1>
```

When the user clicks on the text, however, a script changes the style to toggle between paragraph styles 1 and 2:

```
if (myText.className == "1")
    myText.className = "2";
else
    myText.className = "1";
```

As a result, every time you click on the text area, the font family, size, and spacing change, as you can see in Figures 6-3a and b.

This page doesn't work with Navigator.

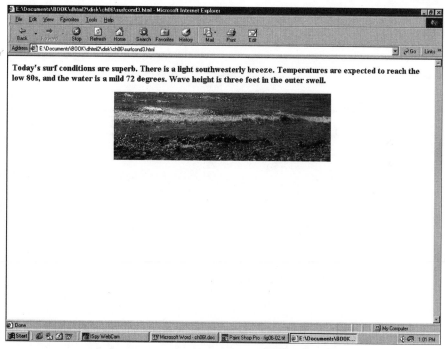

Figure 6-3a: Clicking on the text changes the style sheet that it uses. Here you can see the original text appearance.

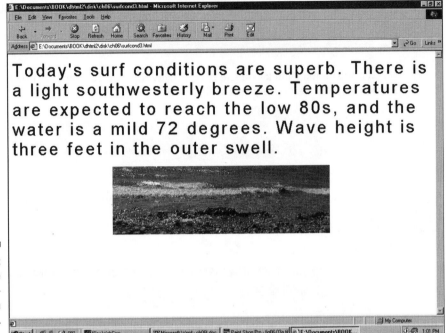

Figure 6-3b:
This is the
text appear-
ance after a
click.

Listing 6-4   The surfcond3.html Source Code

```
<HTML>
<HEAD>
<STYLE type="text/css">
<!--P.1 {font-size:20; font-family:times; font-weight:bold}
P.2 {font-size:40; font-family:arial; letter-spacing:.3em}-->
</STYLE>
<SCRIPT>
function changeText() {
     if (myText.className == "1")
         myText.className = "2";
     else
         myText.className = "1";
}
</SCRIPT>
</HEAD>
<BODY onclick="changeText()">
<P id=myText CLASS=1>
Today's surf conditions are superb. There is a light southwesterly breeze.
          Temperatures are expected to reach the low 80s, and the water is a
          mild 72 degrees. Wave height is three feet in the outer swell. </P>
<CENTER><IMG src=surf.jpg></CENTER>
</BODY>
</HTML>
```

Checking Out All the Hot Spots

Chapter 3 tells you how to create a page in which text appears each time the mouse is clicked, which makes for an interactive presentation. Showing and hiding areas is a very effective way to alter a page based on user actions. You can use this technique in many ways.

One way is to create special hot spots on a page. For example, you can display annotation text as a user moves over areas in a bitmap or over text on a page.

You can see a sample of these annotations in hints.html in the ch06 folder (see also Listing 6-5). In this example, I use a client-side image map to define hot spots on an image of a painting. Moving the mouse pointer over the hot spots displays text that describes the hot spot. For example, moving the pointer over the candy kisses brings up a message explaining that part of the painting (see Figure 6-4).

Figure 6-4:
Moving the mouse pointer over the painting brings up messages that explain parts of the picture.

Listing 6-5	The hints.html Source Code

```
<HTML>
<HEAD>
<TITLE>Mouse Over Hints</TITLE>
<SCRIPT>
function hintCandy() {
    tCandy.style.visibility = "visible";
}
function hideCandy() {
    tCandy.style.visibility = "hidden";
}
function hintArtist() {
    tArtist.style.visibility = "visible";
}
function hideArtist() {
    tArtist.style.visibility = "hidden";
}
```

(continued)

Listing 6-5 *(continued)*

```
</SCRIPT>
</HEAD>
<BODY>
<img src=pears.jpg USEMAP="#map1" ISMAP>
<MAP NAME="map1">
    <AREA SHAPE="POLYGON" COORDS="21,167, 35,143, 46,166, 22,167"
            onmouseover="hintCandy()" onmouseout="hideCandy()">
<AREA SHAPE="POLYGON" COORDS="67,168, 76,148, 96,170, 67,168"
            onmouseover="hintCandy()"

onmouseout="hideCandy()">
<AREA SHAPE="POLYGON" COORDS="72,10, 56,37, 67,39, 41,58, 27,52, 12,20, 14,7, 72,10"
            onmouseover="hintArtist()" onmouseout="hideArtist()">
</MAP>
<DIV id="tCandy" style="position:absolute; left:30; top:210; width: 20%; font-
            size:12pt; background-color:yellow; visibility:hidden">
Candy kisses decorate the foreground, perhaps suggesting Halloween.</DIV>
<DIV id="tArtist" style="position:absolute; left:100; top:20; width: 20%; font-
            size:12pt; background-color:yellow; visibility:hidden">
The artist is reflected in mirrors on mirrors.</DIV>
</BODY>
</HTML>
```

You see two interesting parts to this page. First, the explanatory text is positioned with a <DIV> tag; the text is initially invisible. The background is set to yellow to help the text stand out and appear more like a standard Windows ToolTip. The following is the HTML code for a sample section of text:

```
<DIV id="tCandy" style="position:absolute; left:30; top:210; width: 20%; font-
            size:12pt; background-color:yellow; visibility:hidden">
Candy kisses decorate the foreground, perhaps suggesting Halloween.</DIV>
```

Next, you see code to hide and show this div based on where the user moves the mouse pointer. The code is based on an image map, using the same approach that I demonstrate in Chapter 3. The following is the script that shows and hides one of the explanatory divs. It simply changes the visibility property for the object.

```
function hintCandy() {
    tCandy.style.visibility = "visible";
}
function hideCandy() {
    tCandy.style.visibility = "hidden";}
```

When you create text areas that you want to display based on user actions, make the areas visible so that you can see all the items on the screen. Position them at the location where you want them to appear. Then make them invisible and add the code to show them. Doing it this way is much easier than having the images initially invisible and having to guess at where to put them.

Navigator requires the `<AREA>` tag to have an HREF in order to process mouse events. That, of course, means that a jump takes place whenever the user clicks on the hot spot. To prevent all that jumping around, set the HREF to call the JavaScript function for showing the hint instead of setting it to a URL.

```
<AREA SHAPE="POLYGON" COORDS="21,167, 35,143, 46,166, 22,167"
            href="javascript:hintCandy()" onmouseover="hintCandy()"
            onmouseout="hideCandy()">
```

Navigator also uses a different method for showing and hiding divs. In particular, instead of setting `style.visibility`, you set the element `visibility` property to either `"show"` or `"hide"`, as shown in the following line of code:

```
document.tCandy.visibility = "show";
```

You can see the Navigator version by loading hints_nn.html.

You can also change visibility to create animation effects. For example, you can set up a series of text and images that display when you load a page and cycle through them by using `window.setInterval`. As an example, I show you how to create an introductory page for the *Surf Aliens* movie. (Load divshow.html from the ch06 folder or refer to Listing 6-5.) The introductory page contains text in the center with the movie name and a series of spans that surround the text with key points about the film. The page cycles through these messages one at a time. The result is an attention-grabbing animated effect that uses very little bandwidth.

First, you set up a series of spans to surround the movie title. You can see these spans at the end of Listing 6-6. Notice that they all have the same id — sp1. (You find out why in a moment.)

Now that you have several spans with important marketing facts about the movie, you can animate them. To do so, create a collection for all the elements named sp1. Use the same trick that I describe in Chapter 5 to get a collection of all the radio buttons in a particular group. The following is the script, taken from the `init` function:

```
msgSet = document.all.item("sp1");
numMsg = msgSet.length;
```

Next, you use `setInterval` repeatedly to call the function that cycles through the spans. In the following code, you cycle images every 1.5 seconds:

```
window.setInterval("showNext()", 1500);
```

The function `showNext` does all the interesting work in this page. It uses a counter to keep track of the current item to show and begins by making that element visible, as follows:

```
msgSet(curMsg).style.visibility = "visible";
```

Next, showNext hides the previously shown element. To do so, showNext first checks to determine whether element number 0 was just shown. If so, it hides the last element in the collection. Why? Because there is no element –1. Instead, after the last element is shown, element number 0 is shown again. That way, the page continually loops through all the elements. So if you have just shown element number 0, the previous element was the last in the list. The following is the code:

```
if (0 == curMsg)
    msgSet(numMsg-1).style.visibility = "hidden";
else
    msgSet(curMsg-1).style.visibility = "hidden";
```

Finally, you increment the counter. You use the mod function to keep the counter values valid — that is, between 0 and one less than the number of elements in the collection, as follows:

```
curMsg = (++curMsg % numMsg);
```

When you load the page, the various messages circle around the title in the middle, as you can see in Figure 6-5.

Figure 6-5:
Every 1.5 seconds, a different message appears around the movie title.

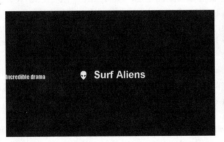

Navigator doesn't let you get a collection of similarly named elements, so instead you need to use the layers collection, which gives you a collection of all positioned <DIV>, <SPAN>, and <LAYER> tags. Because I don't want the span containing the words *Surf Aliens* to show and hide, the show and hide code loops through all but the last span in the collection:

```
function showNext() {
  //show the message
  document.layers[curMsg].visibility = "show";
  //hide the previous
  if (1 == curMsg)
      document.layers[numMsg].visibility = "hide";
  else
      document.layers[curMsg-1].visibility = "hide";
  //Increment the counter without exceeding the bounds
  curMsg = (curMsg % numMsg) + 1;
}
```

<BGSOUND> is an Internet Explorer-only tag, so I use the <EMBED> tag to play the MIDI file:

```
<EMBED SRC="../media/sj1.mid" HIDDEN=FALSE VOLUME=100 LOOP=TRUE AUTOSTART=TRUE
          NAME=music_embed MASTERSOUND>
```

Now, theoretically, setting AUTOSTART to true makes the MIDI file play automatically when the page loads, but that has never worked for me. (Although it does for other folks. . . .) If it doesn't play for you, change HIDDEN to true, and then double-clicking on the MIDI file starts it playing.

Because Navigator doesn't support the WebDings font, I also removed the WebDings character that draws the alien head.

You can view the entire Navigator version of this file by loading divshow_nn.html.

Listing 6-6	The divshow.html Source Code

```
<HTML>
<HEAD>
<TITLE>Animation Through DIVs</TITLE>
<SCRIPT>
var msgSet;
var curMsg = 1;
var numMsg;
function init() {
    //Get all of the message spans
    msgSet = document.all.item("sp1");
    numMsg = msgSet.length;
    window.setInterval("showNext()", 1500);
}
function showNext() {
//show the message
msgSet(curMsg).style.visibility = "visible";
//hide the previous
if (0 == curMsg)
msgSet(numMsg-1).style.visibility = "hidden";
else
msgSet(curMsg-1).style.visibility = "hidden";
//Increment the counter without exceeding the bounds
curMsg = (++curMsg % numMsg);
}
</SCRIPT>
</HEAD>
<BODY BGCOLOR=black onload="init()">
<BGSOUND SRC="../media/sj1.mid" LOOP=INFINITE>
<SPAN style="position:absolute; top:45%; font-family:WebDings; color:white; font-
          size:35pt; "><CENTER>...<FONT FACE=Arial><B>  Surf Aliens
          </B></CENTER></SPAN>
<SPAN id=sp1 style="position:absolute; top:20%; font-size:20pt; font-family:impact;
          color:yellow; visibility:visible">
<CENTER>Nonstop action</CENTER>
```

(continued)

Listing 6-6 (continued)

```
</SPAN>
<SPAN id=sp1 style="position:absolute; top:48%; left:0; font-size:20pt; font-
              family:impact; color:yellow; visibility:hidden">
Incredible drama
</SPAN>
<SPAN id=sp1 style="position:absolute; top:80%; font-size:20pt; font-family:impact;
              color:yellow; visibility:hidden">
<CENTER>Rocking sound track</CENTER>
</SPAN>
<SPAN id=sp1 style="position:absolute; top:48%; left:80%; font-size:20pt; font-
              family:impact; color:yellow; visibility:hidden">
Great effects
</SPAN>
</BODY></HTML>
```

Jamming with the Style Council

Earlier in this chapter, I show you how to dynamically change the style for individual elements. You can also change a style sheet to affect all the elements of a particular style on the page. Changing a style sheet is very powerful. You can use this technique to instantly make all headings turn blue, make all items of a particular style get a highlighted background, or do anything else you fancy.

To change a style sheet, you use the `styleSheets` collection. Each style sheet on the page appears in this collection. As with all the other collections, `document.styleSheets(0)` is the first style sheet on the page, `document.styleSheets(1)` is the second style sheet, and so on.

The `addRule` command adds a new style to the style sheet. You can also use this command to change an existing style. Its format is as follows:

```
document.styleSheets(n).addRule(style item, style definition)
```

For example, suppose that you want to add a new style, P.1, to the first style sheet on the page. You want this new style to be `{font-size:10pt; color: red}`. You would use the following script:

```
document.styleSheets(0).addRule("P.1", "{font-size:10pt; color: red}");
```

If P.1 already existed, the new style definition would replace the old one.

You can use this command to make a page in which the font changes based on window size. First, set up a style sheet that defines the base font. Do so by setting a style for . (a period), which stands for the default font, as follows:

```
<STYLE type="text/css">
<!--. {font-size:12}-->
</STYLE>
```

Next, create a function that changes the style sheet based on the window size. The function begins by choosing the new font size, as follows:

```
if (document.body.offsetWidth < 200)
    txtSize = "10pt";
else if (document.body.offsetWidth < 400)
    txtSize = "14pt";else
    txtSize = "18pt";
```

This code simply checks the width of the page to determine which font size to use. Next, the function changes the style definition for the base font, as follows:

```
document.styleSheets(0).addRule(".", "font-size:" + txtSize);
```

The only thing that's left is to call this function when the window size changes. You also call it when the page is first loaded, using the following script:

```
<BODY onresize="changeSize()" onload="changeSize()">
```

Load stylechange.html from the ch06 directory to try out this page (see Listing 6-7). Be sure to change the size of the browser and watch the text change size (see Figures 6-6a and b). (The size of the text depends on the size of the browser.)

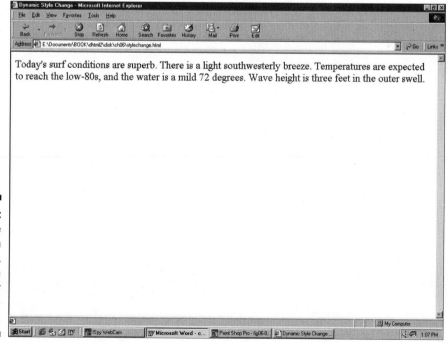

Figure 6-6a:
In this figure and in Figure 6-6b, you can see the browser in two different sizes.

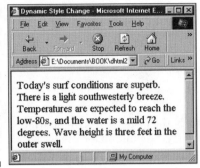

Figure 6-6b:
Note how
the font size
decreases
when the
browser
window
gets
smaller.

Navigator doesn't support dynamic addition to style sheets, and thus this sample doesn't work in Navigator.

Listing 6-7   The stylechange.html Source Code

```
<HTML>
<HEAD>
<TITLE>Dynamic Style Change</TITLE>
<STYLE type="text/css">
<!--. {font-size:12pt}-->
</STYLE>
<SCRIPT LANGUAGE="JScript">
function changeSize() {
    var txtSize;
    if (document.body.offsetWidth < 200)
        txtSize = "10pt";
    else if (document.body.offsetWidth < 400)
        txtSize = "14pt";
    else
        txtSize = "18pt";
    document.styleSheets(0).addRule(".", "font-size:" + txtSize);
}
</SCRIPT>
</HEAD>
<BODY onresize="changeSize()" onload="changeSize()">
Today's surf conditions are superb. There is a light southwesterly breeze.
        Temperatures are expected to reach the low 80s, and the water is a
        mild 72 degrees. Wave height is three feet in the outer swell.
</BODY>
</HTML>
```

The onresize event fires any time that the size of an element changes. By adding script that process the onresize for the <BODY> tag, you can adjust the page based on changes to the page size.

The Super Duper Page Reshaper

Although the page I describe in the preceding section is powerful, Internet Explorer 5.0 introduces a far simpler and way cooler way to make such changes. When you describe the CSS properties for an element, you can use expressions instead of exact values. For example, suppose that you want to resize the font based upon the screen size. You could use HTML such as the following:

```
<BODY style="font-size:expression(document.body.offsetWidth / 20)">
```

Whenever the page size changes, the font size automatically changes as well. Automatically changing font size is really great. It lets you create all types of dynamic effects. For example, you could have one object that's always justified to another object. Or you could easily right-justify elements on a page or position an object a few pixels above the bottom margin, no matter what the size of the browser.

For an example of this technique in action, check out stylechange2.html, shown in Listing 6-8.

Navigator doesn't support `expression`.

Listing 6-8	The stylechange2.html Source Code

```
<HTML>
<HEAD>
<TITLE>Dynamic Style Change</TITLE>
</HEAD>
<BODY style="font-size:expression(document.body.offsetWidth / 20)">
Today's surf conditions are superb. There is a light southwesterly breeze.
          Temperatures are expected to reach the low-80s, and the water is a
          mild 72 degrees. Wave height is three feet in the outer swell.
</BODY>
</HTML>
```

Finding Your Inner Text

I show you many techniques for changing the appearance of the page in the preceding sections of this chapter, but I saved the best for last. Not only can you change the color, size, and visibility of items, but you can also dynamically read and change the HTML code itself. In other words, you can dynamically add new text and even new HTML code to a page. This capability is one of the most powerful features of Dynamic HTML. Using it, you can do pretty much anything that you want to a page. You can add new images, add tables, change text, and read in ads from a database. The sky is the limit.

As always, to read or change the text for an element, you need a named element. Then you use one of three commands: `innerText`, `innerHTML`, or `outerHTML`. These commands set or retrieve HTML code and are typically used on divs, spans, and anchors.

For example, to get the text inside an element, you can use the following code:

```
txt = elName.innerText;
```

To change the text, use this code:

```
elName.innerText = txt;
```

The `innerText` command returns (or sets) the text that's associated with an element. This text doesn't contain any of the HTML tags; it just contains the text. For example, suppose that you have the following code:

```
<SPAN id=sp1 onclick="showIt()">Hello, here is <EM>some text</EM></SPAN>
```

The `innerText` command returns this: Hello, here is *some text*. Use `innerText` to find the text inside an item or to change the text to some HTML code without any formatting information.

By contrast, `innerHTML` returns the entire HTML stream. For the previous HTML code, it returns this: Hello, here is `<EM>some text</EM>`. Use `innerHTML` when you need to know all the HTML tags inside an element or when you want to change what is in an element to include formatting information or HTML tags, such those for images.

Like `innerHTML`, `outerHTML` returns the full set of HTML code for an element. But instead of just showing what is inside an element, it shows the HTML code for the element as well. To continue the example that I presented a moment ago, this command returns this: `<SPAN id=sp1 on click="showIt( )">Hello, here is <EM>some text </EM></SPAN>`. The `outerHTML` command is extremely powerful. You can use it not only to find out everything there is to know about an element but also to change the element itself. For example, you can use it to completely rewrite a page, including all formatting information. You can remove an `<IMG>` tag and replace it with a button. You can then replace the button with some text. Anything is possible.

Be very careful when using the `outerHTML` command. If you change the name of the element, the script that attempts to access that element no longer works.

Navigator doesn't support any of these methods. You can get a similar effect, however, by keeping the HTML text inside strings and dynamically inserting those strings into layers. You've seen that technique in action in several examples, such as surfcond_nn.html.

Reading the values

The easiest way to see how the innerText, innerHTML, and outerHTML commands work is to write a page that uses them. Take a look at inner.html in the ch06 folder (see Listing 6-9). This code contains a span with some text in it. When you click on the text, a message box appears showing the innerText, innerHTML, and outerHTML values for the span. See Figure 6-7.

Figure 6-7:
When you click on the text, a message box appears showing the innerText, innerHTML, and outerHTML values.

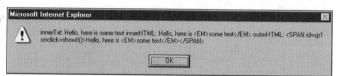

| **Listing 6-9** | **The inner.html Source Code** |

```
<HTML>
<HEAD>
<TITLE>Inner Text</TITLE>
<SCRIPT>
function showIt() {
    var txt;
    txt = "innerTxt: " + sp1.innerText + " ";
    txt += "innerHTML: " + sp1.innerHTML + " ";
    txt += "outerHTML: " + sp1.outerHTML + " ";
    alert(txt);
}
</SCRIPT>
</HEAD>
<BODY>
<SPAN id=sp1 onclick="showIt()">Hello, here is <EM>some text</EM></SPAN>
</BODY>
</HTML>
```

Writing the values

Of course, these commands are much more interesting when they are used to change the text inside a page. Take a look at surfcond5.html in the ch06 folder (see Listing 6-10). This page contains two anchors. When you click on the page, the text inside the anchors changes. For one anchor, innerText is used to change the text, as follows:

```
txtCond.innerText = "lousy";
```

For the other anchor, innerHTML is used to change and italicize the text, as follows:

```
txtWave.innerHTML = "<I>forty</I>";
```

You can see the results in Figures 6-8a and b.

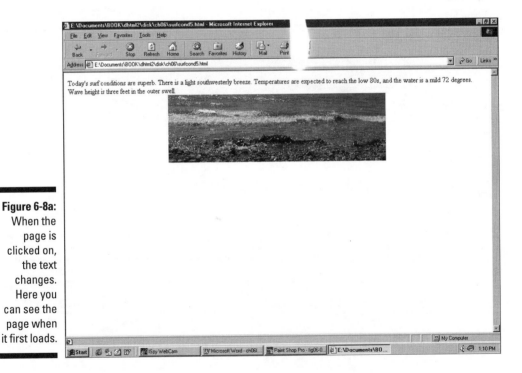

Figure 6-8a:
When the page is clicked on, the text changes. Here you can see the page when it first loads.

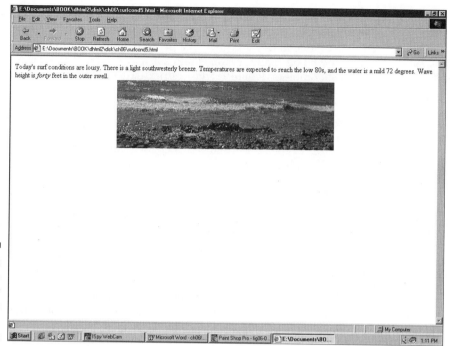

Figure 6-8b:
Here is the
page after
the text has
changed.

Listing 6-10   **The surfcond5.html Source Code**

```
<HTML>
<HEAD>
<SCRIPT LANGUAGE="JScript">
function changeText() {
    txtCond.innerText = "lousy";
    txtWave.innerHTML = "<I>forty</I>";
}
</SCRIPT>
</HEAD>
<BODY onclick="changeText()">
Today's surf conditions are <A id=txtCond>superb</A>. There is a light southwesterly
          breeze. Temperatures are expected to reach the low 80s, and the water
          is a mild 72 degrees. Wave height is <A id=txtWave>three</A> feet in
          the outer swell.
<CENTER><IMG src=surf.jpg></CENTER>
</BODY>
</HTML>
```

Creating a form letter

A popular game in the '70s gave one person a story with missing verbs, nouns, and so on. That person would ask another for these various words, and when complete, would read the story. The results were typically hilarious. You can use `innerText` to achieve the same result with a Web page.

To create such a page, you create text with a variety of anchors. These anchors contain placeholder text that indicates what type of word to type in. When the user types a word, it replaces the placeholder text. The following is some HTML code in this format:

```
Hello <A id=bWord>[name]</A>,<BR>
Do you like <A id=bWord>[adjective]</A> cats? I hope so because we are ready to
            deliver <A id=bWord>[number]</A> cats to your home in
<A id=bWord>[city]</A>.
```

Note that all the anchors have the same `id`. That way, you can easily create a collection of them.

You can also create a span, called *highlight,* to act as a cursor. The span points to the next word to enter and indicates what type of word should be entered.

When the page loads, a collection is created for all the words that need to be filled in. Then a special helper function, `initTxt`, is called. This function performs a number of duties. First, it updates the highlight span to prompt the user to enter the particular type of word. To do this, the function reads the placeholder text that's inside the current span. It then changes the `innerText` command for the highlight span to create the following message:

```
highlight.innerText = "^Type a " + curitem.innerText + " here";
```

Next, the `initTxt` function moves the highlight span below and to the right of the blank word. To do so, it checks `offsetLeft`, `offsetTop`, and `offsetHeight`. It can't check position using the style properties, because the initial position was never set. (Check out Chapter 4 for more information.) The following is the code:

```
highlight.style.pixelLeft = curitem.offsetLeft;
highlight.style.pixelTop = curitem.offsetTop + curitem.offsetHeight;
```

Next, `initTxt` clears the text where the word should be typed.

The second part of the program traps `onkeypress` events. The function that processes `onkeypress` inserts the keys that are typed directly into the current blank word that's inside the HTML page. If the key pressed was Enter, the word index is updated and `initTxt` is called again. In short, Enter moves the cursor to the next blank word in the page. After the last blank word is filled, the highlight span is hidden. The code is as follows:

```
function typing() {
    if (window.event.keyCode == 13) {
        curIdx++;
        if (curIdx < blankWords.length)
            initTxt();
        else
            highlight.style.visibility = "hidden";
    }
    curitem.innerText += String.fromCharCode(window.event.keyCode);
```

Eventually, the page is broken into a series of areas that the user gets to type in. The program iterates through these areas and lets the user directly type into the page. The innerText command is used both to get the type of word that should be typed in and to fill in the page as the user types.

To run the page, load insert.html from the ch06 folder (see Listing 6-11). As you can see in Figure 6-9, the user types to fill in the various blanks in the page. It sure is different than in the old days.

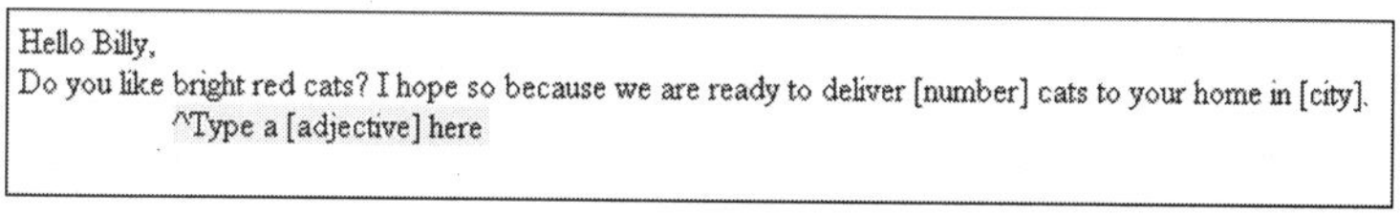

Figure 6-9:
When the user enters a new word, it is inserted into the page, and the highlight span jumps to the next blank word.

Hello Billy,
Do you like bright red cats? I hope so because we are ready to deliver [number] cats to your home in [city].
      ^Type a [adjective] here

Listing 6-11   **The insert.html Source Code**

```
<HTML>
<HEAD>
<SCRIPT>
//Start with the element inside the letter body
var curIdx = 0;
var curEl;
var blankWords;
var curitem;
function init() {
    blankWords = document.all.item("bWord");
    initTxt();
}
//Initialize the question
```

(continued)

Listing 6-11 *(continued)*

```
function initTxt() {
    curitem = blankWords(curIdx);
    highlight.innerText = "^Type a " + curitem.innerText + " here";
    highlight.style.pixelLeft = curitem.offsetLeft;
    highlight.style.pixelTop = curitem.offsetTop + curitem.offsetHeight;
    curitem.innerText = "";
}
function typing() {
    if (window.event.keyCode == 13) {
        curIdx++;
        if (curIdx < blankWords.length)
            initTxt();
        else
            highlight.style.visibility = "hidden";
    }
    curitem.innerText +=
            String.fromCharCode(window.event.keyCode);
}</SCRIPT>
</HEAD>
<BODY onload="init()" onkeypress="typing()">
Hello <A id=bWord>[name]</A>,<BR>
Do you like <A id=bWord>[adjective]</A> cats? I hope so because we are ready to
            deliver <A id=bWord>[number]</A> cats to your home in
<A id=bWord>[city]</A>.
<SPAN id=highlight style="background-color:yellow; position:absolute; left: 0; top:
            0; width:15%">
Type here
</SPAN>
</BODY>
</HTML>
```

Part II

All the World's a Stage

The 5th Wave   By Rich Tennant

"HONEY! OUR WEB BROWSER GOT OUT LAST NIGHT AND DUMPED THE TRASH ALL OVER MR. BELCHER'S HOME PAGE!"

In this part . . .

You can find a lot of cheesy Web pages out there with blinking lights that are screaming for attention. Sometimes you may think that you're shopping for a polyester suit in Las Vegas. That's because, prior to version 4.0 browsers, it was hard to create dynamic multimedia content for the Web without tying up phone lines for hours. In this part, you find out about many cool techniques for creating high-impact Web sites.

You start by reading about effects and transitions. These let you take HTML code and add photo-manipulation style filters, such as lights and drop shadows — all without using JPEGs and other bandwidth-consuming techniques. You also see how to add presentation-style transitions to pages.

Next, you see how to add sound to your page, including WAV and MIDI files. You then find out about movement and synchronization and see how to get all types of great animated effects without needing a Ph.D. Finally, you explore vector graphics.

Chapter 7

Filter Up, Please

• •

• •

*M*icrosoft Internet Explorer contains many features that help you create very cool Web sites without consuming huge amounts of bandwidth. In this chapter, you find out about one of my favorite features: filters. By adding a few extra parameters in the style property, you can have text invert when you mouse over it, sweep lights across the text in your document, or blend text on top of images and images on top of text.

Have you ever spent hours in Photoshop tweaking effects on text for a title on your page? Here, you see how to get similar effects on your Web page by operating directly on HTML text rather than by including images.

The visual effects all come about by filling in the `filter` parameter for the style property. Filters have four great attributes:

✔ They operate directly on HTML code, so you can get cool visual effects without having to download images. As a result, bandwidth usage is dramatically reduced.

✔ They are completely programmable, so you can apply them and modify them in response to events.

> ✔ Because they operate directly on HTML code, what they apply to can change dynamically. You can change text, change an element's size, or read in a value from a database. It doesn't matter — the effects still work.
>
> ✔ They are easy to use.

Visual effects modify the appearance of HTML that is on a page. For example, you can shine lights on text, create glowing letters, or add a drop shadow to help text stand out on top of an image. Or you can gray an image when it can't be selected.

Netscape Navigator does not support Cascading Style Sheets (CSS) transitions and effects, and thus none of the samples or materials in this chapter applies to Navigator. You can fake some of the effects by creating animated GIFs, but trust me, the end result isn't worth the effort.

Something in the Way She Moves "Effects" Me Like No Other

The basic idea behind effects is simple: Web authors often use bitmaps to get rich text effects. But unlike text, these bitmaps are costly to download and create. You need to use sophisticated image-editing tools to work with them. You can't easily translate them into other languages or change the text when the marketing department comes up with the new slogan *du jour*. However, you can author the text portion of a Web page with tools ranging from Notepad to Visual InterDev. You can easily translate text into any language or bring it down dynamically from a server. And text is very small to download.

Effects give you the best of both worlds. You can take some text and apply an effect to it, giving you many of the same capabilities that you would get from an image-editing package. And although the effects are mostly used to manipulate text, they can, in fact, apply to a broad range of HTML elements, including spans, divs, buttons, table cells, and images.

To add an effect to an HTML element, you need to do only two things:

1. **Figure out which element you want to apply an effect to.**

2. **Add the filter property to the `style` parameter, along with the name of the effect that you want to apply.**

For example, one of the effects is the alpha effect. This effect makes an element partially transparent, allowing you to get a glimpse of what is behind it — like looking through a colored fog. You can see this effect in Chapter 4 with the alien2.html page. There, the text with the scene names has an alpha effect applied to it. As a result, you can see part of the image showing through the text.

The alpha effect takes one parameter: opacity. An opacity of 0 means that the element becomes completely transparent — and thus invisible. An opacity of 50 means that the element is half transparent — you can see as much through it as you do of the element itself. And an opacity of 100 means that the element has no transparency — just as if you didn't apply the effect.

The following code shows you how to apply a 50 percent opacity to an element on the page:

```
<IMG src="mypic.jpg" style="left:20; filter:alpha(opacity = 50)">
```

As you can see, you simply add the filter to the `style` parameter.

Table 7-1 lists the various effects that you can apply. Throughout this chapter, you see how to use many, though not all, of the filters. Have some fun and experiment with different ways of using effects on your Web pages.

When applying effects to spans and divs, you usually need to set a width for the span or div. If the effect isn't working, make sure that you have set the width. For example, you can add `width:20%` to the `style` parameter.

Table 7-1	The Internet Explorer Effects
Effect	*Description*
Alpha	Controls the transparency level for an element. Part of what is behind the element shows through the element. Typically used for elements that overlap other elements.
Blur	Adds a motion blur to an element. Essentially, the element appears as if it is moving. Often used for heading 1 and other large text.
Chroma	Makes a particular color in an element transparent. This is most often used on images. For example, you can apply it to a PNG image to get an effect that's similar to a transparent GIF file. (By the way, PNG stands for Portable Network Graphics. It's a format for compressing images. Like the JPEG format, it is 24-bit and highly compressed. Like the GIF format, it is lossless, so you don't lose any details in images when they are compressed.)

(continued)

Table 7-1 *(continued)*

Effect	Description
DropShadow	Creates a shadow formed by offsetting the element. This is used to create the appearance of a shadow as well as to add a silhouette to text, thereby helping it to stand out when placed over other elements. It is similar to letter-boxing.
FlipH	Flips the element horizontally.
FlipV	Flips the element vertically.
Glow	Adds a fiery glow around the outside of the visible portions of the element. For example, you can use this filter to create glowing text.
Grayscale	Grays an element.
Invert	Inverts the colors in an element. For example, black becomes white. Often used to highlight an element when the mouse pointer passes over it.
Light	Shines a set of colored lights on the element. You get to pick the type, number, and color of lights. Used for creating wild color patterns as well as for highlighting portions of the element.
Mask	Makes the displayed portion of the element transparent and the transparent sections solid. Typically used to make transparent text. As a result, the letters appear filled with whatever is behind the text, such as a rich texture.
Shadow	Creates a shadow that falls away from an element, just like a real shadow does.
Wave	Creates a ripple like distortion of the element, as if waves were moving across it. If you say "doo doo doo" repeatedly and wave your hands as the filter applies, you can convince yourself that you are watching *Wayne's World*.
XRay	Grays the image and shows just the edges.

Who knows what evil lurks in the hearts of men?

Here's how to apply a filter to an element. Begin by applying a drop shadow to some text. As you can see in this section, drop shadows set off text from the background, making the text easier to read and giving it a bit of a 3-D look.

There must be something going on around here

When you see filters for the first time, you may think that some type of trickery is going on. After all, something must be going on to make boring old HTML text suddenly start glowing. Well, filters don't require sacrificial chickens or eyes of newt. Instead, they rely on an interesting low-level interface that Internet Explorer provides.

The browser figures out how the element should look. But before it gets around to displaying the element on the screen, it passes the image to the filters. The filters then manipulate that image directly. For example, the light filter goes through all the math to calculate what happens when lights are shined onto the image. After the filter finishes manipulating the image, it passes the image back to the browser. The browser then displays it.

The drop shadow effect takes three parameters: `offx`, `offy`, and `color`. The `offx` and `offy` parameters indicate how many pixels away from the original image the offset image appears. For example, if you set `offx` to 5 and `offy` to 3, the offset image — that is, the shadow — appears 5 pixels to the right and 3 pixels down from the original. Likewise, if you set `offx` to 5 and `offy` to –3, the offset image appears 5 pixels to the right and 3 pixels above the original.

Set the color to the one that you want for the shadow. You can set the value as one of the color constants, such as blue or gray, or as an RGB value in #RRGGBB format.

The following HTML code creates a cyan drop shadow that appears three pixels to the right and three pixels down from the original text (see Figure 7-1). Note that the filter applies to all of the HTML text inside the span, as follows:

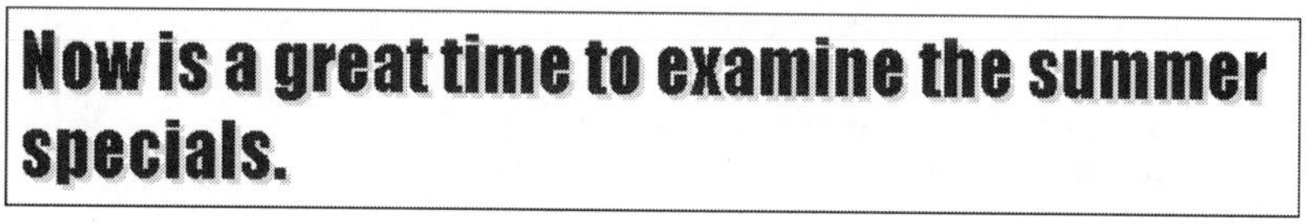

Figure 7-1:
A drop
shadow.

Now is a great time to examine the summer specials.

```
<SPAN style= "font-size: 40; font-family: impact; filter:dropshadow(offx=3, offy=3,
          color=cyan)">
Now is a great time to examine the summer specials.
</SPAN>
```

You can find the complete list in Listing 7-1 or load drop1.html from the ch07 folder on the enclosed CD-ROM.

Listing 7-1   **The drop1.html Source Code**

```
<HTML>
<HEAD>
<TITLE>Drop Shadow</TITLE>
</HEAD>
<BODY>
<SPAN style= "position:absolute; font-size: 40; font-family: impact; filter:drop-
           shadow(offx=3, offy=3, color=cyan)">
Now is a great time to examine the summer specials.
</SPAN>
</BODY>
</HTML>
```

You can find many great uses for drop shadows. You can use them simply to draw attention to some text, as I do in drop1.html. But you can also use them for letter-boxing and other effects. For example, suppose that you have some text that overlaps an image. Text is made from a single color, but images usually have many colors in them. If some of the colors in the image are similar to the color of the text, you may have trouble reading the text. Adding a small drop shadow makes a world of difference — all of a sudden, the letters stand out over the background. This technique, often called *letter-boxing,* is frequently used in subtitled movies. The following HTML code uses a drop shadow on text that labels an image:

```
<IMG src="scene2.jpg" style="position:absolute; left:50; top:80">
<SPAN style="position:absolute; left:110; top:170; font-family:impact,sans-serif;
           font-size:20pt; letter-spacing:.2em;
           color:yellow;filter:dropshadow(offx=2, offy=2)">Scene 2</SPAN>
```

You can also get great text effects with drop shadows. If you add a drop shadow that is 1 or 2 pixels to the right and down from text, the text looks like it is raised from the page. When you use this technique, choose a color that seems like a natural shadow for an object — like a black shadow on white text.

If you create text that is the same color as the background and then apply a drop shadow, the text looks *embossed* — like the letters are pushed up from behind the surface. For example, suppose that the background is white. Create some white text with a gray drop shadow. The text looks like it is embossed in the page. The following HTML code achieves this effect:

```
<SPAN style="position:absolute; left: 300; width: 40%; font-size:40; color:white;
           filter:dropshadow(offx=2, offy=1, color=gray)">
<B>Embossed</B>
</SPAN>
```

If you change directions for the drop shadow and instead have it appear to the left of and above the original text, the text appears as if it is carved into the screen.

To get a 3-D font, put two drop shadows on the text. (You find out how multiple effects work when you read "Don't you ever break the chain," later in this chapter.) Put a dark shadow down and to the right and a light shadow up and to the left. The following HTML code shows you how to do this trick:

```
<SPAN style="position:absolute; width: 100%; color:gray; filter:dropshadow(offx=2,
          offy=1, color=black) dropshadow(offx=-1, offy=-1, color=white)">
<B>3-D Letters</B>
</SPAN>
```

Figure 7-2 shows these various techniques in action. To the left, you can see an image with a letter-boxed title on top of it. Note how easy it is to read the text even though it is on top of an image. To the right, you see a column showing embossed, carved, raised, and 3-D text effects, all made using the drop shadow. Be sure to load drop2.html from the ch07 folder or check out Listing 7-2.

Figure 7-2:
You can see various uses of drop shadows, including the creation of letter boxes, embossed text, carved text, and 3-D text.

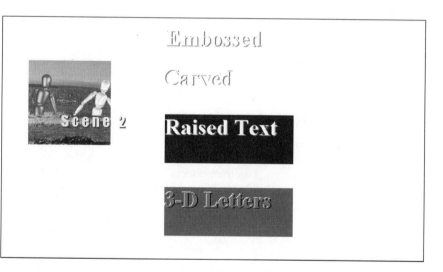

Listing 7-2   The drop2.html Source Code

```
<HTML>
<HEAD>
<TITLE>Drop Shadow</TITLE>
</HEAD>
<BODY>
<IMG src="../media/scene2.jpg" style="position:absolute; left:50; top:80">
<SPAN style="position:absolute; left:110; top:170; font-family:impact,sans-serif;
          font-size:20pt; letter-spacing:.2em; color:yellow;
          filter:dropshadow(offx=2, offy=2)">Scene 2</SPAN>
```

(continued)

Listing 7-2 *(continued)*

```
<SPAN style="position: absolute; left: 300; width: 40%; font-size:40; color:white;
        filter:dropshadow(offx=2, offy=1, color=gray)">
<B>Embossed</B>
</SPAN>
<SPAN style="position: absolute; left: 300; top: 20%; width: 40%; font-size:40;
        color:white; filter:dropshadow(offx=-2, offy=-1, color=gray)">
<B>Carved</B>
</SPAN>
<SPAN style="position:absolute; font-size: 40; background-color: black; left: 300;
        top: 40%; width:30%; height:20%">
<SPAN style="position:absolute; color:white; width: 100%; filter:dropshadow(offx=2,
        offy=1, color=gray)">
<B>Raised Text</B>
</SPAN>
</SPAN>
<SPAN style="position:absolute; font-size: 40; background-color: green; left: 300;
        width:30%; height:20%; top: 70%">
<SPAN style="position:absolute; width: 100%; color:gray; filter:dropshadow(offx=2,
        offy=1, color=black) dropshadow(offx=-1, offy=-1, color=white)">
<B>3-D Letters</B>
</SPAN>
</SPAN>
</BODY>
</HTML>
```

Don't you ever break the chain

You can apply as many effects as you like to a single element. Applying multiple effects is called *chaining,* because each effect is linked to the next, just like links in a chain. Chaining effects is simple. Instead of putting one effect in the style parameter, insert several effects. For example, the following code applies two drop shadows to make 3-D text:

```
<SPAN style="position:absolute; width: 100%; color:gray; filter:dropshadow(offx=2,
        offy=1, color=black) dropshadow(offx=-1, offy=-1, color=white)">
```

Note that you do not use the word *filter* twice. Instead, you start with *filter:* and then list all the filters.

As another example, check out alien2.html from the ch04 folder. There, an alpha effect and a drop shadow effect were applied to the text on top of the images. The alpha effect lets part of the image show through the text, leading to a smooth-looking label. The drop shadow effect letter-boxes the text. The following is the HTML code from that page:

```
<SPAN style="position:absolute; left:110; top:170; font-family:impact,sans-serif;
        font-size:20pt; letter-spacing:.2em; color:cyan; filter:alpha(opac-
        ity=70) dropshadow(offx=2, offy=2)">Scene 1</SPAN>
```

The more that you experiment with chaining filters, the more interesting combinations you find.

Looking through a glass onion

The mask effect makes visible parts of an element turn transparent, and the transparent parts become visible. As a result, you can look through one element to see what lies behind it. It's like looking through a stencil.

For example, suppose you have some text on top of a picture of some buildings. If you mask the text, it becomes transparent — you can see through the text to the picture of buildings. The result is that the letters look like they are made out of buildings. Likewise, you can put masked text on pictures of bricks to get letters made out of bricks. (Don't use straw for letters. The wolf could huff and puff and blow them down.)

This technique lets you get rich-looking letters without needing to download large images. You can take a tiny image of an object (such as a rock or water), tile it, and then use it to provide the texture for text.

When you use a mask effect to create textured text, use the smallest image that you can for the texture and then tile it. You can tile an image behind any HTML element by setting the background-image property for the `style` parameter. For example, the following code tiles the image brick.jpg across the back of a span:

```
<SPAN style="background-image:url(brick.jpg)">
```

Also, make sure that the element containing the text completely covers the image. For example, if the span containing the background image is 100 pixels by 200 pixels, make sure that the span containing the text you are masking is 100 pixels by 200 pixels. After the mask is applied, the parts of the span that didn't contain text turn to a single color, blocking out what is behind it. Thus, the span seems like a solid area with textured text.

To demonstrate this filter, begin by creating a span with a tiled image in the background, as follows:

```
<SPAN style="background-image:url(img1.jpg);width:60%;height:30%">
```

Next, you put some text inside of this span. Put the text in a span of its own, and make that span the same size as the one with the background image. That way, borders don't appear after the effect applies. You apply the mask effect to this span as follows:

```
<SPAN style="position:absolute; height:100%; width:100%; filter:mask(color=white);
             font-size:20pt; font-family:impact">
Don't look now, but there might be an alien on the board behind you. Run to the Surf
             Aliens Web site to find out.
</SPAN>
```

What happens? If there were no mask effect, the text inside the second span would appear on top of a repeating picture of waves. But because a mask effect is applied, the text becomes transparent and the repeating bitmap beneath it shows through. The result is a page where the words seem to be filled with waves, as shown in Figure 7-3. (To see the page, load surf1.html from the ch07 folder or look at Listing 7-3.)

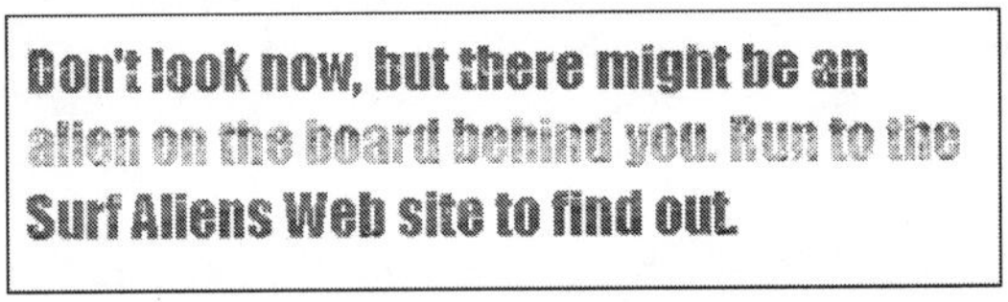

Figure 7-3:
The words appear to be filled with a bitmap texture.

Don't look now, but there might be an alien on the board behind you. Run to the Surf Aliens Web site to find out.

Listing 7-3	The surf1.html Source Code

```
<HTML>
<BODY>
<SPAN style="background-image:url(../media/img1.jpg);width:60%;height:40%">
<SPAN style="position:absolute; height:100%; width:100%; filter:mask(color=white);
            font-size:20pt; font-family:impact">
Don't look now, but there might be an alien on the board behind you. Run to the Surf
            Aliens Web site to find out.
</SPAN>
</SPAN>
</BODY>
</HTML>
```

You may wonder why the page uses two spans. After all, wouldn't it be simpler just to put the background image on the span that has the text inside it? Unfortunately, that approach doesn't work. When you put the background image on the span, every bit in the span has a color set. The mask filter would see that every bit in the span was set, and the filter would therefore turn every bit in the span transparent.

To make transparent text, put the text in its own span and position the span on top of the elements that you want to see through the text. Apply the mask effect to the span itself, not to the elements beneath it.

Adding a drop shadow to masked text makes the edges crisper, thereby making the text easier to read. Crisp edges are especially important when using photographs for the underlying texture, because photographs often have large expanses with gradual color changes. Such gradual color changes make it hard to see the text boundaries, especially if the colors are similar to the color of the background.

When you apply a drop shadow to masked text, set the `positive` parameter to 0. This parameter is specifically designed for use with masks. Normally, drop shadows offset the visible bits. When `positive` is set to 0, the drop shadow applies to the transparent bits. Because the text has a mask on it, the drop shadow applies to the text rather than to the element background.

The following HTML code shows you how to set the `positive` parameter:

```
<SPAN style="position:absolute; height:100%; width:100%; filter:mask(color=white)
        dropshadow(color=black, offx=1, offy=1, positive=0); font-size:20pt;
        font-family:impact">
```

You can see this code in action by loading the surf2.html page from the ch07 folder.

Masks aren't restricted to showing images beneath them. You can have a mask that shows text from another span, animated GIF files, or any other HTML element. One very effective technique is to put a mask on top of a simple animation; the letters come alive.

Get with the program

As with everything else in Dynamic HTML, you can control effects through script. Doing so is a two-part process. First, you need to get access to the effect. Then you need to change its properties.

Because filters are part of the `style` tag, they don't have `id`s. Thus, you need to access them through a collection, not by name. Believe it or not, the collection to use is the `filters` collection. This collection maintains a list of all the filters that are set up for a particular element. Remember that all collections are *zero indexed,* which means that the first filter that's applied to an object is filter number 0, the second is filter number 1, and so on.

After you use the `filters` collection to access a filter, you can write script to manipulate the filter properties. For example, suppose that you want to change the color of the drop shadow on an element named `foo`. You could use the following script:

```
foo.filters(0).color = "green";
```

This script says, "Given the element named `foo`, find the first filter in its collection. Then change the `color` property for that filter to green."

In addition to all the properties that are available for each effect, you can also change the `enabled` property, which controls whether the effect is active. For example, to turn off an effect, you can use the following script:

```
foo.filters(0).enabled = false;
```

Effects are active by default. You can, however, make effects initially inactive by setting this property to 0 in the `style` parameter, as follows:

```
style="filter:alpha(opacity=30, enabled=0)"
```

The most efficient way to turn a filter on or off is by changing the `enabled` property. You can change filters on elements in another way. If you haven't yet set a filter or if you want to eliminate a filter and replace it with a different filter, you can set the `filter` property for the `style` object. For example, the following code puts an alpha filter on an element named `foo`:

```
foo.style.filter = "alpha(opacity=30)";
```

Back in the highlight again

Dynamically applying filters is a great way to highlight items as you move the mouse pointer over them. For example, consider the menu system from Chapter 3 (menu.html). There, you change the color of text when the user moves the mouse pointer over it. Inverting the text is much more striking. Furthermore, changing text color only works on text. Effects apply to images as well, so you can use an effect to highlight an image in a button bar just as easily as highlighting text in a menu bar.

You can update the menu.html file from Chapter 3 so that it uses a series of bitmap buttons to change what is displayed. To start, eliminate the table that is used in Chapter 3 and replace it with a series of images by using the following HTML code:

```
<A HREF="choice1.html"><IMG src="../media/icon1.jpg" onmouseover="mHigh()"
        onmouseout="mBack()"></A>
```

As before, you process `onmouseover` and `onmouseout` messages. Only this time, you invert the image using a filter when the user moves the mouse pointer over the image. The following shows the code that makes this action happen. It dynamically adds a filter to the element over which the mouse pointer has moved:

```
event.srcElement.style.filter = "invert";
```

When the user moves away from the element, the filter is removed with the following line of script:

```
event.srcElement.style.filter = "";
```

You can find the complete source code in Listing 7-4, or load menu2.html from the ch07 folder. As you move the mouse pointer over the images, they invert (see Figure 7-4). Clicking on the images changes the page that's displayed inside the `IFRAME` on the page. Moving away stops the inversion.

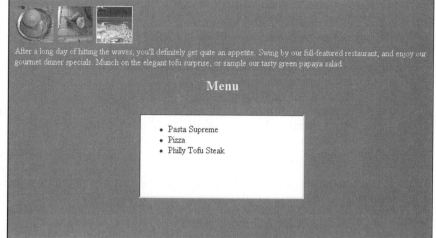

Figure 7-4:
Moving the
mouse
pointer over
the bitmaps
inverts
them.

Listing 7-4	The menu2.html Source Code

```
<HTML>
<HEAD>
<BASE TARGET = menuFrame>
<SCRIPT>
function mHigh() {
   event.srcElement.style.filter = "invert";
}
function mBack() {
   event.srcElement.style.filter = "";
}
</SCRIPT>
</HEAD>
<BODY ALINK=gray LINK=gray VLINK=gray BGCOLOR=gray>
<A HREF="choice1.html"><IMG src="../media/icon1.jpg" onmouseover="mHigh()" onmouse-
            out="mBack()"></A>
<A HREF="choice2.html"><IMG src="../media/icon2.jpg" onmouseover="mHigh()" onmouse-
            out="mBack()"></A>
<A HREF="choice3.html"><IMG src="../media/icon3.jpg" onmouseover="mHigh()" onmouse-
            out="mBack()"></A>
<BR>
<FONT COLOR=yellow>
After a long day of hitting the waves, you'll definitely get quite an appetite. Swing
            by our full-featured restaurant, and enjoy our gourmet dinner spe-
            cials. Munch on the elegant tofu surprise, or sample our tasty green
            papaya salad.
<BR>
<CENTER>
<H2>Menu</H2>
<BR>
<IFRAME name=menuFrame>
</IFRAME>
</BODY>
</HTML>
```

Love is love, not fade away

The alpha effect is extremely useful when you have overlapping elements on a page. The effect allows the obscured element to partially bleed through the top element, thereby adding more visual continuity. You see a sample of that effect in alien2.html.

The alpha effect takes a single parameter that indicates the level of opacity. To see it in action, you can modify the hints.html page from Chapter 6. This sample uses a client-side image map to display annotations about an image as the user moves the mouse pointer over the image. The annotations are the hints. You make the annotations semitransparent by using the alpha effect. That semitransparency shows some of the underlying painting through the hint.

To make the annotations semitransparent, simply apply the alpha effect to the hints, as you can see in the following HTML code:

```
<DIV id="tArtist" style="position:absolute; left:100; top:20; width: 20%; font-
        size:12pt; background-color:yellow; visibility:hidden;
        filter:alpha(opacity=70)">
The artist is reflected in mirrors on mirrors.</DIV>
```

Run the page by loading hints2.html from the ch07 folder. As you move the mouse pointer over the candy kisses or the artist, you see the hints appear, with the painting showing through beneath them (see Figure 7-5).

Figure 7-5:
The text that describes the artist is blended on top of the painting.

In many other situations, you can get great results by using the alpha effect. For example, you can create buttons that fade in as you move closer to them. (Or if a user just ordered a huge amount of goods from your Web site, you can fade out the Cancel button if the user moved the mouse pointer toward it.) Likewise, the alpha effect is very nice for blending several images into each other.

Take a walk on the wild side

If you like watching old spy movies, you've seen the *shadow effect.* The sinister agent stands beneath a street lamp. His shadow falls across the sidewalk at an angle, eventually fading into nothingness. In the corner, next to a brick building, someone lights a match. In the brief glow, you see . . . whoops, I lost myself for a moment. That's pretty much what the shadow effect does. You give it an angle measurement and a color, and it casts a shadow of the given color in that direction.

For an example of shadow in action, check out alien2.html from the ch04 folder. There, an eerie green shadow casts from the title text. The following is the key HTML code:

```
<SPAN style="position:absolute; left: 100; font-family:WebDings; color:white; font-
         size:35pt; filter:shadow(color=#00C000, direction=135)">...<FONT
         FACE=Arial><B>  Surf Aliens </B></SPAN>
```

Another cool effect is the *glow effect.* It causes static like streams of light to grow outward from an object and is very effective when applied to text.

Glow takes two parameters: the color of the glowing light and the strength of the glow. The larger the strength value, the wider the glow reaches. The glow effect is a great one to animate. Changing the strength over time makes fonts come alive. You can see a snapshot of this effect in Figure 7-6. The following is the HTML code that adds the glow effect:

```
<DIV id=d1 style="position:relative; width=40%; color:cyan; filter:glow(color=cyan)">
```

Figure 7-6: The two pieces of large text continually glow as you watch the page. Note that the outline of the black font is glowing.

To see the glow in action, load glow.html from the ch07 folder. You can find the complete source code in Listing 7-5.

Listing 7-5	The glow.html Source Code

```
<HTML>
<HEAD>
<STYLE TYPE="text/css">
<!--H1 { font-size: 70pt; font-family: Arial, sans-serif; font-weight: bold; }-->
</STYLE>
<SCRIPT>
var glowAmt = 0;
var direction = 1;
var maxGlow = 15;
function doGlow() {
    d1.filters(0).strength = glowAmt;
    glowAmt += direction;
    if ((glowAmt >= maxGlow) || (glowAmt == 0))
        direction *= -1;
}
function init() {
    window.setInterval("doGlow()", 200);
}
</SCRIPT>
</HEAD>
<BODY onload="init()" BGCOLOR=black TEXT=white>
<CENTER>
<DIV id=d1 style="position:relative; width=40%; color:cyan; filter:glow(color=cyan)">
<H1> Solid </H1>
<FONT COLOR=black>
<H1> Hollow </H1>
</FONT>
</DIV>
<BR>
<FONT SIZE=6>
Don't get caught surfing naked. Get fully equipped at the Surf Salon with all of the
            clothes and wet suits that you need.
</BODY>
</HTML>
```

The glow animation is accomplished by changing the strength value over time. First, setInterval is used repeatedly to call a function, as follows:

```
window.setInterval("doGlow()", 200);
```

The doGlow function alters the glow strength over time. It increases the strength to a certain number and then decreases it. When the strength reaches 0, it starts increasing again. Thus, the glow is always going from 0 to some value, back to 0, back to the value, and so on. This constant rotation gives a smooth animation of the glow. The code is as follows:

```
d1.filters(0).strength = glowAmt;
glowAmt += direction;
if ((glowAmt >= maxGlow) || (glowAmt == 0))
    direction *= -1;
```

For a fun look, create text using the same color as the background color. Apply a glow filter to the text. The text becomes invisible, but its edges glow. You can see this effect in Figure 7-6.

The glow effect spreads light up, down, left, and right. When using glow on text, try to add a nonbreaking space ( ) to the left and to the right of the element. This space provides some extra glowing room so that when the effect spreads to the left or the right, it isn't cut off by the element's border.

Chapter 8

Web Pages, Hollywood Style

In This Chapter

▶ Transitioning elements

▶ Combining transitions

▶ Using the alpha blend transition

▶ Creating page-to-page transitions

*T*ransitions let you provide a visually appealing change from one element to another. If you've ever watched television or seen a James Bond movie, you've certainly seen transitions. Think about the introduction to a show. The camera wildly chases along the Miami skyline. Then, from nowhere, letters fade in on top of the image, spelling out the names of the stars. Or maybe vertical stripes start to move through one actor's name, and as the stripes move, the name of another actor comes into place. Both of these are examples of transitions. Likewise, if you've used a presentation package such as Microsoft PowerPoint or a multimedia authoring tool such as Macromedia Director, you may have seen transitions used to "sparkle" from one slide or scene to another. Transitions give a sense of sophistication and visual appeal to a site. In this chapter, you add them to your Web pages.

Netscape Navigator does not support Cascading Style Sheets (CSS) transitions and effects, and thus none of the samples or material in this chapter applies to Navigator.

Da da da da da da . . . Wipe Out!

Like effects, transitions modify the visual appearance of elements on a page. But unlike effects, transitions aren't designed for making permanent changes to an element's appearance. Instead, they let you make a smooth change between how an element appears at one time and how it appears after you change it. For example, suppose that you have an image on the screen showing a picture of your child at his first birthday. You want to change the image to show a picture of your kid at his fifth birthday. You could apply a transition so that the first picture smoothly dissolves into the second.

Adding a transition to a page is easy. Simply follow these steps:

1. **Choose the HTML element to which you want to add a transition.**

2. **Add a transition property to the** `style` **parameter for that HTML element.**

   I explain how to complete this step shortly.

3. **Set up the element the way you want it to appear initially.**

   For example, you may want it to be invisible, or you may have some introductory text or a first picture that you want to show.

4. **Call the** `Apply` **method on the transition.**

   This step tells the element that it is about to transition. Microsoft Internet Explorer freezes the way the element appears on the screen.

5. **Change the element to make it look like you want it to after the transition is complete.**

   For example, you can change an image from the first birthday to the fifth birthday.

6. **Call the** `Play` **method on the transition.**

   This step tells Internet Explorer to transition from the way that the element looks when you call `Apply` to the new appearance. For example, this method may cause a four-second-long transition in which the new picture wipes over the old picture from left to right.

Now add a transition to a page. First create a page with some text in it, as follows:

```
<CENTER><H1>Surf Pals</H1>
<FONT SIZE=5>
Are you ready<BR>
to enter the<BR>
<FONT SIZE=7 COLOR=red><I>
Surf Zone</I><BR>
<FONT SIZE=5 COLOR=yellow>
?
<BR>
<FONT SIZE=5>
The only site where gaming surfers congregate.
</CENTER>
```

This script brings up a page with some simple text in it that advertises a Web site.

Now, you add a transition to it. Decide what you want to transition. Keep the first and last lines — *Surf Pals* and *The only site where gaming surfers congregate.* in this example — always visible. Then make the rest of the text transition in.

To transition in the text, you need to create an element that represents just the text that you want to transition. The easiest way to do so is to create a named div or a span. The following HTML code wraps the inner text — the part that you want to transition — into a div:

```
<DIV id=myDiv style="position:relative;width:50% ">
<FONT SIZE=5>
Are you ready<BR>
to enter the<BR>
<FONT SIZE=7 COLOR=red><I>
Surf Zone</I><BR>
<FONT SIZE=5 COLOR=yellow>
?
</DIV>
```

Because the text is now wrapped into a div, you can hide it, change it, and otherwise manipulate it. You can also add a transition to it. To do so, add the following to the `style` parameter:

```
filter:revealTrans(duration=3, transition=2)
```

This script tells the browser that a filter is going to be applied to the HTML element. The filter's name is `revealTrans`, which happens to be the name of the transition filter. You pass two values to it: duration and transition. *Duration* indicates how long the transition should last, in seconds. *Transition* indicates what type of a transition is to occur, as shown in Table 8-1. Thus, the HTML code that you add makes a three-second transition that circles in.

Is that all? Of course not; you just covered Steps 1 and 2. Next, you need to set up the element the way that you want it to appear initially. Have the page start out so that the div is not visible and then have the text transition in. You can make the div initially invisible by using the following code:

```
<DIV id=myDiv style="position:relative; width:50%;
visibility:hidden;
filter:revealTrans(duration=3,
transition=2)">
```

Next, you add the script to apply and play the transition. You do so when the page first loads with the following HTML:

```
<BODY BGCOLOR=black TEXT=yellow onload="init()">
```

Table 8-1	Transition Values
Transition	*Value*
Box in	0
Box out	1
Circle in	2
Circle out	3
Wipe up	4
Wipe down	5
Wipe right	6
Wipe left	7
Vertical blinds	8
Horizontal blinds	9
Checkerboard across	10
Checkerboard down	11
Random dissolve	12
Split vertical in	13
Split vertical out	14
Split horizontal in	15
Split horizontal out	16
Strips left down	17
Strips left up	18
Strips right down	19
Strips right up	20
Random bars horizontal	21
Random bars vertical	22
Random	23

Now you can take care of Steps 4, 5, and 6 inside the function init() as
follows:

```
function init() {
    myDiv.filters(0).Apply();
    myDiv.style.visibility = "visible";
    myDiv.filters(0).Play();
}
```

What happens here? First, you apply the transition. To do so, you need to
find the transition itself. Just like you did with the effects, you access the
transition by using the filters collection. The first filter for the element is
filters(0). In this case, you have only one filter on the element, so you can
just interact with filters(0).

If you have only one transition on an element, you can refer to the transition
by its type. For example, if you have a revealTrans on the element named
myDiv, you can apply the transition with myDiv.filters.revealTrans.
Apply(). Or you can refer to the transition as myDiv.filters(0).Apply().

After you apply the transition, you can change the element to how you want
it to appear after the transition is complete. In this case, myDiv was invisible
when the page loaded, but you can make it visible. Thus, when the transition
plays, the text in the div appears out of nothingness.

Having done that, you call the Play method, which makes the transition go.

To check out the sample in action, load trans1.html from the ch08 directory
(see Listing 8-1). Look at Figure 8-1, and you can see the new text from the div
appear as the text transitions in.

Figure 8-1:
The text in
the div
transitions,
using the
circle in
transition
style.

| Listing 8-1 | The trans1.html Source Code |

```
<HTML>
<HEAD>
<SCRIPT>
function init() {
    myDiv.filters(0).Apply();
    myDiv.style.visibility = "visible";
    myDiv.filters(0).Play();
}
</SCRIPT>
</HEAD>
<BODY BGCOLOR=black TEXT=yellow onload="init()">
<CENTER><H1>Surf Pals</H1>
<DIV id=myDiv style="position:relative; width:50%;
visibility:hidden; filter:revealTrans(duration=3,
transition=2)">
<FONT SIZE=5>
Are you ready<BR>
to enter the<BR>
<FONT SIZE=7 COLOR=red><I>
Surf Zone</I><BR>
<FONT SIZE=5 COLOR=yellow>
?
</DIV>
<BR>
<FONT SIZE=5>
The only site where gaming surfers congregate.
</CENTER>
</BODY>
</HTML>
```

To apply a transition to text, as I do in trans1.html, the text must be in a span or a div where the width is set. Why? It's just one of those rules.

Back-to-back adventures

When the transition finishes, the `onfilterchange` event fires. You can process this event to kick off another transition. For example, suppose that you want to have nonstop transitions for the page from trans1.html. As soon as the new text transitions in, you want it to transition out, and so on.

Setting up your page with nonstop transitions is easy. You simply handle the `onfilterchange` event. When it fires, kick off the next transition. You can see this strategy in action in the trans2.html file located in the ch08 folder (see Listing 8-2).

The following code from trans2.html handles the `onfilterchange` event:

```
<SCRIPT FOR="myDiv" EVENT="onfilterchange">
    init();
</SCRIPT>
```

Listing 8-2	The trans2.html Source Code

```
<HTML>
<HEAD>
<SCRIPT>
function init() {
    myDiv.filters(0).Apply();
    if (myDiv.style.visibility == "hidden") {
        myDiv.style.visibility = "visible";
    }
    else {
        myDiv.style.visibility = "hidden";
    }
    myDiv.filters(0).Play();
}
</SCRIPT>
<SCRIPT FOR="myDiv" EVENT="onfilterchange">
    init();
</SCRIPT>
</HEAD>
<BODY BGCOLOR=black TEXT=yellow onload="init()">
<CENTER><H1>Surf Pals</H1>
<DIV id=myDiv style="position:relative; width:50%;
filter:revealTrans(duration=3, transition=2);
visibility:hidden">
<FONT SIZE=5>
Are you ready<BR>
to enter the<BR>
<FONT SIZE=7 COLOR=red><I>
Surf Zone</I><BR>
<FONT SIZE=5 COLOR=yellow>
?
</DIV>
<BR>
<FONT SIZE=5>
The only site where gaming surfers congregate.
</CENTER>
</BODY>
</HTML>
```

As you can see, this code calls the `init` function. In trans1.html, `init` simply kicked off the transition. In trans2.html, it does the same thing, only it flips the visibility flag of `myDiv` each time that it is called. Thus, the first time it is called, it transitions from blank to displayed. The next time it is called, it transitions from displayed to blank. This cycle continues indefinitely or until you shut down Internet Explorer. The following is the code:

```
function init() {
    myDiv.filters(0).Apply();
    if (myDiv.style.visibility == "hidden") {
        myDiv.style.visibility = "visible";
    }
    else {
        myDiv.style.visibility = "hidden";
    }
    myDiv.filters(0).Play();
}
```

Never try to play a transition again before it has completed. You get all types of nasty error messages. Instead, make sure that the first transition has finished before playing it again. You can do this in two ways. First, you can wait for the `onfilterchange` message and kick off subsequent transitions from that handler, as shown in trans2.html. If you don't want to kick the transition off immediately, you can set a variable to true when you handle `onfiltechange` and only run the transition again if that variable is true. (Of course, you need to change the variable to false as soon as you start the next transition on the element.) This approach is called *establishing a semaphore*.

The other approach is to check the value of the transition's status. If the status is 0, the transition is not currently playing. For example, the following script prevents any problems from occurring when you try to replay a transition before it has finished:

```
if (0 == myDiv.filters(0).status) {
    myDiv.Apply();
    //Change display here
    myDiv.Play();
}
```

Low-sparkled high-heel boys

Transitions are also great for creating slide shows. In Chapter 3, you create a page called food2.html. Every time the user clicks, a new bullet point appears on the screen. You can enhance the page so that each bullet point transitions in. You use the random dissolve transition, which makes the old item sparkle into the new one.

To set up the page this way, add a transition to each bullet point. For example, the following HTML code adds a random dissolve transition to the first bullet point:

```
<SPAN id=bullet style="width:20%; visibility:hidden;
filter:revealTrans(duration=3,transition=12)">Elegant meals
</SPAN>
```

Each time the user clicks, you find the next element to show. You start the transition, show the element, and then play the transition. The following code, taken from the `nextBullet function`, shows how you do this:

```
curEl.filters(0).Apply();
curEl.style.visibility = "visible";
curEl.filters(0).Play();
```

The page also contains code for figuring out which bullet is next. It uses the good old "find a collection for everything with a common name" trick that you use in many sample programs throughout this book. If you find the code confusing, the key to remember is that it creates a collection of all the bullets. Each time the user clicks, the code looks for the next bullet in the collection and displays it.

Check out the page by loading food5.html from the ch08 folder (see Listing 8-3). Be sure to click several times on the page background so that you can see the bullet points sparkle in (see Figure 8-2).

Listing 8-3	The food5.html Source Code

```
<HTML>
<HEAD>
<SCRIPT>
var curBullet = 0;
var curEl;
var collBullets;
var numBullets;
function nextBullet() {
    //Make the next bullet visible
    if (curBullet < numBullets) {
        curEl = collBullets(curBullet);
        curEl.filters(0).Apply();
        curEl.style.visibility = "visible";
        curEl.filters(0).Play();
        curBullet++;
    }
}
function init() {
    //Get the collection of bullets
    collBullets = document.all.item("bullet");
    numBullets = collBullets.length;
}
</SCRIPT>
</HEAD>
<BODY BGCOLOR=black TEXT=white onclick="nextBullet()"
onload="init()">
Click anywhere to show bullets.<BR>
<FONT SIZE=5><SPAN id=bullet style="width:20%;
visibility:hidden;filter:revealTrans(duration=3,
transition=12)">Elegant meals</SPAN><BR>
<SPAN id=bullet
style="width:20%; visibility:hidden;
filter:revealTrans(duration=3, transition=12)">
Fast service</SPAN><BR><SPAN id=bullet style="width:20%;
visibility:hidden; filter:revealTrans(duration=3,
transition=12)">
Good vibes</SPAN>
</BODY>
</HTML>
```

Elegant meals
Fast service

Figure 8-2:
As you click,
new bullet
points
sparkle onto
the screen.

Sweet transitions from Transylvania

Just as you can change effect properties through script, you can also change transition values through script. In fact, the process is pretty much the same. You just use the `filters` collection to get access to the transition. From there, you can change the duration or the transition type.

For example, you can set the first transition on the `myDiv` element to be a wipe right with the following code:

```
myDiv.filters(0).transition = 6;
```

You can use this code to create a page that cycles through all the available transitions. Watching the page is a great way to figure out what each transition looks like.

First, you create a div that contains two images. You can put a transition on the div by using the following code:

```
<DIV id=myDiv style="position:relative; width:165;
height:130; filter:revealTrans(duration=2.5)"
onfilterchange="doTrans()">
<img id=img1 src="img1.jpg"
style="position:absolute;left:0;top:0;visibility:hidden">
<img id=img2 src="img2.jpg"
style="position:absolute;left:0;top:0;visibility:hidden">
</DIV>
```

You can play a transition when the page loads; you then wait for the onfilterchange event. When this event fires, you play the next transition. Each time you play a transition, you change the transition type by cycling through the numbers 0 through 23. You can also switch from whether img1 or img2 is visible. Thus, the transitions also move back and forth between these two images. The following script changes the transition type, setting the new type to the value from a counter named curTrans:

```
myDiv.filters(0).transition = curTrans;
```

As you can see from the code in Listing 8-4, controlling transitions is pretty easy. Be sure to run transall.html from the ch08 folder to see the page in action. It loops through all the available transitions. You can see one of these instances in Figure 8-3.

Figure 8-3:
The image
of the
sunset
appears
using the
strips left
down
transition.

Listing 8-4   The transall.html Source Code

```
<HTML>
<HEAD>
<SCRIPT>
var maxTrans = 23;
var curTrans = 0;
function doTrans() {
    //Change the transition
    myDiv.filters(0).transition = curTrans;
    txt1.innerHTML = curTrans.toString();
    myDiv.filters(0).Apply();
    if (curTrans % 2) {
        img1.style.visibility = "hidden";
        img2.style.visibility = "visible";
    }
    else {
        img2.style.visibility = "hidden";
        img1.style.visibility = "visible";
    }
    if (++curTrans > maxTrans)
        curTrans = 0;
    myDiv.filters(0).Play();
}
```

(continued)

Listing 8-4 *(continued)*

```
</SCRIPT>
</HEAD>
<BODY BGCOLOR=black TEXT=yellow onload="doTrans()">
<CENTER><H1>Transition Demo</H1>
<DIV id=myDiv style="position:relative; width:165;
height:130; filter:revealTrans(duration=2.5)"
onfilterchange="doTrans()">
<img id=img1 src="../media/img1.jpg"
style="position:absolute;left:0;
top:0;visibility:hidden">
<img id=img2 src="../media/img2.jpg"
style="position:absolute;left:0;
top:0;visibility:hidden">
</DIV>
<BR>
This is transition number <A id=txt1>17</A>.
</CENTER>
</BODY>
</HTML>
```

Working on the chain gang

You can chain transitions if you like. For example, you can combine a checkerboard and a circle out to get a checkerboard that circles out.

Chaining transitions involves three parts. First, you need to set up several transitions on the element itself. That part is easy. You just list as many transitions as you want inside the `style` parameter. For example, to have a checkerboard that circles out, use the following HTML code:

```
<DIV id=myDiv style="position:relative; width:165;
height:130; filter:revealTrans(duration=2.5,
transition=3)
revealTrans(duration=2.5, transition=10)">
```

Next, however, comes the tricky part. If you want both transitions to play at the same time, you must apply and play both of them individually. For example, the following script plays the checkerboard and the circle out transitions at the same time:

```
myDiv.filters(0).Play();
myDiv.filters(1).Play();
```

Finally, you get to the trickiest part. You get a script error if you try to apply a transition while it is in the middle of playing. If you play two transitions at once, make sure that both have finished before you try playing them again.

Take care of this potential problem with the `onfilterchange` handler. Instead of waiting for one transition to end before playing the next, wait for both transitions to complete. When both have completed, start the next transitions. But because of the mysterious ways in which Internet Explorer works, you can't start the next transitions immediately. You need to give Internet Explorer a momentary rest. Thus, you call the next transitions by using a `setTimeout`. The `setTimeout` gives Internet Explorer a chance to process the messages it needs to and prepare for the next chained transitions. (Leaving out the `setTimeout` won't cause errors, but sometimes only one of the chained transitions displays.) For example, the following code waits for two transitions to complete:

```
if (++cnt == 2) {
    cnt = 0;
    Window.setTimeout("doTrans()", 1)
}
```

Load chain.html from the ch08 folder, or look at Listing 8-5, to see the complete HTML code for a page with chained transitions. You can see the circling out checkerboard in Figure 8-4.

Figure 8-4:
The combination of a checkerboard and a circle out transition.

Listing 8-5	The chain.html Source Code

```
<HTML>
<HEAD>
<SCRIPT>
var curTrans = 0;
var cnt = 0;
function doTrans() {
    //Change the transition
    myDiv.filters(0).Apply();
    myDiv.filters(1).Apply();
    if (curTrans) {
        img1.style.visibility = "hidden";
        img2.style.visibility = "visible";
    }
    else {
        img2.style.visibility = "hidden";
        img1.style.visibility = "visible";
    }
    curTrans = !curTrans;
    myDiv.filters(0).Play();
    myDiv.filters(1).Play();
}
function changed() {
    if (++cnt == 2) {
```

(continued)

Listing 8-5 *(continued)*

```
            cnt = 0;
            window.setTimeout("doTrans()", 1)
    }
}
</SCRIPT>
</HEAD>
<BODY BGCOLOR=black TEXT=yellow onload="doTrans()">
<CENTER><H1>Chained Transition Demo</H1>
<DIV id=myDiv style="position:relative; width:165;
height:130; filter:revealTrans(duration=2.5,
transition=3)
revealTrans(duration=2.5, transition=10)"
onfilterchange="changed()">
<img id=img1 src="../media/img1.jpg"
style="position:absolute;left:0;
top:0;visibility:hidden">
<img id=img2 src="../media/img2.jpg"
style="position:absolute;left:0;
top:0;visibility:hidden">
</DIV>
</CENTER>
</BODY>
</HTML>
```

Blending into the background

In the earlier sections of this chapter, I show you the revealTrans transition. It provides many different styles of transitions ranging from wipes to circle ins. You can use one other type of transition — the *alpha blending* transition. This transition gradually fades one element in on top of another. It is just like the alpha effect, only it operates as a transition.

The alpha transition is a great way to bring an image into a page or to fade in a series of buttons.

The alpha transition is called blendTrans. Its only parameter is the duration. The following is an example of applying blendTrans to a div:

```
<DIV id=myDiv style="position:relative; width:165;
height:130; filter:blendTrans(duration=2.5)"
onfilterchange="doTrans()">
```

As you can see, applying the alpha transition is no different than applying any other transition. To see the alpha transition in action, load trans4.html from the ch08 folder (see Listing 8-6). It smoothly fades one image into another, as you can see in Figure 8-5.

Figure 8-5:
The sunset fades into the ocean, courtesy of the alpha transition.

Listing 8-6	The trans4.html Source Code

```
<HTML>
<!--From Dynamic HTML For Dummies by Michael I. Hyman-->
<HEAD>
<SCRIPT
var curTrans = 0;
function doTrans() {
    myDiv.filters(0).Apply();
    if (curTrans % 2) {
        img1.style.visibility = "hidden";
        img2.style.visibility = "visible";
    }
    else {
        img2.style.visibility = "hidden";
        img1.style.visibility = "visible";
    }
    curTrans++;
    myDiv.filters(0).Play();
}
</SCRIPT>
</HEAD>
<BODY BGCOLOR=black TEXT=yellow onload="doTrans()">
<CENTER><H1>Transition Demo</H1>
<DIV id=myDiv style="position:relative; width:165;
height:130; filter:blendTrans(duration=2.5)"
onfilterchange="setTimeout('doTrans()',1)">
<img id=img1 src="../media/surf1.jpg"
style="position:absolute;left:0;top:0;visibility:hidden">
<img id=img2 src="../media/sun.jpg"
style="position:absolute;left:0;top:0;visibility:visible">
</DIV>
<BR>
This is transition number <A id=txt1>0</A>.
</CENTER>
</BODY>
</HTML>
```

You can also chain the alpha transition with the reveal transition. You can easily modify the chain.html file to do so by using the following HTML code to define transitions for the div:

```
<DIV id=myDiv style="position:relative; width:165;
height:130; filter:revealTrans(duration=2.5,
transition=3)
blendTrans(duration=2.5)" onfilterchange="change()">
```

Instead of creating a checkerboard that circles out, this code creates an alpha blend that circles out, as you can see in Figure 8-6. To see this combination in action, check out chain2.html in the ch08 folder.

Figure 8-6: The area within the circle alpha blends in over time, leading to a nice chained transition.

Cheap tricks of the trade

Now you know just about everything about transitions. Here are a few more tricks that you should also know:

✔ **If you can't get the transition to apply to a span or a div, make sure that you have set a width.**

✔ **To transition from one image to another, you can try one of two approaches: (a) change the `src` property for the image so that a different image is loaded, or (b) use two `<IMG>` tags and switch which is visible.**

The latter approach forces the images to be loaded when the page is loaded and thus provides better perceived performance.

✔ **Don't have wasted space in the element that you are transitioning.**

This rule is particularly relevant for divs and spans, where you may have a few words and a ton of blank space. The transition takes more machine cycles than it needs to. It also doesn't look very good, because most of the time is spent going from nothing to nothing. If you explicitly set the width and height of a span or div to which you are applying a transition, make it use as little area as necessary. This rule also applies to effects.

✔ **To transition from text to text, instead of having several divs or spans that you hide and show, consider using** innerText **or** innerHTML **to change the contents of the element between the** Apply **and the** Play **calls.**

✔ **If you are applying the same transition or effect to several objects, use a style sheet.**

A style sheet makes your pages smaller and easier to read. (See Chapters 2 and 6 for more information on style sheets.) For example, check out Listing 8-7. It defines a style for spans called trans. This style sets up the width, visibility, and the transition. The bullet points are defined using this style, with HTML code such as the following:

```
<SPAN id=bullet>Elegant meals</SPAN>
```

As a result, the source HTML is smaller, easier to understand, and faster to download.

Listing 8-7	The food6.html Source Code

```
<HTML>
<HEAD>
<STYLE TYPE="text/css">
<--#bullet {width:20%; filter:revealTrans(duration=3,
transition=12); visibility:hidden}-->
</STYLE>
<SCRIPT LANGUAGE="JScript">
var curBullet = 0;
var curEl;
var collBullets;
var numBullets;
function nextBullet() {
    //Make the next bullet visible
    if (curBullet < numBullets) {
        curEl = collBullets(curBullet);
        curEl.filters(0).Apply();
        curEl.style.visibility = "visible";
        curEl.filters(0).Play();
        curBullet++;
    }
}
function init() {
    //Get the collection of bullets
    collBullets = document.all.item("bullet");
    numBullets = collBullets.length;
}
</SCRIPT>
</HEAD>
<BODY BGCOLOR=black TEXT=white onclick="nextBullet()"
onload="init()">
<FONT SIZE=5><SPAN id=bullet>Elegant meals</SPAN><BR>
<SPANid=bullet>Fast service</SPAN><BR>
<SPAN id=bullet>Good vibes</SPAN>
</BODY>
</HTML>
```

The Page Is White, the Page Is Black

You need to know about more than one type of transition. "Sure," you say, "that's what you said the last time. Are these things related to tribbles?" Although transitions, tribbles, and trouble all start with *tr,* they are, in fact, unrelated.

The last of these transitions is *page-to-page transitions.* All the transitions that I've described so far in this chapter apply to individual elements on a Web page. You can also create transitions that apply to the entire page and that fire automatically when a page is loaded or when a page exits.

To set up the transition to run automatically when you load a page, use the following syntax:

```
<META HTTP-EQUIV = "Page-Enter" CONTENT =
"revealTrans(transition=3, Duration=2.0)">
```

To specify a transition to apply when leaving the page, you can do the same thing. However, use `Page-Exit` instead of `Page-Enter`, as follows:

```
<META HTTP-EQUIV = "Page-Exit" CONTENT =
"revealTrans(transition=3, Duration=2.0)">
```

Note that the `<META>` tag must be placed in the head, not in any other part of the page.

You can specify any transition, just as you would when setting a transition for an element. For example, check out page2page.html from the ch08 folder. This page is the same as the alien2.html page from Chapter 4. Only now, when you first browse to it, the page transitions in using a circle in transition. The only difference is the `Page-Enter` `<META>` tag. Load the page, or check out Figure 8-7 to see what it looks like.

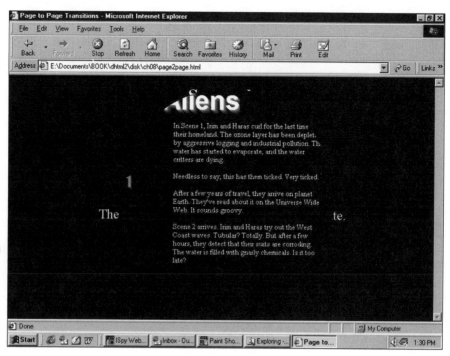

Figure 8-7:
The page
circles in
when it is
loaded.

Chapter 9

Touch Me, See Me, Hear Me

● ●

In This Chapter

▶ Adding sounds to your Web page

▶ Playing several sounds at once

▶ Playing a sound dynamically

▶ Changing the volume and balance on a sound

● ●

*J*im Morrison leaned in close to the microphone. Sweat dripped from his brow as he seductively brushed his long hair away from his eyes. He paused. He stared at the crowd. And then he sang, "Music is your special friend." And indeed, whether or not you like the Doors (or the Who, for that matter), music can add some extra pizzazz to your site. In this chapter, you find out about some of the fundamentals of adding sound to your Web pages.

Microsoft Internet Explorer provides two main ways to incorporate music into your page: the built-in sound tag `<BGSOUND>` and the ActiveMovie control. Netscape Navigator lets you add sounds by using the `<EMBED>` tag or by adding links to Real Audio files.

Pump Up the Jam

Adding sounds to your Web page is easy. You simply use the `<BGSOUND>` tag, as shown in the following format:

```
<BGSOUND SRC=soundfile VOLUME=volumelevel BALANCE=panamount
LOOP=loopcount>
```

As with any HTML tag, you don't need to include all the parameters. By far, `SRC` is the most important parameter. Pass it the name of the sound file that you want to play. The file can be a Real Audio (RA) file, a MIDI file, or a WAV file.

The VOLUME parameter sets the volume for the sound. The value can range from –10,000 to 0, where 0 is the loudest. The BALANCE parameter indicates how much of the sound appears in the left and right speakers. Set to 0, the sound plays equally from both speakers. If you set it to –10,000, the sound comes completely from the left speaker. Similarly, if you set it to 10,000, the sound comes completely from the right speaker. The LOOP parameter indicates how many times the sound should play. By default, the sound plays once. You can set it either to a number or to INFINITE. If you set it to INFINITE, the sound loops indefinitely — or at least until you go to a new page.

Does this sound too good to be true? Not at all. Check out Listing 9-1 or load bksound.html from the ch09 folder on the enclosed CD-ROM to see a sample page that includes a repeating MIDI file, using the following line of HTML code:

```
<BGSOUND SRC="bkgd.mid" LOOP=INFINITE>
```

Theoretically, you are supposed to put <BGSOUND> tags within the document head. But you don't really have to.

Listing 9-1   The bksound.html Source Code

```
<HTML>
<HEAD>
<BGSOUND SRC="bkgd.mid" LOOP=INFINITE>
</HEAD>
<BODY BGCOLOR=black TEXT=white>
<H1>Alien Rock</H1>
Just when you thought it was safe. Disco disappeared. Punk
paled. Rap rusted. The streets were once more safe, filled
with the sounds of silence. And then it happened.
Alien surf rock descended and ruled.
</BODY>
</HTML>
```

Because <BGSOUND> is an Internet Explorer-only tag, you need to use a different tag to play sounds in Navigator. In particular, the <EMBED> tag allows you to play sounds. When using it, you can set the parameters shown in Table 9-1. You can see the <EMBED> tag in use by checking out Listing 9-2 or loading the bksound_nn.html file from the ch09 folder.

Table 9-1   <EMBED> Parameters

Parameter	Meaning
SRC	The sound file to play.
HIDDEN	Set to TRUE to hide the sound playing control; FALSE to show it. FALSE is the default.

</HTML>What's that sound?

You can play many different types of sounds. The three most commonly used types on the Web are MIDI, WAV, and RA. MIDI (Musical Instrument Device Interface) files are the smallest type of music files to play. They don't contain a recording of a sound. Instead, they contain information about the musical notes and instruments that are needed to play a song. The file may contain information such as "play middle A on a clarinet for five seconds." The actual sound depends on how your sound card plays a clarinet sound.

By contrast, WAV files contain a recording of a song. The song sounds exactly the same regardless of where it is played. However, this sound file is much larger than a MIDI file.

Instead of simply having a couple of notes, WAV files can take over 160,000 bytes to represent one second of sound. Of course, you can reduce the size of WAV files in many ways, but in general, they get quite large. Real Audio (RA) files are a highly compressed type of audio file designed especially to be downloaded from the Internet.

MIDI files work well for music but can't produce any special-effect sounds or voice. WAV files work well for special effects and voices. You can also use them for music, but if you're just trying to play a background theme song, use a MIDI file instead. Real Audio files provide very good compression.

Parameter	Meaning
VOLUME	A number between 0 and 100 that sets the volume.
LOOP	Set to a number to loop the sound file or set to TRUE to make it loop infinitely.
AUTOSTART	Set to TRUE to play the file automatically as soon as it is downloaded.

Listing 9-2   The bksound_nn.html Source Code

```
<HTML>
<!--From Dynamic HTML for Dummies by Michael I. Hyman-->
<EMBED SRC="../media/bkgd.mid" HIDDEN=FALSE VOLUME=100 LOOP=TRUE AUTOSTART=TRUE>
</HEAD>
<BODY BGCOLOR=black TEXT=white>
<H1>Alien Rock</H1>
Just when you thought it was safe. Disco disappeared. Punk paled. Rap rusted. The
          streets were once more safe, filled with the sounds of silence. And
          then it happened. Alien surf rock descended and ruled.
</BODY>
```

Mixing the Night Away

Playing one sound file at a time is interesting, but not nearly as interesting as having several sound files play together. In fact, you can even play sounds dynamically in response to mouse-overs or other events.

Playing more than one sound at a time is simple. You simply include more than one `<BGSOUND>` tag. For example, the following HTML code causes two sounds to play at once. The first is a MIDI file that loops infinitely. The second is a WAV file that plays once.

```
<BGSOUND SRC="bkgd.mid" LOOP=INFINITE>
<BGSOUND SRC="rock.wav">
```

You can check out a page that plays two sounds at once by loading bksound2.html from the ch09 folder.

To play several sounds at once on a Navigator page, include multiple `<EMBED>` tags, as you can see in the bksound2_nn.html file in the ch09 folder.

Just playing two sounds at once is interesting, but it is far more interesting to control *when* they are played. For example, you can set up a MIDI file that plays in the background to establish a mood for your page. Then you can play WAV files in response to user actions, such as moving the mouse pointer over portions of the page. Follow these steps:

1. **Add as many** `<BGSOUND>` **tags as you expect to have sounds play at once.**

   In other words, if you plan to have as many as five sounds playing at once, place five `<BGSOUND>` tags on the page.

2. **Provide an** `id` **for each** `<BGSOUND>` **tag.**

3. **To play a sound, set the** `SRC` **property for one of the** `<BGSOUND>` **tags.**

For example, suppose that you want to have a background sound and an accent sound that fires in response to mouse pointer movements. You first set up the `<BGSOUND>` tags, as shown in the following HTML code:

```
<BGSOUND SRC="bkgd.mid" LOOP=INFINITE VOLUME=-500>
<BGSOUND id=snd2 >
```

As you can see, the `SRC` property for the second sound is not set. As a result, nothing plays for that sound when the page is loaded. When you want the second sound to play, just set the `SRC` parameter, as shown in the following script:

```
snd2.src = sndName;
```

As soon as this line executes, the second sound starts playing.

Check out bksound3.html from the ch09 folder to see this technique in use (Listing 9-3 shows bksound3.html). In particular, this page traps mouse-movement events on specific words on the page. When the user moves the pointer over those words, extra sounds play.

Changing the <EMBED> properties dynamically has no effect with Netscape Navigator.

Listing 9-3	The bksound3.html Source Code

```
<HTML>
<HEAD>
<SCRIPT>
function playSnd(sndName) {
    snd2.src = sndName;
}
</SCRIPT>
<BGSOUND id=snd1 SRC="../media/bkgd.mid" LOOP=INFINITE VOLUME=-500>
<BGSOUND id=snd2 >
</HEAD>
<BODY BGCOLOR=black TEXT=white>
<H1>Alien Rock</H1>
Just when you thought it was safe. <A onmouseover="playSnd
('../media/rock.wav')">Disco disappeared.</A> <A onmouseover=
"playSnd('../media/rock2.wav')">Punk paled.</A> Rap rusted. The
streets were once more safe, filled with the sounds of
silence. And then it happened.
Alien surf rock descended and ruled.<BR>
</BODY>
</HTML>
```

Sound and Vision

In addition to setting the SRC property for a <BGSOUND> tag, you can also set the volume, balance, and loop count. Suppose that you have a <BGSOUND> named foo. To change the volume, you could use the following script:

```
foo.volume = -500;
```

To change the balance, you can use the following script:

```
foo.balance = -10000;
```

Finally, to make the sound loop infinitely, you can use the following script:

```
foo.loop = "INFINITE";
```

If you change the loop count on a sound, the change only takes effect if the sound is playing. For example, if the loop count is "INFINITE", the sound always plays. Changing the loop count to " " stops the sound as soon as the loop is finished (although sometimes it takes one more play through before it finally decides to quit).

If, on the other hand, the loop count is 1 and you change the value to "INFINITE" after the sound finishes playing, the sound doesn't loop. It already looped once, and that was that. You can't tell it to start playing again after it has stopped.

The following example shows you how to use the tags and files that are presented in this chapter. You create a page that contains buttons for increasing and decreasing the volume of a sound. The page also contains a button to stop the infinitely looping sound.

First, the page contains two sounds, a MIDI file and a WAV file. Both loop infinitely, as follows:

```
<BGSOUND id=snd1 SRC="bkgd.mid" LOOP=INFINITE VOLUME=-1000>
<BGSOUND id=snd2 SRC="rock.wav" LOOP=INFINITE>
```

The page also contains three buttons. One button increases the volume, one lowers the volume, and one stops the second sound. The following HTML code sets the button that increases the volume:

```
<INPUT type=BUTTON value="Louder" onclick=
"changeVolume(100)">
```

As you can see, this code calls a function named changeVolume and passes it the value 100. The changeValue function simply takes the value passed to it and uses it to increment the sound's volume. The following is the key script from the changeVolume function:

```
snd1.volume += amt;
```

If you pass changeVolume a positive number, the volume increases. If you pass it a negative number, the volume decreases.

The button that stops the second sound simply clears the loop count, using the following script:

```
snd2.loop = "";
```

To try this file, load bksound4.html from the ch09 folder (see Listing 9-4). Be sure to click on the Louder and Softer buttons several times to hear the volume change.

Listing 9-4	The bksound4.html Source Code

```
<HTML>
<HEAD>
<SCRIPT>
function changeVolume(amt) {
    snd1.volume += amt;
}
function loopRock() {
    snd2.loop = "";
}
</SCRIPT>
<BGSOUND id=snd1 SRC="../media/bkgd.mid" LOOP=INFINITE VOLUME=-1000>
<BGSOUND id=snd2 SRC="../media/rock.wav" LOOP=INFINITE>
</HEAD>
<BODY BGCOLOR=black TEXT=white>
<H1>Alien Rock</H1>
Just when you thought it was safe. Disco disappeared. Punk
paled. Rap rusted. The streets were once more safe,
filled with the sounds of silence. And then it happened.
Alien surf rock descended and ruled.<BR>
<INPUT type=BUTTON value="Louder" onclick=
"changeVolume(100)">
<INPUT type=BUTTON value="Softer" onclick=
"changeVolume(-100)">
<INPUT type=BUTTON value="Stop Rock" onclick="loopRock()">
</BODY>
</HTML>
```

What about ActiveMovie?

Another way to play sounds with Internet Explorer is with the ActiveMovie control. The ActiveMovie control is a sophisticated control that plays both sound and video. It provides several key features that are not available through the use of the <BGSOUND> tag:

✔ You can play the same sound several times, programmatically. As a result, you can download the sound once and then play it as many times as you want whenever you would like.

✔ You can *seek* within the sound, thereby playing specific portions of the sound. For example, you can start the sound playing from three seconds after its beginning.

✔ You can stop or pause the sound during the middle of playing. By contrast, with <BGSOUND>, the whole sound plays to its end. You have no way of stopping it.

Using the ActiveMovie control is more involved than using the <BGSOUND> tag. First, you need to instantiate the control, as shown in the following HTML:

```
<OBJECT id=snd1 CLASSID="CLSID:05589FA1-C356-11CE-BF01-00AA0055595A"
                style="visibility:hidden">
<PARAM NAME="FileName" VALUE="../media/rock.wav">
</OBJECT>
```

Then you need to add script to play the file. (Note that instead of having a sound file, you can just as easily play a video. Just make the control visible and set the FileName to a video file.) Before you actually play the file, though, you need to make sure that the machine has a sound card and you need to make sure that the file has downloaded enough that it can play, as you can see in the following script:

```
function playSnd() {
    //Is there a sound card?
    if (snd1.issoundcardenabled()) {
        //Has enough downloaded that it can play?
        if (snd1.readyState >= 3)
            snd1.Run();
    }
}
```

To listen to a Web page that plays sound using ActiveMovie, load amovie_sound.html from the ch09 folder.

Chapter 10

Time After Time

In This Chapter

▶ Using a sequencer to execute an action after a delay

▶ Repeatedly executing an action

▶ Synchronizing a series of actions

▶ Running a series of actions in response to a user event

I look at a great many Web pages, and frankly, most of them are boring. Why? Nothing happens. After all, how interesting is a page that lists 20 favorite albums or shows a picture of a pet cat? Some sites, however, use animation to draw your attention. When done well, animation can add plenty of flavor to a page. When done poorly, it gives you a headache or at least makes you shout "Puhleaze."

And speaking of headaches, let me rant for a moment about Mike's Web Authoring Rule No. 4:

Rule No. 4: Timing is everything.

In other words, most Web pages are static. The page changes very little after it downloads. In Chapters 2, 4, and 6, you see that adding a little animation through `window.setInterval` and `window.setTimeout` can liven up a page. Adding more sophisticated time-based changes can pull in a viewer and dramatically increase the appeal of a Web page. But if your timing is off, your page can end up looking like a cheaply dubbed movie shot with a stroboscope: Everything jerks around.

In this chapter, I show how to use `window.setTimeout`, `window.setInterval`, and the sequencer control to add sophisticated timing to a page.

Synchronicity

For simple timing tasks or for pages that must work on both Microsoft Internet Explorer and Netscape Navigator, use `window.setTimeout` and `window.setInterval`. For more complex timing needs, you can use the *sequencer control,* which combines the capabilities of `window.setTimeout` and `window.setInterval`. Essentially, the sequencer control lets you schedule when a function should run, how often it should be called, and what the pause should be between calls. So you can say the following:

> Execute function `foo` in three seconds. At four seconds, execute function `bar`. Then call `bar` 25 times in a row, every 50 milliseconds.

Do these instructions sound complex? Well, if you don't use the sequencer control, they are. Fortunately, the sequencer control lets you add complex timed behaviors to a Web page without getting a huge headache.

In this chapter, I show you a number of pages that change over time. I start by showing you how to use `window.setTimeout` and `window.setInterval` to do so. Then I show you how to use the sequencer.

I start with a simple page where a word shows up 3.5 seconds after the page first loads (see Figure 10-1). To do so, I create a hidden div. I set a timer that fires after 3.5 seconds. At that point, I show the div. You can see the code for this page in Listing 10-1 or by loading time1.html from the ch10 folder on the CD.

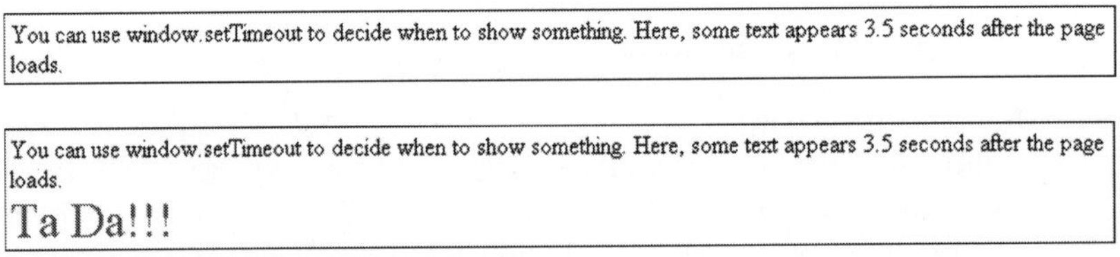

Figure 10-1:
You can see the page when it loads, and a few seconds later, the words *Ta Da!!!* appear.

You can use window.setTimeout to decide when to show something. Here, some text appears 3.5 seconds after the page loads.

You can use window.setTimeout to decide when to show something. Here, some text appears 3.5 seconds after the page loads.

Ta Da!!!

Listing 10-1	The time1.html Source Code

```
<HTML>
<HEAD>
<SCRIPT>
function showIt() {
   tada.style.visibility = "visible";
}

function start() {
   window.setTimeout("showIt()", 3500);
}
</SCRIPT>

</HEAD>
<BODY onload="start()">
You can use window.setTimeout to decide when to show something. Here, some text
               appears 3.5 seconds after the page loads.
<DIV id=tada style="position:relative;visibility:hidden">
<FONT SIZE=6 COLOR=red>
Ta Da!!!</DIV>

</BODY>
</HTML>
```

Doing a similar page in Navigator is easy. Just change the line that shows the `<DIV>` to:

```
document.tada.visibility = "show";
```

You can load time1_nn.html from the ch10 folder on the CD to see the Navigator version in action.

Actually, you can easily modify the page to make it work in both Internet Explorer and Navigator. All you need to do is check the browser version to decide how to control the visibility of the `<DIV>`.

Slightly More Complex Timing

In the preceding example, only one element changed over time. In this section, I make a slightly more complex example. In it, several `<DIV>`s become visible at various times. Is creating this example hard? Heck no. I just put several `window.setTimeout` lines in a function.

```
show(d1);
window.setTimeout("show(d2)", 1500);
window.setTimeout("show(d3)", 3000);
```

The `show` function takes the name of the element to show as an argument and changes that object's visibility, as shown in the following line:

```
obj.style.visibility = "visible";
```

What are these mysterious objects named d1, d2, and d3? They're simply <DIV>s containing text, such as the following:

```
<DIV id=d1 style="position:absolute; left:30px; top:10px; font-size:30pt; color:red;
            visibility:hidden">
This is your brain</DIV>
```

You can see this page in action by loading time2.html from the ch10 folder on the CD. Also, be sure to check out Figure 10-2, where you can see the three different messages that appear on the screen at different times.

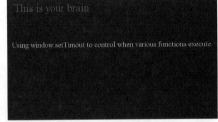

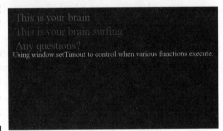

Figure 10-2 :
You can see the page when it first loads, after two seconds, and after the final message appears.

You can easily create a version of this page for Navigator. Simply change the way the <DIV>s are shown to the following:

```
obj.visibility = "show";
```

Also, instead of passing in the name of the element to show, prefix the name with `document`, as shown in the following line:

```
show(document.d1);
```

You can run this file by loading time2_nn.html from the ch09 folder. As with seq1_nn.html, you can easily modify this page so that it works with Internet Explorer as well.

 Navigator is very sensitive about what it considers to be layers. Perhaps I merely encountered a bug, but I did find that if I had <FONT> tags within a <DIV>, the <DIV> would not show up in the layers collection. Thus, you may note that I use Cascading Style Sheets (CSS) styles for all the <DIV> tags in the time2_nn.html file.

And Now, for Something Completely Different

Well, actually, I don't do something completely different in this section. But I do make a page that is much more interactive than the ones in the preceding examples. This time, I make a page that has a countdown timer in it. The countdown timer starts with the value 5 and counts down to 1, changing the value every second. It starts counting after two seconds elapse. You also change the color of some text every 2.5 seconds, starting as soon as the page loads.

Why is this page more complex than before? Well, it contains two repeated actions. Each repeated action starts at a different time. And one of the repeated actions lasts for only a certain amount of time.

To create this page, I use window.setTimer as well as window. setInterval. These two functions are very similar. window.setTimer, as you know, calls a function after a certain amount of time. window. setInterval calls a function repeatedly, with a delay between each invocation.

To achieve the countdown timer, I start by calling a function to make the countdown happen. I use window.setTimeout so that the counter starts after two seconds. I also immediately start the function that changes colors on the text, by calling window.setInterval, as shown in the following code:

```
window.setTimeout("startCountDown()", 2000);
window.setInterval("changeColor()", 2500);
```

The startCountDown function then calls window.setInterval to call another function, named countDown, every second, as shown in the following code:

```
siID = window.setInterval("countDown()", 1000);
```

Note that the return value of `window.setInterval` is stored in a global variable. This value is an identifier for the particular interval timer. You can pass the value to `window.clearInterval` to stop the timer.

The `countDown` function displays a counter that goes from 5 to 1. When the counter hits zero, the interval timer is stopped, as shown in the following code:

```
if (cnt == 0)
window.clearInterval(siID);
```

You can see the complete program by looking at Listing 10-2. Or you can load the page by opening time3.html from the ch10 folder. Figure 10-3 shows the page a few seconds after it has started.

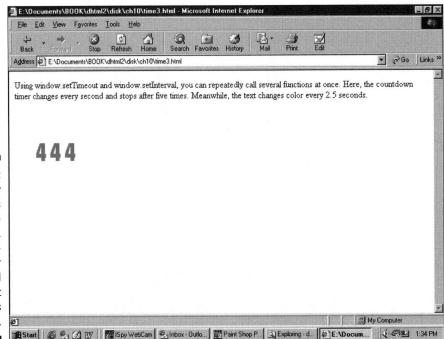

Figure 10-3: A few seconds after the page starts, the countdown timer is at 4 and the text color is green.

Listing 10-2	The time3.html Source Code

```
<HTML>
<HEAD>

<SCRIPT>
var siID;
var cnt = 5;
var colors = new Array("gray", "green", "blue", "purple", "black");
var curColor = 0;

function countDown() {
   txt1.innerText = cnt + " " + cnt + " " + cnt;
   cnt--;
   if (cnt == 0)
       window.clearInterval(siID);
}

function changeColor() {
   txt1.style.color = colors[curColor++];
   curColor %= colors.length;
}

function startCountDown() {
   siID = window.setInterval("countDown()", 1000);
}

function start() {
   window.setTimeout("startCountDown()", 2000);
   window.setInterval("changeColor()", 2500);
}
</SCRIPT>

</HEAD>
<BODY onload="start()">
Using window.setTimeout and window.setInterval, you can repeatedly call several func-
            tions at once. Here, the countdown timer changes every second and
            stops after five times. Meanwhile, the text changes color every 2.5
            seconds.
<DIV id=txt1 style="position:absolute; left: 50; top: 120; font-size:40; font-family:
            impact">
</DIV>
</BODY>
</HTML>
```

Note that this program is starting to get complex to code. If I had much more timing going on, creating the page would start to become painful. But don't worry; I'm about to tell you about the sequencer. The sequencer makes it easy to create pages that use very complex timing.

Modulo what?

The *modulo function,* represented in code by %, is a cool math function. It takes two values as parameters and returns the remainder of the first value divided by the second. For example, 3 % 10 is 3. 13 % 10 is 3. 10 % 10 is 0. The modulo function is often used to keep a number within a particular range.

For example, suppose that you have an array called `colors` with five color names in it and an index variable called `curColor` that you use to access array elements. If you find `curColor % colors.length`, you are guaranteed that `curColor` ranges between 0 and `colors.length-1`. Thus, it is always a valid index. If you want `curColor` to go from 0 to the last element in the array and then loop back to 0, you can increment the value of `curColor` and then modulo the result with the length of the `color` array, as is done in the function named `changeColor`.

You can see modulo in use in the `changeColor` function in time3.html.

Naturally, making a version of this page that works with Navigator is fairly easy. The only annoying part is that you need to use the good old write-into-a-layer trick to get the color and the text to change. You can see the full source code by loading time3_nn.html from the ch09 folder or by examining Listing 10-3.

When you dynamically insert text into a layer and use CSS positioning or color commands on the text, Netscape seems to lose the positioning and other style information for the layer into which the text is inserted. This response may be a bug, or it may be a feature. Regardless, the workaround is to provide all the positioning and font information on the text that is inserted, rather than relying on the containing layer.

Listing 10-3   The time3_nn.html Source Code

```
<HTML>
<HEAD>

<SCRIPT>
var siID;
var cnt = 5;
var colors = new Array("gray", "green", "blue", "purple", "black");
var curColor = 0;
var curText = "Countdown";
var curColorText = "<SPAN style='position:absolute;font-size:30pt;left: 50px; top:
            120px;color:black'>"

function writeIt(t) {
```

```
   document.txt2.document.open();
   document.txt2.document.write(t);
   document.txt2.document.close();
}


function countDown() {
   curText = cnt + " " + cnt + " " + cnt;
   writeIt(curColorText + curText + "</SPAN>");
   cnt--;
   if (cnt == 0)
       window.clearInterval(siID);
}

function changeColor() {
   curColorText = "<SPAN style='position:absolute;font-size:30pt;left: 50px; top:
               120px;color:" + colors[curColor++] + "'>";
   writeIt(curColorText + curText + "</SPAN>");
   curColor %= colors.length;
}

function startCountDown() {
   siID = window.setInterval("countDown()", 1000);
}

function start() {
   window.setTimeout("startCountDown()", 2000);
   window.setInterval("changeColor()", 2500);
}
</SCRIPT>

</HEAD>
<BODY onload="start()">
Using window.setTimeout and window.setInterval, you can repeatedly call several func-
               tions at once. Here, the countdown timer changes every second and
               stops after five times. Meanwhile, the text changes color every 2.5
               seconds.
<LAYER id=txt2>
</LAYER>
</BODY>
</HTML>
```

Sequencer

In this section, I show you how to use the sequencer. The sequencer enables you to create very richly timed pages. Although the sequencer is overkill and a little tough to use for simple timings, such as with the first two examples in this chapter, it is invaluable for complex timing.

When you use the sequencer, you create a set of action sets. An *action set* is a group of timed commands that execute together. For example, you may have one set of commands to animate the image of a dog, make some divs visible, and change text on the page. You want that set of actions to occur when the user clicks on a button. Thus, you group those commands into an action set. You may want two transitions to start and lights to sweep across the page when the user moves the mouse pointer over an element. You group those commands into another action set.

Sequencer control to Major Tom

"You know, I was wondering," you ask, "are you sure that CLASSID thing shouldn't have been set to DV84U? That thing you just showed me has way too many bizarre letters in it." Well, that long set of letters is part of how you add ActiveX controls to a Web page.

ActiveX controls are components that conform to the ActiveX standard. (Surprising name for the standard, huh?) They are blurbs of functionality that you can use to enhance the way a program operates. Because all ActiveX controls expose their functionality in a similar way, they can be used in a broad variety of applications. You can use them in Microsoft Office, in Visual Basic, or in soup with a touch of pepper.

ActiveX controls provide a variety of methods that can be used by the application. For example, the sequencer control has a method called play. This method tells the control to begin executing timed commands. But for the application to use this functionality, it needs to know that the control has a method called play.

Think of it this way: You're forming a baseball team with your coworkers. Someone who you've never played with shows up to practice, and you want to figure out which position that person should play. You could try him or her out in different spots to see what works. But most likely, you would have a dialog like that goes something this:

"Hey, what's your name?"

"Pat."

"Good to meet'cha, Pat. Say, how are you at catching pop flies?"

"My brother Renfield is much better at that."

"Well, how about pitching? Have you ever done that?"

And so forth. Eventually you would figure out what type of position Pat would be best at (hopefully something other than benchwarmer).

That's exactly what happens when you put an ActiveX control in an application. The application asks several questions to figure out what capabilities the ActiveX control provides.

Before you can use the ActiveX control, though, you need to tell the application (in this case, Internet Explorer 5.0) which ActiveX control to use. Now, you could just use a name like *sequencer*. But the problem with that name is that I may also create a new control called *sequencer*. So could the kid next door. If you put all those controls on one machine, how would the application know which one to use? That's where that really long set of characters comes in to play. That is called the *class ID*. The class ID is automatically generated when you create an ActiveX control using one of those utilities that programmer types carry in their pockets. The class ID is guaranteed to be unique. Thus, if I make a sequencer control and you make one, the class IDs would be different. So by telling Internet Explorer the class ID for the control to use, you always get the right one. It's like designating a really long social security number.

Thus, the <OBJECT> tag tells Internet Explorer to add an ActiveX control to a page, and the CLASSID parameter indicates exactly which control to use.

You can have as many action sets as you want on a page. You can play any action set whenever you want.

The sequencer is an ActiveX control. (If you're not familiar with using ActiveX controls on Web pages, be sure to read the sidebar "Sequencer control to Major Tom.") The following is the HTML code that's used to add one to your page:

```
<OBJECT ID="seq"
    CLASSID="CLSID:B0A6BAE2-AAF0-11d0-A152-00A0C908DB96">
</OBJECT>
```

I got a message from the action set

To use the sequencer, take the following steps (these are the general steps; more specific guidelines follow):

1. **Determine what you want to modify and when you want to modify it.**

2. **Add the sequencer control to your Web page.**

3. **Create the various action sets.**

4. **Play the action sets.**

As I say in the preceding section, an action set is a group of commands to run. To be exact, an action set is a named group of functions that are called, perhaps repeatedly, at particular times, all with respect to when the action set is played. When you set the timing information for the functions, time 0 means the time at which the action set plays. The action set could be played at 10:00 a.m. Sunday morning. It could also be played at 1:00, 1:01, and 1:02 on a Thursday afternoon — it doesn't matter. Time 0 is always with respect to when it starts playing. Thus, an action set provides a way to synchronize a group of actions, because they are all timed relative to when the action set plays.

For example, if you are a programmer, you may wake up in the morning, brush your teeth while reading *Dilbert,* and then head to the kitchen for a slice of pizza. This breakfast routine is similar to an action set: It is a set of activities that you perform in order. If you wake up late one day, you still perform the same actions in the same order, just at a different time.

You may have several action sets as part of your routine. For example, every other night you may take a shower. (Okay, that's being extreme. Every third night.) Thus, you'd run the shower action set every few days and the breakfast action set when you wake up.

To use the sequencer, you create the action sets and then play them when you want. Creating the action sets is easy after you get beyond one trick. You only put one sequencer on the page, but the sequencer can have many action sets within it. It does so by creating a collection of the action sets. Thus, any time that you refer to an action set, you need to access it via the collection. The following is the syntax for playing an action set:

```
sequencer_name.Item("actionset_name").Play();
```

For example, suppose that you create an action set named DoFirst for a sequencer named seq1. You would use the following script to play the action set:

```
seq1.Item("DoFirst").Play();
```

To create an action set, you use the at command. The syntax for the at command is as follows:

```
sequencer_name.Item("actionset_name").At(time, "function" [,repeat, interval
                [,tiebreak [,tolerance]]]);
```

You can ignore the tiebreak and tolerance parameters: They're for the hard-core Web nerds. All the time measurements are in seconds. Set the time to the time that you want the function to be called. For example, you can use the following script to call a function named closeMe 3.5 seconds after the action set is played:

```
seq1.Item("DoFirst").At(3.5, "closeMe()");
```

Remember to put the function name inside quotation marks.

You can add actions to the action set whenever you want. For example, you may want to add items in response to the user pushing a button or selecting some choice. But most often, you establish the action set by processing the oninit event for the sequencer.

Use the following code to process the oninit event:

```
<SCRIPT FOR="seq" EVENT="oninit">
    //The at commands go here, e.g.
    //seq1.Item("DoFirst").At(3.5, "closeMe()")
</SCRIPT>
```

Delayed for a moment

Now I show you how to create the time1.html program by using the sequencer instead of window.setTimeout.

You can add a sequencer to the page and process its `oninit` event to create an action set. This action set calls the function `showIt` 3.5 seconds after the action set is played:

```
<SCRIPT FOR="seq" EVENT="oninit">
    seq.Item("showThem").at(3.5,"showIt()");
</SCRIPT>
```

Then you play the action set when the page is loaded by running the following script:

```
seq.Item("showThem").Play();
```

That's all there is to it. The words _Ta Da!!!_ appear 3.5 seconds after the page loads. You can see this script in action by loading seq1.html from the ch10 folder (see Listing 10-4).

Listing 10-4	The seq1.html Source Code

```
<HTML>
<HEAD>
<SCRIPT FOR="seq" EVENT="oninit">
    seq.Item("showThem").at(3.5,"showIt()");
</SCRIPT>
<SCRIPT>
function showIt() {
    tada.style.visibility = "visible";
}
function start() {
    seq.Item("showThem").Play();
}
</SCRIPT>
</HEAD>
<BODY onload="start()">
The sequencer makes it easy for you to decide when something should execute. Here,
                some text appears 3.5 seconds after the page loads.
<DIV id=tada style="visibility:hidden">
<FONT SIZE=6 COLOR=red>
Ta Da!!!</DIV>
<OBJECT ID="seq"
    CLASSID="CLSID:B0A6BAE2-AAF0-11d0-A152-00A0C908DB96">
</OBJECT>
</BODY>
</HTML>
```

Ready? Set. Action!

Next, I redo time2.html, once again using the sequencer. To do so, I place several actions in an action set. Doing so is straightforward. You just call the `at` method several times.

For example, you can easily enhance seq1.html so that it displays three separate messages, each at a different time. The following code sets up this action set:

```
<SCRIPT FOR="seq" EVENT="oninit">
    seq.Item("showThem").at(0.000,"show(d1)");
    seq.Item("showThem").at(1.500,"show(d2)");
    seq.Item("showThem").at(3.000,"show(d3)");
</SCRIPT>
```

Check out this page by loading seq2.html from the ch10 folder (see Listing 10-5).

Listing 10-5   **The seq2.html Source Code**

```
<HTML>
<HEAD>
<SCRIPT FOR="seq" EVENT="oninit">
    seq.Item("showThem").at(0.000,"show(d1)");
    seq.Item("showThem").at(1.500,"show(d2)");
    seq.Item("showThem").at(3.000,"show(d3)");
</SCRIPT>
<SCRIPT>
function show(obj) {
    obj.style.visibility = "visible";
}
function start() {
    seq.Item("showThem").Play();
}
</SCRIPT>
</HEAD>
<BODY BGCOLOR=black onload="start()">
<DIV id=d1 style="position:absolute; left:30; top:10; visibility:hidden">
<FONT SIZE=6 COLOR=red>
This is your brain</DIV>
<DIV id=d2 style="position:absolute; left:30; top:60; visibility:hidden">
<FONT COLOR=blue>
This is your brain surfing</DIV>
<DIV id=d3 style="position:absolute; left:30; top:110; visibility:hidden">
<FONT COLOR=green>
Any questions?</DIV>
<DIV style="position:absolute;left:20;top:150">
<FONT COLOR=yellow size=4>
The sequencer lets you easily control when various functions execute.
</DIV>
<OBJECT ID="seq"
    CLASSID="CLSID:B0A6BAE2-AAF0-11d0-A152-00A0C908DB96">
</OBJECT>
</BODY>
</HTML>
```

Repeat after me

Creating action sets with multiple items in them is cool. Adding repeating actions is even cooler. Using `window.setInterval`, as is done in time3.html, you can cause an item to repeat indefinitely. To have the item run a certain number of times, you need to keep track of the iterations with a counter. And as you can see with time3.html, doing so gets ugly in a hurry. But keeping track of the iterations with a sequencer is easy. You simply figure out how often you want to call a function and how long to wait between calls. For example, the following script adds an action that gets called five times in a row, every half-second:

```
seq1.Item("showMe").At(0, "doIt()", 5, .5);
```

To repeat an item indefinitely, pass in –1 as the repeat count. To call the function as fast as possible, as opposed to at specific intervals, pass in 0 for the delay.

Remember that the times specified are in seconds. So if you pass in 1 for the delay, the function is called every second. If you pass in 0.01, the function is called 100 times a second. Note that, if you try using very small values, the system doesn't keep up with what you expect. For example, you can't execute items 1,000 times a second. Typically, you can get as many as 30 calls a second.

Now I show you how to create the time3.html page, using the sequencer. Remember that this page has a countdown timer in it. The countdown timer starts with the value 5 and counts down to 1, changing the value every second. You also change the color of some text every 2.5 seconds. The following calls create the action set:

```
seq.Item("showThem").at(2, "countDown()", 5, 1);
seq.Item("showThem").at(0, "changeColor()", -1, 2.5);
```

Note that countDown is called five times and changeColor is called infinitely. These functions behave just the same as they do in time3.html.

To see this page in action, load seq3.html from the ch 10 folder (see Listing 10-6).

Listing 10-6	The seq3.html Source Code

```
<HTML>
<HEAD>
<SCRIPT FOR="seq" EVENT="oninit">
    seq.Item("showThem").at(2, "countDown()", 5, 1);
    seq.Item("showThem").at(0, "changeColor()", -1, 2.5);
</SCRIPT>
<SCRIPT>
var cnt = 5;
var colors = new Array("gray", "green", "blue", "purple", "black");
var curColor = 0;
function countDown() {
    txt2.innerText = cnt + " " + cnt + " " + cnt;
    cnt--;
}
function changeColor() {
    txt1.style.color = colors[curColor++];
    curColor %= colors.length;
}
function start() {
    seq.Item("showThem").Play();
}
</SCRIPT>
</HEAD>
<BODY onload="start()">
<SPAN id=txt1>
Using the sequencer, you can repeatedly call several functions at once. Here, the
            countdown timer changes every second and stops after five times.
            Meanwhile, the text changes color every 2.5 seconds.</SPAN>
<DIV id=txt2 style="position:absolute; left: 50; top: 120; font-size:40; font-family:
            impact">
</DIV>
<OBJECT ID="seq"
    CLASSID="CLSID:B0A6BAE2-AAF0-11d0-A152-00A0C908DB96">
</OBJECT>
</BODY>
</HTML>
```

The last action hero

In the examples that I present in the earlier sections of this chapter, you always play the sequencer when the page begins. And you create only a single action set. However, you can create as many action sets as you want and play the sequencers whenever you want. This capability is very powerful because it lets you create animated sequences that fire in response to a user's actions.

You can also stop sequencers and pause them. Table 10-1 shows the various methods that are available for the sequencer.

Table 10-1	The Sequencer Methods	
Method	_Meaning_	_Sample_
At(_time, "function"_ [,_repeat, interval_ [,_tiebreak_ [,_tolerance_]]])	Adds a new item to an action set.	`seq1.Item ("foo"). At(1.7, "showIt()");`
Pause	Pauses an action set. Subsequent play commands continue the sequencer running from the current time.	`seq1.Item ("foo"). Pause();`
Play	Runs an action set. This method is ignored if the action set is currently playing.	`seq1.Item ("foo"). Play();`
Seek	Moves to a particular time in the action set. For example, you can skip parts of an action set by seeking after they occur.	`seq1.Item ("foo"). Seek(3.2);`
Stop	Stops the action set. Subsequent plays start from time 0.	`seq1.Item ("foo"). Stop();`

And Now, for Something Completely Real

As a parting gesture for this chapter, I show you how to create a real-world sequencer example. You create a page that displays information about a particular area during the different seasons. You then use the sequencer to make the page appear more like a CD-ROM or a TV show. When the page loads, an alpha transition blends in an image. Then a line of text containing the words _Dateline: August_ appears, one character at a time. Midway through this action, explanatory text that describes the season appears. The explanatory text has the word _winter_ highlighted. Clicking on the word _winter_ kicks off another action set, which transitions to a new image, a new dateline, and a new set of explanatory text.

This example is complex, so I'm going to break it into pieces so that you can see what is going on.

First, you create two different action sets. One action set plays when the page loads. The other plays when the user clicks on the word _winter_. The following code sets up the two action sets:

```
seq.Item("show1").at(0, "trans1()");
seq.Item("show1").at(0, "prep(date1)");
seq.Item("show1").at(2.3, "dateLine(date1)", date1.innerText.length, .2);
seq.Item("show1").at(2.3+date1.innerText.length*.15, "showIt(txt1)");
seq.Item("show2").at(0, "trans2()");
seq.Item("show2").at(0, "prep(date2)");
seq.Item("show2").at(2.3, "dateLine(date2)", date2.innerText.length, .2);
seq.Item("show2").at(2.3+date2.innerText.length*.15, "showIt(txt2)");
```

"Holy cow," you say. "That's a lot of actions." Sure. But this page does a lot.

Notice that there are two action sets. And in fact, the action sets look remarkably similar. The difference is that one operates on date1 and the other on date2.

Each action set begins by calling a transition function. The trans1 function transitions in the first image. Then the trans2 function transitions the first image to the second and hides any text that relates to the first image.

The prep function is an interesting one. It works in conjunction with dateLine. Together, these two functions take an element, read the text from it, and then clear the element; they then replace the text one character at a time. Why bother? It's a cool effect. You author the text the way that you normally author HTML code. But when the page runs, the text appears one character at a time. Using the sequencer, you can control how many characters appear per second. In this case, you show a new character every fifth of a second.

The prep function pulls the original text out of the element and shoves it into a variable. The function then clears the element and makes it visible. The prep function also clears a counter that's used to track which letter needs to appear next. The following is the script:

```
curLetter = 0;
txt = which.innerText;
which.innerText = "";
which.style.visibility = "visible";
```

After prep runs, the element whose name was passed to it is visible and empty. All the text that was in it is stored in a variable named txt.

How do the characters get back in? The dateLine function puts them back in, one at a time, using the following script:

```
which.innerText = txt.substring(0, ++curLetter);
```

In case that script looks like a foreign language, I can describe what it does. First, the script adds one to the current letter. The script then creates a new string that consists of the characters of txt from character 0 (the first character) to the curLetter character. So the first time through, this script creates a string with the first letter in `txt`. The second time through, the script creates a string with the first two letters in `txt`, and so on. This string is then placed directly into the element to provide the element's new text.

Of course, the incremental displaying of characters only works if `dateLine` is called once for each character in the element. That's why the code that creates the action set looks so complex. The following line sets up the calls to `dateLine` for the first action set:

```
seq.Item("show1").at(2.3, "dateLine(date1)", date1.innerText.length, .2);
```

You can see that the repeat count is set to `date1.innerText.length`. In other words, the repeat count is the number of characters in the element. If the element has little text in it, then `dateLine` is only called a few times. If the element is large, `dateLine` is called many more times.

As a result, you don't know when the dateline characters will finish being displayed. For visual interest, you can show the explanatory text only after 75 percent of the characters have been displayed in the dateline. To do so, you set the time when `showIt` is called based on the number of characters. The following line of script does just that. Because each character is shown every 0.2 seconds and `date1.innerText.length` characters are shown, `date1.innerText.length*.15` calculates how long it takes for 75 percent of the characters to appear, as follows:

```
seq.Item("show1").at(2.3+date1.innerText.length*.15, "showIt(txt1)");
```

When possible, design script so that it calculates lengths on the fly, rather than having them hardwired in. (In other words, don't always assume that a piece of text has 11 characters in it. Check the size of the text, and write your scripts to operate accordingly.) For example, the script line that you just looked at works regardless of the size of `date1`. By using this technique, you can author the page as if it were static. You don't need to build the text *Dateline: August* through some ugly code. Rather, you type it into a div as you would any other text. You can see the end result of the page by simply switching visibility on elements and without needing to run scripts.

Be sure to look over Listing 10-7. The page ties together many interesting techniques. It blends in images by using transitions. It checks for clicks on text. Part of the text on the page appears one character at a time. Throughout, the functions dynamically compute timing and other information.

You should also load the page and try it out. Do so by loading seq4.html from the ch10 folder. You can see the letters appearing over time in Figure 10-4.

Although it is possible to make an equivalent page in Navigator by using the same techniques used in time3_nn.html, doing so is a royal pain in the behind.

Figure 10-4:
The first image fades into the second. Next, the letters in the dateline appear, one at a time, just as the image fully fades in. Three-quarters of the way through, additional explanatory text appears.

Listing 10-7	The seq4.html Source Code

```
<HTML>
<HEAD>
<SCRIPT FOR="seq" EVENT="oninit">
    seq.Item("show1").at(0, "trans1()");
    seq.Item("show1").at(0, "prep(date1)");
    seq.Item("show1").at(2.3, "dateLine(date1)",
            date1.innerText.length, .2);
    seq.Item("show1").at(2.3+date1.innerText.length*.15,
            "showIt(txt1)");
    seq.Item("show2").at(0, "trans2()");
    seq.Item("show2").at(0, "prep(date2)");
    seq.Item("show2").at(2.3, "dateLine(date2)",
            date2.innerText.length, .2);
    seq.Item("show2").at(2.3+date2.innerText.length*.15,
            "showIt(txt2)");
</SCRIPT>
<SCRIPT>
var curLetter;
```

```
var txt;
function nextSeason() {
    seq.Item("show1").stop();
    seq.Item("show2").play();
}
//Prepare the dateline
function prep(which) {
    curLetter = 0;
    txt = which.innerText;
    which.innerText = "";
    which.style.visibility = "visible";
}
function trans1() {
    picture.filters(0).Apply();
    img1.style.visibility = "visible";
    picture.filters(0).Play();
}
function trans2() {
    //Hide old stuff
    txt1.style.visibility = "hidden";
    date1.style.visibility = "hidden";
    //Do the transition
    picture.filters(0).Apply();
    img1.style.visibility = "hidden";
    img2.style.visibility = "visible";
    picture.filters(0).Play();
}
//Add one letter each time called
function dateLine(which) {
    which.innerText = txt.substring(0, ++curLetter);
}
function showIt(which) {
    which.style.visibility = "visible";
}
function start() {
    seq.Item("show1").Play();
}
</SCRIPT>
</HEAD>
<BODY onload="start()" bgcolor=black text=white>
<CENTER>
<DIV id=picture style="position:relative; width:320; height:240;
            filter:blendTrans(duration=3)">
<IMG id=img1 src="../media/summer.jpg" style="position:absolute; left:0; top:0; visi-
            bility:hidden">
<IMG id=img2 src="../media/winter.jpg" style="position:absolute; left:0; top:0; visi-
            bility:hidden">
</DIV>
</CENTER>
<SPAN id=date1 style="position:absolute; left:30%; top: 260; font-size:30; font-
            family:impact; color: olive; visibility:hidden">Dateline:
            August</SPAN>
<SPAN id=date2 style="position:absolute; left:30%; top: 260; font-size:30; font-
            family:impact; color: olive; visibility:hidden">Dateline:
            December</SPAN>
```

(continued)

Listing 10-7 *(continued)*

```
<SPAN id=txt1 style="position:absolute; width: 35%; left: 30%; top: 295;
                visibility:hidden">
During the summer, the sun shines endlessly on the clear blue water. The temperature
                ranges from 70 to 80 degrees, and a pleasant breeze blows onto the
                shore. But then comes <A onclick="nextSeason()"
                style="color:aqua">winter</A>.</SPAN>
<SPAN id=txt2 style="position:absolute; width: 35%; left: 30%; top: 295;
                visibility:hidden">
The winter brings frequent snowstorms. School and work are shut down as residents
                take to the streets to dig out pets and cars.</SPAN>
<OBJECT ID="seq"
    CLASSID="CLSID:B0A6BAE2-AAF0-11d0-A152-00A0C908DB96">
</OBJECT>
</BODY>
</HTML>
```

Chapter 11

The Graphic Details

In This Chapter

▶ Understanding the difference between raster and vector graphics

▶ Drawing simple vector graphics shapes

▶ Drawing more complex shapes, such as gradient-filled text

▶ Rotating and scaling graphics

▶ Creating rotating 3-D text

▶ Creating an analog clock

▶ Using the WebDings font

▶ Using VML to create simple shapes

▶ Changing VML colors and strokes

▶ Moving and rotating VML shapes

▶ Creating complex VML shapes and gradients

Some of my favorite Web pages contain nothing but text. When I've been up all night long and I just can't get to sleep, I cruise over to them. They download quickly, and as I read page after page of text describing the latest in lawyer fashions, my head nods to the keyboard. Nothing beats a good nap.

In this chapter, you find out about two Microsoft Internet Explorer components that can take away the snoozes by adding graphics to your Web pages: the structured graphics control and VML.

Netscape Navigator does not support any of the techniques described in this chapter.

Web Graphics 101

You can have two basic types of Web graphics: good graphics and bad graphics. Just kidding. The two categories of Web graphics are raster graphics and vector graphics. *Raster graphics,* more commonly known as *bitmaps,* are the types of images that are used in almost every Web page today. JPEG, GIF,

BMP, and PCX files are all examples of raster graphics. Raster graphics store the value of every dot that needs to appear in an image. If you have a 200 x 200 pixel image, the raster graphic stores a value for each of the 40,000 pixels. For example, the file contains information saying, "The pixel at (20,13) has color value #330058. The pixel at (20,14) has color value #330059."

The pixels that make up an image are determined by the program that created the image. The program could be a drawing or image-manipulation product, such as Photoshop, or a rendering product, such as TrueSpace 3.0. The application that's displaying the graphic (for example, Internet Explorer 5.0) simply takes this precomputed image and pops it on the screen. No thinking is required.

By contrast, *vector graphics* don't tell the computer what values go where. Instead, they tell the computer the commands to use to draw the image. For example, a vector graphic may say, "Draw a green rectangle at coordinate (100,100) that is 50 pixels wide and 20 pixels high." The application displaying the graphic reads these commands and then executes them. So it needs to do some computing.

Which is better? It depends on what you're doing. Vector graphics are often smaller to download and are more flexible than raster images. After all, it doesn't take much to say, "Draw a rectangle that is 400 pixels wide and 400 pixels high. Put a green circle on top of that." On the other hand, reading out the colors for every pixel in a 400 x 400 image takes a great deal of download time.

Vector graphics are *resolution independent*. In other words, they contain the complete description of the commands that are needed to draw an image. That image could be redrawn into a 10 x 10 pixel area or into a 1,000 x 1,000 pixel area. Both take the same amount of information. Because the actual commands needed to draw the object are stored, the object looks good at any size. If you've ever zoomed in really closely on a bitmap, you can see all the individual dots that make it up. That's what happens when you zoom a raster image on a Web page. It becomes blocky, and all the lines get jagged. By contrast, the lines for vector graphics are always smooth. You can shrink them, enlarge them, and twist them, and they always show up looking perfect.

Images such as corporate logos and symbols, office clip art, and stylized graphic design work are easily represented as vector graphics. In fact, such artwork is typically created with products such as Freehand, Illustrator, or PowerPoint; all of these programs are designed to create vector-based art. You know you're looking at an image that works well as a vector graphic if you can say, "A-ha! Mickey's ear is a filled circle, as are his eyes. His mouth is a curve, and his nose is a filled curve."

On the other hand, photorealistic images, such as photographs of people, nature, or a rendered alien landscape, are hard to represent as vector graphics. Such images usually don't have large patterns of geometric shapes. Rather, each dot in the image tends to be a little different from the dot next to it. Representing such images as vector graphics would probably require a different command for each pixel. That's even less efficient than storing the value for each pixel.

Raster images store the color value of every pixel in the image. This type of file gets large quickly. For example, each pixel typically needs four bytes to store the color value. So a 200 x 200 image chews up 160,000 bytes — a file size that takes a while to send on a 28.8 Kbps modem. That's why most raster images are compressed. The most common compression schemes for the Web are GIF, JPEG, and PNG. GIF images store 256 color images; its compression is reasonable and *lossless,* which means that the uncompressed image looks exactly like the original. JPEG and PNG images store 16.7 million color graphics. They use extremely sophisticated compression techniques that compress images to their bare essentials. Like GIF files, PNG is lossless. By contrast, JPEG is *lossy* — images always look a little different when they are compressed. If you crank the JPEG compression factors way up, in fact, you end up with very blocky pictures.

So, use vector images when you want to rotate or scale the image on the fly and when the images look like graphic design work. Use raster images to display images that look like photographs.

If you're using a raster image that, with a bit of cleanup, could easily be represented through vector graphics, definitely consider making the switch. The resulting image should take far less time to download. (***Note:*** Internet Explorer 5.0 supports three vector graphics formats natively: the structured graphics control format introduced in Internet Explorer 4.0, the Windows Metafile Format, and VML. Macromedia's Flash is another common vector graphics engine, and it has a playback control for Internet Explorer and Navigator.) This topic brings up Mike's Web Authoring Rule No. 5:

Rule No. 5: Size matters.

In other words, use whatever capabilities you can to decrease download time. Where applicable, use effects and transitions instead of rendered images and animated GIF files. For non photographic images, use vector graphics instead of raster graphics. These techniques help reduce download time and thus increase the responsiveness of your page. Note that none of these techniques are mutually exclusive. You can mix and match them however you need.

Microsoft has built into its Web browser two different controls for creating vector graphics. Internet Explorer 4.0 and 5.0 contain a powerful control for displaying vector graphics on a page: the structured graphics control. Internet Explorer 5.0 introduces another approach, called *VML* (Vector Markup Language). The VML control interprets, believe it or not, VML, which is a new Web standard for describing vector graphics. Having two control options, of course, brings up the question of the day: Which should you use? Well, if you need your graphics to work with Internet Explorer 4.0 and Internet Explorer 5.0, you should go for the structured graphics control. If you're focused on Internet Explorer 5.0 or you want to use the upcoming standard, use the VML control. Furthermore, you stand a good chance of soon having a variety of tools that can output graphics in VML format.

In this chapter, I show you a little bit about both approaches. I start with the older approach and show you how to create a variety of pictures with the structured graphics control. Then I show you how to use VML.

Using the Structured Graphics Control

The *structured graphics control* lets you describe an image to draw by passing in commands via the <PARAM> tags. It's like having a built-in, ultra-powerful Etch-A-Sketch. To use the structured graphics control, follow these steps:

1. **Figure out where on the page you want the graphics to appear.**

2. **Add a structured graphics control to the page, giving it the desired location and size.**

3. **Pass the drawing commands through the** <PARAM> **tags.**

The following is the HTML code to use to add the structured graphics control to your page:

```
<OBJECT style="height:200; width:200"
CLASSID = "CLSID:369303C2-D7AC-11D0-89D5-00A0C90833E6">
</OBJECT>
```

That looks boring. And, in fact, if you add that code to a page, nothing shows up. To get the good stuff, you need to add <PARAM> tags to tell the structured graphics control what to draw. The basic format for these tags is as follows:

```
<PARAM NAME="LineXXXX" VALUE="command">
```

You tell the control what to draw, one item at a time. Each item that you want to draw needs its own line number. So the first shape drawn is Line0001. The second shape drawn is Line0002. The following is an example that draws two ovals on the screen:

```
<PARAM NAME="Line0001" VALUE="Oval(-100,-100,200,200)">
<PARAM NAME="Line0002" VALUE="Oval(0,0,20,20)">
```

How do you know that two ovals are going to be drawn? Because two Oval commands are used. You can use a wide selection of commands to draw everything from ovals to rectangles to text and splines. You can also choose colors, fonts, and fill styles for what you draw.

Rather than go through every possible command now (although I do that very shortly), I describe just a few of the commands so that you can create a page that displays vector graphics.

You just saw the Oval command. Its syntax is as follows:

```
Oval(left, top, width, height, initialRotation)
```

Notice that, except for the initialRotation parameter, the format is exactly the same as the Oval command that you used with the path control. The oval is drawn within the area from the coordinate specified with the left and top values, with the specified width and height. Figure 11-1 shows you how the oval appears.

Figure 11-1:
The oval touches the sides of the rectangle that starts at the speci-fied corner and has the specified width and height.

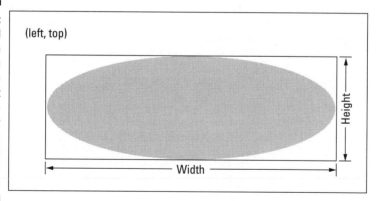

The other parameter is initialRotation. It lets you rotate the oval, as shown in Figure 11-2.

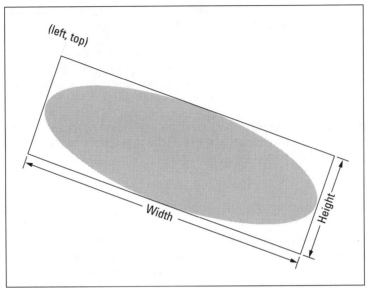

(left, top)

Width

Height

Figure 11-2:
The oval is
rotated.

Another drawing command is `Pie`. This command draws wedge shapes, much like a piece of pie. The command is very similar to `Oval`. However, instead of drawing the complete oval, you can specify where along the oval the wedge begins and how wide the wedge is. You do so by specifying the `startAngle` and `arcAngle` parameters, as follows:

```
Pie(left, top, width, height, startAngle, arcAngle, initialRotation)
```

The angle measurements start with 0 degrees, which is at the three o'clock position. Then the angle measurements proceed counterclockwise. So 90 degrees is at the top of the oval, and 180 degrees is at the left side (nine o'clock position) of the oval. You can see the angle measurements illustrated in Figure 11-3.

You can draw as many objects as you want inside a structured graphics control. Simply figure out where you want them to appear, fill in the appropriate parameters, and draw the objects.

The only tricky thing is figuring out where you want the objects to appear. To do so, you need to understand the structured graphics coordinate system. The center of the control is point (0,0) — the origin. So if you draw an object with its left corner at (0,0), the left corner shows up in the middle of the control. The x-axis increases going right, and the y-axis increases going down, as shown in Figure 11-4.

Figure 11-3:
Drawing a
wedge
using the
Pie com-
mand. The
startAngle
and arc-
Angle
parameters
specify
what the pie
shape looks
like.

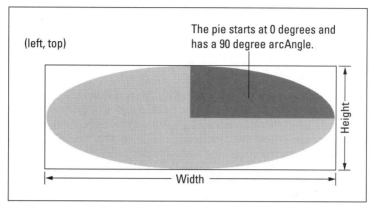

Figure 11-3:
Drawing a wedge using the Pie command. The startAngle and arcAngle parameters specify what the pie shape looks like.

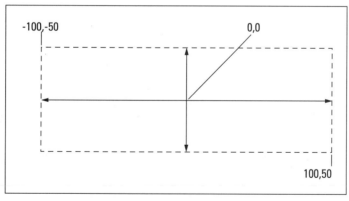

Figure 11-4:
The coordinate system for a control that is 200 pixels wide and 100 pixels high. Point (0,0) is at the center of the control. The x-axis increases going to the right, and the y axis increases going down.

At this point, you may scratch your head and wonder why the coordinate system is the way it is. After all, the HTML page has (0,0) in the upper-left corner but otherwise is the same. A Cartesian coordinate system has (0,0) in the center, but the y-axis values increase going up. It seems as if the coordinate system is a mix of the two — in fact, it is. Placing (0,0) at the center of the control means that if you rotate the control (which you read about later in this chapter), the rotation occurs around the center of the control. That's typically what you want to do when rotating an object. The *y* coordinates increase going toward the bottom of the page because that's the way HTML works.

So although getting used to the coordinate system may be a bit awkward, the system actually makes it much easier to create objects that get rotated.

The objects that are drawn by the graphics commands all have a *line color* — the color that's used for the border of the object — and a *fill color* — the color that's used for the inside of the object. So the oval has its border drawn with the border color, and the inside is drawn with the fill color. You can set these colors with the following commands:

```
SetLineColor(r,g,b)
SetFillColor(r,g,b)
```

In this example, *r, g,* and *b* specify the amount of red, green, and blue for the color. Each value can range from 0 to 255. Therefore, (0,255,0) is bright green, and (128,128,128) is a medium gray.

Now you have enough information to create some simple vector graphics. In fact, you know everything that's necessary to create a radiation symbol. This skill may become very useful if you spend far too much time in front of your computer monitor. The radiation symbol is a big black circle that's filled with three yellow wedges. (Or you can think of it as three black wedges and three yellow wedges.)

You can draw a radiation symbol in a control that is 200 pixels wide and 200 pixels high by using the following code:

```
<OBJECT style="height:200; width:200"
CLASSID = "CLSID:369303C2-D7AC-11D0-89D5-00A0C90833E6">
```

First, draw a black oval for the background. To do so, set the fill color to black, as follows:

```
<PARAM NAME="Line0001" VALUE="SetFillColor(0, 0, 0)">
```

Then draw the oval. You want the oval to fill the entire control. Because the control is 200 pixels wide and 200 pixels high, you thus set its height and width to be 200. (By the way, an oval with the same width and height is a circle.) But where do you put the left and top? The center of the control is at (0,0) — you want the center of the oval to be there. Because the oval is 200 pixels wide, the left position needs to be at –100. (Why? The center of the oval is 100 pixels away from the left, because the width is 200. If the center is at (0,0), then 100 pixels to the left is –100.) Likewise, the top value needs to be –100. The following is the HTML code:

```
<PARAM NAME="Line0002" VALUE="Oval(-100,-100,200,200)">
```

To center an object that is specified with left, top, width, and height parameters, set the left parameter to –width/2 and the top parameter to –height/2. If you want the center to appear at (x, y), set the left parameter to x – width/2 and the top parameter to y – height/2.

Now that you have a black circle on the screen, you need to add the yellow wedges. That's easy. First, set the fill color to yellow, as follows:

```
<PARAM NAME="Line0003" VALUE="SetFillColor(255, 255, 0)">
```

Now you can create the three yellow pie-shaped objects. Because the circle is made up of three yellow pies and three blank pies, for a total of six pies, and the whole circle is 360 degrees, each pie needs to be 60 degrees wide. Start the first pie at 0 degrees. It is to extend 60 degrees. You can then skip 60 degrees for the black wedge. (After all, if nothing is drawn, you see the black from the oval underneath.) The next pie starts at 120 degrees and extends 60 degrees. The final yellow pie starts at 240 degrees and extends 60 degrees. The following is the HTML code:

```
<PARAM NAME="Line0004" VALUE="Pie(-95,-95,190,190, 0, 60, 0)">
<PARAM NAME="Line0005" VALUE="Pie(-95,-95,190,190, 120, 60, 0)">
<PARAM NAME="Line0006" VALUE="Pie(-95,-95,190,190, 240, 60, 0)">
```

That's it! You've now drawn a radiation symbol, as you can see in Figure 11-5. To check out the page in action, load sg1.html from the ch11 folder on the enclosed CD-ROM (see Listing 11-1).

Figure 11-5:
You draw the radiation symbol using the structured graphics control.

Listing 11-1	The sg1.html Source Code

```
<HTML>
<BODY>
<OBJECT style="height:200; width:200"
CLASSID = "CLSID:369303C2-D7AC-11D0-89D5-00A0C90833E6">
    <PARAM NAME="Line0001" VALUE="SetFillColor(0, 0, 0)">
    <PARAM NAME="Line0002" VALUE="Oval(-100,-00,200,200)">
    <PARAM NAME="Line0003" VALUE="SetFillColor(255, 255, 0)">
    <PARAM NAME="Line0004" VALUE="Pie(-95,-95,190,190, 0, 60, 0)">
    <PARAM NAME="Line0005" VALUE="Pie(-95,-95,190,190, 120, 60, 0)">
    <PARAM NAME="Line0006" VALUE="Pie(-95,-95,190,190, 240, 60, 0)">
</OBJECT>
<DIV style="position:absolute; left: 220; height: 300; width:40%; color:red;
font-size:40pt">Danger! Alien surfers were here.
</DIV>
</BODY>
</HTML>
```

Be careful when you type the line numbers for the structured graphics commands. They are read sequentially starting with Line0001. The control stops as soon as it can't find an item with the next expected line number. So if you have Line0001 and Line0003 but no Line0002, the control only reads Line0001. It looks for Line0002, doesn't find it, and stops. Thus, Line0003 and any subsequent lines are never read. Also, be careful when you cut and paste lines. If you have two lines with the same number, only the first is read. So be sure to renumber the lines after pasting.

All the commands that are fit to draw

After you get a taste of using the structured graphics control, it's time to discover the full breadth of the drawing capabilities that it provides. You can see the entire list of drawing commands in Table 11-1.

Table 11-1	The Structured Graphics Control Drawing Commands	
Command	**Usage**	**Sample**
Arc(*left*, *top*, *width*, *height*, *startAngle*, *arcAngle*, *rotation*)	Draws an arc from the *startAngle*, having *arcAngle* size. The arc is a section of the oval that is formed by the bounding box established by the *left*, *top*, *width*, and *height* parameters. An arc is very similar to a pie, except that only the curved part — not the wedge— is drawn, and it is not filled.	`<PARAM NAME= "Line0001" VALUE="Arc (-100,-100,200, 200,0,60,0)">`
Oval(*left*, *top*, *width*, *height*, *rotation*)	Draws an oval based on the area established by the *left*, *top*, *width*, and *height* parameters. Ovals are filled.	`<PARAM NAME= "Line0001"VALUE= "Oval 200,(-100, -100,200,0)">`

Command	Usage	Sample
Pie(x, y, width, height, startAngle, arcAngle, rotation)	Draws a wedge starting at _startAngle_ and ending at _startAngle+arcAngle_. This is a filled subsection of an oval.	`<PARAM NAME= "Line0001" VALUE="Oval (-100,-100, 200,200,0, 60,0)">`
Polygon(n, x@, y@ [..., xₙ, yₙ], rotation)	Creates a polygon that is formed by connecting the _n_ points specified. The last point is connected to the first, and the polygon is closed. Polygons are filled.	`<PARAM NAME= "Line0001" VALUE="Polygon (3,-100,-100, 0,100,100, -100,0)">`
PolyLine(n, x₁, y₁ [..., xₙ, yₙ], rotation)	Creates a line that is formed by connecting the _n_ points specified. Unlike a polygon, the last point is not connected to the first, and the object is not filled.	`<PARAM NAME= "Line0001" VALUE ="PolyLine (3,-100,-100, 0, 100,100,-100,0)">`
Rect(_left, top, width, height, rotation_)	Draws a rectangle with an upper-left corner at (_left, top_) and having the specified _width_ and _height_. Rectangles are filled.	`<PARAM NAME= "Line0001" VALUE="Rect (-100,-100, 200,200,0)">`
RoundRect(_left, top, width, height, arcWidth, arcHeight, rotation_)	Draws a rounded rectangle with an upper-left corner at (_left, top_) and having the specified _width_ and _height_. The corners of the rectangle are rounded by creating a quarter of an oval with the specified _arcWidth_ and _arcHeight_. Rounded rectangles are filled.	`<PARAM NAME= "Line0001" VALUE="RoundRect (-100,-100,200, 200,20,30,0)">`
SetFillColor (_r, g, b_ [, _r2, g2, b2_])	Sets the color that is used to fill in objects. The second set of color values set the background color, which is used with text and gradients. The _r_, _g_, and _b_ values range from 0 to 255.	`<PARAM NAME= "Line0001" VALUE="SetFill Color(255,0, 128)">`
SetFillStyle(_style_)	Defines how objects are to be filled. The _style_ parameter can be one of the following: 0 Null 1 Solid	`<PARAM NAME= "Line0001" VALUE="SetFill Style(11)">`

(continued)

Table 11-1 *(continued)*

Command	Usage	Sample
	3 Hatch horizontal	
	4 Hatch vertical	
	5 Hatch forward diagonal	
	6 Hatch backward diagonal	
	7 Hatch cross	
	8 Hatch diagonal cross	
	9 Horizontal gradient	
	10 Vertical gradient	
	11 Radial gradient	
	12 Line gradient	
	13 Rectangular gradient	
	14 Shaped gradient	
SetFont(*family, height, weight, italic, underline, strikethrough*)	Sets the font to use for text. The parameters are very similar to those that are used with style sheets. Set *family* to the font that you want to use, such as Arial. The *height* parameter indicates the size of the font, using the same coordinates as the structured graphics control. The *weight* parameter ranges from 0 to 700, where 300 is normal and 700 is extra bold. Set *italic*, *underline*, and *strikethrough* to 1 to choose those particular font styles.	`<PARAM NAME= "Line0001" VALUE="SetFont (Arial,40,500, 0,0,0)">`
SetGradientFill(*startX, startY, endX, endY, strength*)	Sets the region that is used for a gradient fill. The start point is set to the foreground color, and the end point is set to the background color. The gradient then smoothly goes between the two colors. The *strength* value varies the appearance of the gradient.	`<PARAM NAME= "Line0001" VALUE="Set GradientFill (-100,-100, 100,100,1)">`
SetHatchFill (*transparent*)	Determines whether a hatch fill is transparent. Set the value to 0 to make the fill transparent.	`<PARAM NAME= "Line0001" VALUE="Set HatchFill(0)">`

Command	Usage	Sample
SetLineColor(*r, g, b*)	Sets the color that is used to draw lines and the outlines of objects. The *r, g,* and *b* values range from 0 to 255.	```<PARAM NAME= "Line0001" VALUE="SetLine Color(255,0, 128)">```
SetLineStyle (*style = [,linewidth]*)	Defines how lines and shape outlines are drawn. The *linewidth* parameter sets how many pixels wide the line should be. The default is 1. The *style* parameter can be one of the following: 0 Not drawn 1 Solid 2 Dash	```<PARAM NAME "Line0001" VALUE="SetLine Style(1)">```
SetGradientShape (*n, x1, y1 [..., x_n, y_n]*)	Defines the polygon that is used when the fill style is 14 (shaped gradient).	```<PARAM NAME= "Line0001" VALUE="Set GradientShape (3,100,100,0, 100,100,-100, 0)">```
Text (*'string', x, y, rotation*)	Draws text. The lower-left corner of the text is placed at the *x, y* location that is specified. Unlike all other objects, where the rotation is about the object center, the rotation is about the lower-left corner of the text.	```<PARAM NAME= "Line0001" VALUE="Text ('Hello Mom', 3,-100,0)">```

You can create rich illustrations with the structured graphics control. For example, take a look at sg2.html from the ch11 folder (see Listing 11-2). It incorporates the radiation symbol as well as a logo. The logo uses a triangle for the letter *A*, followed by the letters *LIEN SURF PATROL*. The logo is filled with a green gradient, and two red lines appear over the top of the letters, as shown in Figure 11-6.

Figure 11-6:
This page uses two structured graphics controls. Note the gradient that's used for the Alien Surf Patrol logo.

Listing 11-2   **The sg2.html Source Code**

```
<HTML>
<BODY>
<OBJECT style="height:200; width:200"
CLASSID = "CLSID:369303C2-D7AC-11D0-89D5-00A0C90833E6">
    <PARAM NAME="Line0001" VALUE="SetFillColor(0, 0, 0)">
    <PARAM NAME="Line0002" VALUE="Oval(-100,-100,200,200)">
    <PARAM NAME="Line0003" VALUE="SetFillColor(255, 255, 0)">
    <PARAM NAME="Line0004" VALUE="Pie(-95,-95,190,190, 0, 60, 0)">
    <PARAM NAME="Line0005" VALUE="Pie(-95,-95,190,190, 120, 60, 0)">
    <PARAM NAME="Line0006" VALUE="Pie(-95,-95,190,190, 240, 60, 0)">
</OBJECT>
<OBJECT style="height:55; width:400"
CLASSID = "CLSID:369303C2-D7AC-11D0-89D5-00A0C90833E6">
    <PARAM NAME="Line0001" VALUE="SetFillStyle(13)">
    <PARAM NAME="Line0002" VALUE="SetLineStyle(0)">
    <PARAM NAME="Line0003" VALUE="SetFillColor(0, 255, 30, 0, 0)">
    <PARAM NAME="Line0004" VALUE="SetGradientFill(-200, -25, 200, 25, 1)">
    <PARAM NAME="Line0005" VALUE="Polygon(3, -200, 25, -175, -25, -150, 25)">
    <PARAM NAME="Line0006" VALUE="SetFont('Impact', 50, 500, 0, 0, 0)">
    <PARAM NAME="Line0007" VALUE="Text('LIEN SURF PATROL', -150, 25)">
    <PARAM NAME="Line0008" VALUE="SetLineStyle(1)">
    <PARAM NAME="Line0009" VALUE="SetLineColor(255,0,0)">
    <PARAM NAME="Line0010" VALUE="PolyLine(2, 0, 0, 140, 0)">
    <PARAM NAME="Line0011" VALUE="PolyLine(2, -50, 15, 135, 15)">
</OBJECT>
</BODY>
</HTML>
```

If a gradient-filled object touches the border of the structured graphics control, you see a dark line at the border. You can work around this bug by making the structured graphics control large enough that the object filled with the gradient doesn't cross the border. For example, the second structured graphics control in sg2.html is 55 pixels high, so the gradient-filled text doesn't hit the border of the control.

You can see the commands that are used to draw the logo by looking through the <PARAM> tags for the second object on the page. For example, the following commands draw the red lines:

```
<PARAM NAME="Line0008" VALUE="SetLineStyle(1)">
<PARAM NAME="Line0009" VALUE="SetLineColor(255,0,0)">
<PARAM NAME="Line0010" VALUE="PolyLine(2, 0, 0, 140, 0)">
<PARAM NAME="Line0011" VALUE="PolyLine(2, -50, 15, 135, 15)">
```

This code sets the line style to solid and the color to red, and it draws two lines.

Creating the gradient, on the other hand, is a little trickier. (In case you are wondering, a *gradient* is a smooth change from one color to another. For example, a summer sky fades from a deep blue to a pale blue as it moves toward the horizon.) Follow these steps to fill shapes with gradients:

1. **Set the fill style to one of the gradient fill types (9, 10, 11, 12, 13, or 14).**

2. **Set the foreground and background color by supplying two colors to** SetFillColor**.**

3. **Use** SetGradientFill **to indicate which point should start with the foreground color and which point is to start with the background color.**

   Gradients blend from the foreground color to the background color. The gradient blends colors starting with these two points. For example, suppose that the foreground color is green and the background color is red. You would indicate that (0,0) should be green and (100,30) should be red. All other points blend smoothly between these two.

4. **Draw shapes.**

   They are now painted with a gradient rather than a solid color.

Looking at the second object in sg2.html, you can see the following lines of code. They set up a gradient that fills a polygon and some text.

```
<PARAM NAME="Line0001" VALUE="SetFillStyle(13)">
<PARAM NAME="Line0002" VALUE="SetLineStyle(0)">
<PARAM NAME="Line0003" VALUE="SetFillColor(0, 255, 30, 0, 0, 0)">
<PARAM NAME="Line0004" VALUE="SetGradientFill(-200, -25, 200, 25, 1)">
<PARAM NAME="Line0005" VALUE="Polygon(3, -200, 25, -175, -25, -150, 25)">
<PARAM NAME="Line0006" VALUE="SetFont('Impact', 50, 500, 0, 0, 0)">
<PARAM NAME="Line0007" VALUE="Text('LIEN SURF PATROL', -150, 25)">
```

Is Notepad your favorite paint program?

The structured graphics control provides a powerful, easy-to-read, textual representation of an image. There's only one problem. Most people have a hard time thinking of images in terms of coordinates of fundamental shapes. Drawing a picture using a drawing program is much easier. Many drawing programs, such as PowerPoint, Freehand, and Illustrator, support vector graphics. Using these tools, you can easily draw pictures. Fortunately, Microsoft provides a tool to convert vector files that were created with these packages. You simply save images in the WMF format. (This acronym stands for Windows Metafile Format, not something that you'd see in a personal ad.) You can then use the metafile converter to turn the picture into the structured graphics control's textual representation. Note, however, that depending upon the drawing package that you use, some simple shapes may end up generating huge structured graphics data. This especially happens if your drawings include gradients. You can find the metafile converter in the Microsoft Internet SDK (Software Development Kit), which you can find by going to Microsoft's home page at www.microsoft.com.

The sg2.html file is very small, yet it adds rich graphics to a page. You can find far more interesting vector graphics by looking through vector clip art libraries, such as those shipped with Microsoft Office.

Twist and shout

When you place a GIF or JPEG file on a page, it just stays there. You can move its position on the screen and you can resize it, but that's about it. Structured graphics, on the other hand, have much more flexibility. You can resize them without loss of detail. (When you zoom in on an image, by contrast, it gets very blocky, and eventually you can see big rectangles for the individual pixels.) You can rotate them around the *x, y,* and *z*-axes. And, of course, you can move them around as well. These capabilities let you create very cool animations. For example, you can spin the radiation sign or flip the company logo around.

The structured graphics control has a wide variety of methods that you can use to change its appearance. These methods are shown in Table 11-2. Later in this section, you use the `rotate` and `scale` methods to manipulate a structured graphics control.

Table 11-2	Structured Graphics Control Manipulation Methods	
Method	*Use*	*Sample*
Clear	Clears all graphics that are in the control and resets the line colors, fill styles, and so on to the defaults. This method is typically used in conjunction with the script interfaces.	`Sg1.Clear();`
Rotate(*x, y, z*)	Rotates the structured graphic control about the (0,0) point. You can also rotate about the *x, y,* and *z*-axes. Rotation angles are specified in degrees.	`Sg1.Rotate` `(30,0,15);`
Scale(*x, y, z*)	Zooms or shrinks the structured graphic elements by the specified amount. Note that this change doesn't affect the size of the control. Instead, it changes the size of the graphics that are displayed inside the control. For example, setting the *x* value to 2 doubles the width of the graphics. You can set the *z* value, but it is ignored by default.	`Sg1.Scale` `(2,0,0);`
SetIdentity	Resets the control to its initial scale, rotation, and translation. It is similar to `Clear`, but the graphics in the control are not cleared. This method is typically called to get the control back to a known (that is, initial) state after a series of modifications.	`Sg1.Set` `Identity();`

Transform 4 x 4 (*array[16]*)	This hard-core nerd method lets you pass in a 4 x 4 transformation matrix to use for manipulating the graphic elements. If you've taken enough computer graphics classes to know how to set up a 4 x 4 transform matrix, you can use this method to control manipulations and to get effects such as pinches and shears. If you don't know how to set up one of these matrixes, you can just pass in random values and watch the graphics turn freaky.	`Sg1.Transform`
		`4x4(new Array`
		`(1,0,0,0,0,`
		`2,0,0,1.2,1.2,`
		`1.2,1,1,1,`
		`1,1));`

Translate(*x, y, z*)	Shifts the position of the graphic within the control. This method doesn't move the control itself but instead moves the structured graphic image that's visible within the control.	`Sg1.Translate` `(-20,10,0);`

Sit on it and scale

By manipulating structured graphics, you can zoom in and zoom out of a picture, and you can rapidly rotate the picture in any direction based on events. These capabilities let you create cool-looking pages without having to download large animated GIF files. You can achieve many different types of effects, including the following:

- Have an image appear to fly toward the user by starting it very small and repeatedly scaling it until it fills the screen
- Have an image disappear by starting it large and repeatedly scaling it smaller
- Have an image tumble away by rotating it while scaling it smaller
- Have an image move across the screen, flip, and move back by translating it and then rotating it 180 degrees when it hits the side of the screen
- Spin an object when the user moves the mouse pointer over it

You can use some of these techniques to make your structured graphics livelier. In particular, you can begin with the radiation sign being very small and have it zoom into the screen and start rotating around the z axis. You can also rotate the logo around the y-axis, making it look like 3-D text.

1. **When the page loads, first shrink the radiation sign to 10 percent of its original size, using the following script:**

   ```
   rad.Scale(.1,.1,.1);
   ```

2. **Every tenth of a second, increase the size of the radiation sign by executing the following script:**

   ```
   rad.Scale(1.1, 1.1, 1.1);
   ```

3. **Finally, rotate the sign every tenth of a second, starting 1.2 seconds after the page loads. Keep the sign rotating until the user leaves the page. The following sequencer line sets up this rotation:**

   ```
   seq.Item("sg").at(1.2, "rotate(rad,0,0,6)", -1, .1);
   ```

   The `rotate` function calls the `rotate` method on the object that's passed in. In this case, it rotates the radiation symbol (`rad`) by six degrees around the z-axis.

For fun, you can also rotate the text. This time, start rotating it around the y-axis five seconds after the page loads. The following sequencer line sets up the text rotation:

```
seq.Item("sg").at(5, "rotate(logo,0,12,0)", 30, .15);
```

Note that you rotate the text 30 times. Each time, it rotates 12 degrees. Thus, at the end of the rotation it has rotated 360 degrees — back to where it started.

You can see this script in action by loading sg3.html from the ch11 folder (see Listing 11-3). Figure 11-7 shows the radiation sign and the rotating logo.

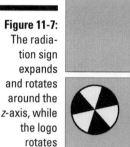
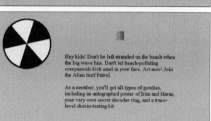

Figure 11-7: The radiation sign expands and rotates around the *z*-axis, while the logo rotates around the *y*-axis.

Listing 11-3	The sg3.html Source Code

```
<HTML>
<HEAD>
<SCRIPT FOR="seq" EVENT="oninit">
    seq.Item("sg").at(0, "scale()", 23, .1);
    seq.Item("sg").at(1.2, "rotate(rad,0,0,6)", -1, .1);
    seq.Item("sg").at(5, "rotate(logo,0,12,0)", 30, .15);
</SCRIPT>
<SCRIPT LANGUAGE="JScript">
function scale() {
    rad.Scale(1.1, 1.1, 1.1);
}
function rotate(which, x, y, z) {
    which.Rotate(x,y,z);
}
function start() {
    rad.Scale(.1,.1,.1);
    seq.Item("sg").Play();
}
</SCRIPT>
</HEAD>
<BODY bgcolor=silver onload="start()">
<OBJECT id=rad style="height:200; width:200"
CLASSID = "CLSID:369303C2-D7AC-11D0-89D5-00A0C90833E6">
    <PARAM NAME="Line0001" VALUE="SetFillColor(0, 0, 0)">
    <PARAM NAME="Line0002" VALUE="Oval(-100,-100,200,200)">
    <PARAM NAME="Line0003" VALUE="SetFillColor(255, 255, 0)">
    <PARAM NAME="Line0004" VALUE="Pie(-95,-95,190,190, 0, 60, 0)">
```

(continued)

Listing 11-3 (continued)

```
        <PARAM NAME="Line0005" VALUE="Pie(-95,-95,190,190, 120, 60, 0)">
        <PARAM NAME="Line0006" VALUE="Pie(-95,-95,190,190, 240, 60, 0)">
</OBJECT>
<OBJECT id=logo style="position:absolute; left: 250; top: 50; height:55; width:400"
CLSID = "CLSID:369303C2-D7AC-11D0-89D5-00A0C90833E6">
    <PARAM NAME="Line0001" VALUE="SetFillStyle(13)">
    <PARAM NAME="Line0002" VALUE="SetLineStyle(0)">
    <PARAM NAME="Line0003" VALUE="SetFillColor(0, 255, 30, 0, 0, 0)">
    <PARAM NAME="Line0004" VALUE="SetGradientFill(-200, -25, 200, 25, 1)">
    <PARAM NAME="Line0005" VALUE="Polygon(3, -200, 25, -175, -25, -150, 25)">
    <PARAM NAME="Line0006" VALUE="SetFont('Impact', 50, 500, 0, 0, 0)">
    <PARAM NAME="Line0007" VALUE="Text('LIEN SURF PATROL', -150, 25)">
    <PARAM NAME="Line0008" VALUE="SetLineStyle(1)">
    <PARAM NAME="Line0009" VALUE="SetLineColor(255,0,0)">
    <PARAM NAME="Line0010" VALUE="PolyLine(2, 0, 0, 140, 0)">
    <PARAM NAME="Line0011" VALUE="PolyLine(2, -50, 15, 135, 15)">
</OBJECT>
<SPAN style="position:absolute; left: 250; top: 150; width: 400; font-size:20">
Hey kids! Don't be left stranded on the beach when the big wave hits. Don't let beach
            -polluting creepazoids kick sand in your face. Act now! Join the Alien
            Surf Patrol.<BR><BR> As a member, you'll get all types of goodies,
            including an autographed poster of Irim and Haras, your very own
            secret decoder ring, and a trace-level dioxin-testing kit.
</SPAN>
<OBJECT ID="seq"
        CLSID="CLSID:B0A6BAE2-AAF0-11d0-A152-00A0C908DB96">
</OBJECT>
</BODY>
</HTML>
```

HTML code lets you change the size and position of text. The structured graphics control lets you do that and rotate text as well. Doing so creates great logo effects. Spinning around the *z*-axis lets you draw text at any angle. Spinning around the *x* or *y*-axis makes text look 3-D.

When you rotate text, remember that 180 degrees creates a mirror image of the text and 360 degrees returns the text to its original position. Thus, to spin a text through one revolution, you need to spin it so that the number of rotations times the angle for each rotation equals 360.

Reverse commute

You can rotate an object around the *x, y,* or *z*-axes. To rotate an object one way and then rotate it back to its original position, you need to use a trick. If you are only rotating along one axis, you can get back to the original position by rotating the same number of times, but with a negative angle. In other words, suppose that you rotate six degrees around the *z*-axis ten times in a row. You end up rotating the graphic 60 degrees. To get back to where you started, you can rotate ten times by –6 degrees.

This tactic doesn't work, however, when you rotate around more than one axis at a time. For example, suppose that you rotate a graphic with the following line of script:

```
Sgl.Rotate(60, 0, 120);
```

In this case, you are rotating 60 degrees around the *x*-axis and 120 degrees along the *z*-axis. You may think that you could use the following code to get back to where you started:

```
Sgl.Rotate(-60, 0, -120);
```

But guess what? You don't! Here's why. When you rotate around several axes, the control first rotates by the *x* amount, then the *y* amount, and then the *z* amount. So the first command rotates the control by 60 degrees around the *x*-axis and then 120 degrees around the *z*-axis. The second command rotates by –60 degrees around the *x*-axis and –120 degrees around the *z*-axis. You can see the results in Figure 11-8.

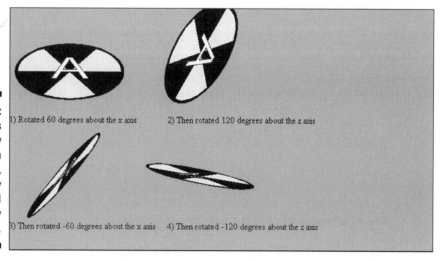

Figure 11-8:
An object is rotated by (60,0,0), then by (0,0,120), then by (-60,0,0), and then by (0,0,-120).

1) Rotated 60 degrees about the x axis   2) Then rotated 120 degrees about the z axis

3) Then rotated -60 degrees about the x axis   4) Then rotated -120 degrees about the z axis

But what you want to do is to rotate along the *x* axis by 60 degrees, then along the *z* axis by 120 degrees, then along the *z* axis by –120 degrees, and then along the *x* axis by –60 degrees. In other words, you want to repeat the initial steps in reverse and use negative angles. You can see these results in Figure 11-9.

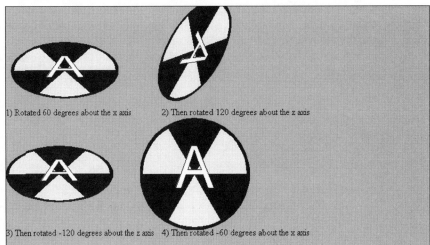

1) Rotated 60 degrees about the x axis
2) Then rotated 120 degrees about the z axis
3) Then rotated -120 degrees about the z axis
4) Then rotated -60 degrees about the x axis

Figure 11-9:
The object
returns to its
original
state.

To see a live page that rotates an object and then returns it to its original
position, check out sg4.html from the ch11 folder.

The page rotates an object by using this script:

```
which.Rotate(x,0,0);
which.Rotate(0,y,0);
which.Rotate(0,0,z);
```

The rotation is reversed by calling the following script:

```
which.Rotate(0,0,-z);
which.Rotate(0,-y,0);
which.Rotate(-x,0,0);
```

Some cool things to try out

In the preceding sections of this chapter, I show you the basics of using the
structured graphics control. In this section, I want to show you some cool
tricks using it. First, I show you how to make 3-D text. I then demonstrate the
power of animating overlapping structured graphics. Finally, I show you how
to use fonts for pictures.

3-D text tricks

I show you how to use structured graphics to rotate text in the "Twist and shout" section earlier in this chapter. This maneuver gives a 3-D feel to text and gives you complete control over how text appears on a page. You can get an interesting effect by repeating some text several times, each time having rotated it a different amount around the y-axis. For example, in Figure 11-10, you can see the word *Surf* repeated four times. It looks as if the text is rotating in 3-D. In fact, it looks like each word is on top of a corner street sign.

Figure 11-10:
The words
look like a
three-
dimensional
road sign.

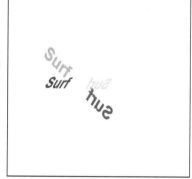

Here's how this effect works. Four structured graphics controls all contain the same text. The first control isn't rotated. The next control is rotated 90 degrees around the y-axis. As a result, it appears to be straight through the page. The next control is rotated 180 degrees, so it is a mirror image of the first control. And the fourth control is rotated 270 degrees, making it a mirror image of the second control. As a result, the text repeats, with two pieces along the x-axis and two pieces along the z-axis. (The text that is rotated 90 and 270 degrees about the y-axis appears to be straight along the z-axis.) Now, when these four controls start out, you don't see the text that is rotated 90 and 270 degrees. But that's okay. Soon you rotate all the controls, and then the spinning of each piece of text gives a strong 3-D look. The following script does the initial rotation:

```
SG1.Rotate(0, 270, 0);
SG2.Rotate(0, 180, 0);
SG3.Rotate(0, 90, 0);
```

After the controls are set up, they are all repeatedly rotated by the same amount, giving them their 3-D look. You can see the full code in Listing 11-4.

Listing 11-4	The spin.html Source Code

```
<HTML>
<HEAD>
<SCRIPT FOR="seq" EVENT="oninit">
    seq.Item("rotate").at(2.000,"rotateIt()", -1, .1);
</SCRIPT>
<SCRIPT>
function rotateIt() {
    SG1.Rotate(2,3,1);
    SG2.Rotate(2,3,1);
    SG3.Rotate(2,3,1);
    SG4.Rotate(2,3,1);
}
function init() {
    SG1.Rotate(0, 270, 0);
    SG2.Rotate(0, 180, 0);
    SG3.Rotate(0, 90, 0);
    seq.Item("rotate").play();
}
</SCRIPT>
</HEAD>
<BODY onload="init()">
<OBJECT id=SG4
STYLE="POSITION:ABSOLUTE; HEIGHT: 195; LEFT: 5%; TOP: 25%; WIDTH: 195; Z-INDEX: 0"
CLASSID = "CLSID:369303C2-D7AC-11D0-89D5-00A0C90833E6">
<PARAM NAME="Line0001" VALUE="SetLineStyle(0)">
<PARAM NAME="Line0002" VALUE="SetFillColor(64, 64, 255)">
<PARAM NAME="Line0003" VALUE="SetFillStyle(1)">
<PARAM NAME="Line0004" VALUE="SetFont('Arial', 40, 700, 0, 0, 0)">
<PARAM NAME="Line0005" VALUE="Text('Surf', -95, 0)">
</OBJECT>
<OBJECT id=SG1
STYLE="POSITION:ABSOLUTE; HEIGHT: 195; LEFT: 5%; TOP: 25%; WIDTH: 195; Z-INDEX: 0"
CLASSID = "CLSID:369303C2-D7AC-11D0-89D5-00A0C90833E6">
<PARAM NAME="Line0001" VALUE="SetLineStyle(0)">
<PARAM NAME="Line0002" VALUE="SetFillColor(0, 255, 255)">
<PARAM NAME="Line0003" VALUE="SetFillStyle(1)">
<PARAM NAME="Line0004" VALUE="SetFont('Arial', 40, 700, 0, 0, 0)">
<PARAM NAME="Line0005" VALUE="Text('Surf', -95, 0)">
</OBJECT>
<OBJECT id=SG3
STYLE="POSITION:ABSOLUTE; HEIGHT: 195; LEFT: 5%; TOP: 25%; WIDTH: 195; Z-INDEX: 1"
CLASSID = "CLSID:369303C2-D7AC-11D0-89D5-00A0C90833E6">
<PARAM NAME="Line0001" VALUE="SetLineStyle(0)">
<PARAM NAME="Line0002" VALUE="SetFillColor(255, 0, 255)">
<PARAM NAME="Line0003" VALUE="SetFillStyle(1)">
<PARAM NAME="Line0004" VALUE="SetFont('Arial', 40, 700, 0, 0, 0)">
<PARAM NAME="Line0005" VALUE="Text('Surf', -95, 0)">
</OBJECT>
<OBJECT id=SG2
STYLE="POSITION:ABSOLUTE; HEIGHT: 195; LEFT: 5%; TOP: 25%; WIDTH: 195; Z-INDEX: 2"
CLASSID = "CLSID:369303C2-D7AC-11D0-89D5-00A0C90833E6">
<PARAM NAME="Line0001" VALUE="SetLineStyle(0)">
<PARAM NAME="Line0002" VALUE="SetFillColor(255, 255, 0)">
<PARAM NAME="Line0003" VALUE="SetFillStyle(1)">
<PARAM NAME="Line0004" VALUE="SetFont('Arial', 40, 700, 0, 0, 0)">
<PARAM NAME="Line0005" VALUE="Text('Surf', -95, 0)">
</OBJECT>
<OBJECT ID="seq"
    CLASSID="CLSID:B0A6BAE2-AAF0-11d0-A152-00A0C908DB96">
</OBJECT>
</BODY>
</HTML>
```

For fun, add four more controls, rotated to 45, 135, 225, and 315 degrees. Also, rotate one control at a time until it hits the next. Then stop it and rotate the control that it just hit, to give a domino-type effect.

Ticking away the moments that make up a dull day

Structured graphics controls are transparent, which means that you can see through any part of the control where graphics aren't drawn. Thus, you can put these controls on top of text and see the text behind them. You can overlap several controls to create animated scenes. For example, you can create an analog clock by creating a clock background out of structured graphics and then putting an hour, minute, and second hand on top. To make the clock tick, you just rotate each of the hands every hour, minute, and second.

Rotating the hands is easy — just call the `rotate` method on each control. Likewise, making them rotate every proscribed time amount is also easy — you simply use the sequencer.

You can see the source code for such a clock in Listing 11-5. The page contains four structured graphics controls and a sequencer. The background of the clock, `rad`, is made from the radiation symbol from the previous example. The `secondHand`, `minuteHand`, and `hourHand` objects are all structured graphics controls that contain a rectangle for the various clock hands.

Listing 11-5	**The clock.html Source Code**

```
<HTML>
<HEAD>
<TITLE>Alien Clock</TITLE>
<SCRIPT FOR="seq" EVENT="oninit">
    //Initialize everything
    var curDate, curSec, curMinute;
    curDate = new Date();
    curSec = curDate.getSeconds();
    curMinute = curDate.getMinutes();
    //Preset the various hands
    secondHand.Rotate(0,0,curSec*6-90);
    minuteHand.Rotate(0,0,curMinute*6-90);
    hourHand.Rotate(0,0,(curDate.getHours()%12)*30-90);
    //Compute starting time for next hand move
    nextMinute = 60 - curSec;
    nextHour = (30 - curMinute%30)*60;
    seq.Item("sg").at(0, "rotate(rad,6)", -1, .1);
    seq.Item("sg").at(0, "rotate(secondHand,6)", -1, 1);
    seq.Item("sg").at(0, "showTime()", -1, 1);
    seq.Item("sg").at(nextMinute, "rotate(minuteHand,6)", -1, 60);
    seq.Item("sg").at(nextHour, "rotate(hourHand,3)", -1, 1800);
```

(continued)

Listing 11-5 *(continued)*

```
</SCRIPT>
<SCRIPT>
var nextMinute, nextHour;
function rotate(which, z) {
    which.Rotate(0,0,z);
}
function showTime() {
    timeArea.innerText = new Date();
}
function start() {
    showTime();
    seq.Item("sg").Play();
}
</SCRIPT>
</HEAD>
<BODY bgcolor=silver onload="start()">
<OBJECT id=rad
CLASSID = "CLSID:369303C2-D7AC-11D0-89D5-00A0C90833E6"
STYLE="position:absolute;left:0; top:0; width:200; height:200">
    <PARAM NAME="Line0001" VALUE="SetFillColor(0, 0, 0)">
    <PARAM NAME="Line0002" VALUE="Oval(-100,-100,200,200)">
    <PARAM NAME="Line0003" VALUE="SetFillColor(255, 255, 0)">
    <PARAM NAME="Line0004" VALUE="Pie(-95,-95,190,190, 0, 60, 0)">
    <PARAM NAME="Line0005" VALUE="Pie(-95,-95,190,190, 120, 60, 0)">
    <PARAM NAME="Line0006" VALUE="Pie(-95,-95,190,190, 240, 60, 0)">
</OBJECT>
<OBJECT ID="secondHand"
    CLASSID = "CLSID:369303C2-D7AC-11D0-89D5-00A0C90833E6"
    STYLE="position:absolute;left:0; top:0; width:200; height:200">
    <PARAM NAME="Line0001" VALUE="SetLineStyle(0)">
    <PARAM NAME="Line0002" VALUE="SetFillColor(0,0,255)">
    <PARAM NAME="Line0003" VALUE="SetFillStyle(1)">
    <PARAM NAME="Line0004" VALUE="Rect(-5,-2,100,4,0)">
</OBJECT>
<OBJECT ID="minuteHand"
    CLASSID = "CLSID:369303C2-D7AC-11D0-89D5-00A0C90833E6"
    STYLE="position:absolute;left:0; top:0; width:200; height:200">
    <PARAM NAME="Line0001" VALUE="SetLineStyle(0)">
    <PARAM NAME="Line0002" VALUE="SetFillColor
    (255,0,128)">
    <PARAM NAME="Line0003" VALUE="SetFillStyle(1)">
    <PARAM NAME="Line0004" VALUE="Rect(-5,-3,85,6,0)">
</OBJECT>
<OBJECT ID="hourHand"
    CLASSID = "CLSID:369303C2-D7AC-11D0-89D5-00A0C90833E6"
    STYLE="position:absolute;left:0; top:0; width:200; height:200">
    <PARAM NAME="Line0001" VALUE="SetLineStyle(0)">
    <PARAM NAME="Line0002" VALUE="SetFillColor(0,255,128)">
    <PARAM NAME="Line0003" VALUE="SetFillStyle(1)">
    <PARAM NAME="Line0004" VALUE="Rect(-5,-3,65,6,0)">
</OBJECT>
<SPAN id=timeArea style="position:absolute; left:0; top:210; color:white;
font-size:20">
</SPAN>
<OBJECT ID="seq"
    CLASSID="CLSID:B0A6BAE2-AAF0-11d0-A152-00A0C908DB96">
</OBJECT>
</BODY>
</HTML>
```

The clock ticking is done with the sequencer. The background rotates every tenth of a second. (After all, you would hate for the clock to look boring.) Because a minute contains 60 seconds, you want the second hand to turn 360 degrees in 1 minute. Dividing 360 by 60, you get six degrees per second. Thus, you rotate the second hand by six degrees every second. Likewise, you rotate the minute hand six degrees every minute. The hour hand moves 360 degrees every 12 hours. Thus, it moves 30 degrees every hour — that is, every 3,600 seconds. Rather than wait that long to move it, you can move it 15 degrees every half-hour. For good measure, you can also print the current time beneath the clock every second. The following script sets up all these actions in a sequencer:

```
seq.Item("sg").at(0, "rotate(rad,6)", -1, .1);
seq.Item("sg").at(0, "rotate(secondHand,6)", -1, 1);
seq.Item("sg").at(0, "showTime()", -1, 1);
seq.Item("sg").at(nextMinute, "rotate(minuteHand,6)", -1,
60);
seq.Item("sg").at(nextHour, "rotate(hourHand,15)", -1,
1800);
```

You need to take two other steps to get the clock to work. First, you need to initialize the rotations for the hands. After all, the minute hand may move every minute, but that isn't too interesting if the hand points to 0 minutes after the hour when it is 12:37. This initial rotation is done inside the `oninit` handler, as you can see in the following script:

```
curDate = new Date();
curSec = curDate.getSeconds();
curMinute = curDate.getMinutes();
//Preset the various hands
secondHand.Rotate(0,0,curSec*6-90);
minuteHand.Rotate(0,0,curMinute*6-90);
hourHand.Rotate(0,0,(curDate.getHours()%12)*30-90);
```

One step remains. You need to figure out the first time to move the minute and hour hands. After all, you don't want to move them a minute after the page loads. You want to move them every time the minute (or hour) changes. To do so, I've added some code to offset the start time for the hand movement. The minute hand starts when the second hand next reaches 12:00. The hour hand starts moving at the next half-hour mark. (For example, if the clock page is loaded at 12:37, the hour hand first moves at 1:00, or 23 minutes later.)

The code for aligning hand movements is in the `oninit` handler. The following script computes how many seconds are left until the next minute and how many minutes are left until the next hour:

```
nextMinute = 60 - curSec;
nextHour = (30 - curMinute%30)*60;
```

That's pretty much it. When the page loads, the clock hands move to their starting positions and then regularly update themselves. You can see the clock in action by loading clock.html from the ch11 folder. When the page runs, you see something like what is shown in Figure 11-11.

Figure 11-11:
The clock ticks away while the radiation sign turns into a spinning clock face.

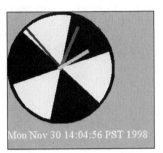

Mon Nov 30 14:04:56 PST 1998

Shamalama WebDings dong

In the early days of the IBM PC, few people had graphics cards. They were hideously expensive, and color monitors were even more expensive. Instead, people used characters to draw images. The PC fonts included some extra characters, such as vertical and horizontal lines, which were made especially for this purpose. Menu drop-down boxes, dialog boxes — complete with shadows — and even charts were all drawn with these characters.

Today, no one uses characters for creating user-interface elements, but they are still very useful for Web graphics. Microsoft provides a special font — WebDings — with Internet Explorer 5.0. This font contains a variety of characters that you can use to spice up your Web pages, including pictures of buildings, no-smoking signs, buses, police cars, hearts, eyes, and much more. For example, if you need an arrowhead (or better yet, an alien head), you can find it in the WebDings font. These special characters are called *glyphs*. Using the glyphs makes much smaller Web pages and saves you a great deal of time in trying to figure out how to draw copyright signs and other symbols. Figure 11-12 shows one of the many glyphs that are available in the WebDings font.

You use the WebDings font several times in Chapter 4 to add an alien head to a page. However, you use it as plain HTML text in those examples. Using the structured graphics control, you can rotate, scale, and fill glyphs. For example, check out sg5.html in the ch11 folder (see Listing 11-6). This page uses the WebDings font and the structured graphics control to create a green alien head that scales and rotates. Unlike HTML text, you can set the color of the outline and the fill, and you can fill the glyphs with gradients and patterns.

Figure 11-12:
This page
is created
with a text
character
from the
WebDings
font.

Listing 11-6	The sg5.html Source Code

```
<HTML>
<HEAD>
<SCRIPT FOR="seq" EVENT="oninit">
    seq.Item("sg").at(0, "scale(logo, 1.1)", 25, .1);
    seq.Item("sg").at(1, "rotate(logo,0,0,6)", 60, .05);
    seq.Item("sg").at(6, "rotate(logo,0,6,0)", 60, .05);
</SCRIPT>
<SCRIPT>
function scale(which, amt) {
    logo.Scale(amt, amt, 1);
}
function rotate(which, x, y, z) {
    which.Rotate(x,y,z);
}
function start() {
    logo.Scale(.1,.1,.1);seq.Item("sg").Play();
}
</SCRIPT>
</HEAD>
<BODY bgcolor=silver onload="start()">
<OBJECT id=logo style="position:absolute; left: 250; top: 0; height:200; width:200"
CLASSID = "CLSID:369303C2-D7AC-11D0-89D5-00A0C90833E6">
    <PARAM NAME="Line0001" VALUE="SetLineStyle(1)">
    <PARAM NAME="Line0002" VALUE="SetLineColor(0, 255, 30)">
    <PARAM NAME="Line0003" VALUE="SetFillColor(0, 128, 30)">
    <PARAM NAME="Line0004" VALUE="SetFont('WebDings', 100, 500, 0, 0, 0)">
    <PARAM NAME="Line0005" VALUE="Text('...', 0, 0)">
</OBJECT>
<OBJECT ID="seq"
    CLASSID="CLSID:B0A6BAE2-AAF0-11d0-A152-00A0C908DB96">
</OBJECT>
</BODY>
</HTML>
```

To use the glyphs, set the font to WebDings and then type any characters that you need. For example, the following lines of script draw an alien head:

```
<PARAM NAME="Line0004" VALUE="SetFont('WebDings', 100, 500, 0, 0, 0)">
<PARAM NAME="Line0005" VALUE="Text('...', 0, 0)">
```

If you want a rotating bicycle, just change Line0005 to the following:

```
<PARAM NAME="Line0005" VALUE="Text('b', 0, 0)">
```

Writing this code is certainly much easier than drawing a bike by hand with the PolyLine and PolySpline commands.

Use the Character Map program to see all the different glyphs in a font. You can find this program in the Accessories menu. Clicking on a character lets you see it zoomed in. Double-clicking on it adds the character to an edit area. You can then copy the characters from the edit area and paste them into your HTML file.

Va-Va-Va-VML

As I mention earlier in this chapter, VML is an upcoming standard for vector graphics. You can find the complete standard documentation for VML on the W3C Web site at www.w3.org/TR/NOTE-VML. (W3C stands for World Wide Web Consortium. It does not stand for Water Closet Water Closet Water Closet. VML stands for Vector Markup Language. Bunches of other markup languages exist, too, such as XML, SGML, and FEFIFOFUML.)

Similarly to the structured graphics control, VML consists of a series of textual commands for describing a graphic design. But unlike the structured graphics control, these commands are incorporated directly into a Web page using custom tags. Thus, they are very tightly integrated with the Web page.

To use VML, you must first incorporate the VML object into your Web page. Note that VML isn't downloaded with every Internet Explorer 5.0 configuration. You can find out whether it is installed, as well as install it, by following these steps:

1. **Go to the Control Panel and double-click on Add/Remove Programs.**

2. **Double-click on Microsoft Internet Explorer 5.0.**

3. **Select Add a Component to Internet Explorer and click OK.**

4. **Scroll down until you see Vector Graphics Rendering (VML). If a checkmark appears in the checkbox, you already have it installed. You can just quit out of the dialog boxes. If not, check the checkbox and continue.**

5. **Click the Next button and follow the directions.**

After you install the VML control, you can use it in your pages. As with the structured graphics control, you need to add an `<OBJECT>` tag to include the control:

```
<object id="VMLRender" classid="CLSID:10072CEC-8CC1-11D1-986E-00A0C955B42E"></object>
```

Next, you need to declare a namespace that all the VML tags can use. Okay, I admit it. I geeked there for a moment. HTML has a certain set of tags that it understands — the tags that I tell you about in the earlier chapters of this book, such as `<P>`, `<DIV>`, and `<SCRIPT>`. But VML also uses a set of tags, such as `rect`, `roundrect`, and `oval`. You need a way to distinguish between these two sets of tags. That's exactly what a namespace does. A *namespace* lets you create a prefix for a tag to say that the tag relates to something particular. For example, to set up a namespace for VML, you write the following code:

```
<xml:namespace ns="urn:schemas-microsoft-com:vml" prefix="v"/>
```

This confusing syntax says that a formal namespace definition called `schemas-microsoft-com:vml` exists and that any time you precede a tag with the letter v, it means that the tag relates to that definition. So, for example, `v:rect` is a tag from the VML space, not an HTML tag.

The namespace declaration is an XML command. You find out a little bit more about XML in Chapter 13. In brief, XML stands for Extensible Markup Language, and it's a cool standard for defining your own tags to represent whatever information you want.

Finally, you need to tell Internet Explorer how to process the VML tags. To do so, you set up a style sheet rule indicating that anything from the VML namespace should be processed by the VML control:

```
<style>
   v\:* { behavior: url(#VMLRender)}
</style>
```

Note here that the v refers to the prefix defined in the `xml:namespace` command, and the `#VMLRender` refers to the `id` of the VML control. You find out more about the behavior keyword in Chapter 12.

After you jump through these hoops, you can incorporate VML commands into your page. One such command is the `oval` command, which draws an oval at the location you specify. You tell it where to show up by using the CSS positioning commands. For example, you could do something such as the following:

```
<v:oval style="width: 2in; height: 2in"/>
```

This command draws a 2 x 2 inch oval on the screen. Note that unlike the structured graphics control, you can use any of the coordinate measurements that CSS allows — very nice, of course.

You can also specify a `fillcolor` attribute to set the color of the object, as shown in the following line:

```
<v:oval style="width: 2in; height: 2in;" fillcolor="blue"/>
```

The `fillcolor` can be one of the HTML colors or a hex value, such as #FF00FF.

To check out this oval, look at Figure 11-13. You can load the example yourself by opening vml1.html from the ch11 folder, and you can check it out by examining Listing 11-7.

Figure 11-13:
An oval drawn with VML.

Listing 11-7	**The vml1.html Source Code**

```
<HTML>
<style>
  v\:* { behavior: url(#VMLRender); position:absolute }
</style>
<BODY>
<xml:namespace ns="urn:schemas-microsoft-com:vml" prefix="v"/>
<object id="VMLRender" codebase="vgx.dll" classid="CLSID:10072CEC-8CC1-11D1-986E-
          00A0C955B42E"></object>
<v:oval style="width: 2in; height: 2in;" fillcolor="blue"/>
</BODY>
</HTML>
```

On the highway to VML

VML contains a number of tags for drawing shapes. I show you the `oval` tag in the preceding section. Other useful tags are `line`, `polyline`, `curve`, `arc`, `rect`, and `roundrect`. For example, the following VML draws a rectangle and a rounded rectangle:

```
<v:rect style="width: 1in; height: 3in; left: 1in; top: 1in" fillcolor="red"/>
<v:roundrect style="width: 1in; height: 1in; left: 2in; top: 2in;" fillcolor="#ff0066"/>
```

You can add further control to the shapes by specifying the *strokecolor* (the color of the shape's outline) and the *strokeweight* (how big the outline is). For example, the following VML draws a rectangle with a 0.1-inch wide blue border and red fill inside:

```
<v:rect style="width: 1in; height: 3in; left: 1in; top: 1in" fillcolor="red"
        strokeweight=".1in" strokecolor="blue"/>
```

As with the structured graphics control, you can also specify a rotation angle for an object. Do so by using the CSS rotation property. For example, the following VML rotates a rectangle by 20 degrees:

```
<v:rect style="width: 1in; height: 3in; left: 1in; top: 1in; rotation:20deg"
        fillcolor="red" strokeweight=".1in" strokecolor="blue"/>
```

To check out these shapes and attributes in action, load vml2.html from the ch11 folder (see Figure 11-14). You can find a complete listing for vml2.html in Listing 11-8.

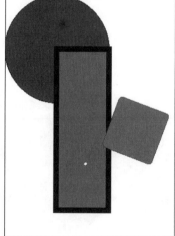

Figure 11-14:
Vml2.html draws a rectangle, round rectangle, and oval with various border and fill styles.

Listing 11-8	The vml2.html Source Code

```
<HTML>
<style>
  v\:* { behavior: url(#VMLRender); position:absolute }
</style>
<BODY>
<xml:namespace ns="urn:schemas-microsoft-com:vml" prefix="v"/>
<object id="VMLRender" codebase="vgx.dll" classid="CLSID:10072CEC-8CC1-11D1-986E-
        00A0C955B42E"></object>
<v:oval style="width: 2in; height: 2in" fillcolor="blue"/>
<v:rect style="width: 1in; height: 3in; left: 1in; top: 1in" fillcolor="red"
        strokeweight=".1in"/>
<v:roundrect style="width: 1in; height: 1in; left: 2in; top: 2in; rotation:20deg"
        fillcolor="#ff0066" strokecolor="#0000ff"/>
</BODY>
</HTML>
```

Texture fills

Instead of filling an object with a solid color, you can fill it with a bitmap texture with the `fill` tag. This trick lets you provide extremely rich textures for the various geometric primitives. The `fill` tag can go inside any of the other shape primitives, just as you can put a `<TD>` tag within a `<TABLE>` tag. Here's a quick sample:

```
<v:fill src="../media/scene1.jpg" type="tile"/>
```

The `fill` tag takes the name of a source image and a type. `Type` can be `tile`, to cause the images to be tiled to fill up the shape, or `frame`, to stretch the image to fill the shape (see Figure 11-15).

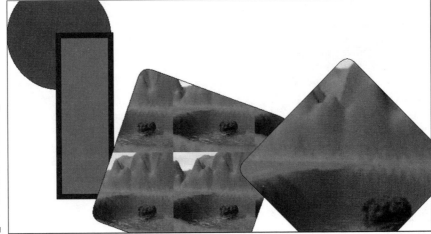

Figure 11-15:
A rounded rectangle is filled with a tiled and framed image.

Load vml3.html from the ch11 folder to see bitmap fills in action. To peek behind the scenes, look at Listing 11-9.

Listing 11-9	The vml3.html Source Code

```
<HTML>
<style>
    v\:* { behavior: url(#VMLRender); position:absolute }
</style>
<BODY>
<xml:namespace ns="urn:schemas-microsoft-com:vml" prefix="v"/>
<object id="VMLRender" codebase="vgx.dll" classid="CLSID:10072CEC-8CC1-11D1-986E-
            00A0C955B42E"></object>
<v:oval style="width: 2in; height: 2in" fillcolor="blue"/>
<v:rect style="width: 1in; height: 3in; left: 1in; top: 1in" fillcolor="red"
            strokeweight=".1in" href="vml1.html"/>
```

```
<v:roundrect style="width: 3in; height: 3in; left: 2in; top: 2in; rotation:20deg">
  <v:fill src="../media/scene1.jpg" type="tile"/>
</v:roundrect>
<v:roundrect style="width: 3in; height: 3in; left: 5in; top: 2in; rotation:45deg">
  <v:fill src="../media/scene1.jpg" type="frame"/>
</v:roundrect>
</BODY>
</HTML>
```

Moving violations

You can animate VML objects by changing their parameters from script. To change the color of an object, give the object an id and then change its fill color, as shown in the following code:

```
oval.fillcolor = "purple";
```

To change its position, use the same commands you would use for any HTML element. For example, you can set the position with code such as:

```
oval.style.left = "4in";
```

Or you can change the rotation with code such as:

```
oval.style.rotation = "55deg";
```

Vml4.html, shown in Listing 11-10, animates a number of VML objects. You can load the page from the ch11 folder, and you can get a sneak preview in Figure 11-16.

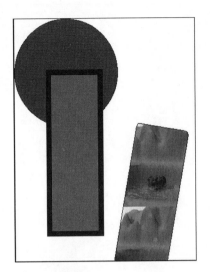 

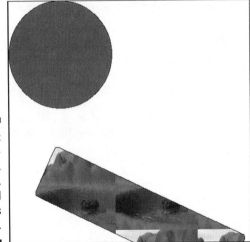

Figure 11-16:
One rectangle moves, one rotates, and the oval changes colors.

Listing 11-10	The vml4.html Source Code

```
<HTML>
<head>
<style>
  v\:* { behavior: url(#VMLRender); position:absolute }
</style>
<script>
var rot=0;
var direction = 1;
var color = 0;
var colorarray = new Array("blue", "red", "green", "yellow", "purple");

function Init() {
   window.setInterval("MoveRect()",200);
   window.setInterval("RotateSquare()", 100);
   window.setInterval("ChangeColor()", 500);
}

function ChangeColor() {
   oval.fillcolor = colorarray[color++];
   color %= 5;
}

function MoveRect() {
   curpos = rect1.style.pixelLeft;
   if (curpos > 500)
      direction = -1;
   if (curpos < 10)
      direction = 1;
   curpos = curpos + direction*5;
   rect1.style.pixelLeft = curpos;
}

function RotateSquare() {
   rot += 5;
   square1.style.rotation = rot + "deg";
}
</script>
</head>
<BODY onload="Init()">
<xml:namespace ns="urn:schemas-microsoft-com:vml" prefix="v"/>
<object id="VMLRender" codebase="vgx.dll" classid="CLSID:10072CEC-8CC1-11D1-986E-
            00A0C955B42E"></object>
<v:oval id="oval" style="width: 2in; height: 2in" fillcolor="blue"/>
<v:rect id="rect1" style="width: 1in; height: 3in; left: 1in; top: 1in" fillcolor=
            "red" strokeweight=".1in" href="vml1.html"/>
<v:roundrect id="square1" style="width: 1in; height: 4in; left: 2in; top: 2in;
            rotation:20deg">
   <v:fill src="../media/scene1.jpg" type="tile"/>
</v:roundrect>
</BODY>
</HTML>
```

VML's bells and whistles

VML includes a very fancy language for describing shape outlines. You can build shapes out of lines, beziers, and all types of curves. To use this language, you first define a shapetype. Then you use the shape object to create an object of that type. (By the way, a *bezier* is not a type of lingerie. It is a special type of curve that is often used in computer graphics. Now that I think about it, maybe it should be a type of lingerie.)

When you create a shapetype, you first define the coordinate system that you want to use when describing the shape. You establish the units in the path by coordsize parameters. The first coordsize parameter indicates how many coordinate units comprise the width of the entire shape, and the second parameter indicates how many units make up the height. For example, if you set coordsize to (100,100), then (0,0) means the upper left of the object and (100,100) means the lower right. You can also set the coordinate for the upper-left corner by using the coordorigin parameter.

Next, you establish the path that defines the shape outline. To do so, you use a variety of cryptic drawing commands. The following table shows a few of these commands.

Command	Meaning
m	Start a path
l	Draw a line to a particular coordinate
c	Draw a curve
qx	Draw an elliptic quadrant
e	Close up the curve

Explaining all these parameters is way beyond the scope of this book. (You wouldn't want me to get migraines, would you?) Be sure to check out the description of them in the VML specification on the W3C Web site.

In the interim, here's a simple shapetype that creates a rhomboid. It starts the path at (20,0). It then moves from there to (80,0), then to (100,60), and then (0,60). Finally, the path closes by connecting back to the beginning:

```
<v:shapetype id="sh1" coordsize="100, 100" path="m20,0l80,0,100,60,0,60e"/>
```

After you define a shapetype, you can use it as many times as you want. Just use the shape tag to create an instance of the shapetype. For example, the following draws the rhomboid:

```
<v:shape type="#sh1" style="width: 1in; height: 3in; left: 1in; top: 1in" fillcolor="red"/>
```

Another fancy feature you can use is a gradient fill. As with the structured graphics control, gradient fills let you make very attractive color swaths. You make them with the fill tag, but instead of setting a bitmap, you set up a gradient. Just set the color2 attribute to the secondary fill color. Set type to either gradient or gradientradial. If you're feeling experimental, you can also set the method attribute to linear or sigma.

For example, the following code fills a shape with a linear gradient that goes from red to blue:

```
<v:shape type="#sh1" style="width: 1in; height: 3in; left: 1in; top: 1in" fillcolor=
        "red"><v:fill color2="blue" type="gradient"/>
</v:shape>
```

Load vml5.html from the ch11 folder to look at some gradient-filled shapes, which are shown in Figure 11-17. You can see the complete source code in Listing 11-11.

Figure 11-17:
Linear and radial gradient-filled shapes.

Listing 11-11	The vm15.html Source Code

```
<HTML>
<head>
<style>
  v\:* { behavior: url(#VMLRender); position:absolute }
</style>
</head>
<BODY>
<xml:namespace ns="urn:schemas-microsoft-com:vml" prefix="v"/>
<object id="VMLRender" classid="CLSID:10072CEC-8CC1-11D1-986E-00A0C955B42E"></object>
 <v:shapetype id="sh1" coordsize="100, 100" path="m20,0l80,0,100,60,0,60e"/>
 <v:shape type="#sh1" style="width: 1in; height: 3in; left: 1in; top: 1in" fillcolor="red">
  <v:fill color2="blue" type="gradient"/>
 </v:shape>
 <v:shape type="#sh1" style="width: 1in; height: 1in; left: 2in; top: 1in; rotation:
              20deg" fillcolor="red">
  <v:fill color2="white" type="gradientradial"/>
 </v:shape>
</BODY>
</HTML>
```

Of course, creating fancy shapes would be much easier with a tool that emits VML. Perhaps by the time you finish reading this book, one will be on the market. But can I tell you what that tool will be? Of course not. They might come after me. Yeah. And then I'd have to eat the page this hint is printed on, from every copy of the book sold.

Part III
Data, Data Everywhere

The 5th Wave   By Rich Tennant

"We're researching molecular/digital technology that moves massive amounts of information across binary pathways that interact with free-agent programs capable of making decisions and performing logical tasks. We see applications in really high-end doorbells."

In this part . . .

This part mainly focuses on incorporating data into your pages. You find out about data binding — a powerful tool for automatically updating parts of your page based on a database. You create behaviors — a powerful new feature in Internet Explorer 5.0 for creating custom interactions. You learn how to persist information from a page. And finally, you discover how to create pages that work with multiple browsers, including Internet Explorer and Netscape Navigator.

Chapter 12

Ain't Misbehavin'

In This Chapter

▶ Extending pages by creating behaviors
▶ Processing events with behaviors
▶ Exposing behavior properties

*L*et me start with a warning: The techniques that I cover in this chapter just don't work with Netscape Navigator. And if you believe my Ouija Board Predictor of Technology Futures, they won't work with Navigator for a while. That's a bummer, because this chapter lays the foundation for some very cool things that I use throughout Part III — behaviors.

You may notice that the programs throughout this book use quite a bit of script for controlling the Dynamic HTML object model. Although using script lets you control all aspects of the way a Web page behaves, this approach has a few problems. First, it limits the number of people who can create interactive Web pages. You, as a *Dynamic HTML For Dummies,* 2nd Edition reader, know how to script Web pages. You're happening. But folks that you work with (or, more likely, work for) probably don't know how to.

Furthermore, every time you come up with a cool new user interface gadget (such as a floating toolbar), you need to copy over a bunch of code and HTML to incorporate it in other Web pages. So not only do you need to figure out how to incorporate your cool control, but you also need to remember where you put the code and how it works. The technical word for this is *pain in the butt.*

Behaviors get rid of the PITB factor. You, as a hip DHTML scripter, can create all types of new controls to use on a Web page. But instead of having to copy and paste them into pages, you can make up new tags or new styles to represent them.

For example, suppose that you make a neat drag-and-drop toolbar. You can create a new tag, `<MYTOOLBAR>`, to represent this toolbar. And if you put this tag into a page (along with some goodies so that the browser knows where to find the code that makes this tag work), the page suddenly has a new cool toolbar. If you want your buddies to use your toolbar, all you need to do is show them how to incorporate the tag. You don't have to teach them tons and tons of script. Or maybe you want an image to do something special when you mouse over it. You can add a special style to the image to hook it up to a behavior.

In other words, behaviors provide a way for you to extend the capabilities of the browser by using simple tags and styles rather than complex scripts.

If you're a real hotshot, you can even write your behaviors in C++ and have them magically appear in the browser.

What Is a Behavior?

Loosely put, a *behavior* is a tag or style that you create to extend the browser. What does the tag or style do? Anything you want it to. Just as `<B>` makes a word bold and `<INPUT>` adds a user interface control, your behaviors can do just about anything. (Well, anything that you can do in the browser. They're probably not going to help you find a date or learn how to pick clothes that match.) Not only can your tag do anything, but you can name your tag anything, too.

What happens if you use a behavior in an earlier browser or in Netscape Navigator? Absolutely nothing. That's one of the beautiful things about behaviors. If the browser doesn't understand a tag it encounters, it ignores it. So Internet Explorer 5.0 understands all the cool features you provide with behaviors, and other browsers just ignore them. Although it may look a bit shabbier, your page shows up in other browsers without causing nasty script errors.

Behavior with Style

Using behaviors involves two steps: incorporating them into your page and creating them. I start by showing you how to add a behavior to your page. (That's the easy part.)

Take a normal page with an image in it and then add a rollover behavior. Then if you yell at an image of a dog, it rolls over. (Just kidding.) The image is a normal image until you mouse over it. As soon as you do, it inverts. This action provides quick visual feedback to the viewer of your page.

You add this capability to a plain old Web page by adding a few simple commands. All you do is put an image on the page and give it a behavior style, as shown in the following HTML:

```
<IMG src="../media/scene1.jpg" style="behavior:url(imageroll1.htc)">
```

To check out this page in action, load imageroll1.html from the ch12 folder. You can see the complete listing in Listing 12-1.

Listing 12-1	The imageroll1.html Source Code

```
<HTML>
<TITLE>A simple style based behavior</TITLE>
<BODY>
<CENTER>
<P>Mouse over the image and watch it change</P>
<IMG src="../media/scene1.jpg" style="behavior:url(imageroll1.htc)">
</CENTER>
</BODY>
</HTML>
```

"Wow," you say, "Is that really all?" Of course not. The command you add says that the image has a particular behavior. The script for that behavior doesn't actually appear on the page. But just because the page doesn't have any script on it doesn't mean that script isn't executing. In fact, when the image loads, you mouse over it, or you mouse off it, script executes. But the script itself is stored in the behavior file.

Thus, the page that you author is simple. All the complex stuff is stored in the separate behavior script. The hardcore nerds write the behaviors. The HTML designers who wear black and smoke clove cigarettes use the behaviors but never need to see the code. (Even HTML designers who wear other colors and don't smoke can use behaviors to avoid writing scripts.)

Pass the Not-Quite-So-Hard Stuff

If you just read the preceding section and now know how to use a behavior in a page, you're probably wondering how to create the behavior. Fortunately, creating a behavior isn't that much harder than creating any other type of a script. You decide which events to process and what to do when those events occur.

Behaviors are always stored in their own separate file with an .htc extension. (This extension stands for *html control*. Despite rumors to the contrary, it is not an anagram for controlled substances the designers may have inhaled.) Behaviors start with a list of events to process. For example, here is the beginning of the imageroll1.htc file:

```
<ATTACH EVENT="onmouseover" HANDLER="event_onmouseover"/>
<ATTACH EVENT="onmouseout" HANDLER="event_onmouseout"/>
```

What does this script mean? Simple. This behavior traps the `onmouseout` and `onmouseover` events for the object that the behavior is applied to. When the user mouses over the element, for example, the behavior grabs the `onmouseover` event and calls the `event_onmouseover` function within the behavior.

Next, the behavior contains script showing what to do with the various events it processes. What does the `event_onmouseover` function do? For imageroll1, it inverts the image using a filter, as shown in the following code:

```
function event_onmouseover(){
 event.srcElement.style.filter = "invert";
}
```

You can find the complete listing for the behavior in Listing 12-2.

Behaviors are really very simple. They just process events on the element to which they are applied.

Listing 12-2   **The imageroll1.htc Source Code**

```
<ATTACH EVENT="onmouseover" HANDLER="event_onmouseover"/>
<ATTACH EVENT="onmouseout" HANDLER="event_onmouseout"/>
<script>
function event_onmouseout(){
 event.srcElement.style.filter = "";
}

function event_onmouseover(){
 event.srcElement.style.filter = "invert";
}
</script>
```

Processing Properties

In addition to processing events, behaviors can also access the various properties on an element. To do so, just manipulate the element's properties like you normally would. For example, make a new rollover behavior that changes the image `SRC` property. The initial image is stored in the `SRC` property of the `<IMG>` tag. You need to also provide an additional property, called `MouseOn`, that lets the user set the alternative image, as shown in the following HTML:

```
<IMG ID=I1 src="../media/scene1.jpg" MouseOn="../media/scene2.jpg"
        style="behavior:url(imageroll2.htc)">
```

In the behavior, you read this property. You then set the image source to this alternative image when the user mouses over the image, as shown in the following script:

```
function event_onmouseover(){
  event.srcElement.src = event.srcElement.MouseOn;
}
```

To restore the image on the onmouseout event, just reset the value of the SRC property. One tricky thing that you need to do, though, is keep the original value of the SRC property around so that you can restore it. To do so, we'll have some code that executes as soon as the behavior is set up. The code will find the value of the src property and store it in a property called Default:

```
this.Default = this.src;
```

In most of the samples in this book, you trap the onload event for the document to perform initialization. But you can't do this step for behaviors. Instead, if they need to initialize, put in code that executes when the behavior is initialized (as was done in the example you just looked at) or trap some message on the element upon which the behavior is placed. You could trap the onload event for the image element, but that event only fires when the image is fully downloaded. On a modem, that could be long after the image is ready to process events. Instead, trap the onreadystatechange event. This event gets sent when the image element is initialized and then again at various points as the image is downloaded.

You can check out this example by loading imageroll2.html from the ch12 folder. You can find the complete listing for the HTML file and the .htc file in Listings 12-3 and 12-4.

Listing 12-3   The imageroll2.html Source Code

```
<HTML>
<BODY>
<CENTER>
<H1>Alien Surf Shop Home Page</H1>
<P>Mouse over the image and watch it change</P>
<IMG ID=I1 src="../media/scene1.jpg" MouseOn="../media/scene2.jpg"
          style="behavior:url(imageroll2.htc)">
</CENTER>
</BODY>
</HTML>
```

| Listing 12-4 | The imageroll2.htc Source Code |

```
<ATTACH EVENT="onmouseover" HANDLER="event_onmouseover"/>
<ATTACH EVENT="onmouseout" HANDLER="event_onmouseout"/>
<script>
function event_onmouseout(){
 event.srcElement.src = event.srcElement.Default;
}

function event_onmouseover(){
 event.srcElement.src = event.srcElement.MouseOn;
}

this.Default = this.src;</script>
```

Adding with a Tag

All the behavior examples that I present earlier in this chapter add a behavior to an element by using a style parameter. You can also create your very own tag names and use behaviors to make those tags do something interesting.

For example, in the preceding section I have you create some image rollover effects with behaviors. These effects are always applied to an <IMG> tag. But what if you want to create a new tag, called <ROLLIMAGE>, that represents a rollover image? Not surprisingly, you can do so. You just need to go through a couple of steps.

First, you need to set up a namespace to use for your new tag. I briefly describe namespaces in Chapter 11. HTML has a certain set of tags that it understands, such as <P>, <DIV>, and <IMAGE>. If you want to create new tags, you need to do so in a way that won't interfere with the browser's reading of HTML tags. So you make a namespace. The namespace has something called a *longname* and a *prefix*. The prefix is an abbreviation for the longname. You put this prefix before tags to indicate that the tag is from that namespace. For example, ps:Yo, indicates that the Yo tag is part of the ps namespace. The longname should be something that uniquely identifies the namespace. Typically it is a URL, but really, it can be anything.

To create your own tag, you first need to set up a namespace for your tags. You do so with the xml:namespace tag. You can use something such as the following HTML to set up a namespace for the rollover tag you're going to create:

```
<xml:namespace ns="imageroll3.htc" prefix="ro"/>
```

This bizarre syntax says that the name `imageroll3.htc` uniquely identifies this namespace. Anytime a tag has `ro:` before it, the tag is from this namespace. For example, `<ro:IMG>` means an `IMG` tag from the `ro` namespace. `<ro:GAIN>` means a `GAIN` tag from the `ro` namespace. What do these tags do? Whatever you program them to. That is, a `<ro:IMG>` tag has nothing to do with an `<IMG>` tag. You are free to make the tag do whatever you want it to.

To make tags do something, you associate a behavior with all the tags from the namespace, as shown with the following HTML:

```
<STYLE>
   ro\:* { behavior: url("imageroll3.htc")}
</STYLE>
```

Now, any tags from the `ro` namespace automatically have the imageroll3.htc behavior applied to them.

You can use namespaces and behaviors to create your special `<ROLLIMAGE>` tag. Have the tag take the same parameters that the `<IMG>` tags have taken so far. For example, the following HTML sets up a rollover image:

```
<ro:ROLLIMAGE src="../media/scene1.jpg" MouseOn="../media/scene2.jpg">
```

This tag has no inherent visuals. To provide visuals, you need to alter the behavior so that it inserts the appropriate HTML tags into the page. Doing so turns out to be easy. When the behavior instantiates, you just insert an `<IMG>` tag into the page:

```
this.innerHTML = "<IMG src=" + this.src + ">";
```

The behavior traps any mouse movement over this image. When you handle such events, you just change the image's `SRC` property. This arrangement is the same as with imageroll2.htc, except that the element that is getting the mouse messages is a child of the `<ROLLIMAGE>`. Thus, you need to check the parent to get the appropriate properties:

```
event.srcElement.src = event.srcElement.parentElement.MouseOn;
```

To see this page in action, load imageroll3.html. You can see the complete listing for the HTML file in Listing 12-5 and for the behavior in Listing 12-6.

Listing 12-5   **The imageroll3.html Source Code**

```
<HTML>
<xml:namespace ns="imageroll3.htc" prefix="ro"/>
<STYLE>
  ro\:* { behavior: url("imageroll3.htc")}
</STYLE>
<BODY>
<CENTER>
<H1>Alien Surf Shop Home Page</H1>
<P>Mouse over the image and watch it change</P>
<ro:ROLLIMAGE src="../media/scene1.jpg" MouseOn="../media/scene2.jpg">
</CENTER>
</BODY>
</HTML>
```

Listing 12-6   **The imageroll3.htc Source Code**

```
<ATTACH EVENT="onmouseover" HANDLER="event_onmouseover"/>
<ATTACH EVENT="onmouseout" HANDLER="event_onmouseout"/>
<script>
//The mouse over and out event will occur on the child image, not the container
//since the container has no visual representation
function event_onmouseout(){
 event.srcElement.src = event.srcElement.parentElement.src;
}

function event_onmouseover(){
 event.srcElement.src = event.srcElement.parentElement.MouseOn;
}

this.innerHTML = "<IMG src=" + this.src + ">";
```

Chapter 13

The Data That Binds Us

*M*any of the techniques that you have seen in previous chapters reduce the number of times that you need to go to the server for new information. For example, you've created animations, added new text to a page, and changed a page's layout, all without asking the server for a new page. These techniques have concentrated on the design aspects of a page. But what about the data in the page itself? After all, many Web pages are designed explicitly to show information, whether it's the time for a movie, the price for a car, or a list of available books about Dynamic HTML authoring.

You typically interact with such a page by filling out a form describing the information that you are looking for. You then send this request to the server. The server processes the information in the form, creates a new page containing the requested data, and sends that data to the browser. All the data lookup is done by some fancy server-side facility. To make slight changes, such as sorting by a certain value or expanding to see more information about a certain item, you end up sending a new query to the server. The server processes it and sends back more information.

This scenario brings up Mike's Web Authoring Rule No. 6:

Rule No. 6: Reduce, recycle, reuse.

In other words, reduce the number of times that you need to request information from the server by reusing what you already have and processing it on the client side. That's what the data-binding services are all about.

Data binding lets you associate HTML elements with fields in a database. The browser automatically fills in the elements with the values from the database. You can then easily move back and forth through the database and update the elements. If you data-bind a table to a div, the text that's inside the table is shoved inside the div. That way, you can easily store different pieces of HTML code and access the code to show it programmatically. If you data-bind to an image, the source for the image is read from the database.

Suppose that you have a database of wines. The database contains an HTML description of the wine, complete with hyperlinks, the name of an image that shows the bottle, and an order reference number. You could dynamically create a page with this information for all the wines in the database.

Processing the data is all done on the client side. You read the data once, and then you can process it in any way that you like without having to get additional information from the server.

You can access the data by using either the Tabular Data Control (TDC) or the Remote Data Service (RDS). The TDC lets you access read-only data that's stored in text-formatted databases. The RDS services provide full client/server database capabilities using Open Database Connection (ODBC). With these services, you can do everything that you would ever want, including writing data back to the server. In this book, I use the TDC capabilities. They are easy to use and provide a great deal of power without the complexity of the RDS. Of course, it is even better with the PLMT, TLA, KAOS, and WKRP.

Netscape Navigator does not support any of the techniques described in this chapter.

Bind — James Bind

You take the following five basic steps to bind data to HTML elements with TDC:

1. **Put the Tabular Data Control on your Web page.**

2. **Tell the TDC the name of the data file.**

3. **Fill in the** `datasrc` **property for the element that you want to bind to.**

4. **Fill in the** datafld **property for the element or elements that you want to populate with information from the database.**

5. **Set the** dataformatas **property for text-based elements, such as tables and divs.**

Adding the TDC is like adding any other ActiveX control. The following is the HTML code:

```
<OBJECT ID="tdc" CLASSID="CLSID:333C7BC4-460F-11D0-BC04-0080C7055A83">
</OBJECT>
```

Pass in the name of the data file by setting the DataURL field with a <PARAM> tag. For example, if your data is in a file called names.txt, you would use the following HTML script:

```
<PARAM NAME="DataURL" VALUE="names.txt">
```

If you want to access several tables at once, add several TDCs. Give each a unique id.

Next, select the element to which you want to bind the data. The element should be one of the types listed in Table 13-1. Fill in the datasrc property, giving it the name of the TDC, preceded by a pound sign (#). For example, to bind a div to the TDC named *tdc,* use the following HTML code:

```
<DIV datasrc="#tdc">
```

Table 13-1	Elements to Which You Can Bind Data
A	INPUT TYPE=RADIO
APPLET	INPUT TYPE=TEXT
BUTTON	LABEL
DIV	MARQUEE
FRAME	OBJECT
IFRAME	SELECT
IMG	SPAN
INPUT TYPE=CHECKBOX	TABLE
INPUT TYPE=HIDDEN	TEXTAREA
INPUT TYPE=PASSWORD	

The `datasrc` parameter tells which data-binding control contains the database of values. Databases are composed of records, and each record contains fields. Therefore, you also need to tell the element which field to use by setting the `datafld` parameter. For example, the following line of code gets data from the first column in the database opened by the `tdc` control:

```
<DIV datasrc="#tdc" datafld="Column1">
```

Now the text inside the div is taken from the first column in the first record in the database. As you move through the database, the text inside the div is updated automatically.

By default, the data in the database is treated as pure text. If you are sending the data into an element that understands HTML code (such as a span or a div), you can place HTML code in the database and have it appear as HTML code inside the element. To do so, set the `dataformatas` parameter to "html", as shown in the following script:

```
<DIV datasrc="#tdc" datafld="Column1" dataformatas="html">
```

Have you ever seen a database go this way and that way?

As soon as you have followed the steps that I just outlined (in the preceding section), the data from the first record shows up on your page. But what happens if you want to show data from a different record? That's easy. You use one of the four movement methods shown in Table 13-2. All these methods and properties apply to the `recordset` property of the TDC.

Table 13-2	Movement Methods and Friends	
Method	*Meaning*	*Sample*
BOF	BOF stands for *beginning of file*. It is a property that is set to true if the database is at the beginning of the file — that is, just before the first record. Use this method to prevent reading from before the beginning of the database.	`(!tdc.recordset.BOF)` `tdc.recordset.MovePrevious();`

Method	*Meaning*	*Sample*
EOF	This close friend of BOF stands for end of file. This property is set to true if the database is at the end of the file — just after the last record. Use it to prevent reading after the end of the database.	if (!tdc. recordset.EOF) tdc.recordset. MoveNext();
MoveFirst	Moves to the first record in the database.	`tdc.recordset. MoveFirst();`
MoveLast	Moves to the last record in the database.	`tdc.recordset. MoveLast();`
MoveNext	Moves to the next record in the database. If you try to move beyond the end of the file, you get an error message.	`tdc.recordset. MoveNext();`
MovePrevious	Moves to the previous record in the database. If you try to move before the beginning of the file, you get an error message.	`tdc.recordset. MovePrevious();`

For example, suppose that you have a TDC named *tdc.* You've bound it to a div. You now want what shows up in the div to come from the next record in the database. To do this, you can use the following script:

```
tdc.recordset.MoveNext();
```

By telling the TDC to advance to the next record, you automatically update the div and any other elements that are tied to the database. Thus, you don't need to worry about all the different places in which the database is used. The data-binding services take care of that for you. You can have all types of HTML elements tied to the database, and they all update simultaneously as you move through the database.

Note that you get an error message if you try to read before the beginning of the database or if you try to read after the end of the database. To avoid this problem, check the BOF and EOF properties before moving, as shown in the following script:

```
if (!tdc.recordset.EOF)
    tdc.recordset.MoveNext();
```

When you are at the end of the file (or the beginning of the file), there is no data because there is no corresponding record. So moving to the end of the file or the beginning of the file blanks out any bound elements. You can avoid this situation by immediately moving to the first or last record if you have reached the beginning or end of the file, as shown in the following code:

```
tdc.recordset.MoveNext();
//If we just moved off the end, back up
if (tdc.recordset.EOF)
    tdc.recordset.MoveLast();
```

I want my CSV

The TDC reads data in comma-separated value (CSV) format. Each field is separated by a comma, and each record is separated by a hard return. For example, the following contains two records, each with three fields:

```
Michael,3/1/95,Gold
Sarah,3/10/98,Platinum
```

Unfortunately, commas and hard returns are frequently used in text, especially in HTML text. Thus, you may want to change the separators to different values. The percent (%) and pipe (|) symbols are frequently used for the field and record separators.

To change the separators, set the FieldDelim and RowDelim parameters in <PARAM> tags. For example, the following makes the TDC treat % as the field delimiter and | as the record delimiter:

```
<OBJECT ID="tdc" CLASSID="CLSID:333C7BC4-460F-11D0-BC04-0080C7055A83">
    <PARAM NAME="DataURL" VALUE="names2.txt">
    <PARAM NAME="FieldDelim" VALUE="%">
    <PARAM NAME="RowDelim" VALUE="|">
</OBJECT>
```

The TDC supplies default names for each field in a database. That way, you can associate each field with an HTML element. By default, the first field is Column1, the second is Column2, and so forth. You can supply more meaningful names if you want. Put these names in the first record and then set UseHeader to true with HTML code such as the following:

```
<OBJECT ID="tdc" CLASSID="CLSID:333C7BC4-460F-11D0-BC04-0080C7055A83">
    <PARAM NAME="DataURL" VALUE="names2.txt">
    <PARAM NAME="UseHeader" VALUE="1">
</OBJECT>
```

For example, the following code names the first column Name, the second Date, and the third Prize:

```
Name,Date,Prize
Michael,3/1/95,Gold
Sarah,3/10/98,Platinum
```

A tale of light bindage

The information in the preceding sections can help create a simple data-binding example. You use a database to pump HTML into a div. You then add Previous and Next buttons to move through the database. The database itself has a single field for each record, containing some HTML code. To see the page in action, load data1.html from the ch13 folder on the enclosed CD-ROM (see Listing 13-1). When you load the page, text from the first record appears on the screen — filling in the div. When you click on the Previous and Next buttons, different text from the database displays, as you can see in Figure 13-1.

Figure 13-1:
Here you can see the page when it starts and after clicking on Next.

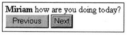

Listing 13-1   **The data1.html Source Code**

```
<HTML>
<HEAD>
<TITLE>Data Binding</TITLE>
<SCRIPT>
function next() {
    tdc.recordset.MoveNext();
    //If we just moved off the end, back up
    if (tdc.recordset.EOF)
        tdc.recordset.MoveLast();
}
function prev() {
    tdc.recordset.MovePrevious();
    //If we just moved before the beginning, back up
    if (tdc.recordset.BOF)
        tdc.recordset.MoveFirst();
}
</SCRIPT>
</HEAD>
<BODY>
<DIV id=myDiv DATASRC="#tdc" DATAFLD="column1" DATAFORMATAS="HTML">
</DIV>
<INPUT TYPE="Button" VALUE="Previous" onclick="prev()">
<INPUT TYPE="Button" VALUE="Next" onclick="next()">
<OBJECT ID="tdc" CLASSID="CLSID:333C7BC4-460F-11D0-BC04-0080C7055A83">
    <PARAM NAME="DataURL" VALUE="names.txt">
</OBJECT>
</BODY>
</HTML>
```

In the raw

You can use the TDC without having to do data binding. For example, you may want to read text from a database, manipulate it with JavaScript, and then send it to an HTML element.

To use the TDC in this fashion, follow these steps:

1. **Add the TDC to the page as I describe in the section "Bind — James Bind."**

2. **Don't bind the TDC to any elements; instead, use the `Fields` property of the `recordset` to access the data.**

   For example, you can get the value of the first field in the current record with `foo=tdc.recordset.Fields.Item(0).Value;`, or you can get the third field with `foo= tdc.recordset.Fields.Item(2).Value;`.

3. **Use the movement commands, as before, to move through the records database.**

It takes all types

Earlier in this chapter, you saw how you can bind a database to several HTML elements at once. You simply associate different fields with the different elements. All the elements update at once as you navigate through the database.

You can see this process in action. Start with the data1.html page. Now add an image element and then bind the image element to one of the fields in the database, as follows:

```
<IMG DATASRC="#tdc" DATAFLD="column2">
```

Note that you don't need to do anything special to the image to tell it to read its source URL value from the database. That happens automatically.

Also, as you can see by looking through Listing 13-2, you don't need to change the script to handle the additional element and the additional field. The only change that you make is to add the image to the HTML code and to make a new database. The new database has two fields in each record, as you can see in Listing 13-3. The first field contains some HTML text, and the second field contains the name of a JPEG file.

Now, when you move through the page, an image appears along with a description of the scene corresponding to the image, as you can see in Figure 13-2.

Figure 13-2:
A span and
an image
are bound to
the data-
base. You
can see
the two
elements
updating as
the user
moves
through the
database.

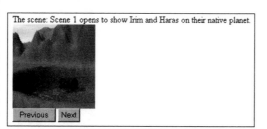

Listing 13-2   The data2.html Source Code

```
<HTML>
<HEAD>
<TITLE>Data Binding</TITLE>
<SCRIPT>
function next() {
    tdc.recordset.MoveNext();
    //If we just moved off the end, back up
    if (tdc.recordset.EOF)
        tdc.recordset.MoveLast();
}
function prev() {
    tdc.recordset.MovePrevious();
    //If we just moved before the beginning, back up
    if (tdc.recordset.BOF)
        tdc.recordset.MoveFirst();
}
</SCRIPT>
</HEAD>
<BODY>
The scene: <SPAN DATASRC="#tdc" DATAFLD="column1" DATAFORMATAS="HTML">
</SPAN><BR>
<IMG DATASRC="#tdc" DATAFLD="column2"><BR>
<INPUT TYPE="Button" VALUE="Previous" onclick="prev()">
<INPUT TYPE="Button" VALUE="Next" onclick="next()">
<OBJECT ID="tdc" CLASSID="CLSID:333C7BC4-460F-11D0-BC04-0080C7055A83">
    <PARAM NAME="DataURL" VALUE="names2.txt">
</OBJECT>
</BODY>
</HTML>
```

Listing 13-3	The names2.txt Source Code

```
Scene 1 opens to show Irim and Haras on their native planet., ../media/scene1.jpg
In Scene 2 <B>Irim</B> visits the scenic West Coast for a quick surf.,../media/scene2.jpg
Haras gets <FONT color=blue>ticked</FONT> in Scene 3., ../media/scene3.jpg
```

A Sorted Affair

One of the benefits of the Microsoft Internet Explorer data-binding services is that you can sort and filter data without having to send a new request to the server. For example, you may want to sort a database by the names of employees. Or you may want to show only data that relates to sales in a particular country.

The general format is to provide a semicolon-separated list of the fields by which you want the data sorted. Adding a minus sign (–) means that you want to sort inversely. For example, the following code sorts the database by Column1 and then by Column3 within Column1:

```
tdc.sort = "Column1;Column3";
```

Call the `reset` method to update the `recordset` for the new sort order as follows:

```
tdc.reset();
```

For example, the data3.html page contains a button that sorts data that's shown in a table. It sorts by the data in the second column, in reverse alphabetic order. The script is as follows:

```
function sdown() {
    tdc.sort = "-column2";
    tdc.reset();
}
```

When you sort text, all the characters are sorted, including HTML tags. So if you have an HTML tag at the beginning of a field, that field is sorted as if it starts with the left bracket character (<), even if you have set `dataformatas` to HTML.

You can also filter the data. This capability is very powerful: You can pull in a whole database of information and look at portions of it whenever you want without having to go to the server again. For example, you could have a database of companies showing the contact names, the sales rep, and the state.

You could show the companies that a particular rep manages without having to do a query on the server. You could then show all the companies in a particular state, again without having to hit the server.

Filtering is very similar to sorting. You set the `filter` property to an expression to use to filter the data. For example, if you set the `filter` property to `Column3="98*"`, you see only records where the data in the third column starts with the numbers 98.

The general format of the filter expression is

```
Columnn comparison Value
```

The *comparison* can be any of the operators shown in the following list:

```
=

>

>=

<

<=

<>
```

As with sorting, you need to call `reset` after you set the `filter` property.

If you want to compare the value in a column to text, the text must be inside double quotes. You cannot put the text inside single quotes.

For example, the data3.html page (see Listing 13-4) has a button that filters the database to only show names where the zip code starts with 98. The code is as follows:

```
function filterit() {
  tdc.filter = 'Column3="98*"'
  tdc.reset();
}
```

Listing 13-4 **The data3.html Source Code**

```
<HTML>
<HEAD>
<TITLE>Data Binding</TITLE>
<SCRIPT>
function sdown() {
   tdc.sort = "-column2";
   tdc.reset();
}
function filterit() {
   tdc.filter = 'Column3="98*"'
   tdc.reset();
}
</SCRIPT>
</HEAD>
<BODY>
<TABLE DATASRC="#tdc">
<THEAD><TR><TH>Name</TH><TH>State</TH><TH>Zip</TH></TR></THEAD>
<TR><TD><DIV DATAFLD="Column1"></DIV></TD>
<TD><DIV DATAFLD="Column2"></DIV></TD>
<TD><DIV DATAFLD="Column3"></DIV></TD></TR>
</TABLE><BR>
<INPUT TYPE="Button" VALUE="Sort Down" onclick="sdown()">
<INPUT TYPE="Button" VALUE="Filter" onclick="filterit()">
<OBJECT ID="tdc" CLASSID="CLSID:333C7BC4-460F-11D0-BC04-0080C7055A83">
   <PARAM NAME="DataURL" VALUE="names3.txt">
</OBJECT>
</BODY>
<HTML>
```

Note the use of an asterisk (*) in the `FilterValue`. You can use * to mean "match any set of characters," and you can use a question mark (?) to mean "match any single character." In this case, the asterisk means "show any items where the value in Column3 starts with 98." The asterisk and question mark are called *wildcards*. They are good things to take with you to a casino.

Run this page by loading data3.html from the ch13 folder. When it runs, a table appears showing all the records in the database. You can click on the Sort Down button to sort the list alphabetically by name or click on the Filter button to show only those items in which the zip code starts with 98. Figure 13-3 shows the page after the data has been sorted.

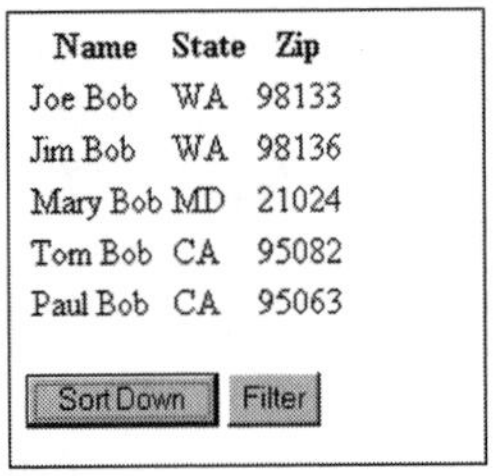

Figure 13-3:
Clicking on
the Sort
Down
button sorts
the data in
the table.

Name	State	Zip
Joe Bob	WA	98133
Jim Bob	WA	98136
Mary Bob	MD	21024
Tom Bob	CA	95082
Paul Bob	CA	95063

Sort Down Filter

Note something else that's interesting about the page. In the earlier samples, the data showed up one record at a time. But here, all the records are displayed at once. That's because, if you bind to an item inside a table, the data-binding services create a new row for every record. This arrangement lets you easily display the contents of the database in a table. The following HTML code is used to do so:

```
<BODY>
<TABLE DATASRC="#tdc">
<THEAD><TR><TH>Name</TH><TH>State</TH><TH>Zip</TH></TR></THEAD>
<TR><TD><DIV DATAFLD="Column1"></DIV></TD>
<TD><DIV DATAFLD="Column2"></DIV></TD>
<TD><DIV DATAFLD="Column3"></DIV></TD></TR>
</TABLE>
```

Note that the `datasrc` parameter is filled in for the table itself. A div is placed inside each `<TD>` to set up a column for each field in the database. The `datafld` parameter is filled in for each of these divs.

Be sure to check out Listing 13-4 to see the entire code for the page.

When you fill a table using the data-binding services, you must set up a table head if you want to label each column. Do not put extra rows in the table body with text to label each column.

You can apply multiple filters, one after the other; the results are cumulative. To start a filter (or a sort, for that matter) from the database, do a reset before you begin the filter or the sort.

XML-Rated Data

In addition to binding to data in comma-separated files, you can also use data binding with XML. What is XML? Even though people have devoted huge books to the subject, the concept of XML is simple. HTML is a great way to represent layout information about a page. But HTML doesn't represent data. Although I can go to my favorite online bookstore and see a list of books and their prices, the underlying information sent to the client is just layout information. I know that the third column in one of the tables is a price, because I know what $9.99 means. But the actual description of the data isn't sent to the page. If I want to sort by prices, I have to ask the online bookstore to send me a new list.

Earlier in this chapter, I show you that the TDC makes this situation nicer, because with TDC I can read in a text file and manipulate the contained data locally. But among other problems, with TDC the file needs to follow strict layout rules, is not a standard format, and I really have to know what each column contains.

XML solves this problem. It is a general (and standard) way of describing data. I make up tags to describe the information I want. For example, I might do something such as the following to describe a book:

```
<BOOK>
    <AUTHOR>Michael Hyman</AUTHOR>
    <TITLE>Dynamic HTML For Dummies</HTML>
    <PRICE>9.99</PRICE>
</BOOK>
```

Are these tags HTML tags? No. They are my own tags that I've designed to represent data. Looking at this, I see that I have a book and a book has an author, title, and price. (If you've ever used a relational database, such as Access, you'll note that the XML data is akin to a relational table with a variety of fields.)

I can read this data from the browser by using the XML capabilities that are built-in to Internet Explorer 5.0. Doing so preserves the semantic information. *Semantic information* is just a really fancy way of saying that after I read in the data, I can ask for the value of the author, or title, or whatever. I don't just have a blob of text that I hope is lined up in some way, and I don't find my information with requests such as "get me the number after the fourth comma in the second line of the file."

Living by the XML rules

XML has some rules that you must follow. Unlike HTML, every tag that begins must have an end. So if I have an `<AUTHOR>` tag in front of some data, I must follow the data with a closing `</AUTHOR>` tag, as shown in the following:

```
<AUTHOR>Michael</AUTHOR>
```

Like HTML, you can have richly hierarchical data. That is, any element can contain further elements, allowing you to represent sophisticated structures. For example, here is another way to represent books:

```
<BOOK>
    <AUTHOR>
        <NAME>
            <FIRST>Michael</FIRST>
            <LAST>Hyman</LAST>
        </NAME>
    </AUTHOR>
</BOOK>
```

Unlike HTML, you can't have overlapped tags. That is, you can do the following in HTML:

```
<B>Hello <I>John</B>, how are you?</I>
```

Note how the bold starts before the italics starts and ends before the italics end. That isn't allowed in XML. You'd need to do something such as the following, in which tags are nested, but not overlapped:

```
<B>Hello <I>John</I></B><I>, how are you?</I>
```

Finally, XML files must have a single root element. (You may think that this makes XML like a carrot. Root is actually a computer science nerd term disguised in common language. Maybe they should have called it a biquadratic interpolator so you'd know it has nothing to do with plants.) What does this mean? Actually, it is really simple. The following XML represents information about two books:

```
<BOOK>
   <AUTHOR>Michael</AUTHOR>
</BOOK>
<BOOK>
   <AUTHOR>Miriam</AUTHOR>
</BOOK>
```

To make this a valid XML file, you need an element to contain these other elements (much as HTML files all are contained within an `<HTML>` and `</HTML>` tag). For example, you might do the following:

```
<INVENTORY>
<BOOK>
   <AUTHOR>Michael</AUTHOR>
</BOOK>
<BOOK>
   <AUTHOR>Miriam</AUTHOR>
</BOOK>
</INVENTORY>
```

Reading XML data

Reading XML data into your page is blissfully easy. You simply add the `<XML>` tag. For example, the following code reads in the XML contained in a file called books.xml:

```
<XML id=books src="books.xml"></XML>
```

You can then use this XML as the source for data binding, just as you use the TDC in this chapter's earlier examples. The only difference is that when you specify the field to bind to, use the XML element name rather than a column number, as shown in the following HTML:

```
<TABLE DATASRC="#books">
<TR>
   <TD><SPAN datafld="TITLE"></SPAN></TD>
   <TD><SPAN datafld="AUTHOR"></SPAN></TD>
</TR>
</TABLE>
```

You can see the results of this page by looking at Figure 13-4. You can find the complete listing for the HTML page in Listing 13-5 and for the XML in Listing 13-6.

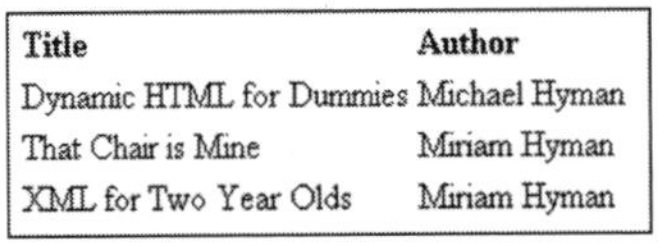

Figure 13-4:
The data-
bound XML
file.

Title	Author
Dynamic HTML for Dummies	Michael Hyman
That Chair is Mine	Miriam Hyman
XML for Two Year Olds	Miriam Hyman

Listing 13-5	The xml.html File

```
<HTML>
<HEAD>
<TITLE>Data Binding to XML</TITLE>
</HEAD>

<BODY>
<!-- Load in the XML -->
<XML id="books" src="books.xml"></XML>

<!-- The data bound table -->
<TABLE DATASRC="#books">
<THEAD><TD><b>Title</b></TD><TD><b>Author</b></TD></THEAD>
<TR>
   <TD><SPAN datafld="TITLE"></SPAN></TD>
   <TD><SPAN datafld="AUTHOR"></SPAN></TD>
</TR>
</TABLE>
</BODY>
</HTML>
```

Listing 13-6   **The XML Data File for books.xml**

```
<INVENTORY>
<BOOK>
    <AUTHOR>Michael Hyman</AUTHOR>
    <TITLE>Dynamic HTML for Dummies</TITLE>
</BOOK>
<BOOK>
    <AUTHOR>Miriam Hyman</AUTHOR>
    <TITLE>That Chair is Mine</TITLE>
</BOOK>
<BOOK>
    <AUTHOR>Miriam Hyman</AUTHOR>
    <TITLE>XML for Two Year Olds</TITLE>
</BOOK>
</INVENTORY>
```

Walking through XML using data binding

The XML example in the preceding section bound the entire set of data into the table in one fell swoop. You can also use the database movement commands (called ADO commands) from Table 13-2, just as you use them in databind1.html to view the data one record at a time. You can see such a page by looking at Listing 13-7 or by loading xml2.html.

Listing 13-7   **The xml2.html Source Code**

```
<HTML>
<HEAD>
<TITLE>Data Binding</TITLE>
<SCRIPT>
function next() {
    books.recordset.MoveNext();
    //If we just moved off the end, back up
    if (books.recordset.EOF)
        books.recordset.MoveLast();
}

function prev() {
    books.recordset.MovePrevious();
    //If we just moved before the beginning, back up
    if (books.recordset.BOF)
        books.recordset.MoveFirst();
}
</SCRIPT>
</HEAD>

<BODY>
<SPAN datasrc="#books" datafld="TITLE"></SPAN> by 
<SPAN datasrc="#books" datafld="AUTHOR"></SPAN><BR>
<INPUT TYPE="Button" VALUE="Previous" onclick="prev()">
<INPUT TYPE="Button" VALUE="Next" onclick="next()">
<XML id=books src="books.xml"></XML>
</BODY>
</HTML>
```

Internet Explorer 5.0 provides a really huge API for reading, searching, and manipulating XML information. You can do all types of really great data manipulation using these capabilities. But I could devote a whole book to the topic (hmm, now there's an idea), and it's too broad to go into here.

Chapter 14

Persistence Is Not Futile

· ·

In This Chapter

▶ Saving user-entered data from pages

▶ Loading data into pages

▶ Saving entire forms

▶ Creating a persistence behavior

· ·

Technically speaking, most Web pages are stateless. ("Oh great," you think. "This chapter starts with something technical. I'm out of here." Well, hold on. It isn't so bad. At least not until the end of the chapter.) What this stateless state means is that every time you go to a particular page, the page has no knowledge that you've been there before. It always brings up the same form, the same menus, or whatever.

Some Web-based applications are more sophisticated, however. For example, when you order books on the Internet, the book vendor probably keeps track of who you are and what you've bought before. Typically, this tracking is done by keeping information about you on the server. When you visit the page, the server detects who you are (using various techniques) and, based upon that information, customizes what you see. Maybe you get news about your special interests, or a list of suggested gifts for someone's birthday, or who knows what.

Another way that Web applications keep track of you is to use something called *cookies*. Cookies are small files saved on your hard disk that can store information. The server can access the cookies it writes. Thus, it can save information onto your machine and then read it back next time you visit a Web page. For example, it could store a list of items you have placed in a shopping cart. (By the way, *cookies* is a short form of the programmer expression *magic cookies*. And, despite some rumors, cookies can't be used to read your financial files or check out what images you might have downloaded from other sites.) But cookies are a pain to create. They're hard to program. They aren't very flexible.

Microsoft Internet Explorer 5.0 provides several built-in behaviors, called the *persistence behaviors,* to help you store information that a user has entered. For example, you can provide a form into which a user types in his name and address. You can then customize subsequent Web pages so as to greet the person by name and to fill in his address automatically if he orders something. Or you may just want to let a user fill out a form, leave, and then continue where she left off when she returns. The persistence behaviors let you accomplish all of these tasks. Thus, like cookies, persistence behaviors let you store and retrieve information on a client machine.

Internet Explorer 5.0 provides four different types of persistence behaviors:

> `saveFavorite` – stores the state of a page when the user adds it to the favorites list. Restores the state when the user returns to the page.
>
> `saveHistory` – saves the state of a page when the user navigates away from it. Restores the state when the user navigates back to it. The information is deleted when Internet Explorer is closed.
>
> `saveSnapshot` – saves and restores form, variable, element and other values.
>
> `userData` – saves and restores any information desired.

In this chapter, I focus on `userData`. It's the most flexible approach, by far, and the only approach suited for creating business applications that need to store information on the client.

Simple Saving

Internet Explorer 5.0 makes saving information from a Web page easy. A special behavior called the `userData` behavior lets you save out values from a page. You first associate this behavior with an element. Then, from script, you can set what to save. Each item has a name and a textual value. When you finish setting what to save, you save the information by using the `save` command.

Loading back the information is similar. You use the `load` command to load in the information file and then use script to look up the values that you want.

The information is stored as an XML file. If you're a real propeller head, you can get to the XML tree and manipulate it, using the XML API.

Note that you can read the information back from any page, which means that you can share the information across pages. Or you can just use it to restore values to an existing page.

To see how the userData behavior works, suppose that you have a page with an edit box in which the user types his or her e-mail name. You can easily save the data that the user types in. Follow these steps to do so:

1. **Set up a style to use the userData behavior.**

    The HTML looks like this:

    ```
    <STYLE>
    .save { behavior:url(#default#userdata_)}
    </STYLE>
    ```

    This behavior exposes an API that lets you save information. The information stays around even if you go to another page or shut down the computer.

2. **Apply this behavior to the object that contains the information you want to save.**

    For example, the following HTML lets you save information from an <INPUT> tag:

    ```
    <INPUT id="username" SIZE="34" class=save>
    ```

    Actually, you aren't restricted to saving information just from the element to which you apply the behavior. You can save information from anywhere. You find out more about that shortly.

3. **Write some script to store the actual information.**

    For example, to store the value that the user typed into the <INPUT> tag, you can use script such as the following:

    ```
    username.setAttribute("name",username.value);
    ```

    The setAttribute command takes two parameters: a name and a value. For example, you might use "email" as the name and then use the e-mail name as the value. Or you might use "phone" as the name and then use the phone number as the value. In computer talk, these are called *name value pairs*.

    You can store as many different name value pairs as you want. For example, the following script stores the value of the <INPUT> field, as well as a phone number:

    ```
    username.setAttribute("name",username.value);
    username.setAttribute("phone", "555-1212");
    ```

4. **After you set up the information to store, you call the save command.**

    The following line of script shows the save command:

    ```
    username.save("mydata");
    ```

The `save` command takes a single string as an argument. You pass in a name for the set of data you are about to store. If you want, you can call `save` several times with different names. That strategy lets you save different data under different headings, or data from different pages under different headings.

For example, you can save all the address information into one area with the following script:

```
username.save("address");
```

And later on, you can save credit card information with the following:

```
username.save("credit_card");
```

You can't call `save` on just any old element on the page. You can only call it on the element to which you apply the `userData` behavior.

Getting the data back

Obviously, the ability to store data is useless if you don't have a way to get it back. Fortunately, Internet Explorer makes it easy to get back the information you saved. (Phew. For a moment you may have thought that Microsoft bought too many of those printer/shredder combinations like the government uses.)

To retrieve information, you first load it, as shown in the following script:

```
username.load("mydata");
```

The command loads in the data associated with that name. Then you can access the data by using `getAttribute`, like this:

```
alert(username.getAttribute("name"));
```

Pulling it all together

Now you can put all this saving and loading data stuff to use in a page. In this section, you create a Web page that lets you type in your name. The page saves this information with the `userData` behavior when you leave the page, refresh the page, or shut down the browser. Any time the page is reloaded, it reloads the name and fills it into the form.

You make this scenario work by trapping the `onload` and `onunload` events. The first event is called after the page loads, and the latter is called when the user moves to a different page, refreshes, or shuts down the browser.

When the user leaves the page, you save out whatever value was typed in as the username, using the following code:

```
function SaveIt() {
   username.setAttribute("username",username.value)
   username.save("mydata");
}
```

As you can see, this code reads the value of the element named `username` and saves it into a file called `mydata`.

When the page is first loaded, you read in the data and reinitialize the input field, as shown in the following code:

```
function RestoreIt() {
   username.load("mydata");
   username.value=username.getAttribute("username");
}
```

You can see this technique in action by loading persist1.html from the ch14 folder. Type in some name for the username. Then shut down the browser and start the persist1.html page again. The name you typed in shows up!

You can see a complete listing for persist1.html in Listing 14-1.

Listing 14-1 The persist1.html Source Code

```
<HTML>
<HEAD>
   <title>Simple Persistence</title>
<STYLE>
.save { behavior:url(#default#userdata)}</STYLE>
<SCRIPT>
function SaveIt() {
   username.setAttribute("username",username.value)
   username.save("mydata");
}

function RestoreIt() {
   username.load("mydata");
   username.value=username.getAttribute("username");
}
</SCRIPT>
</HEAD>
<BODY onload="RestoreIt()" onunload="SaveIt()">
What is your name? <INPUT id="username" SIZE="34" class=save> </BODY>
</HTML>
```

Share it, man

You can use the saved information to restore the state of a page. You can also use saved information in other pages. For example, you might use a page such as persist1.html to gather information about a user. You could then customize later pages with this information, such as greeting the user by name.

In fact, you do exactly that in this section. You read the username saved by persist1.html and use it to customize another page. Doing so is simple. When the page loads, you read in the name. You then insert this name into a <SPAN> in the page, as shown in the following code:

```
function Init() {
   greetings.load("mydata");
   greetings.innerText=greetings.getAttribute("username");
}
```

You can find the complete source for this page in Listing 14-2. To see the page in action, first run persist1.html from the ch14 folder. Type in a username, and then load persist2.html. You're greeted by name. Pretty cool, huh? If you're feeling lazy, of course, you can just check out Figure 14-1.

By default, the persistence information is stored in the directory where the HTML page is viewed. You can change that by giving a path to the save and load command. For example, you could use script such as the following:

```
username.save("../address");
```

This will save in the parent directory of the page. Changing the directory is useful when you are running pages locally, but from different directories, and you want to share information across the pages.

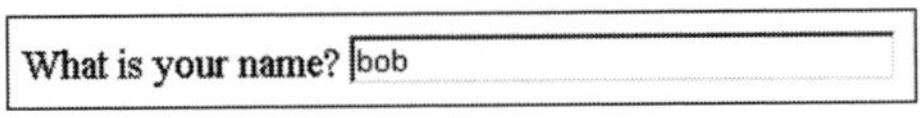

Figure 14-1:
The name entered in persist1.htm l automatically shows up in persist2.html.

What is your name?	bob

Listing 14-2   **The persist2.html Source Code**

```
<HTML>
<HEAD>
   <title>Persisted Information is Global</title>
<STYLE>
.save { behavior:url(#default#userdata)}</STYLE>
<SCRIPT>
function Init() {
   greetings.load("mydata");
   greetings.innerText=greetings.getAttribute("username");
}
</SCRIPT>
</HEAD>
<BODY onload="Init()">
Welcome back <SPAN id="greetings" class=save></SPAN>, it is great to see you again.
I have a great surf board you might like to buy.
</BODY>
</HTML>
```

Saving the Whole World

Although saving one piece of information is nice, most Web forms contain many pieces of information. Fortunately, switching from saving one piece of information to saving many pieces of information is easy. In fact, all you need to do is call setAttribute for everything you want to save. For example, suppose that you have a form with three input fields in it. One stores the name, another the street, and the third the country. You can save out this information with code such as the following:

```
username.setAttribute("name",name.value);
username.setAttribute("street",street.value);
username.setAttribute("country",country.value);
```

Although the preceding code is easy to read, it isn't very general. If you had a form with ten elements on it, you'd need to write ten lines of code. If you had 20 elements, you'd need to write 20 lines of code. A better technique is to use a loop to go through all the elements that you want to save.

For example, suppose that you have a form such as the following:

```
<FORM NAME="myForm" CLASS="save">
  <TABLE WIDTH="50%">
  <TR><TD WIDTH=60>Email </TD><TD><INPUT NAME="email" SIZE="34"></TD></TR>
  <TR><TD>Name         </TD><TD><INPUT NAME="Identity"   SIZE="34"></TD></TR>
  <TR><TD>Street       </TD><TD><INPUT NAME="Address"    SIZE="34"></TD></TR>
  <TR><TD>City         </TD><TD><INPUT NAME="City"       SIZE="34"></TD></TR>
  <TR><TD>State        </TD><TD><INPUT NAME="State"      SIZE="4"> Zip Code
           <INPUT  NAME="ZipCode" SIZE="5"></TD></TR>
  </TABLE>
</FORM>
```

As you can see, this form contains input fields for entering the e-mail name, name, street, city, state, and zip code. You can write a loop to go through all the <INPUT> fields and save out their values. Doing so is, in fact, very easy.

First, you find all the <INPUT> elements on the form:

```
oColl = myForm.tags("input");
```

Next, you loop through these elements. You save the value of any input tag that has a name:

```
for (i = 0; i < oColl.length; i++) {
   //Make sure the element has a name
   if (oColl[i].name != "")
      myForm.setAttribute(oColl[i].name, oColl[i].value);
}
```

This loop just checks each <INPUT> element to see whether it has a name. If so, it saves the value of the element.

Loading back the information uses the same technique, except that instead of calling setAttribute, you call getAttribute. Of course, the layout of the page may have changed sometime after the user saved the information. In that case, you may have <INPUT> tags on the page that don't have information stored for them. In such a case, getAttribute returns null. If you try to use null as the value for an <INPUT> element, you get a script error. So you add a line of code to protect against this condition, as shown in the following script:

```
oColl = myForm.tags("input");
for (i = 0; i < oColl.length; i++) {
   //Make sure the element has a name
   if (oColl[i].name != "") {
      temp = myForm.getAttribute(oColl[i].name);
      if (temp)
         //Set the value
         oColl[i].value = temp;
   }
}
```

To see a page that uses this technique to load and save all the values from a form, check out persist3.html. You can find the complete code for it in Listing 14-3.

Listing 14-3	The persist3.html Source Code

```html
<HTML>
<HEAD>
  <TITLE>Persisting from a form</TITLE>
<STYLE>
.save { behavior:url(#default#userdata)}</STYLE>
<SCRIPT>
//This will save any named attributes in the form myForm
//Assumes unique names
function SaveIt() {
  //Create a collection of INPUT elements on the form
  oColl = myForm.tags("input");
  //Loop through and save them as name, value pairs
  for (i = 0; i < oColl.length; i++) {
    //Make sure the element has a name
    if (oColl[i].name != "")
        myForm.setAttribute(oColl[i].name, oColl[i].value);
  }
  //Now save the data
  myForm.save("mydata");
}

function RestoreIt() {
  //Load the persisted data
  myForm.load("mydata");
  //Walk through the form and set the values
  oColl = myForm.tags("input");
  for (i = 0; i < oColl.length; i++) {
    //Make sure the element has a name
    if (oColl[i].name != "") {
        temp = myForm.getAttribute(oColl[i].name);
        if (temp)
            //Set the value
            oColl[i].value = temp;
    }
  }
}
</SCRIPT>
</HEAD>
<BODY onload="RestoreIt()" onunload="SaveIt()">
<CENTER>
<H1>Alien Surf Shop</H1>
<FORM NAME="myForm" CLASS="save">
  <TABLE WIDTH="50%">
  <TR><TD WIDTH=60>Email </TD><TD><INPUT NAME="email" SIZE="34"></TD></TR>
  <TR><TD>Name          </TD><TD><INPUT NAME="Identity"   SIZE="34"></TD></TR>
  <TR><TD>Street        </TD><TD><INPUT NAME="Address"    SIZE="34"></TD></TR>
  <TR><TD>City          </TD><TD><INPUT NAME="City"       SIZE="34"></TD></TR>
  <TR><TD>State         </TD><TD><INPUT NAME="State"      SIZE="4"> Zip Code <INPUT
            NAME="ZipCode" SIZE="5"></TD></TR>
  </TABLE>
</FORM>
</CENTER>
<HR>
<SPAN>
  <OL><B>To test this feature out</B>
      <LI>Fill in the form<LI>Then close IE5 and/or visit another site<LI>
            Then open this document up again
  </OL></SPAN>
</BODY>
</HTML>
```

Note that a form can have several elements in it, each with the same name. Subsequent attributes overwrite previous ones. For example, if I have two elements named `Address`, the second one overwrites the value of the first. You can write special code to generate unique names if you have this condition. Although doing so is relatively easy when you are saving and restoring from a single page, altering names can cause trouble if you are saving from one page and reading from another. In general, use unique names for elements you plan to save.

It Takes All Types

The persist3.html page works great, but note that it processes only text-entry `<INPUT>` tags. Web pages can contain many other types of entry tags as well, including checkbox `<INPUT>` tags and tags such as `<TEXTAREA>` and `<SELECT>`. Conceptually, handling these various input types is simple. All you need to do is see what type of element you have and decide what to do with it. For example, if you have a checkbox, you want to save the `checked` property. If you have a `<SELECT>`, you want to store the `selectedIndex`.

Although it is conceptually simple to handle all the different input types, doing so involves writing a lot of code. So if you aren't used to looking at big script files, this section may scare you a little. Just take a deep breath. Grab a pop. Run the samples. Say "Cool." And when you're feeling all warm and fuzzy, come back and look at the code.

You're going to write some code that can save all types of element types. In particular, check out Figure 14-2, which shows a form containing many different input elements. You're going to write code that can handle all of them.

Figure 14-2: This form contains many different input elements.

Alien Surf Shop	
Email	mikehy@home.com
Name	Michael
Street	123 Surf Ave
City	Big Wave
State	NK Zip Code

Male ⊙ Female ○ I know it. But I'm not telling ▾
I Like Cats ☑ I Like Dogs ☐
Comments:
Hello everybody.

I break this task into two parts. First, you write code to handle all the different <INPUT> types. Then you write code to handle <TEXTAREA> and other tags. To handle the various input types, you write a function that gets passed the element containing the information to save. Then you check the type property, which tells you whether the element is a radio button, text field, or one of the other input types. After you know what type it is, you can decide what property you need to save.

Take a look at the code:

```
function SaveInputType(obj) {
  //Decide what to save based upon what the INPUT type is
  switch (obj.type) {
  case "text":
  case "hidden":
      myForm.setAttribute(obj.name,obj.value);
      break;
  case "checkbox":
      myForm.setAttribute(obj.name,obj.checked);
      break;
  case "radio":
      //Special case, because radio buttons all have the same name
      //So what we'll do is save the value of the one that is checked
      if (obj.checked)
          myForm.setAttribute(obj.name,obj.value);
      break;
  }
}
```

The only tricky thing is saving radio buttons. In Chapter 5, you discover that radio buttons are special controls. All radio buttons in a group have the same name, and only one radio button in a group can be on at a time. Thus, you check each radio button you encounter to see whether it is checked. If so, you save out the value of the radio button. When you restore the values, you check the value of each radio button you encounter to see whether it is the one that should be checked.

Now that you can save any of the <INPUT> tags, you can write code to handle the other types of tags, as shown in the following code:

```
function SaveType(obj) {
  //Decide what to save based upon what the object is
  switch (obj.tagName) {
  case "INPUT":
      SaveInputType(obj);
      break;
  case "TEXTAREA":
      myForm.setAttribute(obj.name, obj.value);
      break;
  case "SELECT":
      myForm.setAttribute(obj.name,obj.selectedIndex);
      break;
  }
}
```

Note that this code calls SaveInputType if the tag is an <INPUT> tag.

The SaveType function only saves elements that the user can directly modify. You can easily write code to handle other elements, such as <DIV>s, <SPAN>s, and so forth. For example, to save out the value of a <DIV>, you can add code such as this:

```
case "DIV":
   myForm.setAttribute(obj.name, obj.innerHTML);
```

Now that you know how to deal with the various types, saving a form is easy. You loop through all the elements on the form. If they have a name, you call SaveType, passing in the element. Note that previous pages only saved <INPUT> tags, and thus that is all you looked for from the form. Now you need to find all the elements on the form, so you use the myForm.all collection. Here's the code:

```
//Walk though all elements on the form
oColl = myForm.all;
//Loop through and save them as name, value pairs
for (i = 0; i < oColl.length; i++) {
  //Make sure the element has a name
  if (oColl[i].name && (oColl[i].name != ""))
      SaveType(oColl[i]);
}
```

Because you are looping through all the elements in a form, you can easily encounter elements that don't have a name property. You need to check for this situation before you try to find the value of the name property. Otherwise, you end up with a script error. If the element does not have a name property, oColl[I].name returns null. Thus, the if statement ends before you check the value of the name property.

Reading in saved information is akin to writing it. You go through all the elements on the form. If they have a name, you see whether a value is stored. You check the type of the element to determine how to restore the value.

To see a page that can read and restore values from a wide variety of input types, load persist4.html from the ch14 folder. Enter a variety of values into the form, and then shut down the browser. Load the page again, and you see that the values successfully restore. You can see the complete listing in Listing 14-4.

This code does not save <SELECT> tags with multiple selections in them. One way you can handle this case is to use the XML API to write out a richer structure that preserves the information about all the items that are selected.

Listing 14-4	The persist4.html Source Code

```
<HTML>
<HEAD>
  <TITLE>Persisting from a form: all user types</TITLE>
<STYLE>
.save { behavior:url(#default#userdata)}</STYLE>
<SCRIPT>
//This will save any named attributes in the form myForm
//Now handles check boxes, radio buttons, select boxes, and textarea's

function SaveInputType(obj) {
   //Decide what to save based upon what the INPUT type is
   switch (obj.type) {
   case "text":
   case "hidden":
       myForm.setAttribute(obj.name,obj.value);
       break;
   case "checkbox":
       myForm.setAttribute(obj.name,obj.checked);
       break;
   case "radio":
       //Special case, because radio buttons all have the same name
       //So what we'll do is save the value of the one that is checked
       if (obj.checked)
           myForm.setAttribute(obj.name,obj.value);
       break;
   }
}

function SaveType(obj) {
   //Decide what to save based upon what the object is
   switch (obj.tagName) {
   case "INPUT":
       SaveInputType(obj);
       break;
   case "TEXTAREA":
       myForm.setAttribute(obj.name, obj.value);
       break;
```

(continued)

Listing 14-4 *(continued)*

```
        myForm.setAttribute(obj.name,obj.selectedIndex);
        break;
    }
}

function SaveIt() {
    //Walk though all elements on the form
    oColl = myForm.all;
    //Loop through and save them as name, value pairs
    for (i = 0; i < oColl.length; i++) {
        //Make sure the element has a name
        if (oColl[i].name && (oColl[i].name != ""))
            SaveType(oColl[i]);
    }
    //Now save the data
    myForm.save("mydata");
}

function RestoreInputType(obj,val) {
    //Decide how to restore based upon what the INPUT type is
    switch (obj.type) {
    case "text":
    case "hidden":
        obj.value = val;
        break;
    case "checkbox":
        if (val == "true")
            obj.checked = true;
        else
            obj.checked = false;
        break;
    case "radio":
        //Special case, because radio buttons all have the same name
        if (obj.value == val)
            obj.checked = true;
        else
            obj.checked = false;
        break;
    }
}

function RestoreType(obj,val) {
    //Decide what to save based upon what the object is
    switch (obj.tagName) {
    case "INPUT":
        RestoreInputType(obj,val);
        break;
    case "TEXTAREA":
        obj.value = val;
        break;
    case "SELECT":
        obj.selectedIndex = val;
        break;
    }
}
```

```
Function RestoreIt() {
   //Load the persisted data
   myForm.load("mydata");
   //Walk through the form and set the values
   oColl = myForm.all;
   for (i = 0; i < oColl.length; i++) {
       //Make sure the element has a name property and a defined name
       if (oColl[i].name && (oColl[i].name != "")) {
           temp = myForm.getAttribute(oColl[i].name);
           if (temp)
               //Set the value
               RestoreType(oColl[i],temp);
       }
   }
}
</SCRIPT>
</HEAD>
<BODY onload="RestoreIt()" onunload="SaveIt()">
<CENTER>
<H1>Alien Surf Shop</H1>
<FORM NAME="myForm" CLASS="save">
  <TABLE WIDTH="50%">
   <TR><TD WIDTH=60>Email </TD><TD><INPUT NAME="email" SIZE="34"></TD></TR>
   <TR><TD>Name          </TD><TD><INPUT NAME="Identity"    SIZE="34"></TD></TR>
   <TR><TD>Street        </TD><TD><INPUT NAME="Address"     SIZE="34"></TD></TR>
   <TR><TD>City          </TD><TD><INPUT NAME="City"        SIZE="34"></TD></TR>
   <TR><TD>State         </TD><TD><INPUT NAME="State"       SIZE="4"> Zip Code <INPUT
            NAME="ZipCode" SIZE="5"></TD></TR>
   <TR><TD COLSPAN=2> Male <INPUT TYPE=RADIO NAME="Gender" Value="Male">
                     Female <INPUT TYPE=RADIO NAME="Gender" Value="Female">
                     <SELECT NAME=Age>
                           <OPTION VALUE="<13">Under 13</OPTION>
                         <OPTION VALUE=">12<19">Between 13 and 18</OPTION>
                             <OPTION VALUE=">18<35">Between 18 and 35</OPTION>
                             <OPTION VALUE="Non-Committal">I know it. But I'm not
            telling</OPTION>
                         </SELECT></TD></TR>
   <TR><TD COLSPAN=2>I Like Cats <INPUT TYPE=CHECKBOX NAME="Cats" Value="Cats"> I Like Dogs
                   <INPUT TYPE=CHECKBOX NAME="Dogs" Value="Dogs"></TD></TR>
   <TR><TD COLSPAN=2>Comments:<BR><TEXTAREA NAME=TA1 ROWS=5 COLS=38>
                   </TEXTAREA></TD></TR>
  </TABLE>
</FORM>
</CENTER>
<HR>
<SPAN>
  <OL><B>To test this feature out</B>
      <LI>Fill in the form<LI>Then close IE5 and/or visit another site<LI>
              Then open this document up again
  </OL></SPAN>
</BODY>
</HTML>
```

My Brain Hurts. Just Give Me a Behavior

In the earlier sections of this chapter, you find out how to create a page that can read in and save out all of its data. And you unfortunately discover that doing so can involve writing reams of code. Having to carry this code around from page to page can be a real pain. Fortunately, in Chapter 12 I tell you about a great way to hide and reuse code: behaviors. You can write a behavior that hides all the complexity of loading and saving code. If you apply the behavior to an element, it automatically saves its value — and the value of all the elements contained within it — when the page is closed, refreshed, or moved away from. Likewise, it automatically restores the values when the page is loaded.

In fact, such a behavior can be very cool. Suppose that you have a page with three forms on it, and you want to save the values from only two of them. You can apply the behavior to the two forms that you want saved but not to the other form.

Using the custom persist behavior

I begin by showing you how to use the custom persist behavior. (In a little bit I show you how to create it. No peeking!) You can find this behavior in the persist.htc file in the ch14 folder. As I've mentioned, it automatically saves and restores any forms or elements that it is applied to. You begin by incorporating this behavior into your page:

```
<STYLE>
    .save { behavior:url(#default#userdata) url("persist.htc")}
</STYLE>
```

Wait a minute! It looks like the `save` style has two behaviors now. Yup. That's very true. You can combine behaviors together to create new, even more powerful behaviors. In this case, you start with the capabilities that the built-in `userData` behavior supplies. You then extend those capabilities to provide the automatic form- and element-saving features by adding in all the capabilities of the behavior found in persist.htc.

When you use multiple behaviors, they are applied sequentially. Because the persist.htc behavior requires the `userData` behavior, you need to list them in the order shown above.

Now all you need to do to save and restore values is apply this `save` behavior to anything you want to save. For example, you can take the same form used in persist5.html and persist it with the following HTML:

```
<FORM NAME="myForm" CLASS="save">
```

Listing 14-5 shows the complete HTML page that loads and saves data. Note that now that you've put all the nasty code inside a behavior, the HTML page is much easier to understand. It has no code at all! In fact, it is so simple that you can easily imagine adding persistence capabilities to any page.

Listing 14-5	The persist5.html Source Code

```
<HTML>
<HEAD>
  <TITLE>Persisting from a form: all user types</TITLE>
<STYLE>
  .save { behavior:url(#default#userdata) url("persist.htc")}
</STYLE>
</HEAD>
<BODY>
<CENTER>
<H1>Alien Surf Shop</H1>
<FORM NAME="myForm" CLASS="save">
  <TABLE WIDTH="50%">
  <TR><TD WIDTH=60>Email </TD><TD><INPUT NAME="email" SIZE="34"></TD></TR>
  <TR><TD>Name         </TD><TD><INPUT NAME="Identity"    SIZE="34"></TD></TR>
  <TR><TD>Street       </TD><TD><INPUT NAME="Address"     SIZE="34"></TD></TR>
  <TR><TD>City         </TD><TD><INPUT NAME="City"        SIZE="34"></TD></TR>
  <TR><TD>State        </TD><TD><INPUT NAME="State"       SIZE="4"> Zip Code <INPUT
           NAME="ZipCode" SIZE="5"></TD></TR>
  <TR><TD COLSPAN=2> Male <INPUT TYPE=RADIO NAME="Gender" Value="Male">
                    Female <INPUT TYPE=RADIO NAME="Gender" Value="Female">
                    <SELECT NAME=Age>
                        <OPTION VALUE="<13">Under 13</OPTION>
                    <OPTION VALUE=">12<19">Between 13 and 18</OPTION>
                        <OPTION VALUE=">18<35">Between 18 and 35</OPTION>
                        <OPTION VALUE="Non-Committal">I know it, But I'm not
           telling</OPTION>
                    </SELECT></TD></TR>
  <TR><TD COLSPAN=2>I Like Cats <INPUT TYPE=CHECKBOX NAME="Cats"
           Value="Cats"> I Like Dogs <INPUT TYPE=CHECKBOX NAME="Dogs"
           Value="Dogs"></TD></TR>
  <TR><TD COLSPAN=2>Comments:<BR><TEXTAREA NAME=TA1 ROWS=5 COLS=38></TEXTAREA>
           </TD></TR>
  </TABLE>
</FORM>
</CENTER>
<HR>
<SPAN>
  <OL><B>To test this feature out</B>
      <LI>Fill in the form<LI>Then close IE5 and/or visit another site<LI>Then open
           this document up again
  </OL></SPAN>
</BODY>
</HTML>
```

The other shoe drops

As you can see in the preceding section, using the persist.htc behavior is very easy. But writing the behavior involves even more code than Listing 14-5! So if you're feeling dizzy from all the code you just read (if you just read Listing 14-5), be sure to sit down.

How does the persist.htc behavior work? It uses a modified version of the code from persist4.html. First, you change the code so that it can be generically applied to any element. (Why? Well, the code in persist4.html applies just to an element named myForm. You need the code to work with whatever element you apply the behavior to. After all, maybe you're using it on a page that doesn't have a form named myForm. Or maybe you want to save out the values from several forms.) In order to do so, you use a special JavaScript object called this. When a behavior executes, the this object points to the object upon which the behavior is applied. So if you apply the userData behavior to a form named foo, checking the value of this.innerText is the same as checking the value of foo.innerText. And, of course, if you apply the behavior to a form named baz, checking the value of this.innerText is the same as checking the value of baz.innerText.

Here's the modified version of SaveIt. Note that it now finds the collection of all elements contained by the element to which the behavior is applied. (That's what this.all does.) It also calls the save method on the element to which the behavior is applied. (That's what this.save does.)

```
function SaveIt() {
    //Walk though all elements on the element
    oColl = this.all;
    //Loop through and save them as name, value pairs
    for (i = 0; i < oColl.length; i++) {
        //Make sure the element has a name
        if (oColl[i].name && (oColl[i].name != ""))
            SaveType(oColl[i]);
    }
    //Now save the data
    this.save("mydata");
}
```

Next you need to hook up the behavior so that it automatically fires when the page loads and unloads. Before, you did this task by handling the onload and onunload events for the <BODY> tag. But one of the great things about writing behaviors is that users don't have to write event-handling code. Instead, you write the behavior so that it automatically applies.

To start, you have the behavior restore values when the page loads. You use a simple trick to do so. Instead of trying to hook to a page event (a plan that happens not to work very well in this case), you just put a line in the behavior that calls RestoreIt:

```
//Call the restore when the behavior is read in
RestoreIt()
```

This code isn't put inside a function. It's just at the end of the script for the behavior. When the behavior is applied, Internet Explorer processes all the script for the behavior. It encounters the `RestoreIt()` line and calls `RestoreIt()`.

Having the behavior get called automatically when the page unloads is a little trickier. In the behaviors you write in Chapter 12, you use the `<ATTACH>` tag to have an event call a behavior function. You may think that you can do the same thing here, but unfortunately, you can't. Why not? The `<ATTACH>` tag only lets you handle events generated by the element to which the behavior is attached. But most elements don't fire any event before they get destroyed. In fact, you only get that event for the `<BODY>` element. So you need the behavior to somehow handle the `onunload` event for the whole page. You do so by using the `attachEvent` method. This method lets you associate a behavior function with an event. You call it on the window object (which fires the `unonload`). Here's the code:

```
window.attachEvent("onunload", SaveIt);
```

Whenever a user leaves the page, refreshes, or shuts down the browser, the window object fires `onunload`. Because the behavior is attached to this event, the `SaveIt` function gets called. Note that several functions can attach to the same event. Thus, if you use two persist.htc behaviors on a page, both get called when the `onunload` fires.

So far, all of your save and load code has read values associated with `mydata`. If several pages have the same names for elements, they all read and write into the same data set. If a page has several forms on it and the elements in the different forms use the same names, you also end up writing over data. To avoid overwriting, make the behavior more generic. Check the element to which the behavior is applied, and if the element has a `name`, save all the data using that `name`. If it doesn't have a `name` but does have an `id`, save using the `id` value. And if it doesn't have either, fall back on good old" `mydata`". Thus, every element to which the persist.htc behavior is applied ends up saving into its own data area. Here's the code that determines the name to use:

```
if (this.name && (this.name != ""))
   filename = this.name;
else if (this.id && (this.id != ""))
   filename = this.id;
else
   filename = "mydata"
```

You can see the complete code for the persist.htc behavior by looking at Listing 14-6.

Listing 14-6	The persist.htc Source Code

```
<ATTACH EVENT="onload" HANDLER="RestoreIt"/>
<ATTACH EVENT="onbeforeunload" HANDLER="SaveIt"/>
<SCRIPT>
//This will save and restore any named elements that the behavior is attached to. It will
//apply to the element and any elements contained within it. That is, it will traverse through
//elements in a form, table, etc.
//Change SaveType() and RestoreType() to add new types for persistence,
              such as DIVs and so forth

//We are going to get tricky here and use script to attach to the events we need
window.attachEvent("onunload", SaveIt);

function SaveInputType(obj) {
   //Decide what to save based upon what the INPUT type is
   switch (obj.type) {
   case "text":
   case "hidden":
      this.setAttribute(obj.name,obj.value);
      break;
   case "checkbox":
      this.setAttribute(obj.name,obj.checked);
      break;
   case "radio":
      //Special case, because radio buttons all have the same name
      //So what we'll do is save the value of the one that is checked
      if (obj.checked)
          this.setAttribute(obj.name,obj.value);
      break;
   }
}

function SaveType(obj) {
   //Decide what to save based upon what the object is
   switch (obj.tagName) {
   case "INPUT":
      SaveInputType(obj);
      break;
   case "TEXTAREA":
      this.setAttribute(obj.name, obj.value);
      break;
   case "SELECT":
      this.setAttribute(obj.name,obj.selectedIndex);
      break;
   }
}

function SaveIt() {
   //Walk though all elements on the element
   oColl = this.all;
   //Loop through and save them as name, value pairs
   for (i = 0; i < oColl.length; i++) {
      //Make sure the element has a name
      if (oColl[i].name && (oColl[i].name != ""))
          SaveType(oColl[i]);
   }
   //Now save the data
```

```
      //We'll load from the form or element name, if there is one
      if (this.name && (this.name != ""))
          filename = this.name;
      else if (this.id && (this.id != ""))
          filename = this.id;
      else
          filename = "mydata"
      this.save(filename);
}

function RestoreInputType(obj,val) {
   //Decide how to restore based upon what the INPUT type is
   switch (obj.type) {
   case "text":
   case "hidden":
       obj.value = val;
       break;
   case "checkbox":
       if (val == "true")
           obj.checked = true;
       else
           obj.checked = false;
       break;
   case "radio":
       //Special case, because radio buttons all have the same name
       if (obj.value == val)
           obj.checked = true;
       else
           obj.checked = false;
       break;
   }
}

function RestoreType(obj,val) {
   //Decide what to save based upon what the object is
   switch (obj.tagName) {
   case "INPUT":
       RestoreInputType(obj,val);
       break;
   case "TEXTAREA":
       obj.value = val;
       break;
   case "SELECT":
       obj.selectedIndex = val;
       break;
   }
}


function RestoreIt() {
   //Load the persisted data
   //We'll load from the form or element name, if there is one
   if (this.name && (this.name != ""))
       filename = this.name;
   else if (this.id && (this.id != ""))
       filename = this.id;
   else
       filename = "mydata"
```

(continued)

Listing 14-6 *(continued)*

```
this.load(filename);
//Walk through the form and set the values
oColl = this.all;
for (i = 0; i < oColl.length; i++) {
    //Make sure the element has a name property and a defined name
    if (oColl[i].name && (oColl[i].name != "")) {
        temp = this.getAttribute(oColl[i].name);
        if (temp)
            //Set the value
            RestoreType(oColl[i],temp);
    }
}
}

//Call the restore when the behavior is read in
RestoreIt()
</SCRIPT>
```

Chapter 15

Working with Other Browsers

In This Chapter

▶ Wrapping scripts and style sheets in comments
▶ Using the `<NOFRAME>` tag
▶ Finding the browser version
▶ Conditionalizing Dynamic HTML-specific code
▶ Switching frames depending on the browser
▶ Dynamically inserting new HTML code
▶ Using controls with no width or height

*G*uess what? Microsoft Internet Explorer 5.0 isn't the only browser in the world. As a result, many of the cool things that you have seen in this book don't work with other browsers. Your pages may look great when viewed with the latest version of Internet Explorer but may look questionable or be completely worthless in Internet Explorer 3.0 or Netscape Navigator.

You therefore have two choices: You can require all your users to work with a specific browser version, or you can insert code that checks what type of browser is viewing your page and reacts accordingly. In this chapter, you find out about several techniques for adjusting how a page behaves based on the browser that you are using.

The Golden Oldies

You can find many different browsers out there: Internet Explorer 2.0, Internet Explorer 3.0, Internet Explorer 4.0, Navigator 2.0, Navigator 3.0, Navigator 4.0, Mosaic Spider, and many more. The good news is that each new browser introduced great new features. The bad news is that some people still use the old browsers. Thus, pages that take advantage of new features don't work on older browsers.

Some browsers, especially the early versions, don't understand scripts, style sheets, or frames. Fortunately, most people no longer use these browsers, so you can get by with assuming that frames, scripts, and style sheets work. But to be on the safe side, I'm going to show you what to do so that you don't fail miserably with the ancient browsers.

You can't duplicate what a script or style sheet does for a browser that doesn't support these features. In fact, the scripts and style sheet information just show up on your page as if you wanted it to be displayed. So, although you can't get the functionality, you can at least keep the text from appearing on the screen by enclosing the insides of the script and style sheet tags in a comment block. Browsers that understand scripts and style sheets ignore the comments and read the information. The earlier browsers skip everything inside the comments. They don't process the scripts or style data, but they also don't display it directly on the screen. Instead, you see all the normal HTML text, but it lacks interaction and formatting.

For example, the following script has a comment block that's inside the <SCRIPT> tags. On a browser that doesn't understand scripts, nothing appears. A browser that understands scripts processes the code, and the turnBlue function can be called. If you didn't have the comments, the script itself would show up on the Web page.

```
<SCRIPT>
<!--
function turnBlue(elName) {
    elName.style.color = "blue";
}
//-->
</SCRIPT>
```

Likewise, the following comments hide a style sheet definition from browsers that don't understand style sheets:

```
<STYLE TYPE="text/css">
<!--
    P { font-size: 30pt; font-family: AdLib BT; font-weight: normal; text-align:
        center }
//-->
</STYLE>
```

Browsers that understand style sheets can read the style definition. Browsers that don't understand style sheets ignore the whole lot.

Dealing with browsers that don't understand frames is a little trickier. Follow these steps to make your pages display information even if the browser doesn't understand frames:

1. **Add a** `<NOFRAMES>` **tag after the** `</FRAMESET>` **tag.**

2. **Place any HTML code that you would like to appear for browsers that don't support frames.**

3. **End the code with a** `</NOFRAMES>` **tag.**

Browsers that understand frames ignore what is inside the `noframes` section. Browsers that don't understand frames also don't understand the `<NOFRAMES>` tag. Therefore, they ignore it and just display the HTML code that follows — namely, the code between the `<NOFRAMES>` and the `</NOFRAMES>` tags.

You can do two basic things inside the `noframes` section. First, you can tell the user that he is a loser and should get a real browser. You can even point that person to a browser to download. Or you can provide a jump to a page that you've designed that doesn't use frames. The advantage of the latter approach is that your site is viewable by a wider audience. The disadvantage is that you need to create and maintain two different pages — one that works with frames and one that works without frames.

The following HTML code provides a jump if the browser doesn't understand frames:

```
<FRAMESET COLS="100%" ROWS="50%,*">
    <FRAME NAME="Frame 1" SRC="" SCROLLING="AUTO">
    <FRAME NAME="Frame 2" SRC="" SCROLLING="AUTO">
</FRAMESET>
<NOFRAMES>
Dude, get a real browser...<BR>
<A HREF="framefree.html">Click here for a version without frames.</A>
</NOFRAMES>
```

Who Am I?

Although it's a good idea to prepare for browsers that don't understand frames, scripts, and style sheets, you're more likely to encounter browsers that don't understand Dynamic HTML. You can work around this handicap in several ways:

- You can write for the lowest common denominator, HTML 3.2. Your pages may be dull, but they work everywhere.

- You can tell people to get a specific browser, such as Internet Explorer 5.0.

- You can create Internet Explorer 5.0-specific pages and generic pages and dynamically determine which to display by using code on the client side.

✔ You can create Internet Explorer 5.0-specific pages and generic pages and dynamically determine which to display by using code on the server side. This technique is the most reliable and is the best to choose for complex pages, although it does mean maintaining two sets of pages and doing server-side scripting.

✔ You can create a single page and dynamically modify it if the browser is Internet Explorer 5.0.

✔ You can ignore the differences. Elements that use Cascading Style Sheet (CSS) positioning and filters show up as if the CSS information weren't there. The page flows in a strange and potentially awkward fashion, but the bulk of the material is there. Of course, you do need to add some extra code to scripts to keep them from making calls that don't work when run on an old browser.

No matter which of the approaches you use, you need to determine which browser is viewing the page. Fortunately, doing so is easy, especially because Microsoft has kindly included a sample function in the Internet Explorer documentation that returns the version number of Internet Explorer. It returns 0 if the browser is not Internet Explorer.

To see the script, check out the function checkVer in detect.html from the ch15 folder on the enclosed CD-ROM (see Listing 15-1). The script finds the browser name from window.navigator.userAgent. This action returns a string indicating the browser name, the operating system, and more. For example, in Internet Explorer 5.0, the string is Mozilla/4.0 (compatible; MSIE 5.0; Windows 95). All versions of Internet Explorer have MSIE in the string, followed by the version number. In this case, the version number is 5.0.

Listing 15-1   **The detect.html Source Code**

```
<HTML>
<HEAD>
<TITLE>Version Checker</TITLE>
<SCRIPT>
//Returns the IE version number
function checkVer() {
    var appVer, ieLoc;
    appVer = window.navigator.userAgent;
    ieLoc = appVer.indexOf("MSIE");
    if (ieLoc > 0)
        //Internet Explorer
        return parseInt(appVer.substring(ieLoc+5, appVer.indexOf(".", ieLoc)));
    else
```

```
        return 0;
}
function displayVer() {
    var ver;

    ver = checkVer();
    if (ver != 0)
        alert("Internet Explorer " + ver);
    else
        alert("Not Internet Explorer");
}
</SCRIPT>
</HEAD>
<BODY onload="displayVer()">
This page checks the browser version.
</BODY>
</HTML>
```

When looking at this string, you may wonder whether Microsoft programmers have been watching too many Godzilla movies and somehow went off the deep end. Although that may be the case, that's not why *Mozilla* is in the version name. Mozilla was an early code name for Navigator. It was part of what Navigator returned during its early versions, and the word has remained in browsers, including Microsoft's, ever since. It's just one of those strange pieces of computer history that may live on forever.

When the script has the browser name, it checks to see whether *MSIE* is in the name. If it is, the script finds the major version number by looking for the number that follows *MSIE*. (You make the script find the major and minor number by converting the value up to the semicolon into a floating-point number.)

To see the browser detection in action, load detect.html. It brings up a message box that indicates which browser is viewing the page.

Shampooing and Conditionalizing Code

After you know the browser type, you can customize how a page looks. If your page is fairly simple, you can check the browser version before running script that talks to the Dynamic HTML object model. For example, suppose that you have created a page that transitions in text, as you see in Chapter 8. This page calls the Play and Apply methods on the filters collection for an element. Unfortunately, Internet Explorer 3.0 and Navigator don't have a filters collection, much less support for transitions.

To prevent error messages, you can wrap the transition code inside a browser check, as shown in Listing 15-2. The init function determines whether the browser is Internet Explorer 4.0 or later. If so, it performs the transition. If not, the transition code isn't called. In Internet Explorer 3.0 or

Navigator, when the page loads, the HTML text in the body appears. That's because those browsers don't support CSS positioning, and thus the visibility property is ignored. In Internet Explorer 4.0 (or higher), the text transitions in. Thus, the page works in multiple browsers, but it looks better with Internet Explorer 4.0 and Internet Explorer 5.0.

To see the page in action, load condcode.html from the ch15 folder.

Listing 15-2	The condcode.html Source Code

```
<HTML>
<HEAD>
<TITLE>Version Checker</TITLE>
<SCRIPT>
//Returns the IE version number
function checkVer() {
     var appVer, ieLoc;
     appVer = window.navigator.userAgent;
     ieLoc = appVer.indexOf("MSIE");
     if (ieLoc > 0)
          //Internet Explorer
          return parseInt(appVer.substring(ieLoc+5,
               appVer.indexOf(".", ieLoc)));
     else
          return 0;
}
function init() {
     if (checkVer() >= 4) {
          txt.filters(0).Apply();
          txt.style.visibility = "visible";
          txt.filters(0).Play();
     }
}
</SCRIPT>
</HEAD>
<BODY onload="init()">
<SPAN id=txt style="filter:revealTrans(transition=6,
          duration=2);visibility:hidden;width:50%">Welcome to my page!</SPAN>
</BODY>
</HTML>
```

The Invisible Frame Trick

If your page is complex, simply wrapping conditional code around function calls isn't sufficient. For example, if you make extensive use of 2-D positioning, your page isn't going to look very good in less-capable browsers. Instead, you need to make the following two pages:

   ✔ A page that uses 2-D positioning and the full set of Dynamic HTML features

✔ A page that uses tables and anything else that Internet Explorer 3.0 and Navigator provide

Then you need to determine which page to display. One approach is to use a technique that's similar to that for frames: If the browser isn't the one that provides the features you need, provide a link to the other page. Of course, that approach doesn't look very good. Instead, you can use the invisible frame trick, as follows.

1. **Create an entry page that consists of two frames.**

   One frame takes up no space (and is thus invisible), and the other consumes the entire page.

2. **Add browser-detection code to the invisible frame, and have the code decide what to display in the full-screen frame.**

   As a result, when the user goes to the page, he or she always sees a page that's appropriate for his or her browser. The user never knows that several versions of the page exist.

To see this technique in action, load frameswap.html from the ch15 directory (see Listing 15-3). This page contains two frames. The invisible frame uses the following code to switch what is shown in the visible frame:

```
function switchFrames() {
    if (checkVer() < 4)
        parent.frames.item(1).location.href = "ie30page.html";
    else
        parent.mainframe.location.href = "ie40page.html";
}
```

Listing 15-3   **The frameswap.html Source Code**

```
<HTML>
<FRAMESET COLS="100%" ROWS="0,*" FRAMEBORDER=0>
    <FRAME NAME="switcher" SRC="switcher.html" SCROLLING="NO" MARGINHEIGHT=0
           MARGINWIDTH=0 NORESIZE>
    <FRAME NAME="mainframe" SRC="blank.html" SCROLLING="AUTO">
</FRAMESET>
</HTML>
```

The `parent.frames.item(1).location.href` command does the same thing as `parent.mainframe.location.href`. However, the first approach works in Navigator, whereas the second does not.

In Listing 15-3, note that you must set the SRC value for both frames for this technique to work. (That is, you must set what HTML page is displayed in the frames by filling in the `SRC` parameter in the `<FRAME>` tag.) That's why the visible page loads blank.html. As you may guess, blank.html is just an HTML file with an empty body. Listing 15-4 shows the code for the invisible frame.

Listing 15-4	The switcher.html Source Code

```
<HTML>
<HEAD>
<SCRIPT>
function checkVer() {
    var appVer, ieLoc;
    appVer = window.navigator.userAgent;
    ieLoc = appVer.indexOf("MSIE");
    if (ieLoc > 0)
        //Internet Explorer
        return parseInt(appVer.substring(ieLoc+5, appVer.indexOf(".", ieLoc)));
    else
        return 0;
}

function switchFrames() {
    if (checkVer() < 4)
        parent.frames.item(1).location.href = "ie30page.html";
    else
        parent.mainframe.location.href = "ie40page.html";
}
</SCRIPT>
</HEAD>
<BODY onload="switchFrames()">

</BODY>
</HTML>
```

Some early browser releases require the `self.` prefix to be used such as in `self.parent.mainframe.location.href`.

One problem with this technique is that, when you click on the Back button, you go back to the blank page before going to the page before frameswap.html.

Text Implants

Another way to alter a page is to dynamically insert new HTML code if the page is viewed with Internet Explorer 4.0 or beyond. You can do so in the following two ways:

- ✔ **Use `innerHTML`.** Create a set of empty spans in the page. Have a function that checks the browser version and inserts new text into those spans.

- ✔ **Use the data-binding control.** Add a Tabular Data Control (TDC) to the end of the page and have it link to a file containing HTML code. Add spans or divs throughout the page where you want new code to be inserted, and bind them to columns in the database. If the browser is Internet Explorer 4.0 or later, the data-binding control grabs the new HTML code and inserts it into the various spans or divs. Otherwise, the browser doesn't understand what a TDC is, and the blank spans and divs don't appear.

You can see this technique in action by loading condhtml.html from the ch15 folder (see Listing 15-5). With Internet Explorer 3.0, the only thing that's displayed is `Welcome to my page!` With Internet Explorer 4.0 and later, the two divs get filled with HTML code from the file newhtml.txt, as you can see in Figure 15-1. Listing 15-6 shows the contents of newhtml.txt.

Figure 15-1:
New HTML
code is
dynamically
inserted into
the page.

Welcome to my page!
Welcome to the new world!

Hello

Listing 15-5   **The condhtml.html Source Code**

```
<HTML>
<HEAD>
<TITLE>Inserts HTML</TITLE>
</HEAD>
<BODY>
Welcome to my page!
<DIV DATASRC="#tdc" DATAFLD="column1" DATAFORMATAS="HTML">
</DIV>
<DIV DATASRC="#tdc" DATAFLD="column2" DATAFORMATAS="HTML" style="position:absolute;
            left:150; top:150; width:30%">
</DIV>
<OBJECT ID="tdc" CLASSID="CLSID:333C7BC4-460F-11D0-BC04-0080C7055A83" WIDTH=0 HEIGHT=0>
  <param name="DataURL" value="newhtml.txt">
</OBJECT>
</BODY>
</HTML>
```

Listing 15-6   **The newhtml.txt Source Code**

```
<B>Welcome to the new world!</B>,<DIV style="color:green;background-color:yellow">
        Hello</DIV>
```

If you use this technique, remember that any positioning information on elements that are inserted into the divs or spans is relative to the div or the span. Thus, if you want to position an object absolutely with respect to the entire Web page, you need to position the div into which it is being inserted in the upper-left corner of the page.

Under Control

If you use the built-in ActiveX controls (such as the multimedia controls) in your page, set their width and height by using CSS notation, not using the older notation. That is, use the following script:

```
<OBJECT style="height:200; width:200"
CLASSID = "CLSID:369303C2-D7AC-11D0-89D5-00A0C90833E6">
</OBJECT>
```

And don't use this script:

```
<OBJECT width=200 height=200
CLASSID = "CLSID:369303C2-D7AC-11D0-89D5-00A0C90833E6">
</OBJECT>
```

As a result, the object appears properly with Internet Explorer 4.0 and beyond, but it doesn't appear with other browsers — because the default width and height are 0.

Part IV
The Part of Tens

The 5th Wave   By Rich Tennant

AND TO COMPLETE THE MULTIMEDIA EXPERIENCE, WE WANT TO SHIP EACH WORKSTATION WITH THIS SCRATCH 'N SNIFF MOUSE PAD AND A SCENT-RESIDENT RAM CARD.

In this part . . .

No *...For Dummies* book would be complete without the famous Part of Tens. In this part, you can read about the top ten places to find naughty pictures on the Internet. (Whoops, I think that's in Dr. Ruth's book, *Sex For Dummies,* published by IDG Books Worldwide, Inc.)

Actually, you find the top ten Dynamic HTML objects that you need to know about and the top ten style tags. These are things that you are going to use repeatedly. You also find out about the top ten HTML tags and the top ten HTML events. Finally, you read about Mike's famous ten rules for HTML authoring. So grab your favorite HTML code and read away.

Chapter 16

Ten HTML Tags: Don't Leave Home without 'Em

In This Chapter

▶ Reviewing the most common tags

*W*eb pages are filled with tags — those funny-looking commands that are inside angle brackets. Although there are billions of tags (okay, not quite that many), the following are ten that you can't live without:

`<HTML>`: Sure, this tag is boring. But you must use it at the beginning of every page and its good pal `</HTML>` at the end of every page.

`<BODY>`: This tag is where the action is. All the data that gets displayed on the screen shows up between `<BODY>` and `</BODY>`. It's also where you set the background color and the text color for the entire page and where you set up an event handler for when the page loads. For example, the following tag creates a black page with silver text and calls the `init` function as soon as the page loads: `<BODY BGCOLOR=black TEXT=silver onload="init()">`.

`<DIV>`, `<SPAN>`, and `<LAYER>`: To use CSS positioning to place and move text, to place and move whole sections of HTML code, to filter text, or to show and hide whole regions, you need to use a `<DIV>` or a `<SPAN>` tag. If you set the width, you create a column. Divs are closely related to spans. The only difference is that divs start on their own line, whereas spans can be created directly within another text stream. If you are writing pages for Netscape Navigator, you use the `<LAYER>` tag. Like `<DIV>` and `<SPAN>`, it sets up regions for display, but unlike the other two tags, Navigator lets you change the contents dynamically.

`<TABLE>`: This tried-and-true tag is a great way to create columns that are positioned relative to each other. Tables are useful for aligning data, creating columns with different alignment, and displaying data from databases. Related tags include `<THEAD>`, `<TBODY>`, `<TR>`, and `<TD>`.

<FRAMESET>: To show more than one URL at a time or to divide a page into a table of contents and a display area, frames get the job done. Remember not to put frames inside the <BODY> tag. Name the frames to make accessing them later easy. Related tags include <FRAME> and <IFRAME>.

<CENTER>: It's short, it's sweet, and it's been around forever. But <CENTER> remains a great tag. Use it any time that you want to center an element on the page.

: "Give me a break," you say? Of course. This tag's the one that you need to insert lines between elements. It's great for breaking up paragraphs, separating text or images from other images, and generally giving you some space when you need it.

<HEAD>: This tag doesn't do much — except act as the resting stop for background sounds, style sheets, scripts, and titles. If you need any of these elements, be sure to put a <HEAD> tag before your <BODY> tag.

<SCRIPT>: This tag is the key to all interactivity on your page. Put your scripts inside the <SCRIPT> tag. Be sure to set the LANGUAGE parameter to VBScript if you aren't using JavaScript. To handle events on ActiveX controls, use the FOR/EVENT syntax to set up scripts that process those events.

<OBJECT>: Last but not least, this tag lets you add ActiveX controls to your page. Many of these controls are out there just dying to add a burst of functionality to your page. This tag is particularly necessary when adding multimedia controls, XML, or data-binding services to a page.

Chapter 17

Ten Object Model Methods and Properties

In This Chapter

▶ Reviewing the most common methods and properties

*M*anipulating Web pages is all about controlling the Dynamic HTML object model through script. The following are the top ten methods and properties that you need to know about:

style: The style object is available on just about every HTML element. Use it to position and size objects, set the color and size of text, and much more. For example, foo.style.visibility = "hidden" hides an object. See Chapter 18 for a list of the top ten things to do with the style object.

With Netscape Navigator, you don't use the style object. Instead, the related properties (bgColor, visibility, and the position properties) are available from the object itself.

offsetWidth, offsetHeight, offsetLeft, offsetTop: These properties are available on all visual objects such as the body and elements. They return the size of the object and work even if the size hasn't been set using the style object. For example, document.body.offsetWidth returns the width of the body.

The corresponding Navigator properties are width, height, left, and top.

innerText: This method is available on any of the elements that contain HTML code, such as the body, divs, and spans. Use this method to replace the text inside the element, or use innerHTML to replace the HTML code inside the element.

This property isn't available with Navigator. To get the same effects, you use a layer and write into the layer using `document.write`.

src: This property indicates the name of the image file that's used for an image. Changing this property changes what graphic gets displayed on the screen.

`document.all.item(name)`: This is how you create a collection of all items on the page having a given name or `id`. It lets you write scripts that operate on groups of objects at a time, regardless of how many objects are in the group.

This property isn't available with Navigator. Instead, use one of the collections such as `anchors`, `forms`, `frames`, `images`, `layers`, and `links`.

`event`: This object is the key to processing events. Key properties include the following:

x and y (and related `offsetX`, `offsetY`, `screenX`, `screenY`, `clientX`, and `clientY`), which tell the position of the mouse

`keyCode`, which indicates what key has been pressed

`srcElement`, which indicates which object caused the event

Navigator has a different system for processing events. The `event` object gets passed as a parameter to the event handler. Some of the key properties on the `event` object are `layerX`, `layerY`, `pageX`, `pageY`, `target`, `which`, and `modifiers`.

`document.frames`: This object provides a collection of all the frames on the page. Use it to access elements that are in a frame on the page or to change what URL is displayed in a frame.

`filters`: This collection lets you access all the filters that are on an element. Use it to modify filters — that is, the visual effects — as well as to do transitions.

Navigator doesn't support CSS filters.

`document.forms`: This collection gives access to all the items that are on a form.

`className`: This property of elements lets you find or change the style that's used for an element.

The `className` property is not available on Navigator.

Chapter 18

Ten (or So) Properties of the Style Object

● ●

In This Chapter

▶ Reviewing the properties of the `style` object

▶ Reviewing the equivalent Netscape Navigator properties

● ●

The `style` object is one of the most useful objects available for an HTML element. Through it, you can set any of the CSS properties to position, size, and filter elements, as well as to provide complete control over how text appears. The `style` object has well over 40 properties within it. The following are the top ten that you are going use again and again. (Okay, so I'm giving you more than ten this time.)

Property	Meaning	HTML Example	Script Example
`left`	Sets or retrieves the position of the left side of the element. Related properties include `pixelLeft` and `posLeft`. The `left` property returns the position as a string. The string can contain any measurement unit, such as inches (in) or centimeters (cm). For example, if you set the left side of an element to be 2 inches in, `left` returns 2in. This property is available through HTML tags.	`<IMG src="foo. jpg id=foo style "="position: absolute;left: 2in">`	`foo.style. left="3in";`
`pixelLeft`	A numeric value in pixels, this property is only available through scripting.		`foo.style. pixelLeft =-219;`

Property	Meaning	HTML Example	Script Example
posLeft	A numeric value in the same units as those initially set through left. For example, if you set the left position to be 2 inches, posLeft returns 2. This property is only available through scripting.		foo.style. posLeft = 2
top	Sets or retrieves the position of the top of the element. Related properties include pixelTop and posTop. As you can guess, this property behaves similarly to left.	<IMG src="foo .jpg" id=foo style="position: absolute; top:3cm">	foo.style. pixelTop= 35;
width	Sets or retrieves the width of the element. Related properties include pixel Width and posWidth. Once again, this property behaves in the same fashion as left.	<IMG src="foo. jpg" id=foo style="position: absolute; width:30%"	foo.style. width = 200;
height	Sets or retrieves the height of the element. Related properties include pixel Height and posHeight. Needless to say, this property behaves in the same fashion as left.	<IMG id=foo src= "foo.jpg" style= "position: absolute; height:25">	foo.style. height="28px";
fontSize	Sets or retrieves the size for the font. This string can contain measurement units such as "2in". Note that you use font-size in HTML and fontSize in script.	<SPAN id=foo "font-size:2in">	foo.style. fontSize = "22pt";
color	Sets or retrieves the color for the font. Can be set to a color name, such as blue, or to a hex value, such as #FF00C0.	<SPAN id=foo tyle="color: s#FFFF00">	foo.style. color="green";

Property	Meaning	HTML Example	Script Example
filter	Sets or retrieves the effects and transitions for an element. For example, setting filter to "invert" inverts the element. Setting filter to "" clears any filters and transitions. ***Note:*** In the tag format, you would set this as `filter:invert`. Use the `filters` collection on the element to modify any of the properties or call any of the methods for the filters and transitions.	`<SPAN id=foo style="width: 30%; filter: glow">`	`foo.style. filter = "invert";`
visibility	Makes an element visible or invisible. Set to "visible" to make it visible and to "hidden" to hide the element.	`<SPAN id=foo style=" visibility: hidden">`	`"foo.style. visibility = visible";`
background Color	Sets the background color for the element. Can be set to a color name, such as blue, or to a hex value, such as #FF00C0. Note that you use `background-color` in HTML and `background Color` in script.	`<SPAN id=foo style=" background- color: yellow">`	`foo.style. backgroundColor ="#FF00FF";`
font Family	Sets or retrieves the font family to use for text. For example, to use the Impact font, you would set this property to "impact." Note that you use `font-family` in HTML and `fontFamily` in script.	`<SPAN id=foo style="font- family: Arial">`	`foo.style. fontFamily = "impact";`

Navigator doesn't have a `style` object. Rather, the equivalent properties, when they exist, are on the object itself. This list shows the most important properties for manipulating an object's style using Navigator.

Property	Meaning	HTML Example	Script Example
left	Sets or retrieves the position of the left side of the element.	`<LAYER id=foo style="position: absolute;left: 2in">`	`foo.left = 35;`

Property	Meaning	HTML Example	Script Example
top	Sets or retrieves the position of the top of the element.	`<LAYER id=foo style="position: absolute; top:3cm">`	`foo.top= 35;`
width	Sets or retrieves the width of the element.	`<LAYER id=foo style="position: absolute; width: 30%">`	`foo. width = 200;`
height	Sets or retrieves the height of the element.	`<LAYER id=foo style="position: absolute; height: 25px">`	`foo. height = 100;`
font-size	Only available on the element. Not available in script.	`<SPAN id=foo "font -size:2in">`	
color	Sets or retrieves the color for the font. Can be set to a color name, such as blue, or to a hex value, such as #FF00C0. Only available on the element, not in script.	`<SPAN id=foo style="color: #FFFF00">`	
visibility	Makes an element visible or invisible. Set to "visible" to make it visible and to "hidden" to hide the element when used on an element. Set to "show" and "hide" when used from script.	`<SPAN id=foo style="visibility: hidden">`	`foo. visibility = "show";`
back ground-color	Sets the background color for the element. Can be set to a color name, such as blue, or to a hex value, such as #FF00C0. Note that you use background-color in HTML and bgColor in script.	`<SPAN id=foo style="background -color:yellow">`	`foo.bgColor ="#FF00FF";`
font-family	Sets or retrieves the font family to use for text. For example, to use the Impact font, you set this property to "impact." Only available on the element. Not available in script.	`<SPAN id=foo style="font-family: Arial">`	

Chapter 19

Ten Events You've Been Waiting For

In This Chapter

▶ Reviewing the most common events

*E*vents fire whenever the user does something — presses a key, moves the mouse, clicks on a button, and so on. Likewise, events also fire when the page or elements reach certain states — the page loads, a path hits the end, and so on. By processing the events, you can customize how a page behaves. The following are the top ten events that you should know about. Note that they are all in lowercase characters.

onload: Fires when the page (or an element) loads. You are guaranteed that all elements are loaded and available for scripting. Process this event to initialize a page.

onmouseover: Fires when the mouse pointer moves over an element.

onmouseout: Fires when the mouse pointer moves away from an element.

onmousemove: Fires whenever the mouse pointer moves.

onclick: Fires when the user clicks on an element.

onkeypress: Fires when the user presses a key.

onchange: Fires when the user changes a value on an input field, such as by selecting a value in an option list or by leaving a text box after changing its value.

onfilterchange: Fires when a transition (or effect) finishes.

 Not available.

`onerror`: Fires when a scripting error occurs. Lets you process the error rather than having the browser report an error message.

 Not available.

`onresize`: Fires when an element changes size. Typically you process this event for the body, thereby letting you scale other objects when the user resizes the browser.

Chapter 20

Mike's Ten Rules of Web Authoring

. . . .

. . . .

Throughout this book, I share some words of wisdom to help guide you as you create Web pages. Here are those wise pronouncements, summarized in one place.

Rule No. 1: Avoid temptation

Sometimes simple solutions are the best solutions. If you don't need text swirling around, fancy 3-D animations, or blinking buttons to get your point across, don't use them. After all, they just take time and money to create and, when overused, can detract from the content.

Rule No. 2: Good things come in small packages

To display more than a few screens of information on a single page, try one of the following techniques:

✔ Get rid of information that you don't need. For example, use small images rather than full-page pictures.

✔ Add links. Provide short descriptions with links to more information. Essentially, construct a table of contents that is similar to what you would find in a magazine. Move the majority of the material into separate pages. The user gets a live overview but needs to return to the table of contents page each time he or she wants to jump to a different section.

✔ Use frames. Frames let you add a small table-of-contents area that is always present regardless of what page is viewed.

Rule No. 3: Feedback is everything

Small reactions to user actions can make a big difference. For example, you can highlight links as the user moves the mouse pointer over them. That reaction provides extra information that the user has moved on a link, and it reminds him that your page is interesting.

Rule No. 4: Timing is everything

Most Web pages are static. The page changes very little after it downloads. Adding animation can liven up a page, pull in a viewer, and dramatically increase the appeal of a Web page.

Rule No. 5: Size matters

Use whatever capabilities you have to decrease download time. Where applicable, use effects and transitions instead of rendered images and animated GIFs. Use vector graphics instead of raster graphics. These techniques all help reduce download time and thus increase the responsiveness of your page.

Rule No. 6: Reduce, recycle, reuse

Reduce the number of times that you need to request information from the server by reusing what you already have and processing it on the client side. That's what the data-binding services are all about.

Rule No. 7: Think globally

When you are scripting, look for general solutions. For example, suppose that you have filled a table with text items that serve as a menu. You want to highlight the text when the user moves the mouse pointer over it. Instead of setting up an event handler for each cell, set up a handler for the entire table. Use `event.srcElement` to see which item the user just moved the mouse pointer over.

Likewise, if you need to perform an action on a group of elements, such as to turn them all invisible, consider using a collection.

These techniques help you create smaller pages. Furthermore, you can then add and remove elements without needing to change your scripts.

Rule No. 8: Not all machines are created equal

Users have an assortment of different machines with different capabilities. Some users have ultra-hot machines with great graphics cards. Others are using 486s that are held together with chewing gum. Web authors and developers usually have better machines than the typical user. So a decked-out, ultra-chill multimedia page that screams on your Pentium II 266 with 128MB of RAM may look like it was visited by Dr. Freeze if you run it on a 486.

More importantly, check out your pages under these different screen resolutions: 640 x 480, 800 x 600, and 1024 x 768.

Rule No. 9: Not all browsers are created equal

If you can't guarantee that everyone who is visiting your page is using Microsoft Internet Explorer 5.0 (and you can't), protect yourself. Use one of the techniques that I describe in Chapter 15 so that your pages don't generate errors or look terrible when they are used with earlier browsers.

Rule No. 10: Have fun

After all, you most likely only live once.

Part V
Appendixes

The 5th Wave   By Rich Tennant

"Can someone please tell me how long 'Larry's Lunch Truck' has had his own page on the intranet?"

In this part . . .

Okay, you've made it through to the end. Now what? Well, in this part you find three appendixes. Appendi. Appendices. Whatever. The first is a quick guide to HTML. Just add water and you'll know what most of the funny HTML tags mean and do. The next is a quick tour of JavaScript. And finally, you find a guide to all the cool software that comes on the CD.

Appendix A

Tag, You're It: An Overview of HTML Tags

⬤ ⬤

In This Chapter

▶ Understanding HTML fundamentals

▶ Using the `<HTML>` and `<BODY>` tags

▶ Formatting text

▶ Adding images

▶ Adding comments

▶ Creating links

▶ Using the `<HEAD>` tag

▶ Naming elements

▶ Positioning elements

⬤ ⬤

*I*f you've never written an HTML page before, or even if you're somewhat new to it, you may find the look of HTML somewhat confusing. Fortunately, after you see a few simple rules and tags, you can read just about any HTML page.

HTML stands for *hypertext markup language. Hypertext* means that a page can have links on it. Clicking on the links jumps you to other pages. You've seen links in action when you click on one of those blue underlined words on a Web page and jump to some other location. *Markup language* means that special commands indicate how the Web page should appear. When you see titles at the top of the page, letters with different colors, or pictures, they all appear because of markup commands. These commands are called *tags*. Creating a Web page is all about figuring out what tags to put where.

HTML tags all look similar. They appear within angle brackets (<>). So when you look at any of the listings in this book and see things such as <BR> and <BODY>, those are HTML tags. The tags don't appear when you view a page. Instead, they give the browser special formatting instructions. For example, <BR> stands for break. It tells the browser to create a line break and thus to start a new line. Some commands have extra information that can appear within them, called *parameters*. For example, the <BODY> tag begins the portion of the document that you can see. Within it, you can add a variety of parameters, including one for setting the color of the page. Adding a color parameter looks like this:

```
<BODY BGCOLOR=blue>
```

When you see a tag that has a name followed by some other words, with each of those words followed by an equal sign, those other words are parameters.

Some HTML tags are called *grouping tags*. These tags can contain other lines within them. Such tags always have an ending tag counterpart, which has the same name but is preceded by a slash (/). For example, the <SCRIPT> tag indicates the lines that follow are scripts — that is, programs. The section of scripts is followed by a </SCRIPT> tag. Thus, all the lines between the <SCRIPT> and </SCRIPT> tags are script lines.

Such beginning and ending tags are also used for formatting. For example, the <I> tag means to italicize. You place this tag before the first word that you want to italicize and then put the </I> tag after the last word that you want to italicize. In the following line, the word *hello* is italicized:

```
Please say <I>hello</I> when you walk in the door.
```

That's all there is to it. Pages contain text and formatting and organization commands, called tags. To understand HTML, you need to know the key tags.

The capitalization of tags doesn't matter. So <BODY> is the same as <body>.

In the Beginning

All HTML pages start with the <HTML> tag and end with the </HTML> tag. Within the page, you find two main sections. The head, which starts with the <HEAD> tag and ends with the </HEAD> tag, is used for items that don't get displayed in the main part of the page. This is where you set up the page title (which appears on the title bar), sounds, scripts, style sheets, and other non-visual elements.

The body, which starts with the <BODY> tag and ends with the </BODY> tag, is where all the visual stuff appears. It's where you put text, pictures, tables, and the formatting commands. When you look at a page, you are seeing what is in the body.

Thus, a bare-bones page looks something like this:

```
<HTML>
<HEAD>
</HEAD>
<BODY>
Hi! This is my first Web page.
</BODY>
</HTML>
```

Formats R Us

After you've created the skeleton for the page, you can type whatever text you want in the body. It shows up looking like plain text unless you add formatting tags. The most common formatting tags are shown in Table A-1.

Table A-1	Common Formatting Tags	
Tag	*Meaning*	*Sample*
<I>	Makes text italic.	*Make these <I>words italic </I> please.*
<B>	Makes text bold.	Make these <B> words bold </B>please.
 	Inserts a line break.	This forces a new line between words. This is one sentence. This is the next.
<H1>	Inserts a level-1 heading.	Use this tag for the title of a section. The text shows up large and bold, underlined, or otherwise enhanced. You can use many other heading tags as well. Use <H2> for a level-2 heading — one that needs to stand out but is not quite as important as a level-1 head. Likewise, use <H3> for level-3 heads and so on, up to <H6>. <H1>The major heading</H1> Welcome to the first part. <H2>A secondary head</H2>.

(continued)

Table A-1 *(continued)*

Tag	*Meaning*	*Sample*
FONT SIZE=*n* COLOR=*color* FACE= *familyname*>	Font size sets the font to use for a block of text. The size can range from 1 to 7, where 7 is a very large font and 1 is a very small font. Color can be a color name, such as green, or a hex value, such as #FF0080. *Face* indicates the font family to use, such as Arial. You can fill in as many or as few of these parameters as you like. For example, you can just change the face. In that case, the current size and color are used, but the face changes. Or you can set all the parameters.	<Font Size =7> Some large words <font color = blue> in blue </ font> and the default color</FONT> and size.

Place a beginning tag in the text where you want the formatting to begin. Then place the ending tag where you want the formatting to end. You can have several tags apply at once. For example, the following makes some text bold and some text bold and italicized:

```
Hello, <B>bold words and <I>bold italic</I> words</B> mixed together.
```

Remember that the text needs to be inside the body. Listing A-1 shows a simple HTML page.

Listing A-1   **A Simple HTML Page**

```
<HTML>
<BODY>
<H1>Michael's Page</H1>
Hello and <I>welcome</I> to my home page. Here you can learn more about me and
         my interests.
<H2>Career Aspirations</H2>
Beach bum.
<H2>Scuba diving</H2>
Sorry, not one of my interests.<BR>
But if you have any questions, <FONT COLOR=green>just mail me</FONT>.
</BODY>
</HTML>
```

A Picture Is Worth a Thousand Words

Make pages much livelier by adding pictures. You can do so with the `<IMG>` tag. Its format is `<IMG SRC=imagename>`. The image appears wherever you place the tag. If you add a 200 x 200 pixel image, it takes up a 200 x 200 pixel area of the page. (You can change the size of the image using the `<STYLE>` tag, as described in Chapter 4 and later in this appendix.)

For example, to have a picture called dog.jpg, you can use the following HTML script:

```
Here is my dog<BR><IMG SRC="dog.jpg">
```

Please Clear the Table

Tables let you arrange data into orderly rows and columns. Follow these steps to create them:

1. **Begin a table with the** `<TABLE>` **tag.**

   After you start a table, fill out its rows and columns, one row at a time.

2. **Start a row with the** `<TR>` **tag.**

3. **Start each cell in the table with the** `<TD>` **tag.**

4. **Type the HTML code that you want to appear within that cell.**

5. **Finish the cell with the** `</TD>` **tag.**

6. **Repeat Steps 3 through 5 for each cell that you want to add.**

7. **After you finish the row, end it with the** `</TR>` **tag.**

8. **Repeat Steps 2 through 7 for each row that you want to add.**

9. **After you finish the table, end it with the** `</TABLE>` **tag.**

For example, the following HTML code creates a table with three rows and two columns:

```
<TABLE>
<TR><TD>Cell 1</TD><TD>Cell 2</TD><TD>Cell 3</TD></TR>
<TR><TD>Row 2 Cell 1</TD><TD>Row 2 Cell 2</TD><TD>Row 2 Cell 3</TD></TR>
</TABLE>
```

If you want to get fancy, you can label the columns. To do so, add a `<THEAD>` tag right after the `<TABLE>` tag. Then add rows and columns using the `<TR>` and `<TD>` tags. (You usually create a single row of headings.) When you finish with the headings, insert a `</THEAD>` tag and then continue with the normal part of the table.

Hidden Messages

You can add hidden comments to HTML pages. Comments are typically used to do the following:

- ✔ Describe what you are doing so that other HTML authors can understand your page more easily.
- ✔ Prevent an item from being displayed on the page without omitting it from the HTML code.
- ✔ Make it easier for old browsers to read a page. In particular, you can use comments within the `<SCRIPT>` and `<STYLE>` tags to prevent problems with early browsers.

Add a comment by placing `<!--` where you want the comment to begin and `-->` where you want the comment to end, as shown in the following sample:

```
<!-- Hey, this is a comment in an HTML file. -->
```

You can't nest comments. So if you want to put a bunch of HTML code into a comment, make sure that it doesn't contain comments.

Abraham Linking

You've seen many of the markup tags for HTML. Now you need to find out about the other part — hypertext. You create hypertext by telling the browser that clicking on certain words should jump the user to a new HTML page. Setting up links may sound kind of hard, but it turns out to be very easy. You simply use the anchor tag: `<A>`. Place the anchor tag before any words (or images) that you want to turn into a link. Put `</A>` at the end of the words. The words are then highlighted (usually by turning blue and being underlined), and if the user clicks on them, the browser jumps to a new page.

The format for the anchor tag is `<A HREF=link>`. In this case, *link* is the URL for what you want to jump to. For example, to jump to the Microsoft home page, use the following code:

```
<A HREF="www.microsoft.com">Jump to Microsoft</A>
```

To link to a page called family.html that is in the same directory as the page you are editing, use the following code:

```
<A HREF="family.html">My family</A>
```

You can do many other things with links besides jumping to other pages. For example, you can make clicking on a link download a file using the ftp protocol, with HTML code such as the following:

```
<A HREF="ftp:book.zip">Download the book</A>
```

Or you can send e-mail by using code such as this:

```
<A HREF=mailto:mikehy@home.com>Mail the author</A>
```

HTML Groupies

You find two key tags for grouping HTML elements: `<SPAN>` and `<DIV>`. Grouping elements lets you create columns of text, move a set of items at one time, or apply a layout style to some HTML code, all at once. Groups that are created with the `<DIV>` tag start on a new row. Groups that are created with the `<SPAN>` tag continue along in the same line as any text before the `<SPAN>` tag.

To create a span or div, follow these steps:

1. **Put the** `<SPAN>` **or** `<DIV>` **tag in the HTML file.**
2. **Type the HTML code that you want to be in the group.**
3. **Insert a** `</SPAN>` **or** `</DIV>` **tag to end the group.**

For example, the following HTML code uses a `<DIV>` tag to create a column of text that takes up 30 percent of the width of the screen:

```
<DIV style="width:30%">This text will now appear in a column.</DIV>
```

Note that groups can be nested. You can have spans within spans within divs within spans, and so on.

Feed Your Head

So far, all the tags described in this appendix relate to the body — the stuff that the user sees. You use several other tags that belong elsewhere — in the head. (If you are a sailor, you may be wondering whether I have diverted into bathroom humor and plan to talk about flushing the cache, starting paragraphs with the `<P>` tag, and so on. But don't worry. I wouldn't stoop to that level. Just ask Alice.) These tags include ones for setting the title, for playing sounds, and for defining scripts.

I start with a simple tag, the `<TITLE>` tag. It sets what is to appear in the title bar of the browser. Enter `<TITLE>`, followed by some text, and then insert `</TITLE>`. The text between the two tags shows up in the title bar whenever the page is viewed.

Use the `<BGSOUND>` tag to add sounds to your page, as described in Chapter 9. Its format is `<BGSOUND SRC=soundfile>`, where *soundfile* is the name of a MIDI, WAV, or RA file.

When it comes to Dynamic HTML, however, the most important tag that goes in the head is the `<SCRIPT>` tag. You use it to add scripts that customize your page. That's how you make a page do special things as the user interacts with it. You find two basic formats for the script tag. The first lets you define a set of variables or functions that can be called anywhere from a page (that is, you can use the variables and functions within other functions, or you can use them when processing events). The format is as follows:

```
<SCRIPT>
```

You can also use the following format to use VBScript. (Note that VBScript only works with Microsoft Internet Explorer, whereas JavaScript works with both Internet Explorer and Netscape Navigator):

```
<SCRIPT LANGUAGE="VBScript">
```

Then you enter the various scripts, followed by a `</SCRIPT>` tag. For example, the following defines two functions:

```
<SCRIPT>
function turnBlue(el) {
    el.style.color = "blue";
}
function turnGreen(el) {
    el.style.color = "green";
}
</SCRIPT>
```

Note that specifying the language is optional. If you are writing pages to work with Navigator and Internet Explorer, you are better off not specifying a language because Internet Explorer defaults to JScript and Navigator to JavaScript. None of the sample programs in the book specify the language.

The other form of the `<SCRIPT>` tag lets you associate a script with an event, as follows:

```
<SCRIPT LANGUAGE=language FOR=elementname EVENT=eventname>
```

In this script, *language* can be either `JScript` or `VBScript`. Or you can omit the language altogether. *Elementname* is the name of the element on which the event is to occur. *Eventname* is the name of the event. For example, the following code sets up script that runs as soon as the page loads:

```
<SCRIPT LANGUAGE="JScript" FOR="window" EVENT="onload">
        alert("The page is now loaded.");
</SCRIPT>
```

As soon as the page loads, the alert message appears.

Navigator does not support the FOR EVENT syntax.

May I Please See Your ID?

Dynamic HTML operates by changing elements on the page in response to user events. Changing the page is typically done by manipulating specific properties of specific objects. To do so, the object must have a name. In other words, you can't write Dynamic HTML scripts that say, "Do you remember that letter I put on the page a little while ago? Can you please turn it blue?" Instead, you need to say, "This letter is called Miles." And then later, you say, "Make Miles kind of blue."

You can give two types of names to an object: a name and an id. Most of the time, these two operate interchangeably. (You can do some advanced tricks by giving objects names and ids. But that's something you only encounter rarely.)

You add a name or id as a parameter to the element's tag. For example, the following HTML code creates a named image:

```
<IMG NAME="myImg" SRC="family.jpg">
```

You can just as easily give the image an id with the following code:

```
 ID="myImg" SRC="family.jpg">
```

You can then manipulate the image through script, with code such as the following:

```
myImg.style.visibility = "hidden";
```

Elementary Positioning

Dynamic HTML gives you complete control over the size and location of elements through Cascading Style Sheets (CSS). Using CSS is covered in depth throughout this book, especially in Chapter 4.

You can set an object's position and size by using the `style` parameter. The format is as follows:

```
STYLE="position:positionstyle; height:height; width:width; left:left; top:top"
```

Positionstyle can either be relative or absolute. *Relative style* positions the object based on where it would usually appear. *Absolute style* positions it with respect to the entire page. (You can find out more about positioning in Chapter 4.) For example, the following script makes an image appear 20 pixels from the left of the screen, 30 pixels from the top, and 100 pixels wide and high:

```
<IMG SRC="family.jpg" STYLE="position:absolute; left:20px; top:30px; width:100px;
          height:100px">
```

The order of the values doesn't matter. They only must be separated by semi-colons. As with element parameters, you can omit any of the values. For example, the following positions the image but does not change its size:

```
<IMG SRC="family.jpg" STYLE="position:absolute; left:20px; top:30px">
```

By default, position values are in pixels. You can add measurement units to override this. The measurement units are in (inches), cm (centimeters), % (percentages), pt (points), and em (widths of the letter m). For example, the following makes an image appear 2 inches from the left of the screen and 1 centimeter from the top, and the image uses 30 percent of the width of the page:

```
<IMG SRC="family.jpg" STYLE="position:absolute; left:2in; top:1cm; width:30%">

10
```

Appendix B

Tales from the JavaScript

*T*o create Dynamic HTML Web pages, you must know three things: how to create HTML pages with tags, how to use the Dynamic HTML object model, and how to write scripts. In this appendix, I take you on a whirlwind tour of writing scripts using JavaScript. This appendix isn't a substitute for a full-length book on scripting or programming, but it covers the basics.

Scripts appear in the head of the page. Scripts begin with the tag `<SCRIPT>`, followed by the lines of script, followed by the ending tag `</SCRIPT>`.

An Eventful Existence

Adding scripts to a Web page lets you make the page interactive. The user performs an action, such as loading a page, typing on the keyboard, or moving the mouse. This action sends *events* — computer messages that tell the page what the user is up to — to the page. You can write scripts that get called when these events occur. The scripts then change something about the page — perhaps starting an animation when the page loads, changing the color of text as the user moves the mouse pointer over it, or displaying additional information about an image when the user clicks on it.

A script reacts to an event in two basic ways. First, use the following syntax:

```
<SCRIPT FOR=element EVENT=event>
```

Any lines between this tag and the ending `</SCRIPT>` tag are called when the event named *event* fires for the *element*. For example, the following code pops up a message box when the user clicks on an object named `myImg`:

```
<SCRIPT FOR="myImg" EVENT="onclick">
alert("You got it");
</SCRIPT>
```

Netscape Navigator does not support the FOR EVENT syntax.

Note that you can optionally specify the scripting language as shown in the following line:

```
<SCRIPT LANGUAGE="JScript" FOR="myImg" EVENT="onclick">
```

Unless you are using VBScript, you're better off just leaving out the language name.

You can also set up event processing directly inside an HTML tag. In this case, you create a script with a name, using <SCRIPT> tags. You then refer to that name inside the HTML element tag. The syntax is as follows:

```
<ELEMENT message="scriptname">
```

In this case, *ELEMENT* is one of the HTML element tags, such as <BODY>, <SPAN>, <DIV>, <INPUT>, or <IMG>. *Message* is one of the Dynamic HTML messages, such as onclick or onload. *Scriptname* is the name of one of the scripts that you have created.

For example, the following code creates a script called showIt that is called when the page finishes loading:

```
<HTML>
<HEAD>
<SCRIPT>
function showIt() {
    alert("I'm here!");
}
</SCRIPT>
</HEAD>
<BODY onload="showIt()">
Welcome to my Web page.
</BODY>
</HTML>
```

Rolling Up the JavaScript

Like all computer languages, JavaScript is composed of *statements*. Statements are like commands: Walk the dog! Take out the trash! However, instead of ending in exclamation marks, statements end with semicolons. You find many different types of statements. Some initialize values for later use. Others update counters, check values, or print messages.

Statements can be grouped into *functions* — a set of related commands. Functions are building blocks. You combine a set of statements into a function. You then call that function from other places or from other functions. It's like saying "Take out the trash!" rather than "Go to the kitchen! Open the drawer under the sink! Remove the trash can! Go to the bathroom! Remove the trash can! Combine the trash!" and so on. You define the function `TakeOutTheTrash` once. When you call the function later, the computer executes all the commands in that function.

You *define* functions in JavaScript with the function keyword. (A *keyword* is the computer-nerd way of saying a command that the computer understands.) You name the function, add a left brace ({), insert the statements that you want to group into the function, and then add a right brace (}) when you're finished defining the function. For example, the following defines a function called `printName`; the function prints the name of an element that has been clicked on:

```
function printName() {
    alert(window.event.srcElement.name);
}
```

You can *call* this function — that is, cause the statements inside it to execute — any time you want. You simply type the function name, followed by parentheses and a semicolon. The following code calls `printName`:

```
printName();
```

JavaScript programs also contain *variables*. Variables store data — numbers, text, and just about anything else. Variables are often used to get the values from an element for later use. For example, you could use a variable to store the name that a user typed or the initial location of an element. Variables are also useful for shortcuts. For example, suppose that you want to find the name of the element that the user clicked on. You can find this information in Internet Explorer with `window.event.srcElement.name`. However, every time you refer to the name, you would need to type **window.event.srcElement.name**. I've typed it three times so far in this chapter, and my fingers are tired already. Instead, you can store the value in a variable. For example, you can write the following script:

```
elName = window.event.srcElement.name;
```

That line stores the name in a variable named `elName`. Any time you need to refer to the name, you can just use the `elName` variable rather than the laborious `window.event.srcElement.name`.

Assign Your Life Away

To store a value in a variable, you *assign* it using the equal sign (=) command. (Technically, the equal sign, along with the plus sign (+), multiplication sign (*), and other commands, are called *operators*. But you really don't need to know that unless you want to impress computer science pals at a coffee party.) You enter the name of the variable, type the equal sign, and then enter the value that you want to store in the variable. For example, the following script stores the value 5 in a variable named myAge:

```
myAge = 5;
```

The values can come from HTML elements. The following line of JavaScript reads the data that is typed into an edit control called employee from a form named form1. The value is stored in a variable called empName, as follows:

```
empName = form1.employee.value;
```

It's Better to Compute

JavaScript has a variety of math commands that you can use in your program. The most common commands are + (add), – (subtract), * (multiply), and / (divide). You write these commands in a statement from left to right, in the same way you would write any formula. For example, the following line calculates sales tax for a purchase:

```
tax = .08*purchaseAmt;
```

You can combine many math commands into a single statement. For example, the following code calculates the price of a meal, including a tip:

```
price = 1.15*(numPizzas*10.25 + numPops*1.50 + numPies*4.95);
```

Dare to Compare

Many times you need to compare values. You may want to know whether the user just clicked on an image, whether an object is visible, or whether the user tried to order more than his or her credit limit allows. JavaScript provides several commands for doing so: > (greater than), >= (greater than or equal to), < (less than), <= (less than or equal to), == (equal to), and != (not equal to). You typically use such comparisons with an if statement. The if statement performs a statement only if some comparison is true. For example, you may print a message only if the user clicks on an image. Or you may move an element if its *x* position is less than 100. The format is as follows:

```
if (comparison) {
   statements;
}
```

For example, the following code prints a message if a value is less than 3:

```
if (myX < 3) {
   alert("Less than 3");
}
```

You can also decide what to do if the comparison isn't true. Do so with the else clause, as follows:

```
if (comparison) {
   statements;
}
else {
   statements;
}
```

For example, the following script prints one message if a value is equal to 3 and a different message if it is greater than or equal to 3:

```
if (myX == 3) {
   alert("I'm as 3 as a bird now.");
}
else {
   alert("Not 3.");
   myX = myX - 2;
}
```

Note that = and == are very different operators. (In other words, = does not equal ==.) The single equal sign (=) is the assignment operator. It assigns the value of one item to another. However, the double equal sign (==) is the equality comparison operator. It determines whether two items have the same value. Consider the following code:

```
if (myX = 3) {
alert("I'm as 3 as a bird now.");
}
```

Because = is the assignment operator, myX is set to 3, and the alert always displays. Even experienced programmers sometimes make this mistake and use = when they really mean ==.

Crimson and Clover, Over and Over

You may need to repeat a set of statements several times, usually in order to apply the same change to a set of items. You repeat a set of statements with the for loop. Its format is as follows:

```
for (countername = initialvalue; comparison; increment statement) {
   statements;
}
```

As you can see, this command is fairly complex. Typically, you create a counter variable. You compare this value to some other value to determine whether you want to continue with the loop. Then you increment the counter value. For example, the following statement loops ten times:

```
for (i=0; i<10; i = i + 1) {
   sum = sum + i;
}
```

The following events happen:

1. **The for loop begins.**

   This creates a new variable called *i* with an initial value of 0.

2. **The for loop checks the comparison: Is *i* less than 10?**

   Yep — 0 is less than 10.

3. **The statements inside the for loop execute.**

   The value of *i* is added to a variable named sum.

4. **After the statements finish, the increment statement executes.**

   In this case, 1 is added to *i*. So *i* is now 1.

5. **The comparison is checked again: Is *i* less than 10?**

   Yes, 1 is less than 10, so the statements are executed. This cycle continues until *i* is no longer less than 10. Thus, the loop executes ten times.

In Dynamic HTML, for loops are usually used for operating on collections. You often see code such as the following:

```
for (i = 0; i < document.images.length; i++) {
   document.images.item(i).style.visibility = "hidden";
}
```

This script hides all the images that are on the page.

Color Commentary

You can add comments to scripts so that other HTML authors who read the scripts have an idea of what you were up to (and so that you can later remember what you were trying to accomplish). Commenting your code, especially functions, is good practice. On the other hand, remember that all the comments get downloaded to the user. So if you write a few thousand pages of brilliant comments, the user ends up staring at his modem light while all those comments download with the rest of your page.

You can add comments in two ways. To add a single-line comment or place a comment at the end of a statement, use two slashes (//). For example, the following script contains two comments:

```
//This function prints out the type of an event
function printType() {
    alert(event.type); //"on" is not part of name
}
```

You can also create a big block of comments at once. Place a slash and an asterisk (/*) at the beginning of the comments and the reverse (*/) at the end of the comments, as follows:

```
/*
  The following function prints out the type of an event.
  It does so by using the type property of the event method.
  Remember that the value will not include "on". So if called during an
              "onmouseover" event
  This will print out "mouseover"
*/
function printType() {
alert(event.type);
}
```

Arrays and Shine

Variables store single values, such as a name or the *x* position of an element. Sometimes you need to group many values and give them a single name. Grouping makes it easier to access them programmatically. For example, you may want to store all the names of fruits that are sold in a store. Or you may want to store the *x* positions of all the images on your page. You create a set of numbers by creating an array, as follows:

```
myNums = new Array();
```

Think of the array as a stack of boxes. You can store whatever you want in each box. The first box is called *box 0,* the second box is *box 1,* and so on.

This number (0, 1, and so on) is the *index*. You can then set or retrieve values from the array by using brackets ([and]) around the array index.

The following code stores the value 1 in the first element of the array:

```
myNums[0] = 1;
```

The following script determines what value is stored in the third element:

```
foo = myNums[2];
```

Note that the first element is element 0. If *n* items are in the array, the last element is item *n* – 1.

You can find out how many items are in an array by checking its length:

```
numItems = myNums.length;
```

You can also fill in an initial set of values for an array when you create it. Just place the values inside parentheses, separated by commas, as follows:

```
myNums = new Array(1, 2, 3, 7, 6, 8);
```

How Many Parameters Tall?

As I describe earlier, functions are the building blocks for JavaScript programs. You can write functions that operate exactly one way. But you can also make functions more flexible by having them operate on generic elements. For example, suppose that you want to change the text color of an element to blue. You can write the following script to do that:

```
function turnBlue() {
    item1.style.color = "blue";
}
```

This function changes the element named item1 to blue. But it can't change any other element to blue. So if you want to make item2 blue, you need to write a new function. Yuck.

You can get around this tedious work by passing parameters to functions. *Parameters* are named things that the function operates on. When you call the function, you pass in the value. The function then uses that value. You can pass in different values from different parts of the program.

For example, the following code changes the element myFoo to blue:

```
function turnBlue(myFoo) {
    myFoo.style.color = "blue";
}
```

No element named myFoo actually exists on the page. Rather, myFoo is a parameter. (Parameters are also called *arguments*. But that doesn't mean that they fight all the time.) When you call turnBlue, you fill in the value for the parameter by giving it the name of the element that you want to turn blue. The following script turns an element named button1 blue:

```
turnBlue(button1);
```

Similarly, the following code turns an element named Text17 blue:

```
turnBlue(Text17);
```

You can pass as many parameters in as you want. Separate each with a comma. The following function takes four parameters:

```
function rotate(el, x, y, z) {
   el.rotate(x,y,z);
}
```

Shortcuts and More

JavaScript has its roots in Java. And Java has its roots in C and C++. Programmers of C and C++ tend to be real nerds. (I can say that — I program in C and C++, too.) Nerds like to take shortcuts. If you've ever read any articles about computers, you see that they are filled with acronyms: HTTP, URL, IDE, and SCSI, to name a few. After all, why waste time saying something that can be represented with fewer letters? Likewise, programmers like to take shortcuts when coding. JavaScript offers several shortcuts.

To increment the value in a variable, you can use the following code:

```
foo = foo + 1;
```

However, JavaScript provides this shortcut:

```
foo++;
```

You typically see this shortcut in a loop, such as the following:

```
for (i=0; i < 10; i++) {
   //some statement
}
```

Likewise, consider the following code:

```
foo = foo - 1;
```

Instead, you can write this:

```
fooly@=1x2;
```

In fact, any time you want to perform a simple math function on a value, a shortcut is usually available. See the following table.

Instead of this	You Can Use This
a = a + n;	a += n;
a = a * n;	a *= n;
a = a / n;	a /= n;
a = a − n;	a −= n;

To see whether a value isn't true, you can use the following code:

```
if (a != true) {
}
```

Another way to write this statement is as follows:

```
if (!a) {
}
```

You also occasionally see data conversions. If you have a number and you want to turn it into a string, use the toString method, as follows:

```
tName = numVar.toString();
```

Likewise, you can convert a string to an integer with parseInt or to a float with parseFloat. For example, the following script converts a string to a number:

```
myNum = parseInt(myString);
```

Appendix C

About the CD

• •

*H*ere's some of what you can find on the *Dynamic HTML For Dummies,* 2nd Edition CD-ROM:

- ✔ All the sample programs from this book, plus some bonus samples
- ✔ Internet Explorer 5.0
- ✔ Great HTML authoring tools: including HomeSite, Paint Shop Pro, and Cool Edit 96

System Requirements

Make sure your computer meets the minimum system requirements listed below. If your computer doesn't match up to most of these requirements, you may have problems in using the contents of the CD.

- ✔ A PC with a 486 or faster processor
- ✔ Microsoft Windows 95 or later or Microsoft Windows NT 4.0 or later
- ✔ At least 8MB of total RAM installed on your computer (For best performance, we recommend that machines have at least 32MB of RAM installed.)
- ✔ At least 60MB of hard drive space available to install all the software from this CD (You need less space if you don't install every program.)
- ✔ A CD-ROM drive
- ✔ A monitor capable of displaying at least 256 colors

What You'll Find

Here's a summary of the software on this CD. You can examine the contents of the CD just by looking through the directories with Windows Explorer. You'll find five main directories:

- **Cooledit:** Contains Cool Edit 96
- **Homesite:** Contains HomeSite 4.0
- **Msie4:** Contains Microsoft Internet Explorer 4.0
- **Psp:** Contains Paint Shop Pro 5.0
- **Samples:** Contains all the sample programs from this book

Cool Edit, from Syntrillium Software Corporation

Cool Edit is a sound editor. It lets you record and edit sound files, and save them in a variety of formats. Cool Edit supports a broad range of sound editing features, including delay, echo, and pitch effects, as well as cutting and pasting sections of waveforms.

To install Cool Edit, do the following:

1. **Switch to the Cooledit\Win95 folder.**

2. **Double-click on c96setup.exe.**

3. **Click on OK to begin installation.**

   The installation program will check to see if you have previously installed Cool Edit.

4. **Choose where you want to install Cool Edit.**

   By default, it is installed into the C:\cool folder. Click on OK to copy the various files.

5. **The program asks whether you want to use Cool Edit as the default audio editor.**

   If this is the first audio editor you have installed, click on Yes. If you are using a different audio editor as the default editor for sound files, you may want to click on No instead.

6. **Click on Yes when the program asks whether to enable the peak file feature.**

7. **Select the primary and alternative swap folders.**

   These are the folders Cool Edit uses to store temporary files. Because sound files can get very large, you should pick folders that have a lot of available space on them. By default, the program stores files in the C:\WINDOWS\TEMP folder. After you are satisfied with the folder selection, click on OK.

8. **Select the group where you want Cool Edit installed.**

   By default, this is Syntrillium. Click on Add.

9. **Click on Yes to run Cool Edit.**

Because the program on the CD is a shareware version of Cool Edit, you're able to use only a subset of its functionality at any given time. Until you register Cool Edit, every time you run it, you're asked to choose which features you want enabled.

You can find out more about Cool Edit by visiting the Syntrillium Web site at www.syntrillium.com.

HomeSite 4.0, from Allaire

HomeSite 4.0 is a powerful HTML editor. It lets you edit multiple HTML files; provides color syntax highlighting; has wizards for adding ActiveX controls, frames, and tables to your application; and contains a rich set of text editing capabilities. It lets you customize the editing environment, search and replace across multiple files, browse in place, and automatically upload to the Web. And there are many other features as well.

To install HomeSite 4.0, do the following:

1. **Switch to the Homesite folder.**

2. **Double-click on Hs40_ev.exe.**

3. **When the Welcome screen appears, click on Next.**

4. **Read through the License Agreement. Click on Accept if you accept the terms or Cancel if you decide you don't want to install HomeSite after all.**

5. **Type your name and, if you have one, a company name in the User Information screen. Then click on Next.**

6. **Select where HomeSite 4.0 will be installed.**

   By default, it installs in the C:\Program Files\Allaire\HomeSite4 folder. Click on Browse if you want to change where it will be installed. Click on Next to continue with the installation.

7. **If the HomeSite folder didn't exist before, the installation program asks you if you'd like Setup to create the folder for you. Click on Yes to continue.**

8. **Select the components you wish to install. The only options are the program files and the dcoumentation. If you want to save space and already know your way around HomeSite, you probably won't need the documentation. Click on Next to continue.**

9. **Select the program folder where you want the menu shortcut to show up. Click on Next to accept the default and continue.**

10. Finally, the setup program asks you to confirm all the selections you just made. Click on Next to start copying files to your computer.

11. When the installation is complete, a new screen appears telling you that the files have been successfully installed. Click on Finish to automatically run HomeSite 4.0.

12. The first time HomeSite 4.0 runs, it checks which Internet browsers are on your machine and asks what you would like to use for the internal browser. Click on Yes.

Every time you run HomeSite, a splash screen appears, reminding you that HomeSite is shareware. Click on Help to learn how to purchase a licensed version. Click on Continue to run the program.

Browse through the tips or the Help files to learn how to use HomeSite 4.0. You can also find more information at www.allaire.com.

Internet Explorer 4.0, from Microsoft Corporation

If you haven't already installed Internet Explorer 4.0, be sure to do so by switching to the Msie4 folder. Double-click on Ie4setup.exe. An install program walks you through the steps of installing Internet Explorer 4.0.

Paint Shop Pro 5.0, from JASC Inc.

Paint Shop Pro is a shareware graphics viewing and editing tool available for Windows 95 and Windows NT. It lets you read, convert, and save images in over 30 common formats, including JPEG and GIF. It provides a broad variety of editing tools to let you manipulate images, including paint tools; special effects such as sharpen, buttonize, motion blur, pinch, and skew; and much more. You can also capture screens.

To install Paint Shop Pro, do the following:

1. Switch to the Psp\Win95 directory.

2. Double-click on psp501.exe to launch the installation program.

3. Click on Next to bring up the Select Destination Folder screen.

4. By default, the program is installed in C:\Program Files\Paint Shop Pro 5. To accept this location, click on Next. Or, change the location using the file browser in the dialog box, and then click on Next.

5. Click on Next when it asks which options to install.

6. Click on Next to begin installation.

You're asked whether you want to view the Readme. Click on Yes or No.

Installation is now complete. You can run the program from the Windows Start menu.

You can find further information in the help file or by checking the JASC Web site at `www.jasc.com`.

Dynamic HTML For Dummies Sample Programs

All the sample programs from this book are provided on the CD. You can find them by switching to the samples folder. This folder contains a folder for each chapter in the book. Be sure to double-click on default.htm in the samples folder. This contains a brief description and link to all the sample programs in the book, including several bonus sample files.

You can load the sample program directly from the CD. If you want to copy them to your hard drive, use Windows Explorer to copy the samples folder to your hard drive.

If You Have Problems (Of the CD Kind)

I tried my best to compile programs that work on most computers with the minimum system requirements. Alas, your computer may differ, and some programs may not work properly for some reason.

The two likeliest problems are that you don't have enough memory (RAM) for the programs you want to use, or that you have other programs running that are affecting the installation or running of a program. If you get error messages such as Not enough memory or Setup cannot continue, try one or more of these methods and then try using the software again:

- ✔ Turn off any antivirus software that you have on your computer. Installers sometimes mimic virus activity and may make your computer incorrectly believe that it is being infected by a virus.

- ✔ Close all running programs. The more programs you're running, the less memory is available to other programs. Installers also typically update files and programs. So if you keep other programs running, installation may not work properly.

- ✔ Have your local computer store add more RAM to your computer. This is, admittedly, a drastic and somewhat expensive step. However, adding more memory can really help the speed of your computer and allow more programs to run at the same time.

If you still have trouble with installing the items from the CD, please call the IDG Books Worldwide Customer Service phone number: 800-762-2974 (outside the U.S.: 317-596-5430).

Index

• Q •

Notes

Notes

Notes

Notes

Notes

Notes

Notes

From PCs to Personal Finance, We Make it Fun and Easy!

ISBN 0-7645-0435-5
$19.99 US/$28.99 CAN

ISBN 0-7645-5013-6
$19.99 US/$26.99 CAN

For more information, or to order, please call 800.762.2974.

www.idgbooks.com
www.dummies.com

Dummies Books™
Bestsellers on Every Topic!

TECHNOLOGY TITLES

INTERNET

America Online® For Dummies®, 5th Edition	John Kaufeld	0-7645-0502-5	$19.99 US/$26.99 CAN
E-Mail For Dummies®, 2nd Edition	John R. Levine, Carol Baroudi, Margaret Levine Young, & Arnold Reinhold	0-7645-0131-3	$24.99 US/$34.99 CAN
Genealogy Online For Dummies®	Matthew L. Helm & April Leah Helm	0-7645-0377-4	$24.99 US/$35.99 CAN
Internet Directory For Dummies®, 2nd Edition	Brad Hill	0-7645-0436-3	$24.99 US/$35.99 CAN
The Internet For Dummies®, 6th Edition	John R. Levine, Carol Baroudi, & Margaret Levine Young	0-7645-0506-8	$19.99 US/$28.99 CAN
Investing Online For Dummies®, 2nd Edition	Kathleen Sindell, Ph.D.	0-7645-0509-2	$24.99 US/$35.99 CAN
World Wide Web Searching For Dummies®, 2nd Edition	Brad Hill	0-7645-0264-6	$24.99 US/$34.99 CAN

OPERATING SYSTEMS

DOS For Dummies®, 3rd Edition	Dan Gookin	0-7645-0361-8	$19.99 US/$28.99 CAN
LINUX® For Dummies®, 2nd Edition	John Hall, Craig Witherspoon, & Coletta Witherspoon	0-7645-0421-5	$24.99 US/$35.99 CAN
Mac® OS 8 For Dummies®	Bob LeVitus	0-7645-0271-9	$19.99 US/$26.99 CAN
Small Business Windows® 98 For Dummies®	Stephen Nelson	0-7645-0425-8	$24.99 US/$35.99 CAN
UNIX® For Dummies®, 4th Edition	John R. Levine & Margaret Levine Young	0-7645-0419-3	$19.99 US/$28.99 CAN
Windows® 95 For Dummies®, 2nd Edition	Andy Rathbone	0-7645-0180-1	$19.99 US/$26.99 CAN
Windows® 98 For Dummies®	Andy Rathbone	0-7645-0261-1	$19.99 US/$28.99 CAN

PC/GENERAL COMPUTING

Buying a Computer For Dummies®	Dan Gookin	0-7645-0313-8	$19.99 US/$28.99 CAN
Illustrated Computer Dictionary For Dummies®, 3rd Edition	Dan Gookin & Sandra Hardin Gookin	0-7645-0143-7	$19.99 US/$26.99 CAN
Modems For Dummies®, 3rd Edition	Tina Rathbone	0-7645-0069-4	$19.99 US/$26.99 CAN
Small Business Computing For Dummies®	Brian Underdahl	0-7645-0287-5	$24.99 US/$35.99 CAN
Upgrading & Fixing PCs For Dummies®, 4th Edition	Andy Rathbone	0-7645-0418-5	$19.99 US/$28.99CAN

GENERAL INTEREST TITLES

FOOD & BEVERAGE/ENTERTAINING

Entertaining For Dummies®	Suzanne Williamson with Linda Smith	0-7645-5027-6	$19.99 US/$26.99 CAN
Gourmet Cooking For Dummies®	Charlie Trotter	0-7645-5029-2	$19.99 US/$26.99 CAN
Grilling For Dummies®	Marie Rama & John Mariani	0-7645-5076-4	$19.99 US/$26.99 CAN
Italian Cooking For Dummies®	Cesare Casella & Jack Bishop	0-7645-5098-5	$19.99 US/$26.99 CAN
Wine For Dummies®, 2nd Edition	Ed McCarthy & Mary Ewing-Mulligan	0-7645-5114-0	$19.99 US/$26.99 CAN

SPORTS

Baseball For Dummies®	Joe Morgan with Richard Lally	0-7645-5085-3	$19.99 US/$26.99 CAN
Fly Fishing For Dummies®	Peter Kaminsky	0-7645-5073-X	$19.99 US/$26.99 CAN
Football For Dummies®	Howie Long with John Czarnecki	0-7645-5054-3	$19.99 US/$26.99 CAN
Hockey For Dummies®	John Davidson with John Steinbreder	0-7645-5045-4	$19.99 US/$26.99 CAN
Tennis For Dummies®	Patrick McEnroe with Peter Bodo	0-7645-5087-X	$19.99 US/$26.99 CAN

HOME & GARDEN

Decks & Patios For Dummies®	Robert J. Beckstrom & National Gardening Association	0-7645-5075-6	$16.99 US/$24.99 CAN
Flowering Bulbs For Dummies®	Judy Glattstein & National Gardening Association	0-7645-5103-5	$16.99 US/$24.99 CAN
Home Improvement For Dummies®	Gene & Katie Hamilton & the Editors of HouseNet, Inc.	0-7645-5005-5	$19.99 US/$26.99 CAN
Lawn Care For Dummies®	Lance Walheim & National Gardening Association	0-7645-5077-2	$16.99 US/$24.99 CAN

IDG BOOKS WORLDWIDE

For more information, or to order, call (800)762-2974

FOR DUMMIES

BESTSELLING BOOK SERIES

Dummies Books™
Bestsellers on Every Topic!

TECHNOLOGY TITLES

SUITES

Title	Author	ISBN	Price
Microsoft® Office 2000 For Windows® For Dummies®	Wallace Wang & Roger C. Parker	0-7645-0452-5	$19.99 US/$28.99 CAN
Microsoft® Office 2000 For Windows® For Dummies®, Quick Reference	Doug Lowe & Bjoern Hartsfvang	0-7645-0453-3	$12.99 US/$19.99 CAN
Microsoft® Office 4 For Windows® For Dummies®	Roger C. Parker	1-56884-183-3	$19.95 US/$26.95 CAN
Microsoft® Office 97 For Windows® For Dummies®	Wallace Wang & Roger C. Parker	0-7645-0050-3	$19.99 US/$26.99 CAN
Microsoft® Office 97 For Windows® For Dummies®, Quick Reference	Doug Lowe	0-7645-0062-7	$12.99 US/$17.99 CAN
Microsoft® Office 98 For Macs® For Dummies®	Tom Negrino	0-7645-0229-8	$19.99 US/$28.99 CAN

WORD PROCESSING

Title	Author	ISBN	Price
Word 2000 For Windows® For Dummies®, Quick Reference	Peter Wererlet	0-7645-0449-5	$12.99 US/$19.99 CAN
Corel® WordPerfect® 8 For Windows® For Dummies®	Margaret Levine Young, David Kay, & Jordan Young	0-7645-0186-0	$19.99 US/$26.99 CAN
Word For Windows® 6 For Dummies®	Dan Gookin	1-56884-075-6	$16.95 US/$21.95 CAN
Word For Windows® 95 For Dummies®	Dan Gookin	1-56884-932-X	$19.99 US/$26.99 CAN
Word 97 For Windows® For Dummies®	Dan Gookin	0-7645-0052-X	$19.99 US/$26.99 CAN
WordPerfect® 6.1 For Windows® For Dummies®, Quick Reference, 2nd Edition	Margaret Levine Young & David Kay	1-56884-966-4	$9.99 US/$12.99 CAN
WordPerfect® 7 For Windows® 95 For Dummies®	Margaret Levine Young & David Kay	1-56884-949-4	$19.99 US/$26.99 CAN
Word Pro® for Windows® 95 For Dummies®	Jim Meade	1-56884-232-5	$19.99 US/$26.99 CAN

SPREADSHEET/FINANCE/PROJECT MANAGEMENT

Title	Author	ISBN	Price
Excel For Windows® 95 For Dummies®	Greg Harvey	1-56884-930-3	$19.99 US/$26.99 CAN
Excel 2000 For Windows® For Dummies®	Greg Harvey	0-7645-0446-0	$19.99 US/$28.99 CAN
Excel 2000 For Windows® For Dummies® Quick Reference	John Walkenbach	0-7645-0447-9	$12.99 US/$19.99 CAN
Microsoft® Money 98 For Dummies®	Peter Weverka	0-7645-0295-6	$24.99 US/$34.99 CAN
Microsoft® Money 99 For Dummies®	Peter Weverka	0-7645-0433-9	$19.99 US/$28.99 CAN
Microsoft® Project 98 For Dummies®	Martin Doucette	0-7645-0321-9	$24.99 US/$34.99 CAN
MORE Excel 97 For Windows® For Dummies®	Greg Harvey	0-7645-0138-0	$22.99 US/$32.99 CAN
Quicken® 98 For Windows® For Dummies®	Stephen L. Nelson	0-7645-0243-3	$19.99 US/$26.99 CAN

GENERAL INTEREST TITLES

EDUCATION & TEST PREPARATION

Title	Author	ISBN	Price
The ACT For Dummies®	Suzee Vlk	1-56884-387-9	$14.99 US/$21.99 CAN
College Financial Aid For Dummies®	Dr. Herm Davis & Joyce Lain Kennedy	0-7645-5049-7	$19.99 US/$26.99 CAN
College Planning For Dummies®, 2nd Edition	Pat Ordovensky	0-7645-5048-9	$19.99 US/$26.99 CAN
Everyday Math For Dummies®	Charles Seiter, Ph.D.	1-56884-248-1	$14.99 US/$22.99 CAN
The GMAT® For Dummies®, 3rd Edition	Suzee Vlk	0-7645-5082-9	$16.99 US/$24.99 CAN
The GRE® For Dummies®, 3rd Edition	Suzee Vlk	0-7645-5083-7	$16.99 US/$24.99 CAN
Politics For Dummies®	Ann DeLaney	1-56884-381-X	$19.99 US/$26.99 CAN
The SAT I For Dummies®, 3rd Edition	Suzee Vlk	0-7645-5044-6	$14.99 US/$21.99 CAN

CAREERS

Title	Author	ISBN	Price
Cover Letters For Dummies®	Joyce Lain Kennedy	1-56884-395-X	$12.99 US/$17.99 CAN
Cool Careers For Dummies®	Marty Nemko, Paul Edwards, & Sarah Edwards	0-7645-5095-0	$16.99 US/$24.99 CAN
Job Hunting For Dummies®	Max Messmer	1-56884-388-7	$16.99 US/$24.99 CAN
Job Interviews For Dummies®	Joyce Lain Kennedy	1-56884-859-5	$12.99 US/$17.99 CAN
Resumes For Dummies®, 2nd Edition	Joyce Lain Kennedy	0-7645-5113-2	$12.99 US/$17.99 CAN

IDG BOOKS WORLDWIDE

For more information, or to order, call (800)762-2974

FOR DUMMIES
BESTSELLING BOOK SERIES

Dummies Books™
Bestsellers on Every Topic!

TECHNOLOGY TITLES

WEB DESIGN & PUBLISHING

Title	Author	ISBN	Price
Creating Web Pages For Dummies®, 4th Edition	Bud Smith & Arthur Bebak	0-7645-0504-1	$24.99 US/$34.99 CAN
FrontPage® 98 For Dummies®	Asha Dornfest	0-7645-0270-0	$24.99 US/$34.99 CAN
HTML 4 For Dummies®	Ed Tittel & Stephen Nelson James	0-7645-0331-6	$29.99 US/$42.99 CAN
Java™ For Dummies®, 2nd Edition	Aaron E. Walsh	0-7645-0140-2	$24.99 US/$34.99 CAN
PageMill™ 2 For Dummies®	Deke McClelland & John San Filippo	0-7645-0028-7	$24.99 US/$34.99 CAN

DESKTOP PUBLISHING GRAPHICS/MULTIMEDIA

Title	Author	ISBN	Price
CorelDRAW™ 8 For Dummies®	Deke McClelland	0-7645-0317-0	$19.99 US/$26.99 CAN
Desktop Publishing and Design For Dummies®	Roger C. Parker	1-56884-234-1	$19.99 US/$26.99 CAN
Digital Photography For Dummies®, 2nd Edition	Julie Adair King	0-7645-0431-2	$19.99 US/$28.99 CAN
Microsoft® Publisher 97 For Dummies®	Barry Sosinsky, Christopher Benz & Jim McCarter	0-7645-0148-8	$19.99 US/$26.99 CAN
Microsoft® Publisher 98 For Dummies®	Jim McCarter	0-7645-0395-2	$19.99 US/$28.99 CAN

MACINTOSH

Title	Author	ISBN	Price
Macs® For Dummies®, 6th Edition	David Pogue	0-7645-0398-7	$19.99 US/$28.99 CAN
Macs® For Teachers™, 3rd Edition	Michelle Robinette	0-7645-0226-3	$24.99 US/$34.99 CAN
The iMac For Dummies	David Pogue	0-7645-0495-9	$19.99 US/$26.99 CAN

GENERAL INTEREST TITLES

BUSINESS & PERSONAL FINANCE

Title	Author	ISBN	Price
Accounting For Dummies®	John A. Tracy, CPA	0-7645-5014-4	$19.99 US/$26.99 CAN
Business Plans For Dummies®	Paul Tiffany, Ph.D. & Steven D. Peterson, Ph.D.	1-56884-868-4	$19.99 US/$26.99 CAN
Consulting For Dummies®	Bob Nelson & Peter Economy	0-7645-5034-9	$19.99 US/$26.99 CAN
Customer Service For Dummies®	Karen Leland & Keith Bailey	1-56884-391-7	$19.99 US/$26.99 CAN
Home Buying For Dummies®	Eric Tyson, MBA & Ray Brown	1-56884-385-2	$16.99 US/$24.99 CAN
House Selling For Dummies®	Eric Tyson, MBA & Ray Brown	0-7645-5038-1	$16.99 US/$24.99 CAN
Investing For Dummies®	Eric Tyson, MBA	1-56884-393-3	$19.99 US/$26.99 CAN
Law For Dummies®	John Ventura	1-56884-860-9	$19.99 US/$26.99 CAN
Managing For Dummies®	Bob Nelson & Peter Economy	1-56884-858-7	$19.99 US/$26.99 CAN
Marketing For Dummies®	Alexander Hiam	1-56884-699-1	$19.99 US/$26.99 CAN
Mutual Funds For Dummies®, 2nd Edition	Eric Tyson, MBA	0-7645-5112-4	$19.99 US/$26.99 CAN
Negotiating For Dummies®	Michael C. Donaldson & Mimi Donaldson	1-56884-867-6	$19.99 US/$26.99 CAN
Personal Finance For Dummies®, 2nd Edition	Eric Tyson, MBA	0-7645-5013-6	$19.99 US/$26.99 CAN
Personal Finance For Dummies® For Canadians	Eric Tyson, MBA & Tony Martin	1-56884-378-X	$18.99 US/$24.99 CAN
Sales Closing For Dummies®	Tom Hopkins	0-7645-5063-2	$14.99 US/$21.99 CAN
Sales Prospecting For Dummies®	Tom Hopkins	0-7645-5066-7	$14.99 US/$21.99 CAN
Selling For Dummies®	Tom Hopkins	1-56884-389-5	$16.99 US/$24.99 CAN
Small Business For Dummies®	Eric Tyson, MBA & Jim Schell	0-7645-5094-2	$19.99 US/$26.99 CAN
Small Business Kit For Dummies®	Richard D. Harroch	0-7645-5093-4	$24.99 US/$34.99 CAN
Successful Presentations For Dummies®	Malcolm Kushner	1-56884-392-5	$16.99 US/$24.99 CAN
Time Management For Dummies®	Jeffrey J. Mayer	1-56884-360-7	$16.99 US/$24.99 CAN

AUTOMOTIVE

Title	Author	ISBN	Price
Auto Repair For Dummies®	Deanna Sclar	0-7645-5089-6	$19.99 US/$26.99 CAN
Buying A Car For Dummies®	Deanna Sclar	0-7645-5091-8	$16.99 US/$24.99 CAN
Car Care For Dummies®: The Glove Compartment Guide	Deanna Sclar	0-7645-5090-X	$9.99 US/$13.99 CAN

IDG BOOKS WORLDWIDE™

For more information, or to order,
call (800)762-2974

BESTSELLING BOOK SERIES

Dummies Books™
Bestsellers on Every Topic!

TECHNOLOGY TITLES

DATABASE

Access 2000 For Windows® For Dummies®	John Kaufeld	0-7645-0444-4	$19.99 US/$28.99 CAN
Access 97 For Windows® For Dummies®	John Kaufeld	0-7645-0048-1	$19.99 US/$26.99 CAN
Approach® 97 For Windows® For Dummies®	Deborah S. Ray & Eric J. Ray	0-7645-0001-5	$19.99 US/$26.99 CAN
Crystal Reports 7 For Dummies®	Douglas J. Wolf	0-7645-0548-3	$24.99 US/$34.99 CAN
Data Warehousing For Dummies®	Alan R. Simon	0-7645-0170-4	$24.99 US/$34.99 CAN
FileMaker® Pro 4 For Dummies®	Tom Maremaa	0-7645-0210-7	$19.99 US/$26.99 CAN
Intranet & Web Databases For Dummies®	Paul Litwin	0-7645-0221-2	$29.99 US/$42.99 CAN

NETWORKING

Building An Intranet For Dummies®	John Fronckowiak	0-7645-0276-X	$29.99 US/$42.99 CAN
cc: Mail™ For Dummies®	Victor R. Garza	0-7645-0055-4	$19.99 US/$26.99 CAN
Client/Server Computing For Dummies®, 2nd Edition	Doug Lowe	0-7645-0066-X	$24.99 US/$34.99 CAN
Lotus Notes® Release 4 For Dummies®	Stephen Londergan & Pat Freeland	1-56884-934-6	$19.99 US/$26.99 CAN
Networking For Dummies®, 4th Edition	Doug Lowe	0-7645-0498-3	$19.99 US/$28.99 CAN
Upgrading & Fixing Networks For Dummies®	Bill Camarda	0-7645-0347-2	$29.99 US/$42.99 CAN
Windows NT® Networking For Dummies®	Ed Tittel, Mary Madden, & Earl Follis	0-7645-0015-5	$24.99 US/$34.99 CAN

GENERAL INTEREST TITLES

THE ARTS

Blues For Dummies®	Lonnie Brooks, Cub Koda, & Wayne Baker Brooks	0-7645-5080-2	$24.99 US/$34.99 CAN
Classical Music For Dummies®	David Pogue & Scott Speck	0-7645-5009-8	$24.99 US/$34.99 CAN
Guitar For Dummies®	Mark Phillips & Jon Chappell of Cherry Lane Music	0-7645-5106-X	$24.99 US/$34.99 CAN
Jazz For Dummies®	Dirk Sutro	0-7645-5081-0	$24.99 US/$34.99 CAN
Opera For Dummies®	David Pogue & Scott Speck	0-7645-5010-1	$24.99 US/$34.99 CAN
Piano For Dummies®	Blake Neely of Cherry Lane Music	0-7645-5105-1	$24.99 US/$34.99 CAN

HEALTH & FITNESS

Beauty Secrets For Dummies®	Stephanie Seymour	0-7645-5078-0	$19.99 US/$26.99 CAN
Fitness For Dummies®	Suzanne Schlosberg & Liz Neporent, M.A.	1-56884-866-8	$19.99 US/$26.99 CAN
Nutrition For Dummies®	Carol Ann Rinzler	0-7645-5032-2	$19.99 US/$26.99 CAN
Sex For Dummies®	Dr. Ruth K. Westheimer	1-56884-384-4	$16.99 US/$24.99 CAN
Weight Training For Dummies®	Liz Neporent, M.A. & Suzanne Schlosberg	0-7645-5036-5	$19.99 US/$26.99 CAN

LIFESTYLE/SELF-HELP

Dating For Dummies®	Dr. Joy Browne	0-7645-5072-1	$19.99 US/$26.99 CAN
Parenting For Dummies®	Sandra H. Gookin	1-56884-383-6	$16.99 US/$24.99 CAN
Success For Dummies®	Zig Ziglar	0-7645-5061-6	$19.99 US/$26.99 CAN
Weddings For Dummies®	Marcy Blum & Laura Fisher Kaiser	0-7645-5055-1	$19.99 US/$26.99 CAN

IDG BOOKS WORLDWIDE

For more information, or to order,
call (800)762-2974

FOR DUMMIES™
BESTSELLING BOOK SERIES

IDG Books Worldwide, Inc., End-User License Agreement

READ THIS. You should carefully read these terms and conditions before opening the software packet(s) included with this book ("Book"). This is a license agreement ("Agreement") between you and IDG Books Worldwide, Inc. ("IDGB"). By opening the accompanying software packet(s), you acknowledge that you have read and accept the following terms and conditions. If you do not agree and do not want to be bound by such terms and conditions, promptly return the Book and the unopened software packet(s) to the place you obtained them for a full refund.

1. **License Grant.** IDGB grants to you (either an individual or entity) a nonexclusive license to use one copy of the enclosed software program(s) (collectively, the "Software") solely for your own personal or business purposes on a single computer (whether a standard computer or a workstation component of a multiuser network). The Software is in use on a computer when it is loaded into temporary memory (RAM) or installed into permanent memory (hard disk, CD-ROM, or other storage device). IDGB reserves all rights not expressly granted herein.

2. **Ownership.** IDGB is the owner of all right, title, and interest, including copyright, in and to the compilation of the Software recorded on the disk(s) or CD-ROM ("Software Media"). Copyright to the individual programs recorded on the Software Media is owned by the author or other authorized copyright owner of each program. Ownership of the Software and all proprietary rights relating thereto remain with IDGB and its licensers.

3. **Restrictions on Use and Transfer.**

   (a) You may only (i) make one copy of the Software for backup or archival purposes, or (ii) transfer the Software to a single hard disk, provided that you keep the original for backup or archival purposes. You may not (i) rent or lease the Software, (ii) copy or reproduce the Software through a LAN or other network system or through any computer subscriber system or bulletin-board system, or (iii) modify, adapt, or create derivative works based on the Software.

   (b) You may not reverse engineer, decompile, or disassemble the Software. You may transfer the Software and user documentation on a permanent basis, provided that the transferee agrees to accept the terms and conditions of this Agreement and you retain no copies. If the Software is an update or has been updated, any transfer must include the most recent update and all prior versions.

4. **Restrictions on Use of Individual Programs.** You must follow the individual requirements and restrictions detailed for each individual program in the "About the CD" appendix of this Book. These limitations are also contained in the individual license agreements recorded on the Software Media. These limitations may include a requirement that after using the program for a specified period of time, the user must pay a registration fee or discontinue use. By opening the Software packet(s), you will be agreeing to abide by the licenses and restrictions for these individual programs that are detailed in the "About the CD" appendix and on the Software Media. None of the material on this Software Media or listed in this Book may ever be redistributed, in original or modified form, for commercial purposes.

5. **Limited Warranty.**

   (a) IDGB warrants that the Software and Software Media are free from defects in materials and workmanship under normal use for a period of sixty (60) days from the date of purchase of this Book. If IDGB receives notification within the warranty period of defects in materials or workmanship, IDGB will replace the defective Software Media.

   (b) IDGB AND THE AUTHOR OF THE BOOK DISCLAIM ALL OTHER WARRANTIES, EXPRESS OR IMPLIED, INCLUDING WITHOUT LIMITATION IMPLIED WARRANTIES OF MER-CHANTABILITY AND FITNESS FOR A PARTICULAR PURPOSE, WITH RESPECT TO THE SOFTWARE, THE PROGRAMS, THE SOURCE CODE CONTAINED THEREIN, AND/OR THE TECHNIQUES DESCRIBED IN THIS BOOK. IDGB DOES NOT WARRANT THAT THE FUNCTIONS CONTAINED IN THE SOFTWARE WILL MEET YOUR REQUIREMENTS OR THAT THE OPERATION OF THE SOFTWARE WILL BE ERROR FREE.

   (c) This limited warranty gives you specific legal rights, and you may have other rights that vary from jurisdiction to jurisdiction.

6. **Remedies.**

   (a) IDGB's entire liability and your exclusive remedy for defects in materials and workmanship shall be limited to replacement of the Software Media, which may be returned to IDGB with a copy of your receipt at the following address: Software Media Fulfillment Department, Attn.: *Dynamic HTML For Dummies,* 2nd Edition, IDG Books Worldwide, Inc., 7260 Shadeland Station, Ste. 100, Indianapolis, IN 46256, or call 800-762-2974. Please allow three to four weeks for delivery. This Limited Warranty is void if failure of the Software Media has resulted from accident, abuse, or misapplication. Any replacement Software Media will be warranted for the remainder of the original warranty period or thirty (30) days, whichever is longer.

   (b) In no event shall IDGB or the author be liable for any damages whatsoever (including without limitation damages for loss of business profits, business interruption, loss of business information, or any other pecuniary loss) arising from the use of or inability to use the Book or the Software, even if IDGB has been advised of the possibility of such damages.

   (c) Because some jurisdictions do not allow the exclusion or limitation of liability for conse-quential or incidental damages, the above limitation or exclusion may not apply to you.

7. **U.S. Government Restricted Rights.** Use, duplication, or disclosure of the Software by the U.S. Government is subject to restrictions stated in paragraph (c)(1)(ii) of the Rights in Technical Data and Computer Software clause of DFARS 252.227-7013, and in subparagraphs (a) through (d) of the Commercial Computer–Restricted Rights clause at FAR 52.227-19, and in similar clauses in the NASA FAR supplement, when applicable.

8. **General.** This Agreement constitutes the entire understanding of the parties and revokes and supersedes all prior agreements, oral or written, between them and may not be modified or amended except in a writing signed by both parties hereto that specifically refers to this Agreement. This Agreement shall take precedence over any other documents that may be in conflict herewith. If any one or more provisions contained in this Agreement are held by any court or tribunal to be invalid, illegal, or otherwise unenforceable, each and every other provision shall remain in full force and effect.

Installation Instructions

Here's a summary of the software on this CD. You can examine the contents of the CD just by looking through the directories with Windows Explorer. You find five main directories:

- ✔ **Cooledit:** Contains Cool Edit 96
- ✔ **Homesite:** Contains HomeSite 4.0
- ✔ **Msie5:** Contains Microsoft Internet Explorer 5.0
- ✔ **Psp:** Contains Paint Shop Pro 5.0
- ✔ **Samples:** Contains all the sample programs from this book

For information about installing the individual programs, please refer to Appendix C.

Discover Dummies™ Online!

The *Dummies* Web Site is your fun and friendly online resource for the latest information about *...For Dummies*® books on all your favorite topics. From cars to computers, wine to Windows, and investing to the Internet, we've got a shelf full of *...For Dummies* books waiting for you!

Ten Fun and Useful Things You Can Do at www.dummies.com

1. Register this book and win!
2. Find and buy the *...For Dummies* books you want online.
3. Get ten great *Dummies Tips™* every week.
4. Chat with your favorite *...For Dummies* authors.
5. Subscribe free to *The Dummies Dispatch™* newsletter.
6. Enter our sweepstakes and win cool stuff.
7. Send a free cartoon postcard to a friend.
8. Download free software.
9. Sample a book before you buy.
10. Talk to us. Make comments, ask questions, and get answers!

Jump online to these ten
fun and useful things at
http://www.dummies.com/10useful

For other technology titles from IDG Books Worldwide, go to
www.idgbooks.com

Not online yet? It's easy to get started with *The Internet For Dummies*® 5th Edition, or *Dummies 101*®: *The Internet For Windows*® *98*, available at local retailers everywhere.

Find other *...For Dummies* books on these topics:

Business • Careers • Databases • Food & Beverages • Games • Gardening • Graphics • Hardware
Health & Fitness • Internet and the World Wide Web • Networking • Office Suites
Operating Systems • Personal Finance • Pets • Programming • Recreation • Sports
Spreadsheets • Teacher Resources • Test Prep • Word Processing

IDG BOOKS WORLDWIDE
BOOK REGISTRATION

We want to hear from you!

Visit **http://my2cents.dummies.com** to register this book and tell us how you liked it!

- ✔ Get entered in our monthly prize giveaway.

- ✔ Give us feedback about this book — tell us what you like best, what you like least, or maybe what you'd like to ask the author and us to change!

- ✔ Let us know any other *...For Dummies*® topics that interest you.

Your feedback helps us determine what books to publish, tells us what coverage to add as we revise our books, and lets us know whether we're meeting your needs as a *...For Dummies* reader. You're our most valuable resource, and what you have to say is important to us!

Not on the Web yet? It's easy to get started with *Dummies 101*®: *The Internet For Windows*® *98* or *The Internet For Dummies*, 5th Edition, at local retailers everywhere.

Or let us know what you think by sending us a letter at the following address:

...For Dummies Book Registration
Dummies Press
7260 Shadeland Station, Suite 100
Indianapolis, IN 46256-3917
Fax 317-596-5498

BESTSELLING BOOK SERIES